MOTHERS OF THE MUNICIPALITY: WOMEN, WORK, AND SOCIAL POLICY IN POST-1945 HALIFAX

Highlighting women's activism in Halifax after the Second World War, *Mothers of the Municipality* is a tightly focused collection of essays on social policy affecting women. The contributors – feminist scholars in history, social work, and nursing – examine women's experiences and activism, including those of African–Nova Scotian 'day's workers,' Sisters of Charity, St. John Ambulance Brigades, 'Voices' for peace, and social welfare bureaucrats.

The volume underscores the fact that the 1950s and 1960s were not simply years of quiet conservatism, born-again domesticity, and consumption. Indeed, the period was marked by profound and rapid change for women. Despite their almost total exclusion from elected office, a situation that extended into the tumultuous 1970s, women in Halifax were instrumental in creating and reforming programs and services, often amid controversy. *Mothers of the Municipality* explores women's activism and the provision of services at the community level. If the adage 'think globally; act locally' has any application in modern history, it is with the women who fought many of the battles in the larger war for social justice.

JUDITH FINGARD is an adjunct professor in the Department of History at Dalhousie University.

JANET GUILDFORD is an assistant professor in the Departments of History at Mount Saint Vincent University and Saint Mary's University.

Mothers of the Municipality

Women, Work, and Social Policy in Post-1945 Halifax

*Edited by Judith Fingard
and Janet Guildford*

UNIVERSITY OF TORONTO PRESS
Toronto Buffalo London

6 26270 729

© University of Toronto Press Incorporated 2005
Toronto Buffalo London
Printed in Canada

ISBN 0-8020-3922-7 (cloth)
ISBN 0-8020-8693-4 (paper)

Printed on acid-free paper

Library and Archives Canada Cataloguing in Publication

Mothers of the municipality : women, work, and social policy in
post-1945 Halifax / edited by Judith Fingard and Janet Guildford.

Includes bibliographical references and index.
ISBN 0-8020-3922-7 (bound)   ISBN 0-8020-8693-4 (pbk.)

1. Women in community organization – Nova Scotia – Halifax –
History – 20th century.   2. Halifax (N.S.) – Social policy.
I. Fingard, Judith   II. Guildford, Janet

HQ1460.H34M68 2005   362.83′ 525′ 097622509045   C2004-904716-7

University of Toronto Press acknowledges the financial assistance to its
publishing program of the Canada Council and the Ontario Arts Council.

University of Toronto Press acknowledges the financial support for its
publishing activities of the Government of Canada through the Book
Publishing Industry Development Program (BPIDP).

This book has been published with the help of a grant from the Canadian
Federation for the Humanities and Social Sciences, through the Aid to
Scholarly Publications Programme, using funds provided by the Social
Sciences and Humanities Research Council of Canada.

For our own mothers, Jean V. Guildford and in memory of Sue J. Fingard (1905–2004)

Contents

Illustrations follow page 158

Acknowledgments

We would like to thank the Social Sciences and Humanities Research Council of Canada for providing a Strategic Grant which funded a major portion of the research expenses of the project that has culmi-nated in this collection. The Nova Scotia Advisory Council for the Status of Women was our community partner. Research assistance was ably provided by Jennifer Barro, Tanya Gogan and Lana MacLean. We want to thank Margaret Conrad, Joan Sangster, and David Sutherland for their careful reading of the manuscript. We greatly benefited from their suggestions. We are especially grateful for the enthusiasm and dedication of our contributors and their generosity in responding to each other's work.

MOTHERS OF THE MUNICIPALITY

Introduction

JUDITH FINGARD AND JANET GUILDFORD

Four Life Stories

Abigail (Abbie) Amanda Jacques Lane served as city alderman, representing Ward 2 in Halifax from 1951 to 1965. She attributed her first win to a 'kitchen' campaign led and staffed by housewives, and her career at City Hall was characterized by her commitment to housekeeping and mothering the municipality. She served on welfare, housing, and recreation committees and was appointed to library, school, and hospital boards. She advocated slum clearance and affordable rental housing, a public library for the North End, new kitchen equipment for the City Home (the poorhouse and mental hospital), and the appointment of a dog catcher. Her brand of municipal mothering was, however, a version of 'tough love.' She used humour and sarcasm to make her case: 'If there is one thing I've learned in life, it's that if you want anything you have to nag, nag, nag ... I'm persistent, I don't mind getting in anyone's hair.'[1]

Several elements in Lane's background combined to prepare her for a long and successful career in municipal politics. Born in Halifax in 1898, she was brought up by an independent mother who divorced her alcoholic husband and worked for many years at low-waged work to support herself and her daughter. Abbie attended high school and business college in Truro and entered the paid workforce before she was twenty. After she married in 1924 Lane juggled volunteer roles in women's organizations and community agencies and intermittent paid work with the unpaid work of running a household and raising three children. From 1939 to 1945 she was president of the Halifax Welfare Bureau, a private coordinating agency for charity, and was active in other community welfare and service clubs, including the Halifax Club of Business and Professional Women, Zonta International, the Imperial Order Daughters of the Empire (IODE), the Halifax Women of Rotary, the Diocesan Women's Cathedral League, the Junior League, and the Local Council of Women of Halifax. Professionally she was active in the Canadian Women's Press Club, the Association of Canadian Radio Artists, and later the International Association of Women in Radio and TV.

During the Second World War, Lane's volunteer work increased. She earned first aid and home nursing certificates from St John Ambulance and performed hundreds of hours of volunteer service at the Halifax Infirmary. She became a member of the Red Cross Nursing Auxiliary and a volunteer worker in civil defence. She washed diapers in the port nursery, escorted British war brides to Montreal, passed out cocoa and doughnuts at service canteens, and served as master of ceremonies of camp shows. Lane's high profile in Halifax was also due to her work as an actress and journalist. In the mid-1940s she began a twenty-year career as Mary Gillan on the popular CBC radio series *The Gillans*, and served briefly as the women's editor of the *Halifax Chronicle*. She also provided regular commentary on women's affairs for both of the city's private radio stations; in the 1950s she expanded into television with a weekly fifteen-minute program called *Around the Town*.

By the late 1940s, therefore, Lane had become well known as a media personality, a reformer of welfare services, and an advocate for improving the status of women. She had served as a member of the Civic Planning Commission that drafted a master plan for rebuilding Halifax after the war. It was a short step for her to run for municipal office in 1951, and her kitchen campaign defeated the incumbent, a former mayor, by two votes to one. After Lane's death in 1965, her contribution to Halifax and her work with the Canadian Mental Health Association were commemorated with the Abbie J. Lane Memorial Hospital, a successor institution to the Halifax Mental Hospital, which had succeeded the City Home.[2]

While Abbie Lane was the consummate clubwoman who made her mark as a municipal politician, Gertrude Tynes's launching pad was her family. Born Gertrude Phills in Sydney in 1929, she was the fifth of seven children of relatively well-educated immigrants from the Caribbean island of St Vincent. The multi-ethnic industrial community of Whitney Pier, a part of Sydney, provided more support and encouragement for African Canadians than did Halifax. The Phills family thrived in the environment. After their postsecondary education, all seven children enjoyed successful professional careers in teaching, health care, public service, or the church, all except Gertrude leaving the province to pursue careers in more encouraging environments. In recognition of the Phills's excellence as parents, the Order of Canada was presented to Gertrude's father, Isaac, in 1967.

On her graduation from high school in 1948, Gertrude went to the Provincial Normal College in Truro, where she specialized in that most maternalist of teaching subjects, home economics. She then had a thirty-five-year career as a domestic science teacher. Her first circuit was western Nova Scotia; then, beginning in 1954, she switched to Halifax County. The first sixteen of her thirty-one years in Halifax schools were spent in the eight segregated Black schools of the county. In a period of increasing focus on adult education, Tynes also taught sewing classes in the evening in the same communities. As a Black woman she encountered three common forms of overt discrimination in the 1940s and 1950s: when she was a student she was refused service in a Truro restaurant, she had difficulty finding housing in the Halifax metropolitan area, and, until 1970, her employment was restricted to racially separate schools.

Gertrude married twice but her parenting was confined to the classroom. Raised an Anglican, she eventually subscribed to the postwar culture of Black Halifax by becoming a Baptist in 1971 and joining her church choir and ladies' auxiliary. She also volunteered in the African United Baptist Association Women's Institute, the Nova Scotia Home for Coloured Children, the Black Educators' Association, the Black Professional Women's Group, the Nova Scotia Teachers' Union Retired Teachers' Association, the Association of Teachers of Segregated Schools, the Local Council of Women of Halifax, and the National Council of Women of Canada. She was a member of the board of governors of Northwood Manor, the region's first modern non-profit facility for seniors. In 1995 she collaborated with her teaching colleague Doris Evans to produce a book of reminiscences about Nova Scotia's segregated schools and their teachers.[3]

Some women's careers in Halifax were shaped by racial experience; in other cases a religious vocation was the motivating force. For Sister Mary Clare Flanagan, the church opened the doors to a career working with women and children. Born in Boston in 1902, she was one of eight children, five of whom became professional church workers. The close ties between the Sisters of Charity in Boston and Halifax allowed Sister Mary Clare to enter the orders in Halifax in 1922. She taught first in

Halifax and later in Reserve Mines, Cape Breton, where she became involved in the early work of the cooperative movement centred at St Francis Xavier University. From 1939 to 1945 she was principal of St Margaret's School in Dorchester, Massachusetts. On her return to Nova Scotia, Sister Mary Clare began a new career in social work as the superior of St Theresa's Retreat, a refuge for laywomen in need. In 1950, she graduated from the Maritime School of Social Work with its first specialization in the area of medical social work, and she forged close professional links in the social work community. As director of the Home of the Guardian Angel from 1949 to 1969, Sister Mary Clare was the most visible proponent of the deinstitutionalization of children, encouraging infant adoption and foster-home care. Her expertise in the care of children was usefully deployed in her position as chair of the Family and Child Welfare Division of the Halifax Welfare Council. She pioneered in Nova Scotia the belief that institutions were not the best response for homeless children, and she was an early advocate of group homes and daycare. In particular, she was primarily responsible for the closure of St Joseph's Orphanage and the creation of the St Joseph's day care centre. Like many high profile women of her generation, she was active in the Halifax Branch of the Canadian Mental Health Association. In 1969 she entered the Nova Scotia civil service as staff training and development officer in the Department of Social Services, a position she held until her retirement in 1979. On her retirement she was honoured by the province with a Community Service Award as an outstanding pioneer in social work in eastern Canada. Her notion of professionalism led her to become active in the creation of secular professional organizations such as the Welfare Council of Halifax and the Nova Scotia Association of Child Caring Institutions, of which she was a founding member and the first president. She died in 1987.[4]

Neither Sister Mary Clare nor Gertrude Tynes had direct experience of motherhood; Abbie Lane was so busy that her detractors sometimes considered her to be a negligent mother. Brenda Thompson, on the other hand, came to her activism through her experience of single motherhood, a condition that women were likely to try to hide until modern feminism altered notions of parenting. Born in 1963, Thompson became a welfare mother after her daughter was born. Keen to improve their prospects, Thompson took a business management course but could not find any work but that of waitress. She became interested in MUMS (Mothers United for Metro Shelter), established in 1984 by a militant group of low-income single mothers, including escapees from violent partners, to fight for affordable housing. Although MUMS was short lived, it energized Thompson, who gave voice to her experience by writing a user-friendly guide to welfare services entitled *The Single Mothers' Survival Guide*.[5] She found a sympathetic environment at Mount Saint Vincent University, which, more than any other local institution, advanced the interests of women in education in the last quarter of the twentieth century. Thompson completed a BA in women's studies before going to Acadia University in Wolfville, Nova Scotia, to undertake a master's degree in sociology. She wrote about the very subject that had politicized her and catapulted her into public affairs: 'Single Mother Activists on Welfare.'

Brenda Thompson not only added research to the more usual women's organizational activism, but she was also publicly critical of the minister of social services, Edmund Morris, and was willing to resort to the courts to protect her reputation. When she expressed her low opinion of the 'regressive and sexist welfare policies' of the minister, he retaliated by leaking to the media personal information from Thompson's welfare file. After he refused to make a public apology, Thompson laid charges against him with the help of another single mothers' group, Legal Action for Women on Welfare (LAWW), and won her case. The resulting publicity also helped to focus attention on the problems of single mothers in Nova Scotia. Thompson's activism, criticism of the status quo, and fearless pursuit of her right to privacy constituted important new elements in the late-twentieth-century women's movement in Nova Scotia.[6]

These real-life stories allow us to think about the themes of this collection of essays. We have used them, in a sense, to stand for the many hundreds of women – volunteers, professionals, and activists – who doggedly pursued better lives for themselves, their children, and other women. We were struck by the multiple meanings of motherhood and maternalism they embodied – thus, our title, *Mothers of the Municipality*. Some women faced the individual challenges of biological motherhood, such as birthing and then caring and providing for their children, while others created and staffed the regulatory regimes that shaped the social contours of motherhood. Many women in our study made careers helping mothers and their children. The maternalism of the first wave of feminism continued to be a vital element in women's activism in postwar Halifax and helped to shape policies and institutions. In her study of policies affecting single mothers in Ontario, Margaret Little acknowledges the pivotal role played by bourgeois women's organizations in securing state allowances for mothers but criticizes their failure to temper the moralism of their maternalist ideology.[7] While we, too, acknowledge the repressive moralism that is often part of maternalism, this ideal also contains a genuine concern for improving the lives of women and their children and a recognition of women's valuable unpaid reproductive work.[8]

This collection of essays results from a five-year-long research project about women, work, and social policy in post-1945 Halifax. The initial impetus for the research was twofold. The first was the concern of a group of feminist scholars with the severe cutbacks to services for women in the 1990s, especially in the wake of the elimination of the Canada Assistance Plan. Our sense of the direction of change was that hard-won improvements to the condition and status of women were beginning to erode.[9] Our second concern was the amalgamation in 1996 of four municipalities – the cities of Halifax and Dartmouth, the town of Bedford, and the rest of Halifax County – into one unit called the Halifax Regional Municipality (HRM). The creation of the HRM raised anxiety about women's welfare. Would bringing a multiplicity of municipal services into harmony erode even further the already inadequate services for women? We were especially afraid that the restructuring of provincial income-assistance programs that accompanied municipal amalgamation would make things much worse for many women. In her chapter in this volume, Jeanne Fay's analysis of the new programs in Nova Scotia confirms that these fears were justified.

As the project evolved, it developed a life of its own. Additional scholars and activists became associated with the project and conducted research that significantly contributed to our understanding of the historical experience of women in the HRM since 1945. Although a scholarly study of social policy was our central focus, we also wanted to provide information that would help current women's groups negotiate the terms of the new social order so cogently investigated by Sylvia Bashevkin in her comparative political study of neo-conservatism and post-conservatism in Canada, the United States, and the United Kingdom.[10] The Nova Scotia Advisory Council on the Status of Women has been our community partner. The only government agency specifically concerned with policy affecting women, the advisory council generously provided information, research resources, and meeting space. The council also helped us to develop a relationship with Feminists for Just and Equitable Public Policy (FemJEPP), established in 1998 as a provincial coalition of community-based women's groups committed to ensuring women's full participation in the policy process. The relationship with FemJEPP has enriched our work in innumerable ways and deepened our understanding of the importance of just and equitable public policy in the lives of Nova Scotian women.

Four Themes

Four major overlapping and often interactive themes emerged from the case studies undertaken for the project, and one or more of these themes inform or characterize each of the essays in this collection. The first of these, women's activism, is well illustrated by the four stories at the beginning of this introduction. The magnitude and the impact of this activism surprised us and reminded us that the 1950s and early 1960s were not simply a period of quiet conservatism, born-again domesticity, and consumption. While women's activism is central to all the studies in this volume, the impact of the expansion of the state on women's lives is almost as pervasive. Closely associated with this larger role for government, the increasing secularization of the administration of social institutions is another theme that affected women in distinctive ways. The fourth major theme, the militarization of the Cold War era, assumed heightened importance to women in a town like Halifax, which was an armed forces centre.

Women became activists in three, often overlapping, contexts: in women's organizations, through women's volunteer experiences, and in the individual campaigns of women in key positions in the professions, advocacy groups, and politics. We pursued the theme of women's activism in the HRM through our individual research, and also collectively by hosting a one-day workshop in 1999 at which we invited women who had been active in public life in the 1950s to the 1970s to share their experiences and their stories with us and with one another. Most of those women recognized the importance of a woman's culture to the development of their activism and of their life's work. This culture often took the form of guidance and encouragement by their mothers, which was an important reminder that some women's support networks are intergenerational.[11] Many of the essays in this book focus on the first generation after the Second World War, when women became a successful lobby, nationally, provincially, and municipally. By the mid-1970s the nature of the women's movement was changing, with the advent of a new wave of feminist activism and different demands. These essays make it very clear that the women of the 1940s and 1950s were metaphorical mothers of the new wave.

Another theme that emerged from our research was the impact of the expansion of the role of the state – at the federal, provincial, and municipal level – as employer, service provider, and arbiter of fairness for women in education, employment, and family relations. New postwar federal programs contributed to Halifax's expanding role as a national centre for postsecondary education and a regional one for health. In the wake of the publication of the *Report of the Royal Commission on the Arts, Letters, and Science in Canada* in 1951, the city's five universities benefited when Ottawa began to pay a grant of 50 cents per capita to universities and colleges. Further federal funds were available through the Technical and Vocational Training Assistance Act of 1960. When the assistance plan was restructured in 1967, Ottawa agreed to pay 50 per cent of operating costs of postsecondary institutions, financed in part by further tax transfers to the provinces and in part by cash grants. Recruitment of students to take advantage of the enhanced opportunities was facilitated by the Canada Student Loans Act of 1964.[12] All these measures created employment in the education sector and helped to broaden the intellectual, political, and cultural milieu through the activities of faculty and students. At the same time, the introduction of federal health grants beginning in 1948, government-funded hospital insurance in 1958, and medicare in 1969 greatly expanded Halifax's health care establishment and augmented government payrolls in the city. As a growth industry, health care swelled the ranks of women nurses, physicians, social workers, clerical staff, cleaners, and dietary workers, and also created a demand for clinical psychologists, physiotherapists, occupational therapists, nutritionists, dental hygienists, laboratory technicians, and hospital administrators.

Both the provincial and municipal governments turned to experts in welfare and urban planning to expand their services and advise them on how to attain national standards. For example, the Nova Scotia government invited George Davidson of the Canadian Welfare Council to make recommendations for the reform of provincial welfare programs as part of a provincial study of postwar reconstruction, and city of Halifax called on University of Toronto social work professor Alfred Rose to plan the relocation of Africville in the 1960s. The era of the expert culminated in 1970 with 'Encounter on Urban Environment,' a week-long series of meetings with a panel of male experts brought in to tell Haligonians how to reform their city.

Postwar prosperity reached Halifax a little later than most of Canada, and, when it did, it was based on both old and new forms of government services. In the 1950s and 1960s, the baby boom and a program of rural school consolidation encouraged school construction in Nova Scotia and created an insatiable demand for teachers, who were able to bargain more effectively for higher wages than they had in the past. The Nova Scotia Department of Public Welfare significantly reorganized and expanded its services during the same period, providing new jobs for both social workers and clerical staff. Municipal services also underwent growth. Whatever public welfare there was after the war was organized by municipal governments. Until the late 1950s, Poor Law relief shaped the policies in Halifax, Dartmouth, and Halifax County, but gradually all three municipalities developed more modern welfare bureaucracies. With the adoption of the Canada Assistance Plan in 1966 municipal welfare services expanded dramatically. The creation of several public housing projects in the area was also an important development for women. The press reported in 1972, for example, that 108 of the 348 families in Mulgrave Park (a public housing complex in Halifax's North End) were headed by a single parent, usually a woman.[13] Expansion of recreation services and public transit also created employment and increased women's ability to travel greater distances to participate in the paid workforce. However, it is important to note that heavy reliance on government spending for employment increased the area's vulnerability to the cutbacks that began in the 1970s.[14]

Another development between the 1950s and the 1970s was the secularization of sectarian social institutions. Although this change was pervasive and had a major impact on men, women, and children in Halifax, it had a special effect on women because of their work in and reliance on traditional denominational and religious associations and agencies. Whereas the Anglo-Celtic majority remained politically and economically dominant, the major social division between Protestants and Catholics withered in the 1970s. Until then, distinctive sectarian accommodations included alternating Catholics and Protestants in civic office (e.g., mayor, police chief, fire chief) and arrangements for Catholic and Protestant public schools, which in the City of Halifax were administered by a single school board, a practice dating from the introduction of free public schooling in the 1860s. Equally important was the development of parallel Catholic and Protestant voluntary, social, and charitable institutions.[15] Since the 1970s this pattern has broken down, reflecting a number of trends at the local and national level. These included amalgamation of areas of Halifax County where separate Protestant and Catholic schools were not the practice, the expansion of the role of the state in the provision of social services, and gains in the area of human rights, which have broadened the participation of other ethnic and religious groups within the social and political life of the city.

One group of women who were distinctively affected by the decline in denominational service were women in religious orders or closely tied to religious institutions. Catholic nuns, especially the Sisters of Charity, Salvation Army officers, and deaconesses of the major Protestant churches had provided low-cost expertise in social service and had been vested with considerable professional control. Until the 1970s almost all the social institutions that catered to the needs of women and children relied on women motivated by a religious vocation. Yet, as Kathryn McPherson recognized in her study of nursing in twentieth-century Canada, 'religious influence on social services outside Quebec remains an underdeveloped area of historical scholarship.'[16] In Halifax the institutions controlled by religious women included hospitals, orphanages, reformatories, homes for unmarried mothers, schools, and a college. The loss of the delivery of most social services by religious organizations was therefore a mixed blessing as far as women's professional development was concerned since in state-run programs men often replaced women as administrators.

A fourth issue, the frightening weaponry of the Cold War, intimidated most Canadians, but its significance was magnified in Halifax, where the Canadian navy had a high profile. At the same time, military preparedness ensured that naval spending would continue to be very important to the city's economy. A report commissioned by the City of Halifax in 1960 identified the defence services industry as the fastest-growing employer of labour in Halifax since 1921. The armed forces provided year-round employment, and introduced to the area a reserve of labour in the form of armed forces wives who were trained professionals and were recruited from time to time to help ease the shortage of health care and welfare workers. Military spending was largely recession proof.[17] It produced dedicated housing schemes, brought in service personnel and their families of many different racial and ethnic backgrounds, and, when ships were at sea, created a cadre of wives who spent a significant portion of their child-rearing years as single parents. Halifax's naval function had a major impact on the social and political culture of the area, which was reflected by women's activism both in the peace movement and in civil defence.

We believe that the essays in this collection address a significant gap in Canadian historiography, not only in terms of social welfare and women's activism, but also because there are so few community case studies that encompass this period. Very little has yet been written about women's reform work and activism in the years between the two waves of feminism, something this study helps to document. The way such topics are integrated here in a study of Halifax provides a sharper focus and more coherence than can be found in existing collections of essays on Canadian women. Moreover, the contributors themselves bring to the analysis a commanding breadth and depth of knowledge about women in the Halifax area. By taking a community-based approach, we believe that a study centred on the Halifax Regional Municipality will make a valuable contribution to debates about women's history since the Second World War.

This collection owes a debt to feminist scholars, trained in a number of social science disciplines, who have raised questions about women's experiences in Canada since the war. Feminist scholars have been especially interested in women's relationship to the state – a major theme in this collection. A kind of consensus has emerged that, flawed as it is, the welfare state has on balance improved women's access to resources, including both income and services, and expanded government has created significant employment opportunities for women and spurred union organization within the public sector.[18] More recently feminist debates have been addressing the complexities and ambiguities of such questions. The relationship between voluntary organizations and the state has special meaning for women, as does the role of professionalization. Some of the essays ask questions about the relationship between the rights state – that is, the development of new state provisions for the protection of human rights – and the welfare state and how they both connect to the women's movement. Feminists have also debated the impact of the web of shifting and mutating federal and provincial agencies created to bring women's concerns to the policy process – and how many of these initiatives have been smoke and mirrors.[19]

The emergence of feminist scholarship as part of the second wave has generated and stimulated both theoretical and concrete political debates and has provided new concepts for analysing women's lives. A major difference between the first and second wave has been the acknowledgment – sometimes reluctant – of the diversity of women's experience created by race, class, age, sexual identity, and ability. The capacity of the movement to accommodate this diversity has been an important element in the debates. Scholars have also had to address the continuing dichotomy of the public and private in women's lives. Reaping the benefits of the first wave of feminism, Canadian women have made considerable inroads in expanding their power and representation in public and political life. But the persistent economic inequality women face still reflects the unequal sexual division of labour in private life.[20]

The fact that our community is not the more familiar Toronto, Vancouver, or Montreal has forced us to navigate a narrow channel between unique defining features of the historical experience of the region and the 'Canadian-ness' of the historical experience of an economically and politically marginalized region.[21] Although sometimes frustrating, the particular tensions of describing the Halifax case are also often fruitful, producing scholarship that addresses national trends in a particular local context. To date most of the studies of women's relationship to the social policy process have focused on the national level – national women's organizations and federal government policy. However, municipal and provincial governments deliver many of the programs and services most important to women's daily lives, and the policies they develop in the areas of labour law, human rights, social assistance, and education, to name only a few, are of utmost importance to women. The relationship between public welfare and private charitable organizations may also be best addressed through studies at the community level.

The Halifax Regional Municipality (HRM)

Halifax provides us with both differences and similarities with respect to the wider Canadian postwar experience. One of the most profound differences was the failure of large-scale industrialization to take permanent root in the city. The Halifax Explosion of 1917 devastated the industrial North End, and many of the factories were not rebuilt. Deindustrialization has continued ever since, and the shortage of industrial jobs has affected women as well as men. In 1961 the percentage of women working in manufacturing in Nova Scotia was eight percentage points lower (9.2 per cent) than in Canada as a whole (17.1 per cent). Although the regional economy has exhibited continuing weaknesses, Halifax itself has been subject to many of the features of social modernization that apply to more industrialized areas because it is a provincial capital, regional service provider, and local consumer centre. Competitive wage rates have not been one of these features. Between 1949 and 1987, per capita incomes in Nova Scotia were about 70 per cent of the national average.[22] Even the federal government took advantage of the cheaper labour, paying regional rates to federal public servants, which meant that the same work in Halifax commanded a lower wage than in Toronto.[23]

The city's non-industrial economy also meant that the history of labour relations was markedly different from that in other cities. Before the advent of the unionization of the public service in the 1960s, few women were union members, and those who were found that they were subject to an extremely patriarchal labour culture. In 1952, the president of the Halifax-Dartmouth Trades and Labour Council described council member Nellie Bradley as 'a great trade unionist' for her success in securing a settlement for employees of the Lord Nelson Hotel but also, and equally important, for doing a great job for the Canadian Labour Congress convention in Halifax several years earlier, 'when she very ably led our local ladies on the entertaining committee for the visitors.'[24] In 1970 women constituted only 11 per cent of organized workers in Nova Scotia although they were 28 per cent of the permanent workforce.[25] Some unions – the Canadian Union of Public Employees (CUPE), for example – were considered to be very late converts to the rights of female members.[26] The public sector unionization that women increasingly experienced after 1967 was characterized by labour strife that was just as bitter as that affecting industrial workers elsewhere in Canada. For example, nurses employed in the Victoria General and Nova Scotia Hospitals had to strike in 1973 to secure a reasonable settlement. Two years later they were out again. Then as now, nurses were in short supply and their actions and those of other employees in the health sector suggest that the more recent labour conflict between health care workers and the provincial government built on a legacy of the union activism of women in the public sector over the last three decades.

Another legacy of deindustrialization has been demographic: the weakness of Nova Scotia's economy was a major factor in slow population growth. Although Nova Scotians participated wholeheartedly in the baby boom, the province has not received a significant proportion of the immigrants who have come to Canada since the Second World War. Because many working-class immigrants were looking for industrial employment, Halifax was not attractive to them. Whereas European immigration accounted for a third of Ontario's population growth

TABLE 1
Population of the Halifax Regional Municipality, 1941–1996

Year	City of Halifax	Dartmouth	Halifax County/HRM*	Nova Scotia	HRM as % of NS
1941	70,488	10,847	122,656	578,000	21.2
1951	85,589	15,037	162,217	642,600	25.2
1961	92,511	46,066**	225,723	737,000	30.6
1971	122,035†	64,770	261,435	789,000	33.1
1981	114,594	62,333	288,126	847,400	34.0
1991	114,455	67,798	330,846	901,000	36.7
1996	113,910	65,629	342,966	942,700	36.4

Source: All population figures compiled from published reports of the Census of Canada.
* Halifax County included, among other areas, the cities of Halifax and Dartmouth. In 1996 it was transformed into the HRM.
** 1961 figures for Dartmouth reflect a major amalgamation of outlying areas.
† 1971 figures for the City of Halifax reflect municipal amalgamation.

between 1951 and 1961, the Atlantic region lost a million people in the postwar period. Nova Scotia saw thousands of its young people leave the region in search of better economic opportunities in the rest of the country.[27] Nevertheless the population of Halifax has not lacked diversity. Over 2 per cent of the population of the HRM comprises Blacks with a long history as residents. Halifax has always received a trickle of newcomers from each major wave of immigration, bringing Jews from Europe, Lebanese, Greeks, Italians, and Chinese, for example. The expanding health and education sectors attracted highly trained professionals, initially from the United States and the United Kingdom, and later from India, Africa, and the Middle East.

Despite the economic problems that plagued the province, greater Halifax has been a growth area since the 1950s. Between the 1940s and the 1990s the population of the county (both urban and rural) tripled. Urbanization has involved expansion. First Dartmouth and then Halifax incorporated surrounding areas, providing precedents for county-wide amalgamation in 1996.

If the experience of industrialization, labour relations, and population growth set Halifax apart from other Canadian cities, its experience in other areas was more similar to the Canadian norm. Three such areas are particularly important to this study: the continuing process of suburbanization, the roles of women in the family and in the paid workforce, and the emergence of second-wave feminism. Since 1945, suburban development has formed a continuous ring around Halifax Harbour and the Bedford Basin, and has penetrated well into the rural interior and along the Atlantic shore of Halifax County. The fact that the old city of Halifax was built on a small peninsula limited development possibilities. By the middle of the nineteenth century a number of industries had moved across the harbour to Dartmouth, and once regular ferry service was supplemented by harbour bridges in the second half of the twentieth-century, residential development in Dartmouth also increased. Fishing villages on both sides of the harbour and along the Eastern Shore and the South Shore of Halifax County gradually became modest suburbs. In the 1950s, a Nova Scotia government cooperative housing program turned Sackville, an old farming community north of the Bedford Basin, into a residential suburb. The community of Bedford became a very prosperous suburban town. Many communities on the urban periphery, both African Nova Scotian and white, depended on subsistence production, supplemented by occasional waged work in town. Residential suburbs spread slowly around the harbour and the basin and into formerly rural areas in the eastern and western ends of the county. Manufacturers and distributors began to move to the suburbs in the early 1960s, a trend that continues into the twenty-first century. So did residents, resulting in a decline in the population of the City of Halifax and a more gradual decline in Dartmouth after 1971. Yet, even at the end of the twentieth century there were still pockets of the HRM that were distinctly rural.

After the Second World War, women in Nova Scotia, like their sisters across Canada, were moving to the suburbs, marrying in larger numbers and at younger ages, and having more children than their mothers. Birth rates remained very high until the mid-1960s. Thereafter declining rates reflected changing patterns of women's attachment to the paid workforce and the increased availability of effective contraception. Women were also living longer and were more likely to be divorced. From the 1970s onward birth rates continued to decline, average age at marriage increased, and divorce rates remained high.[28] These patterns changed the age composition of the Canadian population, and by the end of the twentieth century the combination of increased longevity and the aging of the baby boom generation significantly changed the demographic profile of the country. In Nova Scotia, where outmigration was such a significant factor, the aging of the population was slightly greater than the national average.[29]

Women in the Halifax area also followed the national trend towards greater participation in the paid labour force. For example, in 1951, married women constituted about 25 per cent of women workers in Canada. By 1961 that had risen to 50 per cent. In the Halifax area over 48 per cent of women in the labour force were married, widowed, or divorced. Despite regional disparity and lower incomes, by 1961 women in the City of Halifax were participating in waged work at a rate comparable to that of women in Montreal. In the City of Dartmouth, rates were even higher, comparable to those of Calgary, Hamilton, Kitchener, and London. Like their counterparts across the country, married women worked because they needed the money and wanted to improve their families' standard of living. By the 1960s, the largest employers of women were governments – municipal, provincial, and federal. This pattern reflected the legacy of early-twentieth-century de-industrialization and the steadily increasing importance of all kinds of government services, including defence, health, education, and regional development.[30]

Women's economic inequality was one of the major factors that spurred Halifax women to become active in the second wave of feminism. Although very little research has yet been done in this area, we know that Halifax feminists took up the new women's agenda, which focused on employment equality, integrity of the body, and access to power. They were especially concerned about the failure of federal and provincial labour legislation to provide equal opportunity and equal wages for women in the male-dominated workforce. Stimulated by the recommendations contained in the *Report of the Royal Commission on the Status of Women* in 1970, the first significant breakthrough for women in Nova Scotia occurred in 1972, when discrimination was legally defined to include discrimination on the basis of sex. This meant that such grievances against employers could be taken to the Human Rights Commission. In terms of wages, however, the scene remained grim, with women in 1975 earning only half the income of men. Feminists recognized that the main problem was the sex segregation of jobs, whereby 'female' jobs were underremunerated in comparison with 'male' jobs. A group of Halifax feminists established Pro-Feminae in 1974 to support the efforts of women to secure training and jobs in fields that were considered non-traditional for women. As an employment agency, funded by what was then the Department of Manpower, Pro-Feminae also tried to educate employers about the abilities of female workers and dispel the myths about women's inability to drive transport trucks, use machine tools, go to sea.[31]

In their efforts to promote sex education, birth control, freedom from male violence, and access to abortion, feminists discovered the lack of unity among women, and much effort had to be spent combatting anti-feminists, anti-choice advocates, and others who had the support of a few prominent women such as municipal politicians Margaret Stanbury and Eileen Stubbs.[32] While sex education and abortion rights remained contested issues, significant strides were made with respect to providing birth control information and protecting victims of sexual assault and male violence against women. Feminists found, however, that they had to defend themselves against charges of extremism. In 1975, for example, a spokeswoman for Halifax Rape Relief, adopting a more moderate tone to quell the criticism, emphasized its counselling and support functions and insisted that 'We are not a militant organization, determined to seek out every rapist in the city.'[33]

As elsewhere in Canada, progress in women's gaining access to the power structures in the city and province was slow.[34] Few women ran for municipal office, and in the realm of party politics the impression among women was that it was more difficult to win the nomination than to win the election.[35] When a candidate for a seat in the provincial legislature emerged, as Muriel Duckworth did in 1974, traditional women's organizations in the city would not rally behind her. When Duckworth asked for its support, the Local Council of Women, for example, hid behind its creed of non-partisanship.[36] In the age of the 'expert,' women also found themselves being sidelined when it came to consultation on political issues. To cite Duckworth's experience again, when she attended a session of the much touted Halifax Encounter on public planning (1970), she boldly stood up and asked why none of the invited discussants were female. Clearly women, let alone feminists, had a job making the male power structure recognize their stake in the future of their city and county. Inasmuch as feminists were more willing to stand up and be counted, they contributed to the new citizen rights movement as well as women's rights. Duckworth chaired the Movement for Citizens' Voice and Action (MOVE), which coordinated citizen participation in the city's planning in the 1970s.[37]

Like second-wave feminists more generally, those in Halifax initially overlooked matters of class and race. This was succinctly demonstrated in the organization of a provincial conference, 'Women Today in Nova Scotia: Our Potential, Opportunities, Priorities,' held at Mount Saint Vincent University in 1974 in anticipation of International Women's Year. While the conference demonstrated the generational differences that could be expected in a general discussion of women's status, it also starkly revealed white middle-class insensitivity. When *The 4th Estate*, a progressive Halifax weekly, reported that the North End Neighbourhood Centre had been asked to find 'two poor black women and two poor white women' to attend the conference, the journalist facetiously opined that 'someone should set up a rental service providing low income people for bourgeois liberal functions.'[38] Although a number of the recommendations of Nova Scotia's own Task Force on the Status of Women in 1976 addressed the needs of minority women, the Nova Scotia Advisory Council on the Status of Women (NSACSW), established in 1977, paid only token attention to the province's minorities, as Janet Guildford's chapter on the NSACSW in the volume makes clear.

The essays that follow explore our four major themes of women's activism, the role of the state, the secularization of services, and the influence of the Cold War in the specific location of Halifax and Nova Scotia – often reflecting the complicated internal relationships between city and province. As a number of the essays point out, provincial legislation determined part of the framework for women's lives, whether the issue was social assistance, daycare, or child protection. Fingard's essay on women's organizations between 1945 and 1975 is designed to provide background for women's activism in Halifax. Similarly, Guildford's essay on the end of the Poor Law sets the context for other changes in social policy in the postwar period. The next cluster of essays, by Tillotson, Morton, and Fay, discusses the reform of services for women and children in Halifax. The chapter about Black women at work by Bernard and Fingard combines many themes – the modernization of services and the expansion of the role of the state, especially in the area of human rights – and examines them from the unique perspective of Black women living on the urban fringe.

The overall organization of the chapters is chronological, and we were struck by the fact that six of them – Fingard's on women's organizations, Morton's two essays on unmarried mothers and daycare, Fay's on mothers on social assistance, Gregor's on the St John Ambulance home nursing program, and Bernard and Fingard's on Black women at work – for reasons integral to their subject, end in the mid-1970s. A coincidence of timing of this magnitude calls for some analysis. First, it reflects the fact that the postwar expansion and reform of welfare programs ground to a halt in the mid-1970s. Second, by that time second-wave feminism was generating new kinds of social and economic experiences for women and new forms of women's activism.

The chapters encourage readers to explore the multiple and overlapping dimensions of themes. Frances Gregor's essay on home nursing programs and Frances Early's on the Voice of Women (VOW) in the 1960s, for example, both investigate aspects of women's response to the Cold War, but Early's work on the VOW also helps us understand how some women in Halifax moved from a more traditional maternal feminism into a revitalized and reformed women's movement. Guildford's study of the Nova Scotia Advisory Council on the Status of Women looks at one of the major institutions of the second wave of feminism in Halifax and Nova Scotia.

It is our hope that readers will find in what follows a new, and inspiring, perception of women and social change in the postwar period.

NOTES

1 C. Bruce Fergusson, *Alderman Abbie Lane of Halifax* (Windsor, NS: Lancelot Press, 1976), 24.
2 Ibid.
3 The biographical information on Gertrude Tynes is based on the video-taped Workshop, sponsored by the Women, Work, and Social Policy in Post-1945 Halifax Project, 7 May 1999; Gertrude Tynes interview by Judith Fingard, 9 Jan. 2001; Charles R. Saunders, *Share and Care: The Story of the Nova Scotia Home for Colored Children* (Halifax: Nimbus Publishing, 1994); and Doris Evans and Gertrude Tynes, *Telling the Truth: Reflections – Segregated Schools in Nova Scotia* (Hantsport, NS: Lancelot Press, 1995).
4 For more information on Sister Mary Clare's role in the Home of the Guardian Angel, see Suzanne Morton's essay 'Managing the Unmarried Mother "Problem": Halifax Maternity Homes,' in this collection. The biographical information on Sister Mary Clare Flanagan was generously supplied by the Sisters of Charity of Saint Vincent de Paul, Halifax, Archives.
5 Brenda Thompson, *The Single Mothers' Survival Guide*, Nova Scotian edition (Halifax: Dal-PIRG, 1991). Thompson is in the process of putting the *Guide* online as this collection goes to press.
6 See Brenda Juanita Thompson, 'Single Mother Activists on Welfare: An Examination of Social Roots of Collective Action in Nova Scotia' (MA thesis, Acadia University, 1992); Linda Christiansen-Ruffman, 'Women's Con-

ception of the Political: Three Canadian Women's Organizations,' in Myra Marx Ferree and Patricia Yancy Martin, eds., *Feminist Organization: Harvest of the New Women's Movement* (Philadelphia: Temple University Press, 1995), 372–93; Thompson, *The Single Mothers' Survival Guide.*

7 Margaret Little, *'No Car, No Radio, No Liquor Permit': The Moral Regulation of Single Mothers in Ontario, 1920–1997* (Toronto: Oxford University Press, 1998).

8 Mariana Valverde, *The Age of Light, Soap, and Water: Moral Reform in English Canada, 1885–1925* (Toronto: McClelland and Stewart, 1991), for example, emphasizes the moral regulation inherent in these reform activities.

9 Recent scholarship strongly confirms our sense of the direction of change in Canada. See, for example, Sylvia Bashevkin, *Welfare Hot Buttons: Women, Work, and Social Policy Reform* (Toronto: University of Toronto Press; Pittsburgh: University of Pittsburgh Press, 2002) and James J. Rice and Michael J. Prince, *Changing Politics of Canadian Social Policy* (Toronto: University of Toronto Press, 2000).

10 Bashevkin, *Welfare Hot Buttons.*

11 The workshop, held on 7 May 1999, was called 'Making a Difference: Halifax Women Remember the 1950s, 60s and 70s.' Participants included researchers Judith Fingard (history), Frances Gregor (nursing), Janet Guildford (history), Suzanne Morton (history), and Jeanne Fay (social work), and activists Dr. Pamela Brown, Sister Mary Jean Burns, Muriel Duckworth, Joan Fraser, Judith Giffin, Dorothy Grantmyre, Fran Maclean, Judge Sandra Oxner, Linda Christiansen-Ruffman, Myrna Slater, Gertrude Tynes, and Sue Wolstenholme. The workshop participants agreed to a video-tape record of the workshop, which will become part of the archival collection of the Women, Work, and Social Policy Project.

12 Kenneth Norrie and Douglas Owram, *A History of the Canadian Economy* (Toronto: Harcourt Brace Jovanovich, 1991), 592–6.

13 *The 4th Estate* (Halifax), 3 Feb. 1972, 12–13. For a slightly later period, see Gerda R. Wekerle, 'The Shift to the Market: Gender and Housing Disadvantage,' in Patricia M. Evans and Gerda R. Wekerle, eds., *Women and the Canadian Welfare State: Challenges and Change* (Toronto: University of Toronto Press, 1997), 170–94.

14 Norrie and Owram, *A History*, 541.

15 See Judith Fingard, Janet Guildford, and David Sutherland, *Halifax: The First 250 Years* (Halifax: Formac, 1999).

16 Kathryn M. McPherson, *Bedside Matters: The Transformation of Canadian Nursing, 1900–1990* (Toronto: Oxford University Press, 1996), 23. A recent exception is provided by Renée Lafferty, 'Child Welfare in Halifax, 1900–

1960: Institutional Transformation, Denominationalism, and the Creation of a "Public" Welfare System' (PhD thesis, Dalhousie University, 2003).

17 Alasdair M. Sinclair, *The Economic Base of the Halifax Metropolitan Area and Some Implications of Recent Population Forecasts* (Halifax: Institute of Public Affairs, Dalhousie University, 1961).

18 See Janine Brody, ed., *Women and Canadian Public Policy* (Toronto: Harcourt Brace, 1996).

19 See, for example, Nancy Christie, *Engendering the State: Family, Work, and Welfare in Canada* (Toronto: University of Toronto Press, 2000); Little, '*No Car*'; Gerard Boychuk, *Patchworks of Purpose: The Development of Provincial Social Assistance Regimes in Canada* (Montreal and Kingston: McGill-Queen's University Press, 1998); and James Struthers, *The Limits of Affluence: Welfare in Ontario, 1920–1970* (Toronto: University of Toronto Press, 1994).

20 Meg Luxton and Ester Reiter, 'Double, Double, Toil and Trouble ... Women's Experience of Work and Family in Canada, 1980–1995,' in Evans and Wekerle, eds., *Women and the Canadian Welfare State*, 197–221.

21 Suzanne Morton, 'Gender, Place and Region: Thoughts on the State of Women in Atlantic Canadian History,' *Atlantis* 25 (Fall 2000): 119–28.

22 Norrie and Owram, *A History of the Canadian Economy*, 541.

23 *The 4th Estate*, 28 Nov. 1974, 5.

24 Minutes, 10 Dec. 1952, Halifax-Dartmouth District Trades and Labour Council, Public Archives of Nova Scotia (PANS), MG 20, 3151-3, 66–7.

25 *Women at Work in Nova Scotia* (Halifax: Halifax Women's Bureau, 1973), 35.

26 *The 4th Estate*, 30 Sept. 1971, 17.

27 Joy Parr, ed., *A Diversity of Women: Ontario, 1945–1980* (Toronto: University of Toronto Press, 1995), 4.

28 Mary Jane Mossman and Morag MacLean, 'Family Law and Social Assistance Programs: Rethinking Equality,' in Evans and Wekerle, eds., *Women and the Canadian Welfare State*, 119.

29 Susan Lilley and Joan M. Campbell, *Shifting Sands: The Changing Shape of Atlantic Canada – Economic and Demographic Trends and Their Impacts on Seniors* (Halifax: Health Promotion and Programs Branch, Atlantic Regional Office, Health Canada, 1999).

30 Canada, *1961 Census, Labour Force, Bulletin 3.1-7*, Labour force 15 years and older, by marital status, schooling, class of worker, and sex for incorporated cities, towns, and villages of 10,000 population and over.

31 *The 4th Estate*, 19 March 1975, 2.

32 Ibid., 6 Dec. 1973, 1; 18 April 1974, 8.

33 Ibid., 30 April 1975, 6.

34 Margaret Conrad, 'Women and Political Culture in Atlantic Canada,' paper

presented to Building Women's Leadership in Atlantic Canada, Mount Saint Vincent University, Halifax, December 2001.

35 *The 4th Estate*, 5 Oct. 1972, 6. See Fingard, 'Women's Organizations: The Heart and Soul of Women's Activism,' in the collection.

36 Minutes, 8 March, 21 March 1974, Local Council of Women of Halifax, PANS, MG 20, 536–8.

37 *The 4th Estate*, 15 Feb. 1973, 5.

38 Ibid., 24 Oct. 1974, 4; 14 Nov. 1974, 8.

Women's Organizations: The Heart and Soul of Women's Activism

JUDITH FINGARD

At the 2000 conference of the Atlantic Council of the Canadian Federation of University Women, delegates expressed concern for the future of women's voluntary organizations. They cited such factors as the aging of the current membership and the lack of time available to younger, working women because of their family obligations and career pressures. One member opined, 'Young women today work during the day and parent and house-keep at night. When do they have time to take on issues such as education and legislation and status of women?' Yet not all delegates made bleak predictions, and most felt that women's organizations were greatly needed: 'Women's support groups are the only way things get done.' A few expressed optimism that organizations would reinvent themselves in the future to meet new exigencies, that what we were seeing was merely a cyclical decline.[1] About the same time, a member of the service-oriented Junior League of Halifax acknowledged that a membership comprised of professionals instead of the stay-at-home mums of an earlier generation meant less time for good works. But, she observed, 'our enthusiasm is as high as ever. The challenge to all of us is to give back to the community.'[2]

The power of women's organizations has long been of interest to historians and other social scientists. For the postwar period, their analyses have focused largely on national organizations. Significantly, however, there has never been a national women's organization in Canada that was anything other than a federation of local affiliates, than the national sum of its community-based constituencies. Among the national organizations that have branches in cities and towns, and intermediate provincial or regional associations, are two that are unique because they also serve as federations or councils of a large majority of different women's organizations. They are the National Council of Women (NCW), a product of first-wave feminism, and the National Action Committee on the Status of Women (NAC), a product of second-wave feminism. Although the NCW has demonstrated remarkable resilience, the younger organization has been far more involved in the concerns generated by the modern feminist agenda. In a sense, NAC replaced the NCW as the voice for women at the national level.

The significance of women's political activism through voluntary association in women's organizations has produced the hypothesis, favoured by Jill Vickers and her associates, that Canadian women's movements, rooted in organizations, have given Canadian women a voice that has reflected feminist influences far more effectively than has women's involvement in party politics. Moreover, the ability of women to sustain this collective approach to women's issues over several generations has legitimized the movement approach and rendered it more of a political constant than an occasional influence. Certainly, in the case of Nova Scotia, it appears that women favoured this form of activism over holding political office. In her analysis of three feminist organizations from the mid-1980s in the province, all of which existed outside the orbit of national federations, Linda Christiansen-Ruffman also illustrates how 'women are organized in groups to realize their political agenda.'[3]

The failure of women to move beyond the hard-won suffrage campaigns of the First World War period and seek political office continuously troubled the Local Council of Women (LCW) of Halifax and its affiliates, especially the secular ones. Unfortunately the LCW's determination to remain non-partisan, together with its tendency to explore too many issues concurrently, meant that the political spadework they undertook was largely ineffectual. The LCW lobbied for a quarter century before the first woman, Kathleen (Mrs H.L.) Stewart, was finally appointed to the Halifax School Board in 1935.[4] They had to wait another two decades to see the first woman, Alderman Abbie Lane, chair the school board. In 1936 the LCW rejoiced in the election of the first woman, Catherine McLean (Mrs M.T.) Sullivan, to the Halifax City Council as alderman for Ward 3. Two years later Mary T. King (later King-Myers) was elected to the Halifax County Council and served in that capacity off and on for many years. Because other women did not put themselves forward as candidates, further progress was delayed until 1951, when Abbie Lane became alderman for Ward 2 of the city.[5]

It was much the same story in neighbouring Dartmouth. In 1952 the first woman, Gladys Guptill, was elected to the Dartmouth Town Council. In the course of her first term she became chair of the Dartmouth School Board and, in her second, deputy mayor. In 1961 Eileen Stubbs, a home and school activist and mother of eight, who had been elected a county councillor in 1958, entered the new Dartmouth City Council. Many vicissitudes later, she became the metro region's first female mayor – for Dartmouth – in 1973. In the meantime, Silvia Hudson was elected to the reconstituted county council in 1967. In all the metro jurisdictions there was little effective follow-up to these political firsts.[6]

As for provincial and federal elections, no female candidates emerged in the metropolitan area before the 1970s. In the immediate postwar period, LCW members urged women to at least join political parties, where they might try to exert reformist influences.[7] Those who did were segregated in women's party organizations that were more like genteel ladies' auxiliaries than political pressure groups. Moreover, as late as 1976, not more than 10 per cent of the presidents of mixed-gender provincial constituency associations of all parties were women.[8]

Why were women so reluctant to enter the political fray, even at the municipal level? Two Halifax clubwomen, representing different generations, speculated about this matter in 1946, when questioned by Catherine Cleverdon, the pioneer historian of female suffrage in Canada.[9] Ella Maud Murray was eighty years old at the time but was still the driving force behind the citizenship committee of the Halifax Local Council of Women, in which she led study sessions and regularly articulated and revised a program of priorities for the council, including women's responsibilities to their communities. A long-time journalist for the Halifax daily press, Murray, who retained her surname in marriage, believed that, with the end of the war, women would have political opportunity but might prove reluctant to take it. She did not see the discouraging factor as male opposition but rather male incompetence. As she put it, women are 'appalled when they think of the task ahead to try to make good on the errors the men have made.' Breaking into the old parties would not be easy because of 'custom'; thus, new parties offered better opportunities. Yet Murray was not optimistic about the opportunities for the CCF because, she speculated, 'Maritimers are not very quick to "cotton to" third parties.'[10] In another letter Murray may have unwittingly identified the reason for women's wariness of party politics. Women had for decades been devoted to their separate organi-

zations, which served 'to broaden and deepen' their thoughts, particularly through participation in the Woman's Christian Temperance
Union, the Council of Women, and the Women's Institutes.[11]

Murray's friend Abbie Lane, also a journalist but younger than Murray, was more critical about men's attitudes towards prospective
female politicians. She felt men feared women's ability, directness, and
impatience with posturing. While suggesting that women's political
education and campaigning skills were promoted within the women's
auxiliaries of the established parties – she herself had been president of
her local Women's Conservative Club – she directly acknowledged the
effective social activism of mainstream women's organizations, 'which
are strictly non-political but who wield a great deal of influence on all
questions of public interest.'[12] Moreover she believed that all women's
clubs agreed that women's advancement depended on women's own
efforts.[13]

Almost a decade later, in 1955, Nova Scotian women were, according to a report to the Provincial Council of Women, still serving their
political apprenticeship through volunteer service. 'Later, and we
hope, not much later,' the report suggested, 'they will be ready in
appreciable number to seek and hold public office in various ways, so
that their potential influence can be really used.'[14] With a focus more
on the ends than the means, the *Report of the Nova Scotia Task Force on
the Status of Women* suggested twenty-one years later that 'volunteer
activities have been an important avenue through which women have
been able to exert pressure for social change, often as a forerunner to
government action.'[15] Women of the 1970s still eschewed party politics
but had exchanged the role of citizen-apprentice for that of citizen-
activist.

I

Because of its role as a federation of women's organizations and its
goal of enhancing women's status in society, the Local Council of
Women of Halifax, founded in 1894, was recognized by the male political establishment as a voice for women's concerns. Until the late
1940s, the LCW set the agenda for activist women under the guidance
of such experienced champions of maternal feminism as Agnes Dennis
and Ella Murray. With their passing in 1947 and 1949, respectively, the
council became more of an information-exchange service for women's
and community issues than an initiator of change. The council – as

well as some of its major affiliates – also named representatives to a number of boards and committees. These appointments provided the female citizen's only direct input into the political process in policy matters that were of vital importance to women, such as public welfare, employment, housing, and community development.[16] Like the new generation of associations that emerged in the 1960s and 1970s, the LCW continued to have financial support from government in the form of a small annual municipal grant until 1970.[17]

For many years following the war, the Local Council of Women enjoyed the support, through affiliation, of most women's and women-centred organizations in the city and environs, though not all affiliations persisted over the longer term. In the council, women found a common ground that was often lacking in other spheres of life. Prominent among the barriers that were overcome through council work was religious difference, a contentious issue in a number of ways. Until the 1960s, the bifurcation of society in the city of Halifax between Catholics and Protestants was remarkably resilient; yet Catholic and Protestant women worked side by side in the LCW. Clubs that were exclusively either Catholic or Protestant readily affiliated with the LCW. Moreover, in a city where racial discrimination was highly visible, Jewish women's organizations affiliated with the LCW in the interwar period. Beginning in the late 1950s, the civil rights movement led to the recognition that gender transcended race, and Black women's organizations were welcomed to affiliate by the early 1960s. The LCW had 87 affiliates at its high point in 1960, but, by all accounts, many organizations remained outside its net.[18] In 1946 prominent clubwoman Abbie Lane had identified 176 women's groups, and a 1975 study completed for the federal Ministry of State for Urban Affairs, under Linda Christiansen-Ruffman's direction, drew on information supplied by 156 such groups in the Halifax metropolitan area.[19]

Two of the LCW's affiliates that provide us with some insight into how women could either work to overcome legal discrimination or contribute to the community through service were the Halifax Club of Business and Professional Women (HCBPW) and the Junior League of Halifax (JLH), each of which, like the LCW itself, had a national and international presence.

The Halifax Club of Business and Professional Women was organized in 1936. Its members were overwhelmingly single working women – 97 of 121 in 1947. Specifically dedicated to the improvement of women's status by securing equal opportunities for women in citizenship and employment, the HCBPW was an advocate for the concerns of modern working women. Unlike some other Clubs of Business and Professional Women in that province – those in Sydney and New Glasgow, for example – the Halifax club rejected 'service' and concentrated on promoting the legislative underpinnings of gender equality. Although its members included the occasional lawyer, physician, or accountant, most were employed in high status 'female' jobs in hospitals and clinics, schools, offices, and welfare institutions. By the 1970s, working women's professional organizations and employee associations and unions had made inroads into the club's natural constituency and the HCBPW was aging: one-third of its members were retired from the workforce.[20]

The Junior League, a contemporary of the Club of Business and Professional Women, was launched in 1932 and incorporated in 1935. For purposes of continuous energy and renewal, it confined its active membership to women under the age of forty-five, thereby escaping the aging membership that afflicted both the HCBPW and the LCW. This approach ran into difficulty when young middle-class married women started to supplement their homemaking with careers. The league then had to rely more on a 'sustainer' group of older women who were former members. The Junior League was a service club with a unique mission to educate its members as community volunteers for its own and other projects. The work it adopted was wide ranging and on the cutting edge of social reform. Although, beginning with church benevolent societies in the early nineteenth century, service to others had always been considered appropriate work for women's groups, the upper-middle-class status of many Junior Leaguers suggests that more than a modicum of noblesse oblige was also involved in their approach to community needs.[21]

As its affiliates, the HCBPW and JLH worked with the LCW on many women's issues. Members doggedly pursued, through their organizational activism, the amelioration of a number of disabilities they suffered as citizens. The right to vote in municipal elections was limited to those who paid local property tax. Since the titular taxpayer was usually the husband, this practice effectively barred most wives from voting in municipal elections. This was a particularly egregious omission, because every other municipality in the province extended that right to spouses. The HCBPW launched a campaign to secure the Halifax civic franchise for the spouses of taxpayers. The issue was taken up by Grace Wambolt, one of the city's few female lawyers, who, like most of her colleagues in the HCBPW, was an unmarried taxpayer unaffected by the restriction. Clubwomen understood the contribution that women, married and single, made to the city because it so often took the form of organizational activism and volunteer work. In terms of deserving the vote, therefore, they noted that 'the average housewife ... gives much unpaid service to the welfare of the community.'[22] The city council made the advocates jump through a number of hoops, and the excruciatingly slow pace with which it decided to support the necessary legislative amendment was not helped by Alderman Abbie Lane's lukewarm attitude. Appalled by voter apathy in general, she speculated that a few more women voters would do nothing to increase the rate of citizen participation in elections.[23] Lane's unpredictable behaviour on issues like this made a mockery of her earlier call for the political unity of women.[24] Her capriciousness was also an early object lesson for those women who thought that female unity on issues crucial to women could be taken for granted.

Another Business and Professional Women's campaign affected women province-wide. Although the LCW's citizenship committee had expressed concern before the war about the exclusion of women from jury service, the HCBPW took up the issue after the war, again under Wambolt's leadership.[25] Rather than putting forward an equal rights argument, Wambolt, who was a HCBPW representative to the LCW, pointed out practical reasons for empanelling female jurors. She thought they were needed in particular in sex-related cases and for the trials of girls, and she thought it entirely inappropriate that any woman should be tried by an all-male jury. Moreover, Wambolt believed, however irrationally, that women were better judges of truth than men.[26] In seeing women's jury duty as a fairly cut-and-dried issue, Wambolt and others reckoned without the masculinist discourse that still envisaged the adult woman in the home, tending to husband and children, and unable to take leave of her domestic responsibilities in order to be part of a protracted courtroom trial. In 1951 a proposed new juries act threatened to make women's exclusion even more explicit. Through patient behind-the-scenes manoeuvring, the provincial branch of the CBPW got that bill defeated. Even so, no Nova Scotian woman was called for jury service until 1960.[27]

Another policy issue that attracted women's organizations after the war was employment for women – opportunities, training, and the full range of items relating to inequality between men and women in the workplace. While the HCBPW focused considerable attention on concerns that had implications for middle-class women in the professions and white-collar jobs, the LCW found itself involved in employment questions that were more relevant to working-class women. These differences reflected the vintage of the organizations themselves. The HCBPW's concerns – equal pay, employee benefits, equal opportunity – had implications for the kind of modern working woman who joined the club. The LCW was still predominantly a bastion of privilege and tradition, which meant that even after the Second World War members were still worrying about 'the servant problem.' That perennial concern of society women took a new direction in 1949 when the LCW was given representation on the local advisory committee of the federal government's National Employment Service (Unemployment Insurance Commission), which focused on working-class jobs and helped to orient LCW interests towards such issues as the minimum wage, part-time work, and the plight of the older worker.

The interest of the Junior League in employment related largely to voluntary work. As an organization that provided and trained female volunteers to work in community projects that both directly and indirectly benefited women and girls, it was unsurpassed on the Halifax scene. While welfare professionals were usually sceptical about the role of volunteers in social agencies, JLH volunteers were considered the exception.[28] Although not all members had the daytime hours available to undertake the plethora of placements organized by the league, enough keen young middle-class married women, with the kind of dedication to good works reminiscent of nineteenth-century ladies' benevolent societies, were available to produce not only a viable corps but a vibrant one. The league's connection to paid employment related to some positions it maintained as part of its projects. In its early years, for example, it made a contribution to the salary of Gwendolyn Shand, one of the foot-soldiers for welfare in her capacity as executive secretary of the Welfare Council (earlier called the Council of Social Agencies) and herself an active clubwoman.

As a service organization, the Junior League was far more active on welfare issues than were the HCBPW and the LCW. Although the league never explicitly defined this as an area benefiting women, women were the major consumers of social assistance. Before the war the league was responsible for the establishment of the Social Service Index – the central clearinghouse for keeping track of those in need and those receiving relief – for the information of charitable agencies.[29] The league saw itself primarily as an initiator and usually withdrew from direct control or support of a project once it was taken over by a community agency. In this case, the JLH supported the index until it received sufficient funding from the Community Chest, the forerunner of the United Way. However, the board of the Welfare Council, which absorbed the index, continued to include a league representative. As a result of its oversight of the index, the league's commitment to the Community Chest was also established before the war. This commitment was expressed through an organizational donation as well as canvassing, which secured JLH representation on the Community Chest board. When the Community Chest adopted a new constitution in the late 1940s, a reform explored by Shirley Tillotson in this collection, the JLH relinquished its representative in order to make way for the participation of other organizations, well satisfied that a number of ex-leaguers were prominent board members.

The first major postwar project to have an impact on the welfare of low-income women in Halifax was a thrift store, the Bargain Box, opened in 1949.[30] The store, which was the league's major fundraising initiative, sustained JLH projects through several decades. The league's interest in children, which produced many excellent projects, culminated from a social policy perspective in 1963 with the establishment of the first of the postwar generation of daycare centres. In its first year, about half the children in the small operation were recommended by welfare agencies. In furtherance of the promotion of stable conditions for daycare, the JLH welcomed provincial legislation setting out appropriate standards for such facilities and promoted its daycare centre as part of its public relations strategy. In 1969, in keeping with its philosophy, the league transferred the management of the daycare centre, then located in Cunard Street School, to the North End Neighbourhood Centre, a product of the war-on-poverty's community-development movement.[31]

Several other projects of the 1960s and 1970s also reached women in need of advice and services. In 1968 the JLH began a placement for its volunteers at St Euphrasia's Home for delinquent girls run by the Sisters of the Good Shepherd. Still on the cutting edge of social reform, in 1969 the league supported the establishment of the Dalhousie legal aid clinic in the old North End, described as 'a very needy section of Halifax.' The following year the league extended its financial support to the Help Line, a twenty-four-hour-a-day telephone resource and rescue service, started in 1969. Soon after the Family Planning Association was established in 1970, the JLH responded favourably to its request for 'board, voluntary and financial support.'[32]

Among other services it promoted were those for the elderly, the vast majority of whom were women. The JLH supported the Soroptimists' Club, a women's service club dating from 1939, which established Meals on Wheels in 1969. The league also got involved in the campaign to establish dedicated housing for senior citizens, which resulted in the development of the Northwood complex between 1967 and 1977. In the mid-1970s the league turned its attention to the rehabilitation of female offenders, lending support to UNISON, an agency for prisoners and ex-prisoners, and serving on its board.[33]

As an activist organization interested in the most progressive of the mainstream reforms of the day, the JLH put its money and its volunteers where its members judged them to be needed, and its policy of short-term sponsorship continued to give it great flexibility. Junior Leaguers did not engage in endless discussion, long delays, concern about appearances, or squeamishness about rolling up their sleeves and getting to work. Their social activism was recognized by the mayor in 1960, when he asked the league to serve on the welfare committee established as part of a civic strategy for future planning.[34]

Although unity among women was a driving force behind the major women's organizations, they recognized that differences had to be acknowledged and that, where they disadvantaged women, measures should be promoted to eliminate discrimination. Problems encountered by women of colour, Aboriginal women, and women with disabilities were added to the agendas of the LCW, the Club of Business and Professional Women, and the Junior League from time to time in the early postwar decades. Not surprisingly, clubwomen's introduction to racial discrimination was provided by the horrors of the Holocaust in Europe as information gradually filtered back after the war. Yet in the immediate postwar years, positive rather than negative aspects of race relations tended to provide the focus. For example, Dr Mildred Glube, one of the LCW's Jewish members, spoke encouragingly in 1947 about the settlement of Jewish children in Canada, and the LCW, both during and after the war, acknowledged the achievements of Black singer Portia White as a local woman of great talent.[35] The need to campaign for human rights was raised by the LCW president in 1951, when she drew attention to examples of racial prejudice in the United States.[36] Soon voices of concern about local circumstances were raised by Gwendolyn Shand and Alice Haverstock, who provided candid information on racial prejudice in their 1955 study of the social status of women in Nova Scotia.[37] In her role as convener of the LCW citizenship committee in 1959, Shand also focused on the problems encountered by First Nations and Black people. The next year Pearleen Oliver, wife of the pastor of Cornwallis Street African Baptist Church, enlightened the council about the deplorable employment opportunities for Blacks, and in 1962 the council learned from Frances Maclean about the work undertaken by the new Halifax Advisory Committee on Human Rights.[38] Maclean was, as Frances Early indicates in her essay in this collection, one of the major influences in the Voice of Women's campaign against racial discrimination.

While the LCW did not express its human rights concerns in gender terms, the more womanist-oriented Club of Business and Professional Women became cognizant by the late 1950s of the need to provide better employment opportunities for minority women. The provincial president proposed in 1960 that the clubs might undertake a 'detailed study of the status of the Indian in Nova Scotia with particular reference to educational facilities for the Indian woman; professional and business opportunities; contribution to Nova Scotia culture and so on.'[39] Accordingly, after due study, the Halifax club decided that Aboriginal women needed job opportunities together with appropriate counselling and guidance, and the HCBPW offered its assistance to the local Indian Affairs officer. As a result, the club assisted in 1961 with the placement of two young Native women in hairdressing jobs in Halifax and remained at least passively interested in the progress of First Nations women. At the same time, the HCBPW, influenced no doubt by the composition of the local population, became concerned about the exclusion of 'negro girls' from the list of ethnic minorities adopted by the national Business and Professional Women as eligible for a national bursary fund.[40] In terms of encouraging minority participation in their own organization, it was not till 1963 that the HCBPW supported a resolution for consideration at its provincial convention that 'we put our words into practice and when seeking to increase our membership we invite those women of other races and nationalities who are plainly interested in the upbuilding of our country to become members.'[41]

The Junior League devoted its interest in 'difference' to those who were mentally and physically disabled. Beginning in the late 1950s, the JLH donated funds and volunteers to existing organizations and facilities that helped people, especially children, who had visual, speech, or cognitive impairments.[42] In 1960 a new project, a sheltered workshop for the handicapped, was started in cooperation with the Polio Foundation. Known as New Leaf Enterprises, the workshop offered training and employment centred on printing, office work placement, and sewing. In keeping with its philosophy, the league withdrew after four years, leaving the project to the Polio Foundation.[43] As its centennial project, the JLH established the Learning Disabilities Clinic, which it turned over to the Halifax School Board in 1970.[44] In 1971 it adopted the pre-existing vision and hearing screening program at the Children's Hospital, which it greatly expanded.[45] Many volunteer opportunities in the 1960s and 1970s involved helping various categories of afflicted children. To the extent that the care of children with physical and mental disorders fell on mothers, the league volunteers helped to ease their burdens.

Given the time and effort that women's organizations devoted to progressive projects and programs, only a portion of which are examined here – they were also active, for example, in culture, recreation, and heritage – it is startling that they receive so little credit from politicians, the public, or historians. For dogged determination in pursuing their aims and fundraising to sustain themselves or, in the case of the Junior League, their services, they set a standard few could match. The results were usually incremental and seldom dramatic but they could be innovative, and they promoted the interests of women at a time when there was little evidence that any other agency was doing so, at least without pressure and participation from these very women's organizations.

There is no evidence in the reports of long-standing women's organizations that the advent of the women's liberation movement was seen as a threat, challenge, or departure from the women's movement they supported. The impact of women's liberation in Halifax was gradual, supplementing rather than displacing the existing network of organized womanhood. The many women's associations that were affiliates of the Local Council of Women had long discussed common issues and ways of working together. They could handle differences – these were nothing new. Furthermore, some members of the older organizations held multiple memberships. By the 1960s their memberships might include the Voice of Women, the key bridging organization between traditional and newer feminist approaches explored by Frances Early in this volume. Many of the well-established women's organizations of the Halifax area were also chapters of national organizations that created the pressure for the establishment of the Royal Commission on the Status of Women in Canada. By presenting briefs to the commission and studying its report, as well as supporting the subsequent work of the Nova Scotia Task Force on the Status of Women, many local organizations – and certainly the Halifax Local Council of Women, the Halifax Club of Business and Professional Women, and the Junior League of Halifax – kept abreast of current developments and participated as they saw fit.

Thereafter, their continuation through the tumultuous years of the 1970s and 1980s indicates that they had a continuing role to play, at least for their own members. To give them their due, they made useful, if sometimes unsuccessful, interventions on behalf of other women from time to time. Like their counterparts elsewhere, they were grappling with the need to shift their 'focus to reflect changing times.'[46] For example, in 1973, the Council of Women at the provincial level teamed up with the Nova Scotia Human Rights Commission to produce a report on pay scales for men and women in the wake of the anti–sex discrimination legislation that took effect in 1972. Its male author sharply concluded that action was 'required to stop some employers from treating women as substandard, second-rate coolies.'[47] In 1979–80 the Junior League revisited its earlier interest in daycare as part of its new child-advocacy strategy and investigated the possibility of starting a centre for infants 'which would include support for mothers to return to school or work.' But the unwed mothers they consulted were not inclined to use such a facility, an indication perhaps that noblesse oblige, no matter how well intended, was not welcome in the era of women's liberation.[48]

Despite some new approaches, the traditional organizations had difficulty attracting members from three new constituencies of women who were in a hurry to influence women's political agenda: the young, especially college women; the disadvantaged, that is, women who bore the social, economic, and racial stigma of marginality; and the activist professional women dedicated to women's liberation. The LCW knew its modus operandi did not accommodate a new generation of women and yet did little to bridge the gap. Although it submitted a resolution to the National Council of Women in 1973 recommending a study of the feasibility of establishing complementary organizations for young women, the LCW did not show much willingness to adapt to new circumstances. After toying with the idea of holding evening instead of daytime meetings, the members ultimately stuck to their normal practices.[49] In 1973 the HCBPW also recognized the need to attract younger women.[50] Of the three organizations featured here, only the Junior League was able to accommodate second-wave feminism in the 1970s:

it was a club designed for young women, and its service orientation gave it contemporary relevance. Indeed, the JLH's own impatience with the inflexibility of its sister organizations was reflected in its withdrawal from the Local Council of Women in 1976.[51]

II

Meanwhile, a plethora of new women's organizations and women-led organizations emerged in the generation that produced the National Action Committee on the Status of Women in 1972. Most of them were overtly feminist, although other major issues relating to race and income also galvanized women to action. They included both short-term ad hoc groups and continuing organizations; they sought and often received government funding.[52] The flavour of women's activism in the Halifax region in the heady days of the 1970s, as second-wave feminism blossomed, can be captured in the activities of three local organizations: the Dartmouth City Mothers' Club (DCMC), the Metro Area Family Planning Association (MAFPA), and the first Nova Scotia Women's Action Committee (NSWAC).

The earliest of these organizations and the shortest lived was the Dartmouth City Mothers' Club, a war-on-poverty group established in 1968. The low-income women who joined together to form DCMC first met at a cooking course offered by the city's Welfare Department in 1966. As homemakers accustomed to having to stretch scarce resources, they chose as their first project a relatively uncontroversial Wheels to Meals program for senior citizens. A variant on the Meals on Wheels program initiated at the same time by traditional women's organizations in Halifax under the direction of the Soroptimists, the Dartmouth club not only prepared the meals but also brought the diners together and entertained them. They enlisted the support of an elite but equally marginalized group of women – the Naval Officers' Wives Association – to provide the transportation, thereby demonstrating that women could cooperate across class lines in community projects.[53]

The Mothers' next project, Information Please, was designed to unlock the secrets of the intimidating social assistance bureaucracy for the benefit of citizens needing access to public services. Before long the DCMC took on an advocacy role for low-income people uncertain of their rights to, for example, decent and affordable public housing. Seen as a positive force for change, the club secured the blessing of the Dartmouth Welfare Department. In 1970, the women took their concerns to

Dartmouth City Council, where an 'encounter' or panel discussion on welfare, housing, education, and recreation issues revealed that tenants, including the club's members, were powerless to influence municipal government because they were still denied the right to run for council.[54] Determined to give citizens on welfare a sense of belonging to the community, the club argued in favour of a guaranteed annual income, family allowances for children for the duration of their schooling, and public housing rent based on net income and the number of dependants. To secure support for their campaign, they felt they had 'to educate the public and the middle class that people are on welfare not because of choice, but because of the system.'[55]

Not only were the Mothers willing to confront their city council, they also joined with other groups and individuals concerned about the powerlessness of poor people and mounted a public demonstration in January 1971 that would cast them as actors rather than victims. Their march in favour of a 'just society' took them to Province House and Halifax City Hall. The momentum established by the DCMC and other welfare groups led to talk of amalgamation into a militant Dartmouth Welfare Rights Committee, which emerged under male leadership.[56] The Mothers prevaricated, committed to pursuing their own encounters with government officials, and perhaps, according to critics, unwilling to give up their leadership role as the pioneer welfare-rights advocates in Dartmouth. In an attempt to change the maternalist image that seemed to be discouraging women from joining the club, but at the same time to protect their strategy for working for change within the system, they abandoned their gender exclusivity and launched a new organization in 1971: Voice of the People.[57]

In the big social issues the Mothers tackled, gender was an important consideration, but ultimately not the deciding one. In a very short time, the leaders of the DCMC honed their skills as debaters and attracted enough press coverage to give them confidence in their ability to pursue their mission. When their membership did not expand as they desired, they assumed that their label was responsible and they changed it. Being women was secondary to being an effective welfare lobby.

Whereas the short-lived DCMC started as a women's club and turned into a mixed-gender group, the area's family planning initiative was first led by men but became dominated by women once the work of counselling began. Early in 1970, the year after the repeal of the relevant sections in the Criminal Code made it possible, the Halifax-Dartmouth Family Planning Association, soon known as the Metro Area

Family Planning Association, was launched following the first family planning workshop for social workers and other welfare professionals. Affiliated with the national Family Planning Association, it benefited for over two years from a federal Local Initiatives Project (LIP) grant.[58] In the 1970s, LIP grants were crucial to the democratization of decision making and research at the community level and also allowed women to provide a range of services unlikely to find funding elsewhere.

The MAFPA had the support of many of the traditional women's organizations and the help of some members of the powerful medical profession. Although some birth control work had been done by the staff of the Grace Maternity Hospital in the years before such work became a legitimate activity, medical services providers realized that low-income women were not getting the information the needed, except at the discretion of social workers or through chance encounters with the gynaecologists.[59] Thus, an early initiative was to train six out-reach workers to go into the field and spread the good word about reproductive rights and the ways and means available. For these work-ers, the MAFPA chose to recruit welfare recipients who knew Halifax's North End well. In July 1971, they visited sixty-eight families in the Mulgrave Park public housing complex. They went well armed with information about a range of programs relating to family-planning needs which were readily available but unknown to the average low-income woman.[60] Progressive journalists, many of whom were women, also helped to publicize the family planning service. The Halifax weekly *The 4th Estate*, for example, not only carried informative and sympathetic articles but used its 'Help Wanted' column to refer to the Family Planning Association a sixteen-year-old pregnant Black girl from the North End who had been expelled from home, citing her case as a vivid example of the failure of the community to effectively publi-cize its services.[61]

The problems of teen pregnancy, the other major issue confronting the MAFPA, were exposed by a timely study of unwed mothers. Funded by the federal Opportunities for Youth program, the study by the Women's Bureau, an organization of university students, indicated that the number of unwed mothers in schools was steadily rising, and that 80 per cent of the clients in the maternity homes – Bethany and Guardian Angel – were high school students. Yet birth control infor-mation was no more available to these sexually experienced teens than it was to their friends who were on the verge of becoming sexually active.[62] Disseminating information was one thing, securing funding for birth control devices another, and the MAFPA found itself having to lobby for Medical Services Insurance coverage for contraceptives.[63] At the same time, the association promoted the teaching of sex education in schools.[64]

In 1974 the association opened a birth control clinic on Gottingen Street in the heart of the old North End. Counselling and examination by a female doctor were available to all comers regardless of age or marital status, and free or low-cost contraceptives were available. Anxious to avoid the problematic association with abortion, the MAFPA made abortion referrals only after extensive counselling and stressed that abortion was not a form of birth control.[65] That same year the MAFPA acquired its first female president, Pamela Brown, who not only headed the organization but also served as one of the two medical consultants at the clinic, both female. She contended that the aim of the MAFPA was 'to provide education and teach responsibility because ignoring the problem of unwanted pregnancies won't make it go away.'[66] But Dr Brown, her colleague, Dr Margaret Casey, and the health care staff did far more than promote family planning; they also made the clinic a women's health centre by providing Pap smears, instruction in breast self-examination, and advice on nutrition and sexuality. The staff included an outreach worker, who followed up on all the patients, and two registered nurses who volunteered their services. Both physicians donated 30 per cent of their consulting fees back to the clinic in an attempt to keep it afloat. The first paid executive director, Barbara Hart, RN, whose earlier work in St John Ambulance is described in the chaper in this volume by Frances Gregor, also acted as a clinic nurse as required. Open three mornings a week, the clinic in its first year served 206 clients, including a few men seeking advice on vasectomies. In acknowledgment of financial support from both Halifax, Dartmouth, and the county, Brown set her sights on a mobile clinic in order to take the family planning message to the doctors' offices of surrounding communities.[67] By 1976, when it occupied new quarters in Veith House, appropriately a former orphanage, the clinic had been able to expand to Spryfield and Dartmouth and was on the point of including Sackville in its orbit.[68] Its services for women and its female activist staff identified the MAFPA as a women's rights group.[69]

While the needs of low-income women were clearly included in the welfare rights and family planning organizations, feminism also needed a watchdog to lobby for greater equality between women and men in law, politics, and employment and to advocate a redefinition of women's role in society. The first women to focus on liberation in the 1970s organized the 1895 Revival Group, aka the Halifax-Dartmouth Women's Caucus, consisting of about two dozen young women identified as 'students, working women, married women, mothers' who recognized their historical antecedents in the late nineteenth-century and discussed 'equal pay for equal work, the unequal minimum wage law, problems of the single-parent family with a female head, child care, birth control, abortion, education, and socialization of women.'[70] From this beginning emerged the Women's Bureau, which researched many of these issues in 1971–2; the Women's Centre, a resource, information, and social centre started in 1973; and A Woman's Place, established in conjunction with the YWCA in 1976.[71] While not all these iterations of feminist social concerns were directly related, they did have in common participation by young, university women – students, new graduates, and faculty women. This membership base meant that turnover was frequent and the ability to sustain organizational frameworks weak.

In the wake of highly publicized and consciousness-raising activities during International Women's Year and the organization of a provincial task force on the status of women, a group of young professional women got together in Halifax late in 1975 to establish the Nova Scotia Women's Action Committee.[72] The original idea was to ensure that 'the spirit' of International Women's Year continued. The NSWAC interacted with the provincial Human Rights Commission, supported the recommendations of the Nova Scotia Task Force on the Status of Women, and lasted long enough to see the organization of the Nova Scotia Advisory Council on the Status of Women, which is discussed by Janet Guildford in the last essay in this collection. Inspired by the National Action Committee on the Status of Women, the NSWAC approved a constitution in 1976 that emphasized its purpose as a political action committee, 'stressing *implementation* rather than further study,' and its composition as a women-only group.[73] Its approximately three years of documented activity consisted of support for human rights legislation, as evidenced in particular in the case of discrimination on the basis of sex against Roberta Ryan, a Cape Breton woman with police training and experience who was not hired for a permanent position with the North Sydney police force in 1973. Ryan lost the case and the committee incurred a hefty legal bill.[74] The NSWAC's educational work consisted of several workshops, such as an equal pay workshop that included expert panels on equal pay complaints and the relationship between collective bargaining and equal pay.

Its political lobbying work centred on the improvement of legislation affecting women. The NSWAC was a persistent proponent of the concept of equal pay for work of equal value and its enforcement by the labour standards mechanism. Another legislative concern was matrimonial property, an area where the committee was willing to commend 'the philosophy of the Married Persons Property Act' but also to condemn the legislation as 'so flawed as to render the bill as a whole unworkable.'[75] Given the timing of its existence, the NSWAC was also a staunch defender of daycare as a social good for all. This position stood in contrast to the province's official policy, which, as Suzanne Morton argues in her chapter on daycare in this volume, approached daycare as a welfare measure for low-income parents. In terms of research, the Women's Action Committee sponsored a project on boards and commissions in the province in order to identify likely female candidates for appointment. It produced an 'Access Kit to Nova Scotia's Boards and Commissions' in 1978. As an advocate of political equality, the committee adopted the position that women should hold half the appointed positions in the province, a far cry from the token representation traditionally given to women through the Local Council of Women and other long-standing women's organizations.[76] Yet its elite interests meant that the NSWAC bore some resemblance to organizations of the LCW generation, which were failing to attract feminists concerned with promoting women's equality.

National events of the late 1960s and early 1970s encouraged women in Halifax to form new networks and take up new causes. Federal commissions and committees and federal legislation, as well as some provincial legislation, supported women's demands for economic equality, control over their own bodies, better quality housing, and a whole range of social services as rights rather than privileges. The range of women's associations expanded considerably – groups fostered by local issues, branches of new national organizations, and special interest groups based on workplace, profession, or neighbourhood. What distinguished the new groups from the older organizations was the relatively short existence of some, their more focused approach, and their state funding. Yet the Local Council of Women, the Club of Business and Professional Women, the Junior League, and many other traditional associations, including the Canadian Federation of University Women (CFUW), also continued their activities, and their survival tends to confirm the prediction of a CFUW member of the current generation, to which I alluded in the introduction – namely, that there has been a cycle of decline and renewal for women's groups. The women's organizations of the first decade of the twenty-first century worry about renewal in much the same way that women's organizations did in the 1970s. Most will survive and regroup, for, as another member of the CFUW noted, 'So long as we have two sexes there will be need of women's organizations. Women need the networks to withstand the constant erosion of society.'[77]

NOTES

1 Survey responses to the question 'What do you see as the future of women's organizations in this region?' Canadian Federation of University Women, Atlantic Council Conference 2000, Dartmouth, 14 Oct. 2000.
2 *Halifax Mail-Star*, 23 Aug. 2000, A8.
3 Jill Vickers, Pauline Rankin, and Christine Appelle, *Politics As If Women Mattered: A Political Analysis of the National Action Committee on the Status of Women* (Toronto: University of Toronto Press, 1993), 68, 283; N.E.S. Griffiths, *The Splendid Vision: Centennial History of the National Council of Women of Canada, 1893–1993* (Ottawa: Carleton University Press, 1993); Linda Christiansen-Ruffman, 'Women's Conceptions of the Political: Three Canadian Women's Organizations,' in Myra Marx Ferree and Patricia Yancey Martin, eds., *Feminist Organizations: Harvest of the New Women's Movement* (Philadelphia: Temple University Press, 1995), 372.
4 Minutes, 21 Nov. 1935, 23 April 1936, Local Council of Women (LCW) Collection, Public Archives of Nova Scotia (PANS), MG 20, 535-11. Prior to the 1970s, clubwomen were more likely to use their husbands' initials than their own given names.
5 Ibid., 15 Oct. 1936; *Minutes and Reports of the First Annual Meeting of the Twenty-Sixth Municipal Council of the County of Halifax*, 1938.
6 *Dartmouth Free Press*, 1 Dec. 1955, 1, 6; 10 Jan. 1957, 1; 18 Sept. 1958, 1; 23 Oct. 1958, 1–2; 24 Oct. 1973, 1; *The 4th Estate* (Halifax), 29 Sept. 1976, 14–15.
7 Minutes, 19 May 1949, LCW, PANS, MG 20, 536-1.
8 *The 4th Estate*, 6 Oct. 1976, 18–19.
9 Catherine L. Cleverdon, *The Woman Suffrage Movement in Canada* (Toronto: University of Toronto Press, 1950; 2nd ed., 1974).
10 Murray to Cleverdon, 20 Nov. 1946, Catherine L. Cleverdon Collection, National Archives of Canada (NAC), MG 30, D160-7.

11 Ibid., Murray to Cleverdon, 30 July 1946. Murray was less enthusiastic about the influence of more doctrinaire groups like the Imperial Order Daughters of the Empire (IODE) and the Catholic Women's League but pointed out that, through their Council of Women affiliation, they became exposed to a wider viewpoint.

12 Lane to Cleverdon, 3 Sept. 1946, Cleverdon Collection, NAC, MG 30, D160-5.

13 Clipping from *New York Times*, 10 Jan. 1946, Cleverdon Collection, NAC, MG 30, D160-5.

14 Gwendolyn Shand and Alice Haverstock, 'Social Status of Women in Nova Scotia,' presented to the Provincial Council of Women (PCW) of Nova Scotia, 26 April 1955, National Council of Women (NCW) Collection, NAC, MG 28, I25 101-7.

15 *Herself / Elle-Même: Report of the Nova Scotia Task Force on the Status of Women* (Halifax: Nova Scotia Department of Social Services, 1976), 59.

16 For example, in 1950 the LCW had representatives on the Citizens' Housing Commission, Council of Social Agencies, Cancer Society, Local Film Council, Playground Commission, and Civic Affairs Committee. Minutes, 16 May 1950, LCW, PANS, MG 20, 536-1. In 1960 it had delegate status with the Welfare Council, Nova Scotia Arts Council, and Nova Scotia Education Association, and sent representatives to the Senior Citizens' Board, Recreation and Playground Commission, Community Planning Association, Unemployment Insurance Commission, and the Halifax Film Council. Minutes, 17 March 1960, LCW, PANS, MG 20, 536-4.

17 Minutes, 18 Sept. 1970, LCW, PANS, MG 20, 536-8.

18 Ibid., 17 March 1960, 536-4.

19 Lane to Cleverdon, 3 Sept. 1946, Cleverdon Collection, NAC, MG 30, D160-5; Linda Christiansen-Ruffman et al., 'Women's Concerns about the Quality of Life in the Halifax Metropolitan Area,' report prepared for the Ministry of State for Urban Affairs, St Mary's University, Halifax, May 1975. In another paper, which focuses mainly on Labrador, Christiansen-Ruffman discusses the Halifax numbers. Of the 156 groups that contributed to this study, 130 were women's organizations; the others were 'considered mainly women's organizations.' Twenty-eight had several branches, including one church group with over forty branches. Linda Christiansen-Ruffman, 'Researching Women's Organizations in the Labrador Straits: Retrospective Reflections,' in Carmelita McGrath, Barbara Neis, Marilyn Porter, eds., *Their Lives the Times: Women in Newfoundland and Labrador, a Collage* (St John's: Killick Press, 1995), 256.

20 The papers of the Halifax Club of Business and Professional Women (MG 20) are deposited at the Public Archives of Nova Scotia.

21 Information on the Halifax Junior League is contained in the annual reports of the president kindly loaned to this project.
22 K.E. Crowell to Mayor J.E. Ahern, 15 Oct. 1947, Halifax Club of Business and Professional Women (HCBPW), PANS, MG 20, 711-5.
23 Clipping from *Halifax Mail-Star*, 16 June 1959, HCBPW, PANS, MG 20, 715-65-8.
24 Clipping from *New York Times*, 10 Jan. 1946, Cleverdon Collection, NAC, MG 30, D160-5.
25 Minutes, 15 Dec. 1938, LCW, PANS, MG 20, 535-11; Minutes, 4 Aug. 1948, HCBPW, PANS, MG 20, 711-5.
26 Minutes, 19 Nov. 1952, 19 March 1953, LCW, PANS, MG 20, 536-2; Minutes, 20 Feb. and 20 March 1958, LCW, PANS, MG 20, 536-4.
27 Minutes, April 1951, HCBPW, PANS, MG 20, 711-5; Minutes, 14 Oct. 1960, LCW, PANS, MG 20, 536-4. A focused club like BPW was in a better position to move forcefully on the issues of the civic franchise and jury duty than was the LCW with its many and sometimes divergent constituencies. The LCW's formal support by resolution for correcting these two gender anomalies came only in 1950 and 1953, respectively, three and four years after the BPW launched its campaigns to right these particular wrongs. Minutes, 18 May 1950, LCW, PANS, MG 20, 536-1; 19 Feb. 1953, MG 20, 536-2.
28 Junior League of Halifax (JLH), Annual Report of the President (Allison Conrod), 1953–4.
29 JLH, Annual Report of the President (Kathleen M. Rainnie), 1934–5.
30 JLH, Annual Report of the President (Kathryn B. McManus), 1949–50.
31 JLH, Annual Reports of the President (Doris Powers), 1963–4, (Mary Lemessurier), 1966–7, (Jean Harrington), 1968–9.
32 JLH, Annual Reports of the President (Jean Harrington), 1969–70, (Peggy Weld), 1970–1, (Peggy Weld), 1971–2.
33 In 1974–5, the Junior League had representation on the boards of the Family Planning Association, Meals on Wheels, Downtown Planning, School for the Blind, Northwood Manor, and UNISON. Annual Report of the President (Marilyn Edgecombe). The Soroptimists' Meals on Wheels initiative is documented in the Halifax club's papers, which are deposited at PANS: see, for example, Minutes, 26 March 1969, Soroptimists' Club, PANS, MG 20, 1698-9. For more details on UNISON, see *The 4th Estate*, 15 March 1973, 24; 28 Jan. 1976, 5.
34 JLH, Annual Report of the President (Mrs Henry B. Ross), 1959–60.
35 Minutes, March 1943, LCW, PANS, MG 20, 535-12; 20 Nov. 1947, MG 20, 536-1; 19 Sept. 1957, MG 20, 536-4.
36 Ibid., 18 Oct. 1951, 536-1.

37 'Social Status of Women in Nova Scotia,' 26 April 1955, NCW, NAC, MG
    28, I25 101-7.
38 Minutes, 15 Jan. 1959, 14 Oct. 1960, LCW, PANS, MG 20, 536-4; 13 Oct.
    1962, MG 20, 536-5.
39 Minutes, 12 Sept. 1960, HCBPW, PANS, MG 20, 711-9.
40 Ibid., 10 April 1961; 16 Nov. 1961, 711-10.
41 Ibid., 13 May 1963, 711-11.
42 JLH, Annual Report of the President (Joan Walker), 1957–8.
43 JLH, Report of the President (Mrs Henry B. Ross), 1959–60; (Doris Powers),
    1963–4; (Fairlie C. Ernst), 1964–5.
44 JLH, Annual Report of the President (Fairlie C. Ernst), 1965–6; (Mary
    LeMessurier), 1966–7; (Jean Harrington), 1969–70.
45 JLH, Annual Report of the President (Peggy Weld), 1971–2.
46 See Agnes M. Richard, *Threads of Gold: Newfoundland and Labrador Jubilee
    Guilds, Women's Institutes* (St John's: Creative Publishers, 1989), 140.
47 *The 4th Estate*, 13 Dec. 1973, 23.
48 JLH, Annual Report of the President (Sandra Backman), 1979–80.
49 Minutes, 11 Feb. 1972, 14 April 1972, 7 Dec. 1973, LCW, PANS, MG 20, 536-
    8; 19 Feb. 1976, MG 20, 536-8a.
50 Minutes, 31 May 1973, HCBPW, PANS, MG 20, 712-18.
51 Minutes, 17 Sept. 1976, LCW, PANS, MG 20, 536-8a.
52 On the nature of feminist organizations in another Maritime setting, see J.
    Estelle Reddin, 'Organizing in a Small Community: Prince Edward Island,'
    in Jeri Dawn Wine and Janice L. Ristock, eds., *Women and Social Change:
    Feminist Activism in Canada* (Toronto: James Lorimer, 1991), 167.
53 *The 4th Estate*, 23 April 1970, 9.
54 Ibid., 7 May 1970, 9.
55 *Dartmouth Free Press*, 11 June 1970, 3.
56 *The 4th Estate*, 28 Jan. 1971, 3.
57 *Dartmouth Free Press*, 3 March 1971, 3; *The 4th Estate*, 11 March 1971, 2.
58 *The 4th Estate*, 9 March 1972, 7.
59 Ibid., 7 May 1970, 2; 13 Aug. 1970, 3.
60 Ibid., 29 July 1971, 11.
61 Ibid., 26 Aug. 1971, 2.
62 Report on Single Mothers in Halifax by Anne Chalecott and Mary Hill, 27
    Aug. 1971, Manpower and Immigration, NAC, RG 118, G1, 286 103-289, 3;
    The 4th Estate, 9 Sept. 1971, 1.
63 *The 4th Estate*, 23 Sept. 1971, 15; 28 Oct. 1971, 15; 9 March 1972, 7.
64 Ibid., 1 Nov. 1973, 1, 19.
65 Ibid., 14 March 1974, 16; 12 Sept. 1974, 5.

66 Ibid., 7 Nov. 1974, 6.
67 *Halifax Mail-Star*, 7 Feb. 1975, 25.
68 Ibid., 29 Sept. 1976, 21.
69 *The 4th Estate*, 9 July 1975, 2.
70 Ibid., 26 Feb. 1970, 13; 26 March 1970, 8 (quotation).
71 For the Halifax Women's Bureau project papers see Manpower and Immigration, NAC, RG 118, G1, vol. 286, file 103-289, parts 1–3; some information on the Women's Centre can be found in the *The 4th Estate*, 27 Sept. 1973, 14; 25 Oct. 1973, 18; 15 Nov. 1973, 17; 17 Jan. 1974, 14; 9 May 1974, 14; 26 May 1976, 10–12, and in minutes, 13 Dec. 1973, 21 Feb. 1974, LCW, PANS, MG 20, 536-8, and 19 Feb. 1976, 536-8a. The papers of A Woman's Place are on deposit at PANS, MG 20, 1343-4, 1498, 1551-2, 1563-4, 1760-3; see also Nova Scotia Women's Action Committee (NSWAC), PANS, MG 20, 1345-4; 1347-22 – 42.
72 Similarly, feminist organizing occurred in other university settings in Nova Scotia. See Angela Miles, 'Reflections on Integrative Feminism and Rural Women: The Case of Antigonish Town and County' in Wine and Ristock, eds., *Women and Social Change*, 56–74.
73 Constitution: Nova Scotia Women's Action Committee, NSWAC, PANS, MG 20, 1346-16.
74 NSWAC, PANS, MG 20, 1345-5, 1345-14, 1346-16, 1346-17.
75 Nova Scotia Women's Action Committee, Summary of Positions, [1978], NSWAC, PANS, MG 20, 1346-16.
76 The best documentation of these NSWAC concerns is contained in NSWAC, PANS, MG 20, 1346-16. Unfortunately the busy members of the organization were not careful about dating their documents.
77 Survey response to the question 'What do you see as the fate of women's organizations in this region?' CFUW, Atlantic Canada Conference 2000, Dartmouth, 14 Oct. 2000.

The End of the Poor Law: Public Welfare Reform in Nova Scotia before the Canada Assistance Plan

JANET GUILDFORD

Historically, destitute women – especially deserted or widowed women with children, and aged or disabled women – have been categorized as part of what has been described as 'the deserving poor.' In the first half of the twentieth century, poor women continued to be the major 'beneficiaries' of public poor relief and private charity, despite the introduction of mothers' allowances, old age pensions, and better jobs. Although the course of welfare history was not determined solely by problems confronting women, reforms at the provincial level had an enormous impact on women and their children. That is why an examination of the development of public welfare bureaucracies is an important part of women's history.

In 1956 and 1958 the Nova Scotia government adopted Social Assistance Acts to replace the Poor Relief Act, which had not been significantly revised since 1879.[1] A campaign to eliminate the Poor Law and close the hated county poorhouses had begun in the 1930s, when municipalities found it impossible to support destitute residents, and it continued as Nova Scotians planned for postwar reconstruction. For Haligonians, the most visible symbol of the Poor Law was the City Home, known simply as the Poorhouse, located at the corner of South and Robie Streets in the city's South End. Throughout the 1940s and 1950s social scientists, social service agencies, and women's organizations kept up a steady barrage of reports highly critical of the poorhouses in Halifax and around the province – institutions dubbed 'mansions of woe' by nineteenth-century reform politician Joseph Howe. Initially the campaign met with little success. As so often happened in Nova Scotia, reform was not realized until there was an infusion of federal funds, in this case following revisions to the federal

Unemployment Assistance Act in 1958. Although provincial welfare officials and historians emphasize the importance of the 1966 Canada Assistance Plan in expanding welfare services, significant change was underway in the late 1950s. During this period the Nova Scotia Department of Public Welfare, established in 1944, and municipal governments used funds from a variety of federal programs to expand and reorganize their services. This paper provides an overview of the campaign to end the Poor Law and the major features of social assistance adopted by the provincial Department of Public Welfare.[2]

A study of public welfare in Halifax provides an opportunity to examine the meagre provisions for women, including elderly women, made by the Poor Law. This attention to gender is particularly pertinent today because in long-term care programs such as nursing homes 'the overwhelming majority of service users and providers are women.'[3] For younger women, the narrow eligibility requirements of provincial mothers' allowances meant that many women had to turn to local Poor Law institutions for their survival. In contrast to national programs, well studied in the Canadian historical literature, the locally administered needs-based Poor Law institutions have been relatively neglected.[4] And unlike the national welfare state, which more often served to protect the male breadwinner's income the programs of provincial and local governments were significant mainly to women in need. Certainly the Nova Scotia Department of Public Welfare – called the Department of Social Services from 1973 until 1987, when it became the Department of Community Services – has been central to the welfare of women in Nova Scotia, and the department and its long-serving deputy minister F.R. MacKinnon play central roles in several of the essays in this collection, especially Jeanne Fay's work on single mothers.

By the standards of the wealthier provinces such as Ontario and British Columbia, Nova Scotia was slow to develop modern social assistance programs.[5] Even the implementation of the federal-provincial cost-shared old age pensions was delayed in the province until 1933.[6] In place of adequate public welfare, Nova Scotians relied on out-migration, subsistence production, occupational pluralism, and private and informal charity to survive the hardships of decades of depression.[7] However, the extent to which Nova Scotia was a 'social service backwater' in the 1940s and 1950s may have been exaggerated.[8] George Davidson, director of the Canadian Welfare Council, commissioned to survey welfare services for the Nova Scotia Royal Commission on Provincial Development and Rehabilitation (the Dawson

Commission) in 1944, was critical of virtually all aspects of the delivery of welfare services in the province and recommended sweeping changes. However, his criticism of Nova Scotia was tempered by the dismal record of most Canadian provinces: 'On the whole, Nova Scotia's services would probably rank among the top four of the Provinces of Canada – equalled or surpassed only by those to be found in provinces which are blessed with more adequate financial resources.'[9]

Nonetheless, Davidson's criticisms of welfare services in Nova Scotia were well deserved. By the end of the Second World War Nova Scotians could turn to a patchwork of largely inadequate federal, provincial, municipal, and private welfare programs for help. These included unemployment insurance and family allowances, fully funded by the federal government. The Nova Scotia Department of Labour provided workmen's compensation for injured workers, and the Department of Public Welfare administered cost-shared pensions for the elderly and the blind, provided provincially funded mothers' allowances, and provided some support for child protection programs.[10] Yet, as a plethora of critics pointed out, those who did not fit these categories were forced to seek aid from private charities or to turn to the local overseers of the poor for a meagre handout or 'indoor relief' in a poorhouse.[11]

Davidson's comments about the relative place of Nova Scotia's social programs in the national context address a continuing paradox in the history of social organization and social thought in the province. Although Davidson condemned the provision of social services in the province, in the course of his study he would have met with a number of social workers, welfare officials, academics, and politicians who shared his ideas and his faith in social scientific research and expertise. Since the middle of the nineteenth century, elite Nova Scotian professionals in the fields of welfare, education, law, and medicine had established training and certification programs, participated in national associations, and contributed to national and international debates and discussions. Yet their voices seem to have had relatively little impact on institutional development in the province, which consistently lagged behind other jurisdictions. It is also significant that there was little evidence of popular opposition to welfare reform in Nova Scotia. The progressive attitudes of professionals and the apparent openness to change of the general population make simple arguments about the conservatism in the province difficult to sustain. Decades of economic depression obviously played an important role. As a 'have not' province, Nova Scotia simply could not afford adequate social welfare programs.

In addition to the constraints placed on provincial initiatives by inadequate government revenues, the Nova Scotia government was severely limited in its ability to participate in federal-provincial shared-cost programs. Nova Scotia's response to the Unemployment Assistance Act of 1956, discussed more fully below, provides a compelling example of such constraint.

To understand that response, we need to know how social assistance was organized and how it was being challenged in the 1930s and 1940s. An important part of that context was the Halifax Council of Social Agencies (CSA). An affiliate of the Canadian Welfare Council, the CSA was established in 1931 by Samuel H. Prince, an Anglican clergyman and sociologist at King's College. It constantly provided all levels of government with research and demands for reform.[12] Another key agency was the Institute of Public Affairs (IPA) at Dalhousie University, under the direction of Lothar Richter, formerly a senior official in the Department of Labour of the German Weimar Republic. The IPA established a Municipal Bureau in 1933 to provide research and training support for municipal governments in the region. The most useful account of the administration of the Poor Relief Act in the 1930s, for example, is a masters thesis in public administration completed in 1938 by Charles H. Thomas under Richter's supervision.[13] Throughout the 1930s and 1940s researchers at the IPA, including Richter himself, produced a series of research publications and conducted welfare surveys on behalf of municipal governments.[14] The growing professional social work community, augmented by the establishment of the Maritime School of Social Work in 1941 and the Nova Scotia Branch of the Canadian Association of Social Workers, also contributed to debates about public welfare. A number of women's organizations, including the Local Council of Women of Halifax, and provincial labour organizations added their voices to the campaign for reform. While there was disagreement and sometimes conflict about the best approach to improving social welfare, the reformers were unanimous in their condemnation of the Poor Relief Act.[15]

Nova Scotia had adopted a system of local poor relief in 1758, but it was the Poor Relief Act of 1879 that provided the basic legislative framework for the provision of welfare services until 1958. In 1879, after legislation requiring municipal incorporation, administrative as well as financial responsibility for poor relief was handed over to municipal governments. The local poor district remained the basic unit of administration. The four hundred or so poor districts in the province varied considerably in area and population, and many of them were too small and too poor to support the needy living within their boundaries, especially in hard times.[16] Municipal councils appointed overseers of the poor in each poor district to collect and disburse the poor rates; their accounts were audited annually by municipal officials. In most poor districts the overseers were permitted to provide either indoor or outdoor relief, except in the City of Halifax, where local bylaws forbade the provision of outdoor relief. Eligibility for relief from a poor district was dependent on meeting stringent 'settlement' requirements in the district. The 1879 Poor Relief Act adopted the provisions of the settlement law of 1864, which required five years' consecutive residence in a poor district without claiming aid if the claimant were over twenty-one years of age. A legitimate child took his or her father's settlement, an illegitimate child either took on the mother's settlement or gained settlement by birth. A married woman took on her husband's settlement if he had one, but otherwise kept her own. When claimants sought relief from a poor district in which they did not have settlement, that district might grant some temporary aid before removing the 'pauper' back to his or her own poor district. The costs of both the relief and the removal were billed to the poor district in which the recipient had settlement. By the 1930s, some poor districts did not force the removal of deserted wives, widows in the first year of widowhood, and the temporarily ill or injured, but the home poor district was charged with costs of relief. In the cases where settlement requirements were met and relief was provided, the overseers of the poor were empowered to bill the claimants' relatives for the cost of the relief, and in some cases to confiscate the claimants' or family members' property.[17]

This system placed an enormous financial burden on local poor districts, and the settlement requirements often led to prolonged and costly legal disputes. Reformers such as Charles Thomas approved of the efforts made by Halifax County in the late 1930s to impose more centralized control. The County Council decided what proportion of the costs of relief each district should pay, and established a standing committee to administer the poor law. In 1937, Halifax County reduced its poor districts from thirty-two to twenty-one in order to try to cut down on administrative costs, and Thomas recommended the elimination of poor districts entirely. In order to encourage greater uniformity of both costs and relief payments, the county paid 57 per cent of relief costs, while the district itself was responsible for the remaining 43 per cent. The county paid the City of Halifax 50 cents a day for each county resident at the City Home, until a new county home opened in 1940 in Cole Harbour.[18]

The City of Halifax lacked provision for 'outdoor relief' – that is, relief that did not entail residence in the city's poorhouse. The city did attempt to make provisions for families in their own homes by funding private charitable organizations such as the Halifax Association for Improving the Condition of the Poor. After 1916 such funding was channelled through the Halifax Welfare Bureau. In 1944–5, for example, the City of Halifax gave a grant of $5000 to the Halifax Welfare Bureau for providing assistance to needy families. Yet, further outdoor relief was needed for people who were 'without settlement' or for families who had no breadwinner but were not eligible for mothers' allowances. One such case, that of a widow with eight children resident in the City Home, was used to illustrate the failings of the Poor Law in Halifax.[19] Although this woman and her family were compelled to live in the City Home, this institution had no facilities for children. Moreover, because it was believed that children from the home suffered discrimination at neighbouring schools because of their pauper status, it was decided that children resident at the home would not attend school.[20] Thus, indoor relief, in effect, helped to reproduce poverty by sustaining a toxic level of social stigma.

In the years leading up to 1958, Halifax's relief system changed in some small ways. In 1949 the City of Halifax was given the legal right to provide outdoor relief to 'needy unemployed employable persons.' In January 1949, the city established a rudimentary welfare administration and began to provide vouchers – not cash – to those who qualified for relief. In 1952, Halifax welfare officer H.B. Jones reported to the Public Welfare Division of the Canadian Welfare Council that he had had little success in pressing for changes. He had asked Halifax City Council's Health and Welfare Committee to increase the level of support and to pay cash instead of vouchers. Both requests were denied.[21]

Until the 1960s, then, needy families were inadequately supplied with income assistance, and had to rely too often on Poor Law institutions, the county or municipal homes. Throughout the province, these poorhouses were an important and troubling aspect of welfare provision. Most of these institutions dated back to the late nineteenth century, and a significant majority of them also served as chronic care mental hospitals. In the 1940s and 1950s, most municipal homes accommodated a miscellaneous population of 'sane paupers' and the 'harmless insane.' Little segregation was effected, and the homes served a mixed population of patients who were mentally challenged or chronically ill, as well as unmarried mothers, prostitutes, juvenile delinquents, and the elderly poor. No provincial financial assistance was available to the municipalities to help with the costs of these institutions and so, in poorer counties, the buildings had been allowed to deteriorate dreadfully.[22]

Conditions in many of these homes were appalling, and they became a favourite target of reformers. There were a number of detailed studies of poorhouses in the 1940s and 1950s. The first of these was completed in 1944 by George Davidson as part of the Dawson Commission Report. After visiting nine of the municipal homes in the province, he wrote: 'In general the institutions present a depressing appearance on the inside ... are poorly and inadequately staffed both as to numbers and as to quality of personnel, and serve, on the whole, as little more than indiscriminate dumping grounds for all the various types of unfortunate misfits who happen to be a burden on the community.'[23] Further, the worst of these homes were 'dark and dismal, evil-smelling and filthy to the point of almost nauseating the visitor who passes through them. What they must be to the poor wretched creatures who are condemned to live the greater portion of their lives in them cannot even be imagined.'[24]

While the provincial government turned to George Davidson of the Canadian Welfare Council for research, the City of Halifax commissioned Frances Weekes, a researcher at the Municipal Bureau of Dalhousie University's Institute of Public Affairs, to investigate welfare services in the City of Halifax on behalf of a civic planning commission established in 1942.[25] In her 1946 report Weekes was especially critical of the conditions she found at the Halifax City Home. She argued that the provision of adequate income-support programs was no longer seen merely as humanitarian, but had become an issue of social and economic efficiency: the role of a modern welfare system was to ensure that people who were in need were supported adequately enough to permit and encourage their rejoining the productive workforce of the country.[26] 'Merely keeping them from starving, through inadequate or humiliating assistance measures, serves only to undermine their health and morale and to prolong their dependency indefinitely.'[27]

Another report, in 1951, was written by a special committee appointed by Halifax City Council. The committee was chaired by Dr Clyde Marshall, the crusading director of the Division of Mental Health in the provincial Department of Health.[28] His report shared and amplified the criticisms offered by Weekes and Davidson.

The four-storey City Home had been opened in 1886, replacing an earlier building destroyed by fire in 1882. A new wing had been added to the building in 1931.[29] Administered by Halifax City Council's Division of Public Charities and Welfare, the home served the City of Halifax, and in some cases Halifax County and the Town of Dartmouth, as a home for the elderly poor, a temporary shelter for unmarried mothers, a chronic care hospital, and a mental hospital. Residents were segregated on the basis of sex and, to some extent, according to mental and physical condition, although staff tended to allocate patients to wards on the basis of their behaviour and the amount of disruption they were likely to cause, rather than medical diagnosis.[30] Mentally ill residents judged disruptive were kept locked up, but other residents were free to move around the building and to use the sex-segregated exercise yards at the front and back of the building, the only activity available until the 1950s.

Although the building was generally clean and well-maintained, conditions were spartan. Washroom facilities on the wards were inadequate and had to be used by the residents for their personal needs and also for dishwashing. The building met contemporary standards in terms of area per patient, but only because all the space was used for bedrooms – none of the rooms were allocated for recreation or occupational therapy.[31]

In 1944 there were 353 residents: 161 adult men, 174 adult women, and 18 children (11 boys and 7 girls). The presence of children in the home violated child protection legislation, which prohibited their placement in the poorhouses, although severely retarded children continued to be committed to poorhouses until the mid-1960s. Two-thirds of the residents were categorized as 'insane' or 'imbecile,' the remaining 111, most of whom were over sixty, as 'sane.'[32] The average length of stay at the hospital was eight years. Eleven of the residents of the City Home were young women who had been admitted under special warrant to be treated for sexually transmitted diseases, which increased during wartime. Under the terms of the Nova Scotia Health Act they were segregated from other residents, and their costs were paid out of a special dominion grant for health purposes. Later that year, arrangements were made to have these cases kept under detention in the Monastery of the Good Shepherd, a Catholic residential institution that provided supervised care for 'delinquent' women.[33] By 1951 the resident population had increased to 381, with roughly equal numbers of men and women. The 251 mentally ill and mentally challenged patients still represented a significant majority of the population. There were still four children under the age of ten at the home.[34]

Conditions for inmates were very unpleasant. No recreation programs were provided, and residents were locked out of the wards during the day, forcing them to sit in the hallways on backless benches. Medical treatment was minimal. 'Non-continuous' psychiatric treatment was provided for the mentally ill; the director of the Psychiatric Division at the Dalhousie Public Health Clinic served as a consultant. Davidson and Weekes commented on the double rows of locked cells, lit only by a small grating in the door, that were used to confine patients when staff deemed it necessary, or for punishment.[35] Weekes was particularly distressed by the situation of one resident: 'One woman inmate, a carrier of typhoid, is kept continuously confined in one of the small cage-like cells which have been described. Her living quarters are most inadequate.'[36]

Securing staff for the City Home under these conditions was difficult, and poorly trained attendants found it difficult to care for the residents. As the Marshall Committee reported, 'This penning-up for a large part of the time with little light and nothing to do, aggravates their aggressiveness and increases the problem of management. Certainly most normal people so restricted in physical activity would do the same.'[37]

Inmates of the wards for 'sane paupers' fared little better than the mentally ill. Admission to the home was on the basis of the judgment of the superintendent. More than half of the 111 residents in this category in October 1944 were not, in fact, destitute but were being fully or partially supported by relatives or friends, old age pensions, workers' compensation, superannuation payments, or other sources.[38] Segregation of the sane and the insane was imperfect, and a small number of 'young sane paupers' lived on the top floor along with 'better-type insane women.'[39] The City Home also provided temporary shelter for those who were not eligible for any of the categories of assistance available from the province.[40]

In 1951 the Marshall Committee focused much of its attention on the inadequacy of the medical and nursing care available to patients. The lack of a consulting physician or psychiatrist, registered nurses, and a dietitian drew severe criticism. The dietitian who surveyed the kitchens and menus reported that the nutritional quality of the food and the facilities for preparation and food service in the institution were inadequate.[41]

By the end of the war both the province and the City of Halifax had

produced plans for a major overhaul of provincial and municipal welfare systems, especially the elimination of the poor district as the unit of
local poor relief administration and the closure of county homes.[42]
George Davidson recommended to the provincial Royal Commission
on Provincial Development and Rehabilitation that responsibility for
poor relief be moved from the municipalities to the provincial government.[43] He also recommended changes to both the mothers' allowance
system and the law as it affected illegitimate children. Davidson felt
that the mothers' allowance program should be broadened slightly to
include one-child families where the father was alive but unable to
work due to disability. He condemned the $80 a month maximum
available to families under the program and argued that free health services should be provided for those on mothers' allowance.[44] Additionally, he urged improving the provisions for unmarried mothers and
their children, claiming that the law provided greater protection for the
overseers of the poor, who might have to assume responsibility for
unmarried mothers and their children, than for the mothers or children
involved. The overseers of the poor had the first right to claim support
from the putative father; Davidson's point was that this right should
belong to the mother.[45]

In 1946 Frances Weekes delivered much the same message to the
City of Halifax: 'The present provisions are almost invariably insufficient' and the most 'imperative need is for outdoor relief.' She recommended that the city establish an income maintenance program, and
that 'outdoor' medical care be provided for all recipients of municipal
and provincial income assistance. Weekes shared the widely held professional opinion that private social agencies should play an important
role in welfare services. In her view, private agencies should supplement public social assistance programs by providing casework services to families. Finally, she supported Davidson's recommendation
that both the provincial and federal governments should take greater
responsibility for aspects of social welfare in Halifax.[46]

In the years immediately after the war, social workers, welfare workers, women's organizations, and the Halifax Council of Social Agencies
kept up the pressure for reform. In January 1947, for example, the council held a meeting on 'Poor Relief in Canada with special reference to the
Poor Relief Act in Nova Scotia' and sent recommendations to its executive committee.[47] In 1950 the members of the Mainland Nova Scotia
Branch of the Canadian Association of Social Workers successfully lobbied local women's organizations such as the Women's Institutes, the

Nova Scotia Council of Women, and the Imperial Order Daughters of the Empire (IODE) to support reform of the Poor Relief Act. Margaret Doolan, a Halifax social worker, explained the shortcomings of the old Poor Law to the provincial annual meeting of the IODE. She drew particular attention to the problems of having untrained and unpaid overseers of the poor make decisions about people's eligibility for relief.[48] There was also some experimentation within the limits of the existing law. For example, by 1958 the Hants County Children's Aid Society, which had been renamed Family and Children's Services, held contracts with all four municipalities in Hants County to administer and provide relief, family casework, and services to children.[49]

The Local Council of Women (LCW) in Halifax regularly monitored affairs at the City Home. In July 1944, the LCW was concerned with the lack of occupational therapy at the home; in 1945 the diet provided for residents was the focus. In 1950, the Halifax Welfare Council's Gwendolyn Shand, a member of the LCW Committee on Laws for Women and Children, recommended improvements to the Nova Scotia Poor Relief Act. Two years later, Dr Alice Kitz reported that the City Home was still overcrowded, and no rehabilitation services were offered. In 1956, when Muriel Duckworth was convener of the LCW's Mental Hygiene Committee, she instituted a program of volunteer visits by the LCW to the City Home, the County Home, and the Nova Scotia Hospital, the provincial psychiatric hospital. Over the next two years, the LCW continued its visiting role, heard from a range of experts, and continued to advocate improvements.[50] The Halifax Branch of the Nova Scotia Division of the Canadian Mental Health Association was also attentive to problems at the City Home. In 1957, the report of the volunteer service in the Halifax City Home, soon known as White Cross, indicated concern with the lack of social activities, reiterating the comments of other critics that it 'is a social tragedy that City Home residents sit and have little or nothing to occupy their time during the hours between rising and retiring.'[51]

The Halifax County Hospital in Cole Harbour, although a much newer building, also got a bad review from the Halifax Branch of the Canadian Mental Health Association. At the time of the association's report in 1955, the building, designed for 425 patients, housed 597, most of them mentally ill. As a result, the wards were overcrowded and 'every inch of space is required for beds.' Although there were four registered nurses and one trained attendant, the majority of general attendants were under twenty years of age – many of them only fourteen or fifteen. Many patients were kept in locked isolation rooms, and restraints were used. Recreation and occupational therapy was also minimal. The biggest difference between the City Home and the Cole Harbour facility was that the latter had a farm, which provided some work for twenty-five of its residents.[52]

Despite reformers' persistence, their hopes were not realized in the first decade after the war. The Poor Relief Act remained in force, despite proponents for reform both within the Department of Public Welfare and outside it.[53] The reasons for the failure of the reformers in the postwar decade are rooted in both the shifting national political mood and local conditions. James Struthers notes the collapse of a similar welfare reform movement in Ontario, which he attributed to a number of factors, including 'unanticipated prosperity' (probably not a factor in Nova Scotia) and the Cold War, which dampened political support for expanding the social safety net.[54] The Liberal government of Nova Scotia shared in this political shift. Premier Angus L. Macdonald, elected as a reformer in 1933, returned to Nova Scotia a much more conservative politician after serving in Mackenzie King's wartime cabinet, and there can be little doubt that his fear of 'state socialism' was a factor in his government's failure to develop progressive welfare policy.[55] By 1947 he had certainly abandoned his former sympathy with labour, and that year's provincial Trade Union Act reflected 'a fierce anti-communism.'[56] In November 1945 and April 1946 Macdonald vehemently espoused a provincial rights position at federal-provincial conferences and, alone among the Maritime premiers, rejected federal government initiatives to expand federal involvement in social welfare.[57] With respect to the welfare institutions, much of the initiative passed to mental health reformers, who concentrated on establishing criteria for municipal hospitals in order to obtain government funding to reform the county homes.

Also militating against a successful campaign for welfare reform was the lack of cohesion among the disparate groups involved. This disunity may be best illustrated by the example of the establishment of the Maritime School of Social Work in 1941. The driving force behind the creation of the school was Samuel Prince, the president of the Halifax Council of Social Agencies. According to Gwendolyn Shand, executive secretary of the council and for many years a close associate, Prince moved more quickly to establish the Maritime School of Social Work than some of his colleagues had anticipated. When pressed to explain his haste, he told them that another group, headed by Lothar Richter of the Institute of Public Affairs, was also considering establishing professional training for social workers. Prince believed that Richter would establish a program modelled on social work training in continental Europe, 'and such schools were not adapted to the Canadian scene at all.'[58] The failure of the Halifax Council of Social Agencies and the Institute of Public Affairs to collaborate on the establishment of social work training may have reflected the suspicions of disloyalty harboured against Lothar Richter, who was a German refugee, during the Second World War. It may also have been a manifestation of philosophical differences about how welfare services should be organized. Richter's scheme was certainly in the tradition of an expanded role for the state, while Prince's approach seems to have been theologically rooted.[59] Whatever the source of their differences, these two organizations did not collaborate or coalesce into a unified movement to train the social workers needed to oversee the reform of public welfare in Nova Scotia.

The breakthrough that critics of the Poor Relief Act were hoping for was slow in coming. In anticipation of change, the Poor Relief Act was superseded by the Nova Scotia Social Assistance Act of 1956, which could not be fully implemented until a new cost-sharing formula was developed. This was achieved in 1958, following a renegotiation of the 1956 federal Unemployment Assistance Act. The new Unemployment Assistance Act established a federal funding program to provide 50 per cent of the cost to provinces of supporting 'unemployed employables' on social assistance. The Canadian Welfare Council had begun a new and vigorous lobby for such a program in 1953. Through persistence and political pressure, the CWC had persuaded a very reluctant Prime Minister Louis St Laurent to hold a federal-provincial meeting on the problem of responsibility for the unemployed who were not eligible for unemployment insurance. When the Unemployment Assistance Act was passed in 1956, four provinces, including Nova Scotia, found its terms unacceptable and refused to participate in the agreement.[60]

Nova Scotia refused to participate because it was ineligible to receive any money under the Act. For a province to qualify for federal funds, more than .45 per cent of its population had to have been receiving municipal or provincial social assistance. Women who were receiving mothers' allowance were not included in this number because they were regarded as unemployable. Under the existing Poor Relief Act, so few people received aid that Nova Scotia could not meet the .45 per cent threshold.

F.R. MacKinnon, director of child welfare at the provincial Department of Public Welfare, argued that Nova Scotia was being penalized for the weaknesses of the Poor Relief Act and the large proportion of mothers' allowance cases in the province. In the mid-1950s the poor relief case load varied from about 1,800 to 2,500. In order to reach .45 per cent of the population, the case load would have had to have been about 3,000. At the same time 1.2 per cent of Nova Scotia's population was 'benefiting from Mothers' Allowances.' Inclusion of mothers' allowance recipients would have enabled Nova Scotia to qualify for the federal cost sharing.[61]

Well before the passage of the Unemployment Assistance Act, the Department of Public Welfare recognized that this requirement would cause problems for Nova Scotia. In September 1955, MacKinnon advised R.M. Fielding, the minister of municipal affairs, that because of the limitations imposed by the Poor Relief Act, Nova Scotia 'need have no qualms about asking for special consideration' from the federal government.[62] MacKinnon, a native of Pictou County, became a long-serving deputy minister in the department. After earning a BA at Mount Allison University and an MA at Harvard, he was appointed executive director of the Colchester County (Nova Scotia) Children's Aid Society in 1937. Two years later, he was appointed assistant director of child welfare for the province, and in 1944 he succeeded Ernest Blois as director.[63]

In 1955, MacKinnon sought advice from George Davidson, who had moved from the Canadian Welfare Council to serve as the deputy minister of welfare in the Department of National Health and Welfare. MacKinnon was pessimistic about the prospect of significant welfare reform in Nova Scotia. He told Davidson

> As you well know the whole problem of municipal relief in Nova Scotia is a difficult one, and there is quite a strong body of thinking which goes something like this: The Poor Law structure is outmoded and outdated and the municipalities generally are not paying adequate relief, and nothing can ever be done by the province to improve the situation as far as setting up relief administration with good welfare principles is concerned. There is a large number of people who feel this way and some of them are very vocal in government circles. It is my own view that some members of the Cabinet have very strong views along these lines.[64]

One solution, MacKinnon suggested, would be to sidestep the Poor Relief Act and set up a new provincial social assistance program parallel to mothers' allowances.[65] Davidson thought this might be a useful approach, although he apparently could not resist reminding MacKinnon that he had recommended to Nova Scotia in the 1940s that the province take over the administration of relief. The present system 'will always be a "skeleton in the closet" and an embarrassment to you as long as the municipalities are left the job of dispensing poor relief, and are not prodded or compelled or persuaded by the province to maintain even minimum standards of decency and humanity in their administration.'[66]

Two factors affected the breakthrough on the federal funding issue for Nova Scotia in 1958. MacKinnon discovered through informal channels that Newfoundland had been able to work out a separate and private arrangement with Ottawa over its participation in the Unemployment Assistance program. He expected, rightly, that Nova Scotia could strike a parallel deal. The second was a direct personal appeal for support to James Band, deputy minister of welfare for Ontario.[67] In 1958 MacKinnon was on loan from the Nova Scotia Department of Public Welfare to the Canadian Welfare Council in Ottawa. He discussed Nova Scotia's problem with Norman Cragg of the CWC's Public Welfare Division, and the two approached 'Jimmy' Band for help. Band had strong connections with the new Conservative administration in Ottawa, especially with the new minister of national health and welfare. At their meeting in Toronto, Band questioned MacKinnon about Nova Scotia's reasons for requesting the elimination of the .45 per cent threshold. According to MacKinnon, after he had answered all the questions to Band's satisfaction, Band told him 'It will be done.'[68] In the 1958 revision of the Unemployment Assistance Act the offending threshold was removed.[69]

Once the threshold for eligibility for federal funding had been eliminated, Nova Scotia agreed to participate in the cost-sharing plan. Over the next eight years, using funds provided under the Unemployment Assistance Act and a number of other federal programs, the Nova Scotia Department of Welfare substantially reorganized and expanded its activities. Professionally administered social assistance programs were established in municipalities across the province, and minimum standards established. With the provision of more accessible 'outdoor relief,' the first steps were taken toward dismantling the network of county poorhouses.

In 1958 the Nova Scotia Department of Public Welfare reorganized existing programs such as mothers' allowances and provided for the transfer of federal and provincial funds for the creation and expansion of municipal social assistance.[70] Ignoring the advice offered by George Davidson in his 1944 report on welfare services in Nova Scotia and repeated in 1955, the provincial government decided to retain the municipal governments' administration of welfare services. Both Mac-Kinnon and Premier Robert Stanfield believed a large role for municipal governments was valuable and necessary.[71] Under the terms of the Social Assistance Act of 1958, municipalities were reimbursed for two-thirds of the funds they spent on municipal social assistance; 50 per cent of the costs were provided by the federal government under the Unemployment Assistance Act, and 16²⁄₃ per cent by the province. In exchange, municipal governments had to meet provincial standards for food allowances, drop residency requirements, and agree to pay for the administration of the programs.[72]

In April 1960 the Mothers' Allowance Act was rescinded and its provisions incorporated into the Social Assistance Act. Eligibility and settlement requirements were relaxed somewhat under the new legislative provisions. For the first time, mothers of Indian children whose husbands were dead or disabled could qualify for mothers' allowances. Regulations respecting deserted and orphaned children were adjusted to create more uniformity in payments.[73] A new disability program was established to provide assistance for those whose handicap was 'so severe that gainful employment is not open to them.' This program was supplementary to the federally funded disability pensions for which the regulations regarding eligibility were more stringent.[74] To prepare social workers for the new programs, annual training conferences and courses were developed for provincial and municipal welfare workers and for the staff of the private child-care institutions that delivered welfare programs. In January 1960, for example, the Department of Public Welfare held a three-day institute on public assistance, conducted by Norman Cragg of the Canadian Welfare Council's Public Welfare Division, for the directors of the divisions of the department and for regional and departmental supervisors. Municipal welfare officers from nine areas of the province attended the final two days of the institute.[75] Two years later, training conferences for municipal welfare officers were inaugurated.[76]

The 1958 Social Assistance Act enabled the municipalities in Nova Scotia to replace the unpaid overseers of the poor with paid welfare officers and to improve social assistance rates. But it did not immediately eliminate the other substantial legacy of the Poor Relief Act, the county poorhouses. Some reforms were introduced. The Department of Public Welfare was able to provide funds for maintaining the residents of the homes on the same basis as municipal social assistance, to set minimum standards for care, and to offer staff training programs. It did not control admissions policies, and many municipalities continued to use their county homes as multi-purpose residences.[77] Although a new program was developed by the department in 1964 to provide for the placement in foster homes or private nursing homes of former county home residents, this process took several years.[78] In 1961, taking advantage of the national hospital insurance program adopted in 1958, the Nova Scotia government proclaimed the Nursing Homes Act to provide separate care for the chronically ill. In 1966 the Hospital Insurance Commission assumed responsibility for the mentally ill. However, only four of the municipal mental hospitals, including two in the Halifax area, were recognized by the commission as mental hospitals. In addition, not all of the residents of the municipal hospitals met the commission criteria for mental illness; in 1966 the Department of Public Welfare took over responsibility for the 870 patients who did not fit these criteria. Fortunately, by this time the department had the funds available under the terms of the Canada Assistance Plan to help provide for their care. A year earlier, in anticipation of the changes to come, the government of Nova Scotia set up a Classification Committee to determine the appropriate care for residents of the homes and guidelines for future admissions.[79] The term 'municipal home' was changed to 'home for the aged,' and the care in these facilities was designed for those requiring personal and nursing care.[80] By the late 1960s the poorhouses had, in theory at least, been replaced by more specialized institutions, and responsibility for the residents had been divided between the Department of Public Welfare and the Nova Scotia Hospital Commission.

In Halifax, one of the first changes under the new system was the opening of Basinview Home, a new facility for seniors. The building, located at the north end of Gottingen Street, was not new. It had been used during the Second World War by the navy for patients suffering from sexually transmitted diseases and later for Hungarian refugees, and was sold by the federal government to the city for one dollar. Officially opened in 1959, the home was designed to provide 'pleasant surroundings for senior citizens without means of self-support, as well as achieving a much needed segregation of mental and welfare patients.'[81] Just over 100 patients were moved from the City Home, renamed the Halifax Mental Hospital, to Basinview, which the *Halifax Mail-Star* compared to a 'comfortable college dormitory.' Recreational facilities and lounges with televisions and pianos, and an interdenominational chapel were part of the new facility.[82] Satisfaction with the home was short-lived. In 1967, the Local Council of Women decided to investigate reports that Basinview was dirty and desolate and infested with cockroaches and rats. A year later, the LCW reported that conditions had improved, but complaints resurfaced in a series of damning reports in *The 4th Estate* in the early 1970s. In 1976, Basinview Home was closed, replaced by the private non-profit Northwood Manor, a new, purpose-built complex farther south on Gottingen Street. Similarly, on the other side of the harbour in Dartmouth, Oceanview Home opened in 1959 in former military barracks at Eastern Passage and took in the 'sane elderly' from the Halifax County Hospital in Cole Harbour. It, too, was replaced by a new building in 1967.[83]

In the early 1960s the Department of Public Welfare entered the field of community development, in particular to address the problems facing racial minorities.[84] Although this initiative was specifically designed to address the impact of racism, there were significant implications for women, who became involved in the community development process as volunteers, child-care workers, teachers, and administrators. The department played a major role in an interdepartmental human rights committee, which was established in 1962 to coordinate the work of a number of provincial government departments.[85] In the spring of 1964, F.R. MacKinnon, now deputy minister of public welfare, discussed the importance of community development as a new and important dimension of the work of the department at the annual staff meeting. The theme of the conference was 'Community Development with special reference to the Negro and the Indian.' The conference discussed recent research and promoted adult education as a tool in community development.[86] It also provides some insight into the ways in which the department was attempting to use economic development programs to expand its services. In 1961 the federal government had passed the Agricultural and Rural Development Act (ARDA), which provided federal funding on a cost-sharing basis for community economic development.[87] George Matthews, social assistance consultant for the Department of Public Welfare, discussed the role that ARDA programs could play in addressing the needs of families and communities in rural areas and announced that his department was negotiating with ARDA for a community development project in Black communities, the largest of which were in Halifax County. These initiatives were not without their critics, who argued that ARDA supported social welfare programs rather than regional development.[88] The Department of Public Welfare also used Department of National Health and Welfare General Welfare Training and Research Grants to support its community development work. Some projects were cost shared on a 50:50 basis with the provinces; others received 100 per cent funding from the federal government.[89]

During the two decades from 1944 to 1964, the Nova Scotia Department of Public Welfare changed dramatically. In the 1960s, it was organized into six divisions, each with its own director, and all reporting to Deputy Minister F.R. MacKinnon. Only two of these divisions, Child Welfare and Old Age Assistance, had existed in 1944. The Old Age Assistance Division administered the supplementary provincial allowance for those receiving the universal federal old age pension, the blind persons' allowances, and disabled persons' allowances. Responsibility for the administration of mothers' allowances had been moved from Child Welfare to the Social Assistance Division created in 1958.[90] The Social Assistance Division also offered support to municipal programs, including municipal homes and the municipal welfare officers. The other divisions included Field Services, to which the staff of the Department of Public Welfare regional offices were attached; Office Services; and the Emergency Welfare Services Division, which handled the department's contribution to civil defence.[91]

The history of social welfare reform in the decades after the Second World War has a new relevance in the early twenty-first century, as hard-won gains have been eroded by cutbacks and 'restructuring' in the Nova Scotia Department of Community Services since the mid-1990s. The programs of the Nova Scotia Poor Relief Act, with their very heavy reliance on the use of county poorhouses, were gradually eliminated after changes were made to the Unemployment Assistance Act in 1958. Between 1958 and 1966 the Nova Scotia Department of Public Welfare, under the leadership of Deputy Minister F.R. MacKinnon, made substantial and often innovative use of a variety of federal funding programs, including those designed for regional economic development. As James Bickerton has argued, 'regional policies were smuggled in through the "back door" as part of the government's "War on Poverty" social-welfare package.'[92] MacKinnon demonstrated considerable political skill in attracting federal funds to the Department of Public Welfare in the decade before the adoption of the Canada Assistance

Plan. He protected his department from the encroachments of other departments and expanded its work into the areas of long-term care for the chronically ill and the aged, human rights, and community development, all of which benefited women in need in Halifax. Today the Nova Scotia Department of Community Services is once again having to fight for its share of federal funding, especially since the Canada Assistance Plan was replaced by the Canada Health and Social Transfers in 1996. Sadly, we seem to be coming full circle. The recently restructured income-support programs of the department, with their inadequacy and attendant stigmatizing effects, offer a stark reminder of how close we still are to the policies that sustained the 'mansions of woe.'

NOTES

I want to thank Shirley Tillotson for her insightful and helpful comments and criticisms throughout the research and writing of this essay.

1 This research is part of the Women, Work, and Social Policy in Post-1945 Halifax Project. An important focus of this research is the amalgamation of four municipal units in 1996, which led to the creation of the Halifax Regional Municipality. Therefore, the evidence of activities and policies at the municipal level are drawn largely from the three municipal units in Halifax County: the county itself, the City of Halifax, and Dartmouth. See Jeanne Fay, 'From Welfare Bum to Single Mum: The Politics of Defining Mothers on Social Assistance in Nova Scotia, 1966–1977' (MSW thesis, Maritime School of Social Work, Dalhousie University, 1997), Appendix A, Synopsis of Statutes and Selected Regulations.

2 Nova Scotians participated in unemployment insurance and received family allowances, both adopted in 1944. See Dennis Guest, *The Emergence of Social Security in Canada*, 2nd ed. (Vancouver: University of British Columbia Press, 1985).

3 Sheila M. Neysmith, 'Towards a Woman-Friendly Long-Term Care Policy,' in Patricia M. Evans and Gerda R. Wekerle, eds., *Women and the Canadian Welfare State: Challenges and Change* (Toronto: University of Toronto Press, 1997), 222.

4 Similar local institutions in the United States have been studied by American feminist historians. See, for example, Linda Gordon, 'The New Feminist Scholarship on the Welfare State,' Linda Gordon, ed., *Women, the State and Welfare* (Madison: University of Wisconsin Press, 1990) and Linda Gor-

don, 'Social Insurance and Public Assistance: The Influence of Gender in Welfare Thought in the United States, 1890–1935,' *American Historical Review* 97, 1 (1992): 19–54.

5 James Struthers, *The Limits of Affluence: Welfare in Ontario, 1920–1970* (Toronto: University of Toronto Press, 1995); Allan Irving, 'The Development of a Provincial Welfare State: British Columbia, 1900–1939,' in Allan Moscovitch and Jim Albert, eds., *The 'Benevolent' State: The Growth of Welfare in Canada* (Toronto: Garamond Press, 1987), 155–74.

6 The federal old age pension program, cost shared with the provinces, was introduced in 1927. Provinces signed on over the next decade: British Columbia in 1926, Manitoba and Saskatchewan in 1928, Alberta and Ontario in 1930, Prince Edwards Island in 1933, Nova Scotia in 1934, and Quebec and New Brunswick in 1936. Kenneth Bryden, *Old Age Pensions and Policy-Making in Canada* (Montreal: McGill-Queen's University Press, 1974), ch. 5.

7 E.R. Forbes and D.A. Muise, *The Atlantic Provinces in Confederation* (Toronto and Fredericton: University of Toronto Press and Acadiensis Press, 1993); E.R. Forbes, 'Cutting the Pie into Smaller Pieces: Matching Grants and Relief in the Maritime Provinces during the 1930s,' in E.R. Forbes, *Challenging the Regional Stereotype: Essays on the 20th Century Maritimes* (Fredericton: Acadiensis Press, 1989), 148–71.

8 See, for example, Margaret Conrad, 'The 1950s: The Decade of Development,' in Forbes and Muise, eds., *The Atlantic Provinces in Confederation*, 393.

9 *Royal Commission on Provincial Development and Rehabilitation*, vol. 4, *Report on Public Welfare Services* (hereafter *Davidson Report*) (Halifax: Government of Nova Scotia, 1944), 22.

10 See the essays by Shirley Tillotson and Suzanne Morton in this collection for further details on child protection in Nova Scotia.

11 *Davidson Report*, 103ff. See also *Statutes of Nova Scotia*, 1923, c. 8; 1930, c. 4; 1931, c. 2. Eligibility for old age pensions and mothers' allowances was determined on the basis of a means test. Old age pension coverage began at seventy and the maximum benefit was $25 a month. Some of the charities operated by both religious and secular organizations received financial support from provincial and municipal governments.

12 Leonard F. Hatfield, *Sammy the Prince: The Story of Samuel Henry Prince, One of Canada's Pioneering Sociologists* (Hantsport: Lancelot Press, 1990); Gwendolyn V. Shand, *A History of the Halifax Welfare Council* (Halifax: Welfare Council, 1960); Lawrence T. Hancock, *The Story of the Maritime School of Social Work, 1941–1969* (Halifax: Maritime School of Social Work, 1992).

13 See Janet Guildford, 'A History of the Institute of Public Affairs, Dalhousie University,' unpublished paper, 1985; Charles H. Thomas, 'The Adminis-

tration of the Poor Law in Nova Scotia, 1749–1937' (MA thesis, Dalhousie University, 1938).

14 The Institute of Public Affairs journal, *Public Affairs*, published the results of much of this research, and the institute also published a series of books with Macmillan. The first in the series was *Canada's Unemployment Problem*, ed. Lothar Richter (Toronto: Macmillan, 1937).

15 Regarding the participation of labour organizations in aspects of welfare reform in Nova Scotia, see Shirley Tillotson, '"When Our Membership Awakens": Welfare Work and Canadian Union Activism, 1950–1965,' *Labour/Le Travail* 40 (1997): 139–79, and Shirley Tillotson, 'Class and Community in Canadian Welfare Work, 1933–1960,' *Journal of Canadian Studies* 32, 1 (1997): 63–92.

16 Thomas, 'The Administration of the Poor Law'; Forbes, 'Cutting the Pie.'

17 Thomas, 'The Administration of the Poor Law,' 17–18, 41.

18 Thomas, 'The Administration of the Poor Law,' ch. 9. In 1940 Halifax County established its own county home and no longer relied on purchasing services from the City of Halifax.

19 Frances Weekes, *Organization of Welfare Services in the City of Halifax. A Memorandum Prepared by the Nova Scotia Municipal Bureau, Dalhousie University* (hereafter *Organization of Welfare Services*) (Halifax: Institute of Public Affairs, 1946).

20 Ibid., 32.

21 H.B. Jones to W.T. McGrath, 25 March 1952, Canadian Welfare Council, National Archives of Canada (NAC), MG 28 110, vol. 347, file 25, 1134-9.

22 The 1879 Poor Relief Act empowered the municipalities to create municipal homes. In 1886 further legislation enabled municipalities and incorporated towns to establish mental hospitals. By 1890, eleven municipal mental hospitals were in operation, all of them doing double duty as poorhouses. Thomas, 'The Administration of the Poor Law,' 42–8.

23 *Davidson Report*, 107.

24 Ibid., 122.

25 Weekes, *Organization of Welfare Services*.

26 Ibid., ii.

27 Ibid., iv.

28 Dr Clyde Marshall was married to a psychologist who taught at Dalhousie University. The other members of the committee were E.J. Cragg and B.O. MacDonald. PANS, RG 35-102, 33, C4, Survey – City Home 1951 with Recommendations (hereafter Survey – City Home).

29 Survey – City Home, 11. Between 1882 and 1886 the Halifax Home was temporarily housed in the former Nova Scotia Penitentiary in the North

End of the city. Judith Fingard, 'The 1880s: The Paradoxes of Progress,' in Forbes and Muise, eds., *The Atlantic Provinces in Confederation*, 108.

30 Survey – City Home, 29.
31 Weekes, *Organization of Welfare Services*, 23–4; Survey – City Home.
32 Weekes, *Organization of Welfare Services*, 22–3.
33 Ibid., 33.
34 Survey – City Home.
35 Weekes, *Organization of Welfare Services*, 25–7.
36 Ibid., 28.
37 Survey – City Home, 30.
38 Weekes, *Organization of Welfare Services*, 29.
39 Ibid.
40 Ibid., 31.
41 Survey – City Home, 33ff.
42 *Davidson Report*; Halifax published a master plan for the city in 1945, which included both Weekes's study and submissions by the Halifax Council of Social Agencies.
43 *Davidson Report*, 5.
44 Ibid., 11–12.
45 Ibid., 18–19, 157.
46 Weekes, *Organization of Welfare Services*, 54, 55–87. Weekes developed her proposal for outdoor relief in Halifax more fully on 88ff, 121–8.
47 PANS, RG 35, Series 30, Section F5, *Annual Report*, Halifax Council of Social Agencies, 1947.
48 *Halifax Mail-Star*, 19 April 1950, 3; 21 April 1950, 6.
49 Author's interview with Harold Crowell, 14 November 1996.
50 See Minutes of the Local Council of Women (LCW), 1944–58, PANS, MG 20, vol. 535–6.
51 Report Re: Volunteer Service at the Halifax City Home, 1956, Canadian Mental Health Association Nova Scotia Division, Halifax Branch, PANS, MG 20, vol. 1476, no. 1.
52 Report of the Committee appointed by the Halifax Branch of the Canadian Mental Health Association to study the brief presented by the Scientific Planning Committee, re the care of the mentally ill in Nova Scotia, PANS, MG 20, vol. 1476, no. 1, n.d. [1950s].
53 The public housing movement in Halifax shared a similar fate in the 1950s. See John Bacher, 'From Study to Reality: The Establishment of Public Housing in Halifax, 1930–1953,' *Acadiensis* 18, 1 (1988): 91–119.
54 Struthers, *Limits of Affluence*, 141.
55 Carman Miller, 'The 1940s: War and Rehabilitation,' in Forbes and Muise, eds., *The Atlantic Provinces in Confederation*, 336.

56 E. Jean Nisbet, '"Free Enterprise at Its Best": The State, National Sea, and the Defeat of the Nova Scotia Fishermen, 1946–1947,' in Michael Earle, ed., *Workers and the State in Twentieth Century Nova Scotia* (Fredericton: Acadiensis Press, 1989), 189. Earle and McKay also noted a significant change in the provincial Liberal government's labour policy from the pioneering Trade Union Act of 1937, the first in Canada 'to require employers to recognize and bargain with unions supported by a majority of their employees, and to provide the check-off of union dues' to 'a conscious effort (especially since 1947) to weaken labour's position in the province as part of a strategy of economic development.' Michael Earle and Ian McKay, 'Introduction: Industrial Legality in Nova Scotia,' in Earle, ed., *Workers and the State*, 14 and 17. The conservatism of Angus L. Macdonald's government was also corroborated by F.R. MacKinnon. Author's interview with F.R. MacKinnon, 10 July 1996.

57 Miller, 'The 1940s,' 336.

58 Gwendolyn V. Shand, quoted in Hancock, *The Story of the Maritime School of Social Work*, 8. See also Hatfield, *Sammy the Prince*.

59 Guildford, 'History of the Institute of Public Affairs'; Hatfield, *Sammy the Prince*. Prince shared a philosophical framework similar to Charlotte Whitton's, while the IPA was closely associated with the new professional elite in Canada that rose to influence during the Second World War. See P.T. Rooke and R.L. Schnell, *No Bleeding Heart: Charlotte Whitton, a Feminist on the Right* (Vancouver: UBC Press, 1987), 112–19; Doug Owram, *The Government Generation: Canadian Intellectuals and the State, 1900–1945* (Toronto: University of Toronto Press, 1986).

60 Senior Scribes of Nova Scotia, *Poverty Poor Houses and Private Philanthropy* (Halifax: Author, 1996), 27–8. F.R. MacKinnon was among the Senior Scribes; James Struthers, 'Shadows from the Thirties: The Federal Government and Unemployment Assistance,' in Jacqueline S. Ismael, ed., *The Canadian Welfare State: Evolution and Transition* (Edmonton: University of Alberta Press, 1987), 3–32; Rodney S. Haddow, *Poverty Reform in Canada, 1958–1978* (Montreal: McGill-Queen's University Press, 1993), esp. ch. 2. F.R. MacKinnon, Director of Child Welfare, Nova Scotia Department of Public Welfare, was closely involved with the CWC's campaign, and throughout the 1950s he maintained regular contact and close association with members of the national staff.

61 PANS, RG 72, vol. 10, Unemployment Assistance file, (no number) Untitled, undated typescript. The accompanying note suggests the author was F.R. MacKinnon.

62 Letter from F.R. MacKinnon to Hon. R.M. Fielding, Minister of Municipal

Affairs, 22 Sept. 1955, PANS, RG 72, vol. 10, no. 23, Re: Federal Provincial Conference.

63 'Who's Who in Welfare,' *Welfare News* 15, no. 2 (1964), 2 and 4.

64 F.R. MacKinnon to Dr George F. Davidson, Deputy Minister of Welfare, Department of National Health and Welfare, Ottawa, 31 Oct. 1955, PANS, RG 72, vol. 10, no. 23, Re: Federal Provincial Conference. MacKinnon believed he had no allies in his campaign to replace the Poor Relief Act with a new system of social assistance. Author's interview with F.R. MacKinnon, 10 July 1996.

65 Author's interview with MacKinnon.

66 George Davidson to F.R. MacKinnon, 4 Nov. 1955, PANS, RG 72, vol. 10, no. 23, Re: Federal Provincial Conference.

67 Struthers, *Limits of Affluence.*

68 Author's interview with F.R. MacKinnon, 10 July 1996.

69 For another account of the changes to the Unemployment Assistance Act see Struthers, *Limits of Affluence*, 177-8.

70 The process of legislative reform had begun in 1954 with amendments to the Poor Relief Act that moved the administration of poor relief from poor districts to municipal units, prohibited the keeping of children under sixteen in poorhouses without the permission of the director of child welfare, and reformed the language of poor relief. 'Person in need' replaced 'pauper,' for example. In 1956 Nova Scotia adopted its first Social Assistance Act, but this legislation had little impact until federal funds were available. Fay, 'From Welfare Bum to Single Mom,' appendix.

71 Author's interview with F.R. MacKinnon, 10 July 1996. MacKinnon explained that the involvement of the municipal government in the provision of welfare services played a vital educational role that could not have been performed had the welfare services been centralized in the Nova Scotia Department of Public Welfare.

72 In the late 1950s and early 1960s *Welfare News*, a quarterly Department of Public Welfare publication for social welfare workers, ran a constant flow of information about the changes in administration, services, and programs.

73 D.J. Coulter, 'Changes in Social Assistance Legislation,' *Welfare News* 11, 2 (1960).

74 Ibid.

75 'Welfare Institute,' *Welfare News* 11, 1 (1960).

76 The main topics of discussion for the first conference reflected both the interests of the employees of the social assistance program and those of their clients, and included the kind of training required for the job, security,

pension plans, salary, sick leave, and vacations for welfare officers, and also the issue of the provision of drugs for recipients of social assistance and how to handle cases of spousal desertion. George Mathews, 'Municipal Welfare Officers Conference,' *Welfare News* 13, 2 (1962).

77 Robert Haley, *History: Homes for Special Care Nova Scotia, 1758–1991* (n.p., n.d.) Nova Scotia Community Services Library Special Collection.

78 *Welfare Services in Nova Scotia* (Halifax: Department of Public Welfare, 1964); Haley, *History*.

79 The government developed six categories of care: acute hospital care, assessment and rehabilitation, extended hospital care, intensive personal care with nursing supervision, limited personal care, and supervisory care. Haley, *History*.

80 Of the 870 residents of the municipal homes for whom the Department of Public Welfare had taken responsibility, 640 were classified as being suitable for homes for the aged. The remaining 230 were classified as retarded. Renovations were carried out in some of the existing municipal mental hospitals, and these were converted into 'specialized homes for the disabled.' Haley, *History*.

81 *Halifax Mail-Star*, 19 July 1959, 17.

82 Ibid.

83 Minutes, 13 Oct., 10 Nov., 8 Dec. 1967, 13 Sept. 1968, LCW, PANS, MG 20, 536-7; *The 4th Estate*, 17 Sept. 1970, 1, 28; 24 Sept. 1970, 3–4; *Dartmouth Free Press*, 12 May 1960, 7; 24 Aug. 1961, 8; 20 Dec. 1967, 2.

84 This work grew out of an interdepartmental committee on human rights established by Conservative premier Robert Stanfield in October 1962 'to give immediate attention to the problems of the Negro in Nova Scotia,' to improve race relations, and to promote the 'freedom and equality of opportunity for all persons without regard to race, creed, nationality, ancestry, or place of origin.' F.R. MacKinnon, 'Human Rights,' *Welfare News* 13, 4 (1962), 3–4.

85 H.R. Banks, 'Human Rights,' *Welfare News* 14, 3 (1963), 11–12. The commitment to human rights by the Department of Public Welfare had little impact on the racist and sexist humour that appeared in *Welfare News*. In the July 1960 issue of the journal the 'best joke from the Canadian Conference [on Social Work] was published. A darkie travelling from the deep south came upon a northern Indian village and the old Indian Chief remarked to his henchmen in audible tones "Midnight man come!" The dark fellow took one look at the Chief and said: "What you talkin' bout boy – Youse about half past eleven youself."' 'Canadian Conference on Social Work,' *Welfare News* 11, 2 (1960).

86 A.G. MacKenzie, 'Annual Staff Conference, Department of Public Welfare,' *Welfare News* 15, 1 (1964), 4–8.

87 The Agricultural and Rural Development Act (ARDA) was the first major regional development program adopted by the federal government. Passed in 1961, it was a 50:50 cost-sharing program aimed at improving economic conditions and potential in the poor, rural, agricultural areas of the country. Della Stanley, 'The 1960s: The Illusions and Realities of Progress,' in Forbes and Muise, eds., *The Atlantic Provinces in Confederation*, 425.

88 James P. Bickerton, *Nova Scotia, Ottawa, and the Politics of Regional Development* (Toronto: University of Toronto Press, 1990), 187–91.

89 Gwen Pickering, 'General Welfare Training and Research Grants,' *Welfare News* 13, 2 (1962), 4–6.

90 Those who had previously met the eligibility requirements for mothers' allowances were now supported by the Provincial Social Assistance Division under the terms of Part I, Group 1 of the Nova Scotia Social Assistance Act. New categories of eligibility had been added to the program, including the wives of prisoners and common-law widows, since 1944. *Welfare Services*, 1964.

91 *Welfare Services*. The 1964 annual report of the Department of Public Welfare was published in a new format, somewhat longer than the version printed in the Nova Scotia *Journal of the House of Assembly*. Women had not fared well in the reorganization and expansion of the Department of Public Welfare. Of the thirty-two senior staff listed in the Departmental Directory in July 1964, only six were women. Only one woman, Gwen Pickering, Director of Office Services, served as a divisional director. Of the twelve Children's Aid directors, Rosemary Rippon of the Lunenburg County CAS was the only woman. On the other hand, nine of the ten superintendents of child-caring institutions in the province were women.

92 Bickerton, *Nova Scotia, Ottawa*, 204.

Democracy, Dollars, and the Children's Aid Society: The Eclipse of Gwendolen Lantz

SHIRLEY TILLOTSON

The 1950s are quite rightly seen as a period of social conservatism, coloured by Canadians' passion for a 'normal' life after decades of war and hard times. But in some aspects of Canadian life, the end of war ushered in welcome – even exciting – change, rather than a comfortable return to a safe past. For welfare work, whether private social work or publicly funded health and welfare programs, a return to normal at the end of the war was unthinkable. If 'normal' means familiar and comforting, if 'normal' refers to a formula for success that had been only temporarily disrupted by the war, then there was no normal welfare system to which social workers and public servants and policy makers could return. In social welfare, the period from 1940 to 1958 was one of fast-paced change, a transformation of sometimes bewildering proportions. It was a time when people engaged in serving the needs of the poor and the vulnerable had constantly to be accommodating new realities. These were decades of possibility, not normalcy, in welfare work.

The record of state policy innovation in this period is well known, a standard theme in Canadian history. Less well understood are the changes in private welfare in the same decades. If we fail to consider the welfare charities in this period, we miss seeing important changes in community organization and welfare practices that flowed from and should be seen as part of the development of the welfare state. In cities across Canada, the decade following the war was full of nasty spats among the community-minded and compassionate, as different components of the welfare community vigorously fought for their vision of what the 'right' mix of public programs and private services should be. In my examination of the conflicts of this period, I have been finding that a process of democratization was under way.[1] As the social rights of citizens expanded, embodied in new social programs, so too did the mechanisms of accountability in welfare ramify, hotly contested all the while. As new means were created by which insiders' control of social services could be challenged, a process began that would lead to the welfare rights movement and the wider democratic claims of the 1960s.

In this essay, I examine a particular conflict in Halifax as an instance of the kind of bitter battle that divided the welfare community in the immediate postwar years, as they experimented with new ways of organizing the public-private division of welfare responsibilities. Such large transformations in political culture are lived out in a myriad of apparently petty struggles, and engage their participants in power relations at multiple levels, from the interpersonal to the institutional to the ideological. In Halifax, the changing relation of public and private in welfare became a fight about firing veteran child welfare worker Gwendolen Lantz. Unmarried and aged sixty-two in 1951, she had been the first professionally trained social worker hired by the Halifax Children's Aid Society (CAS) in 1925. Long-standing dissatisfactions with the CAS, and Lantz's management of it in her role as executive secretary, began to take new, more tactical forms in the spring of 1951. In the Welfare Council,[2] an organization in which social workers from both government and private welfare agencies met to coordinate and plan social services, the decision that Lantz be asked to resign was made in October 1951. To put that decision into action, however, required the help of the Community Chest, the fundraising organization that provided more than 80 per cent of the CAS's operating budget. It took a full year for the Welfare Council to persuade the Community Chest to pressure the board of the Children's Aid Society to ask Lantz for her resignation, which only the CAS board legally could do. Also applying pressure on the CAS board was the Division of Child Welfare of the provincial Department of Public Welfare, whose Director, F.R. MacKinnon, was an influential member of the Welfare Council. In October 1952, Lantz was asked to resign, and she did so. This outcome had involved many-sided relations among four groups: the Welfare Council, the Community Chest, the civil servants in the provincial Department of Public Welfare, and the CAS board. A fifth group, whose role in this story is somewhat shadowy, but arguably important, comprised politicians in Nova Scotia's Liberal and Conservative parties.

The contributions of this complex episode in public-private relations to the making of a more democratic political culture and the gender dynamics of that process can be understood by answering two historical questions that centre on the timing of the campaign to have Lantz dismissed. As many began to acknowledge in 1951–2, there had been problems with Lantz and complaints about the CAS since her arrival. The first question about the timing of her forced resignation, therefore, is how to explain Lantz's security of tenure in the twenty-five years between 1925 and 1950. Why had she been able to resist attacks on her performance for so long, during periods of crisis that saw other social workers embattled and let go from private and municipal agencies in various Canadian cities?[3] The answer to this question links the micropolitics exercised in small communities to the larger and gendered shifts in authority on which the welfare state was based. The second puzzle is why Lantz was not eased out sooner in the postwar period, since the attempt to force her out began in 1948.[4] After an initial inquiry into child welfare in Halifax that year, the momentum of reform slowed. When a second inquiry was launched in 1951, however, the reform process took hold and ran to its conclusion. The second point about timing, therefore, is to explain the different strategic circumstances of 1948 and 1951. In doing this, I hope to show the significance for democratization of the expanding government role in child welfare.

The woman who found herself at the sharp end of these changes in political culture, Gwendolen Lantz, was from Elmwood, in rural Lunenburg County, and had completed her BA at Dalhousie in 1911.[5] She was in her late twenties when, early in 1918, in the aftermath of the Halifax Explosion of December 1917, she joined the dozens of other Nova Scotia women who volunteered to be 'visitors' for the Rehabilitation Division of the Halifax Relief Commission. In this role, she was quickly trained in rudimentary social casework under the supervision of professionals brought in from places such as Montreal and Boston.[6] Apparently unemployed after her spell of volunteer social work, Lantz left Halifax in 1919 to attend the new McGill Department of Social Study and Training. She may have earned one of the diploma certificates offered there. While in Montreal, she worked at the Society for Prevention of Cruelty to Women and Children. That agency was directed by Howard Falk, who had been in charge of the social work operations of the Halifax Relief Commission during the time Lantz worked there. Falk was also the first director of the McGill department.[7]

Perhaps because of these two moments of connection between Falk and Lantz, his views on social work and social workers left their mark on her. Like Falk, Lantz would defend her work with claims that her approach to social work was distinctively 'modern' and her opponents reactionary, even when, by the end of her career, she was battling professionals with at least equally good credentials and much broader experience. Something of Falk's stance as a rather bluntly righteous, albeit eloquent, critic of contemporary welfare work is apparent in Lantz's reports from the beginning.[8] It is a tone that contrasts sharply with the 'pleasing and self-commendatory' language frequently used by representatives of charities in the period.[9] Lantz was entirely willing to disagree bluntly and publicly with other social workers, and, indeed, developed a reputation over time for thinking she was 'the only one in Halifax whose work is beyond criticism.'[10] In the course of her career in Halifax, she would give her board the impression that her conflicts with the city's other child welfare institutions arose because her 'ethical standards' were exceptionally high.[11]

Unlike Falk, who moved from city to city as his energetic but imperious personality cost him support among other welfare workers, Lantz stayed in Halifax.[12] In her first five years, she helped to expand the Children's Aid Society while serving, with some degree of success, the child welfare institutions that had created her position. Accused in 1926 of wanting the CAS to grow too quickly, she pointed out that she and her board had already succeeded in solving the debt problems of the Halifax Infants' Home, and therefore could be trusted to be financially responsible.[13] A stenographer and a second social worker were hired within a year of Lantz's appointment.[14] In 1927, as part of the Community Chest's general program of making charity more 'efficient,' the chest sought to reduce expenses by amalgamating the CAS and the city's family service agency, the Welfare Bureau. Lantz again proved effective in defending her agency, when the case she made for CAS autonomy convinced the 'disinterested party' (a retired marine engineer) who was assigned to study the matter.[15] Perhaps inevitably, however, given the difficult issues that arise in child protection work, her agency attracted criticism even in these early days of her tenure as its director. When the private welfare community was discussing the proposal to fire Lantz in the early 1950s, several veterans of the scene claimed that there had been 'difficulties with the CAS' since just after Lantz was hired.[16] While these may have been conveniently selective memories, Lantz was undoubtedly required from the beginning to operate within a complex network of interagency relationships. She may well have stepped on toes right from the start.

In the 1930s, the CAS faced both reduced financing and an increased demand for its services, as the Depression inhibited charitable giving and threw families into crisis. There were only 13 new wards in 1930, while in 1934, there were 42. With no increase in staff, the number of continuing wards for which casework supervision was required rose from 125 in 1930 to 279 in 1939. The ideal of an appropriate case load was 75, according to a social work study done in the early 1950s; but social workers, from the 1930s onward, frequently carried much larger burdens.[17] In Halifax's CAS, Lantz handled much of the casework load herself, along with the agency's administrative and legal work.[18] Her critics in later years said that women hired as her assistant social workers were treated by Lantz as her messengers, with judgments on cases always reserved for Lantz to make.[19] Carrying an absurdly heavy burden of work, purportedly increased by her reluctance to delegate, Lantz appears to have been under considerable strain during the 1930s. In an extraordinary demonstration of frustrated anger, she reportedly resorted to 'depositing' two mentally disabled children on the steps of City Hall.[20] A more responsible, less dramatic attempt to get support for her work was her agency's application to the Community Chest in 1938 for more than doubled funding. It was refused. City Hall made its first contribution to the CAS in 1938, but the amount was insignificant – $250.[21] The Depression also helped to produce a pattern in the treatment of wards for which Lantz would later be criticized. By 1939, 221 of the CAS's wards were in shelters and orphanages, as against 72 in 1930. This trend went against the professional consensus in favour of foster homes over congregate care settings. But, like the early proponents of foster care, Lantz preferred that foster parents not be paid a fee, and hard times made fewer families able to take in an extra dependant.[22] By the end of her first fifteen years in Halifax, as she turned fifty in 1939, Lantz must have had difficulty imagining a hopeful future in her working life. It is easy to see her as a case of a familiar present-day phenomenon: social worker burnout.

During the war years, evidence began to mount that, under these difficult conditions, Lantz had become defensive and resigned to the inadequacy of the CAS's services. For example, unlike the director of any other CAS or family service bureau in the country, she refused in 1942 to assist in the work of the Dependents' Board of Trustees, which attended to cases of child neglect among armed forces members' families. She argued that to do so would take time away from the CAS's own work, and retorted very sharply to efforts by Canadian Welfare Council director George Davidson to persuade her otherwise.[23] Although she probably worked day and night for the CAS, in 1941–2 she took on the extra responsibility of teaching the year-long course in child welfare at the newly founded Maritime School of Social Work.[24] She continued to complain, with some justification, that the Community Chest's funding of her agency was inadequate, and that she needed a staff of nine rather than two. But she did not take her agency out of the chest, as the Children's Hospital had done, to raise its own funds on the strength of the very powerful appeal of child protection work. She claimed her board lacked the ability to mount such a campaign.[25] She herself was only an intermittent participant in the Community Chest's roster of speakers, and in at least one year refused any involvement at all.[26] In 1943, an outside observer described her as 'completely embittered and disillusioned about the possibilities of anything better ever happening in Halifax.'[27]

At times, her resignation shaded into conservatism. On perhaps the single most important child welfare measure of the war years, the Family Allowance Act of 1944, Lantz expressed the view that parents' poverty was not an appropriate reason to make cash payments to families to meet children's needs. In this view, she congratulated herself, she was alone among Halifax social workers.[28] In fact, she was not. The Welfare Council's Child Welfare Division went on record as opposing these 'children's allowances,' offering the same range of reasons, including Lantz's, that anti-statist English-Canadian social workers had offered in earlier debates.[29] Like Charlotte Whitton, Lantz believed that private agencies should be advocates of 'social legislation.' But legislative programs vary in their content and ideological underpinnings, and her reason for opposing family allowances aligns her with the more conservative and anti-statist current in Canadian social work of the 1940s.[30] She presented herself as an advocate of reform, but resisted new perspectives on the role of the state in welfare work.

In spite of her defensive and sometimes self-righteous attitude, Lantz was certainly conscious of the vast extent by which the demand for social work services to unmarried mothers and neglected children exceeded what she and her one assistant could supply. Despairing of increased funding from the Community Chest, her response was to hunker down. She managed to have her home address suppressed in the City Directory in 1942, 1944, and thereafter (not likely to have been an easy matter). In this way, and in others, she seemed to be trying to protect herself. She refused to talk to Canadian Welfare Council field workers in 1944 and 1951 (and possibly at other times). And, apparently continuing a long-standing practice, she vigilantly filtered the information supplied to her board from other agencies, in order to suppress expressions of dissatisfaction with the agency.[31] In 1951, reporting on past experience, a prominent journalist told the Welfare Council that 'the newspapers' found it almost impossible to get information from Lantz and had come to feel that there was 'a complete lack of interest on the part of the CAS in the city's neglected children.' He added that the newspapers 'have been told again and again that the Society "cannot take action," but they know this is not correct.'[32] She maintained professional ties through the Welfare Council, serving on its executive committee, for example, between 1938 and 1947, but on a social level, Lantz held herself apart. After one year's membership, she withdrew from the city's Club of Business and Professional Women, an organization formed in 1936 to which her social worker peers generally belonged.[33] After 1936, her main personal relationship appears to have been with a woman bookkeeper with whom she lived.[34]

In 1925 Lantz had represented the new wave in social work. Articulate, well-educated, energetic, and extremely sure of herself, she brought to Halifax some of the same reforming energy that the leading lights in Canada's first generation of professional social workers, Charlotte Whitton and Howard Falk, contributed to provincial and municipal welfare work across Canada in the interwar years.[35] Her CAS reports and the scraps of evidence concerning the 1927 inquiry into the CAS/Welfare Bureau amalgamation reveal a kind of well-informed, tough-minded assertiveness that equalled Whitton's and Falk's. The expression of morally righteous anger, for which both of these two better-known figures were noted, appears also to have been part of Lantz's style, expressed in her protests of the 1930s and her reaction to challenges in the 1940s. Peter Stearns has argued that early-twentieth-century attitudes towards anger included the belief (at least for boys and men) that anger in the service of a good cause could be a 'splendid force.' Like both Falk and Whitton, Lantz appears to have carried that style into the 1940s, when a more restrained, bureaucratically suited manner came to be expected of both women and men. But in the interwar years, her willingness to deploy righteous wrath was one of her bulwarks.[36]

Lantz's position was also strengthened, in a paradoxical way, by the consequences of charitable fundraising's failures in Halifax in the early

1930s.[37] Between 1930 and 1934, the Halifax Community Chest's efforts to increase charitable donations met with bitter and repeated defeat. Member agency budgets and staff salaries were cut, and a 'common sense' belief emerged that Halifax had a donation ceiling of about $60,000.[38] In 1938, when Pittsburgh-trained social worker Gwendolyn Shand arrived in Halifax, her impression was of a community that accepted social 'conditions ... apathetically.'[39] Later, Shand would reiterate this perception, calling the 'welfare field' in pre-war Halifax 'passive,' and deploring the fact that there had been then, including herself, only three trained social workers in the city.[40] The stagnation that fundraising failures had induced meant there were few alternatives to Lantz's authority. As one of only two professional social workers before Shand's arrival, Lantz had been able to assert the superiority of her skills and standards in part because of the near absence of similarly qualified critics. Whatever her frustrations with financing, she had been able to hold some kind of moral high ground as the city's private welfare services settled into underfunded inadequacy. Paid only a modest salary at the low end of Canadian social workers' range, foregoing conventional family life, and ultimately provided with only a minimal pension, Lantz was not only hardworking, but apparently self-sacrificing. In this, she was typical of a generation of mainly women social workers whose jobs were secured in part by the respect that their dedication and self-abnegation evoked.[41] Like the clergymen with whom they were associated, discursively and in fact, as providers of care, social workers were expected to eschew monetary motivations for moral and emotional ones.[42] Lantz's position in Halifax was undoubtedly secured in part by her conformity to this feminized model of social work.

In interwar Canada, however, a newer view of social work as skilled, professional work, potentially part of public administration, and worthy of a man's wage in some of its branches, was gaining ground.[43] In Halifax in 1939, forces began to come together that would help support this shift and, in the process, counterbalance Lantz's authority.

The arrival of another Nova Scotian–born social worker, Gwendolyn Shand, was a sign of the forces of change. She was hired in 1938 to serve as the first paid staff member of the Welfare Council and the Social Service Index, a social work case-coordinating agency. Only about five years younger than Lantz, and trained, like Lantz, in the early 1920s, Shand was not of a different 'generation.' Shand came from rural Nova Scotia, too, albeit from the larger community of Windsor. With a master's degree in social work, and with experience in both Montreal and

Pittsburgh, she brought to Halifax an authority at least equal to Lantz's. In fact, with various 'short courses' under her belt from the London School of Economics, Smith College, and the New York School of Social Work, she might conceivably have been condescending towards Lantz.[44] Shand took a brisk sort of 'new broom' view of her role in Halifax's welfare circles, and very shortly found that Lantz, intentionally or not, presented an obstacle to change. The Welfare Council's efforts to push the city to develop a public welfare department, for example, were met with opposition in City Council because some of the city councillors based negative views of social workers on their perceptions of Lantz's 'difficult personality.'[45] Also important in determining the hostility that emerged between Shand and Lantz was that Shand arrived in Halifax at a moment when social work financed by the state was about to expand. Three of the major innovations in social services between 1940 and 1945 were unemployment insurance, with its associated employment services; provincial subsidies for Children's Aid Societies; and family allowances, accompanied by various forms of supervision and education.[46] More enthusiastically than Lantz, Shand would welcome a universalist, and not just a residualist welfare state, and would celebrate the 'broader participation of the social worker in public life.'[47]

In addition to Shand's arrival, two other developments in Halifax welfare circles in the late 1930s and the 1940s also marked the changing character of both private social work and the personnel of the welfare state. One was a new face in the volunteer community: the Halifax Junior League, incorporated in 1935. It was the Junior League that, in 1938, had provided the funds to employ Shand at the Social Service Index and the Welfare Council. An international organization, created for women under forty-five years of age, the Junior League engaged in a wide array of community social and cultural work, and did so with a novel twist. Unlike Rotarians or the Imperial Order Daughters of the Empire, for example, all Junior Leaguers were given a training course in social welfare and community planning called 'Community Needs.' The International Junior League, headquartered in New York, served as consultants and advisers, sending out social workers to give lectures on agencies such as the juvenile courts, children's aid societies, and welfare bureaux. Members of the Junior league prided themselves on being a new breed of volunteer, demonstrating a 'professionalism' in skill and standards, even if 'amateur' in the strict sense.[48] Several of their members, including lawyer Caroline McInnes and well-to-do wife Lillian

Farquhar, would be very active both in the CAS board during the 1940s and, in Farquhar's case, on the Community Chest board, fighting for improved CAS funding. Drawn from Halifax's supremely confident social elite and equipped with modern social work training, a Junior League member would not easily be cowed, even by someone of Lantz's ability and authority.

The other development that threatened Lantz's security at the CAS was the emergence of F.R. 'Fred' MacKinnon as a force in the provincial Department of Public Welfare. He represented the advent of a new generation of social workers, a cohort that included an increased proportion of men, usually relatively young and frequently war veterans, who often displaced more senior women in social work's higher administrative ranks.[49] As Shand would write in 1955, 'many positions which had been traditionally filled by women, are now being invaded by the men.'[50] In Ottawa's Community Chests, Joy Maines retired in 1945, and was replaced by Lieutenant Sidney T. Smith, while in Vancouver's Welfare Federation, Marjorie Bradford left for a United Nations job, leaving the federation to hire Colonel Hugh Allan.[51] In the Canadian Welfare Council, Canada's central and most influential social work body, the employment in 1941 of George Davidson, PhD, as the executive director, to replace Charlotte Whitton, MA, also marked this gender shift in the demography of welfare administrators.[52] In Nova Scotia, the thirty-five-year-old MacKinnon's appointment as the province's director of child welfare in 1944 made him part of this new wave. With a 1935 MA from Harvard, MacKinnon had served as the Colchester County (Nova Scotia) CAS director in 1937. In 1939 the province's deputy minister of welfare had singled him out from among the province's social workers to be the recipient of a Rockefeller Foundation scholarship to study at the University of Chicago and tour North American welfare agencies. On his return, he had been named the assistant director of the Child Welfare Division, and in 1944 replaced as director E.H. Blois, who had been at the helm since 1912.[53] With the departure of Blois and, in 1948, the retirement of long-term deputy minister Frank Davis, MacKinnon became one of the most senior civil servants in the provincial departments of public health and welfare. MacKinnon's dissatisfaction with Lantz would make him one of her most formidable opponents. Indeed, early in his tenure as director of child welfare, in the spring of 1948, he informed the Welfare Council officially and forcibly of his unhappiness with child welfare services in Halifax.[54]

From the archival traces that remain of the campaign to improve Halifax's child welfare practices in the years between 1948 and 1952, it is clear that the tensions between Lantz and the various child-serving agencies in Halifax were not new. But at the same time, women from those agencies seem to have become more willing after 1948 to talk to outside observers about Lantz's 'unfortunate personality' and make the claim that she was doing social work various kinds of harm.[55] The timing of this shift in mood had to do largely with Fred MacKinnon's plans to make his department the real arbiter of social work standards in Halifax. Lantz's iron will, forged through years of embattled self-justification, made her a significant obstacle to these plans. In the years between 1948 and 1952, MacKinnon presided over the creation of new child welfare legislation and collected evidence of Lantz's failings. Both of these undertakings were part of his larger commitment to reforming public welfare in Nova Scotia. In Halifax, this project entailed working through the Welfare Council, where both public and private agencies were represented. In the council, MacKinnon enjoyed considerable support, from both women and men.[56] There was, nevertheless, a gender dynamic in the micropolitics of the welfare reform enterprise.

The new stage in the process of reform in Halifax began in 1948, when MacKinnon announced to the Welfare Council that he was seriously concerned about child welfare services in Halifax. He soon realized, however, that the existing Child Protection Act of 1923 gave him no real authority over the Children's Aid Societies it chartered. For this reason, and no doubt others, he appears to have persuaded the minister that revised legislation was required. The Child Welfare Act of 1950 created a 'grading grant' system, which enabled the provincial director of child welfare to reward satisfactory CASs with a supplement to their operating budget of up to $2,000 per year.[57] While developing this new regulatory tool, MacKinnon also gathered evidence of the problems with Lantz's management of the Halifax CAS. In June 1951, he would supply a dossier of this material to the Welfare Council. While the case against Lantz included accusations of uncooperativeness, MacKinnon was careful to show that the problem was not just interpersonal friction, but that Lantz's personality had real consequences for vulnerable children.

One case illustrated his main points. In November 1946, Lantz had taken into CAS care a boy whose parents had separated and whom she deemed was neglected. She placed him in one of the Halifax orphanages. Just over a month later, in January 1947, his parents reconciled, and asked to have their child returned. Lantz refused, asserting that they could not provide a suitable home. Over the next fifteen months they continued to appeal to Lantz. She persistently rejected their appeals. In March 1948, on the request of the president of the CAS, MacKinnon's department investigated the parents and their home. MacKinnon's department served as the CAS for Halifax County and so had on its staff several social workers who routinely did these sorts of investigations. The two social workers assigned to assessing the case both concluded that the home was 'completely satisfactory' and recommended that the boy be returned to his parents. However, it was only after nearly another full year had passed, in July 1949, *more than two years* after he had been initially apprehended, that Lantz gave consent to have the boy returned to his home. MacKinnon concluded his summary of the case by observing (with what must pass for passion in a civil service memo): 'It is extremely difficult to rationalize this kind of action or to understand [Lantz's] reasoning in this particular case.'[58]

In this story, MacKinnon was illustrating one of the general complaints about Lantz – that she put children in institutions and left them there for so long that their ties to their families and communities were deeply harmed.[59] Whereas in this particular case, the problem appeared to be Lantz's extreme views on the suitability of a biological family, she was also criticized for finding relatively few foster homes acceptable, and for preferring to leave children in orphanages rather than place them in what she judged to be inadequate foster homes. Whether her judgments were sound must remain open to question; certainly, MacKinnon's staff formed different ones. In Lantz's view, for example, Guysborough County was 'very primitive' and therefore unsuitable as a source of foster homes. MacKinnon and his staff offered what seems to have been a more precisely observed perspective. Acknowledging that some parts of the county were indeed isolated and therefore deficient in medical services, they claimed to have found in other parts homes that were perfectly good and open to accepting children.[60]

The question of the availability of foster homes was just one of a series of points of stark disagreement that emerged as the Child Welfare Division of the Welfare Council undertook its 1951 survey of Halifax children's agencies, in an attempt to diagnose problems.[61] Lantz and MacKinnon both were involved in a series of four 'round table' meetings of child welfare workers, convened to discuss this survey in the months of March, April, and May 1951. The survey had found that, in addition to not finding and using enough foster homes, the Halifax

CAS was failing to give adequate casework services to unmarried mothers and their children, and, overall, that the CAS was not working cooperatively with either the children's institutions or MacKinnon's office. In fact, Lantz's abrupt treatment of unmarried mothers meant that these often desperate women showed up at the provincial Department of Public Welfare, seeking the help Lantz had refused them.[62]

In the course of discussions about these charges, Lantz defended her agency as doing the best it could with limited staff. On the staffing shortage point, her critics agreed. But she found a less receptive audience when she suggested to her critics that they should read more up-to-date books on child welfare, and told representatives of the institutions that had paid most of her salary through donations to the CAS for many years that they should hire their own social workers, as comparable institutions in Toronto and Montreal did.[63] On these points, the other social workers met her assertions with detailed arguments, none of which appear to have altered Lantz's convictions. As one veteran welfare volunteer later noted, they found her unwillingness to accept any criticism to be 'baffling beyond words.'[64]

Although the Welfare Council rather than the Department of Public Welfare convened these meetings, civil servant MacKinnon played a key role. Like the sixty-two-year-old Lantz, MacKinnon sometimes based his rhetoric on being the most 'up-to-date' expert in the room.[65] His age (almost twenty-five years less than Lantz's) may have made this claim on his part superficially more plausible. But he had another, more genuine advantage in the argument; as provincial director of child welfare, he was armed with abundant statistics on the performance of other CASs in the province: the numbers of adoptions arranged, foster homes found, and dollars of charitable money per capita raised.[66] He could show how much better every other CAS had done at fundraising. By the end of the round table meetings, it was evident that the group was not going to achieve consensus on who was to blame in Halifax and why, because Lantz absolutely refused to concede any fault. One suspects that few participants in the process had genuinely expected anything else.[67] Lantz, for her part, made very clear her view that MacKinnon compared dismally to his counterpart in Ontario's civil service and that he completely misunderstood the proper relationship between private and public welfare agencies.[68] She had, however, met in MacKinnon someone who matched and sometimes exceeded her in intellectual authority, mastery of pertinent fact, political skill, moral certainty, and sheer strength of will. He represented, moreover, in his gender, youth, and institutional position, the future of social welfare leadership. He wielded the political clout such symbolism conferred, as he worked relentlessly towards making his public agency the arbiter of standards. Lantz made one more defence of her position at a 29 May 1951 meeting of the Child Welfare Division of the Welfare Council. She was given twenty minutes to speak. After her presentation, and a brief wrangle with MacKinnon and one of his departmental staff, MacKinnon moved that the division forward the survey of Halifax children's agencies to the Welfare Council executive. The motion carried. At the 22 June meeting of the council executive, a special committee, chaired by Dr H.B. Clarke, a respected United Church minister, was asked to investigate the CAS and its relationships to other agencies, including MacKinnon's department.[69] Over the summer, Clarke's committee met with the concerned parties and also with representatives of the city's newspapers, to gauge 'public confidence' in the CAS. The report produced in September went decisively beyond general expressions of goals for reform to make very specific complaints about Lantz's management, such as allegations that she did not respond to written complaints from other social work agencies and that there was no communication between her CAS and MacKinnon's department. The report included the recommendation that Lantz be asked to resign. In October 1951 Clarke's committee presented this report for discussion at a well-attended session of the Welfare Council's executive committee. The situation had by now become so sensitive as a public issue that the copies of the Clarke committee report used in this meeting were not allowed to leave the room, and those present were sworn to strict secrecy. After some vigorous discussion, nineteen of the twenty-one members voted to endorse the report's recommendation that Lantz had to be removed from office (the two CAS board members abstaining). Then the council sent the report to the CAS board, with their endorsement.[70]

The process so far had been painful and protracted, perhaps out of a sense that Lantz had to be accorded a full opportunity to respond to criticisms. But there would be yet further delays after October 1951. In this last stage of the story, the playing out of shifts in social work authority gave way to another level of politics.

In 1951–2 the president of the CAS was Richard A. Donahoe. Over the previous decade, Donahoe had frequently served on the CAS board, but this was his first term as its president. When he took the position, he must have known that the CAS was under attack by the provincial Department of Public Welfare. It is therefore useful in

understanding the final stage of the Lantz story to know that Richard
Donahoe had a reason to buck Fred MacKinnon's plans. In 1949, Donahoe had lost the contest for Halifax North in the provincial election to
Harold Connolly, the most senior minister in the Liberal government,
who became in 1950 the minister of public welfare, and Fred MacKinnon's political master. Although Donahoe had failed to unseat Connolly in 1949, Donahoe's party, the Progressive Conservatives, under
the new leadership of Robert Stanfield, had emerged from the political
wilderness to become the official opposition with seven MLAs. In
1949–53, for the first time since 1933, the Conservative Party was pos-
ing a real challenge to Premier Angus L. Macdonald's Liberals. Donahoe would demonstrate his worth to the Conservatives when, in 1955,
he won Halifax South, the seat left vacant by Macdonald's death,
to become the only Conservative elected in any of the four Halifax Peninsula ridings during the 1950s. Donahoe would, in turn, become
minister of public welfare in the Stanfield government after the 1956
election.[71] Already, in 1952, Donahoe was a significant political con-
tender: in the Halifax mayoralty race in April of that year, he beat the
incumbent, John Ahern, a Liberal Party activist who would win Halifax North in 1956.[72] To the Liberals, Donahoe's 1952 mayoralty victory
must have made him seem a real threat to Connolly in the 1953 provincial election. In 1951–2, then, Lantz had a defender in Donahoe, whose
motivations must at least partially have been to challenge plans laid in
Harold Connolly's ministry. At the same time, MacKinnon could not
have been unhappy that, should his campaign produce negative publicity about the CAS, its president was someone his minister would
happily see as guilty by association.

From October 1951, when, as president of the CAS, Donahoe
received the Welfare Council's recommendation to force Lantz's resignation, until October 1952, when she resigned, Donahoe stalled. He
told the council that the problem lay in the constitutions and mandated
responsibilities of the various child-serving agencies, not in personalities, and that another survey by an independent outsider would see
things differently. The council agreed that another survey by someone
independent would be desirable, but then found that this concession
had simply given the CAS a means of delaying action. The CAS put
roadblocks in the way of launching the survey they had asked for.
When, finally, in the spring and summer of 1952, the council and Community Chest organized an assessment of the CAS and its relations to
other agencies by a very prominent Canadian social worker, Bessie

Touzel, Lantz refused Touzel's request for information and, later, Donahoe disputed whether Touzel's findings really amounted to a survey.[73] In the very last stages of discussions, in September 1952, when the council had secured the support of the chest, after much effort, and the chest had delivered a financial ultimatum to the CAS, Donahoe was still arguing that to see firing Lantz as the solution to the CAS's weaknesses was unfair to Lantz.[74] In the final stages of this struggle, key decisions were made in at least one unminuted meeting between the three presidents of the chest, the council, and the CAS. Donahoe, as president of the CAS, stood in the way of firing Gwendolen Lantz.[75] He had resisted the proposal to do so since the summer of 1951, and had become identified as the person whose compliance had to be obtained before 'the situation,' as it had come to be known, could be resolved.[76]

That there was a partisan dimension to this struggle is sustained by more than just inference, although its backroom nature makes explicit evidence scarce. I began to look for party loyalties among the key players after I read a comment made in February 1952 by the president of the Community Chest, Marshall Wilson, to a visiting expert from the Canadian Welfare Council.[77] Wilson, a prominent business executive and a friend of federal Liberal MP (and former CAS president) Sam Balcom, told the visiting expert that he was 'convinced that there are political implications' to the delays. This is no more than a suggestive hint, but two other facts support the notion that the ministry staff had significant backing from the minister and thus that old enmities from the hustings might have been at play. One is that in 1951, the department took the step of withholding the provincial grant to the Halifax CAS. This step was so unusual and dramatic that it was unlikely to have been undertaken without the minister's knowledge and approval.[78] The other fact – a more explicit one – is that, in May 1952, the acting minister, R.M. Fielding, gave his blessing, albeit subtly, to the proposed termination of Lantz's employment.[79] This evidence strongly suggests that the Liberals backed MacKinnon's campaign. In this context, Donahoe's remarkably stubborn defence of Lantz, involving a variety of stalling tactics and bold-faced attempts to deny accumulated evidence, seems to have been as much a defence of his own political image as it was credible support for an unfairly persecuted victim. To be the man at the helm of the CAS when Lantz was fired could have led to his name being linked with the failings of the CAS. Once Donahoe had begun to defend Lantz, he must have felt he had to continue to argue that there were solutions other

TABLE 2
Revenue sources shown in the operating budget of the Halifax
Children's Aid Society, 1943–1951 (rounded to even dollars)

Year	Community Chest	Province	City
1943	$4,183	$1,750	$500
1944	$9,091	$1,500	$1,000
1945	$6,450	$2,000	$1,000
1946	$9,215	$1,666	$916
1947	$10,000	$2,000	$1,000
1948	$9,625	$2,000	$1,000
1949	$10,733	$2,000	$1,000
1950–1 (16 mos.)	$14,460	$4,000	$1,333

Source: Journals of the House of Assembly, vols. 1944–52, Part
II, Appendix 23

than her dismissal. Otherwise, he was open to being described by his political enemies as not caring about the welfare of neglected children. Something similar had happened at least once before in Canadian politics, in 1934, when Ontario premier George Henry was attacked by his political opponents for the failures of the York County CAS, of which Henry was president.[80] An element of partisan politics, then, may well have delayed and embittered this fight.

Party politics may also have helped drive the reform process led by MacKinnon. The pressure for changes to the CAS was possible only because the CAS was not simply a private charity, but was also the agent of government-mandated and government-funded child-protection work. In 1943, the provincial government had begun to make grants in support of the CAS's operating budget, which covered staff salaries and other operating expenses. These grants were still relatively insignificant in the immediate postwar years, when charitable donations paid for over 80 per cent of the Halifax CAS's operating budget (see table 2). But most of the money spent on CAS wards (in the 'maintenance budget') came from per capita fees set by legislation and paid by government. As a result, many people thought that the CAS was a government service.[81] There was, therefore, a risk to the government's reputation if a CAS fell into public disrepute. And yet, the mechanisms of enforcing government standards in CAS work were weak, when, in the Halifax case, the provincial contribution to the operating budget was so small. The grading grants in the 1950 Child Welfare Act certainly gave the provincial officials some new leverage.[82] Nonetheless, in Halifax, the real financial clout remained in the hands of the Community Chest. And the Community Chest would not on its own have forced the ouster of Gwendolen Lantz.

If Lantz's personality had been one obstacle to CAS reform and, in 1951, party politics became another, the most fundamental was the conservatism of the Community Chest fundraising system. As Gwladys Kennedy admitted in April 1952, the chest's budget committee had been concerned about 'the whole matter' of the CAS for 'several years,' but had not protested, 'hoping things would correct themselves.'[83] The Halifax Community Chest was reluctant to intervene in the social work practices of member agencies. They were not unique among Canadian federated fundraisers in this respect. Chests had to be sensitive to agencies' fears that joining a federated appeal would mean the surrender of autonomy.[84] The fears were not merely irrational; chests promised donors that their contributions would be used 'efficiently,' which meant that the chests' budget committees undertook to judge whether some member agencies' services overlapped with or duplicated other services available in the community. In Vancouver in 1943, the Welfare Federation ejected the Disabled Veterans Association, which ran a clubroom for its clientele. The federation had been studying duplication of services, and had concluded that there was too much overlap among the veterans' agencies it funded.[85] Chest management of agencies could be even more intrusive. For example, left-wing political meetings at federation-funded community centres in Vancouver attracted hostile public attention in 1950 and prompted the federation board to prohibit the use of agency facilities for political activities.[86] But especially in the years between 1950 and 1953, when public concern about the proliferation of multiple appeals was making chests avid to recruit hold-out agencies, chests tried to avoid appearing to manage heavy handedly the affairs of those already in the fold.[87]

The conservatism of the chests also came from a fundraising bias: public criticism of member agencies was to be avoided, especially around campaign time. But public relations considerations tied agencies and fundraisers together like partners in a three-legged race. While the agencies ultimately needed the fundraisers more than fundraisers needed them, a successful fundraising campaign did depend on the cooperation of the member agencies. Some canvassers came from agency boards; agency staff served as speakers and sources of promotional information; some agencies would host tours for the public.[88] 'Popular' agencies, which usually meant child-serving ones, could seriously embarrass the chest by leaving it.[89] In many cities in the postwar years, agencies were shifting from the supplicant mode of the Depression era to a more assertive posture. Chests began to hear demands from more agencies for funding that was adequate to hire qualified, professional staff and provide a high standard of service.[90] The ferment Fred MacKinnon initiated in the Halifax Welfare Council was just one example of this larger process, in which social workers sought better funding for their agencies or other, related goals and used the threat of bad publicity or other forms of pressure to try to extract concessions from the chests.[91]

Conflicts between a social work perspective and a fundraiser perspective were consolidating in a pattern of polarization in the first decade after the war, and bedevilling relations between Community Chests and Welfare Councils everywhere.[92] Halifax's council was one of the more alienated from its city's chest, and so the potential for conflict was very high. The Halifax chest had little official representation from member agencies on its board and budget committee. One of the CAS board members, Junior League member Lillian Farquhar, found this feature of the Halifax welfare structure especially frustrating as she struggled, starting in the early 1940s, to have the chest grant to the CAS increased to pay for more staff. The board's response expressed the fundraiser's perspective: that Halifax had limited resources for charity and that the CAS was being given its fair share of the funds that the chest was able to raise. In 1943, however, Farquhar discovered that the chest had a substantial surplus carried over from year to year as a kind of 'rainy day' reserve fund and a source of interest income. She was outraged, telling the Canadian Welfare Council's George Davidson that 'the Community Chest has no right to withhold public funds which are given for the purpose of helping the agencies and alleviating suffering.' A member of a wealthy family, Farquhar threatened to withdraw her own donation and suggested menacingly that other donors might be similarly moved.[93] She felt, as her New York adviser reported, that 'the sense of trusteeship of the public money is apparently unthought of by this board.'[94] She also fought a prolonged, and, by 1950, a successful battle to have the chest's board membership change on a rotating basis and include designated positions for an increased number of agency representatives, nominated by the Welfare Council.[95] Both in seeking, as a donor, to make the chest more accountable and in attempting, as a member, to diversify the constituencies represented on its board, Farquhar was trying to insist on more democratic welfare practices.

The CAS 'situation' thus pitted social workers against fundraisers and raised important issues of accountability. The Welfare Council was determined to force the issue, even while aware of the consequences for fundraising. At one of the crisis points in the 1951–2 events, the council president accused the chest of being 'afraid of' the October 1951 report.[96] The council president knew chest fundraising depended on presenting the agencies as faultless providers of essential services. Exposure of the Lantz record would have highlighted the falsity of those images. When, finally, the chest accepted that it would have to threaten to cut off its support of the CAS in order to force Lantz's resignation, it tried to do so before the fall fundraising campaign.[97] This suggests that, like Donahoe, the chest thought that newspaper coverage of the Lantz/CAS story risked damaging the images of those who did the firing, as well as bringing to light questions of the adequacy of the CAS's work over the previous twenty-five years. These were matters that fundraisers were loathe to expose.

Aware of the chest's reluctance to take on the CAS problem, the Welfare Council delayed officially transmitting the council report to the chest until May 1952.[98] In fact, they only did so when they had concrete evidence that their support for the firing of Lantz could be presented as *preventing* bad publicity. In April 1952 Welfare Council President Fred Fraser got a call from Frank Doyle, associate managing editor of the city's leading daily, the *Chronicle-Herald*. Doyle, whose long-term political loyalties had probably been formed in his years with the old Conservative dailies, the *Herald* and the *Mail*, told Fraser that the *Chronicle-Herald* had been receiving increasing numbers of complaints about the CAS but had not published them. If something was not done soon to remedy the problem, he said, the newspapers would have to speak out. He knew of the survey and knew that the CAS had been sitting on the recommendation to fire Lantz since the preceding October. It seems likely that Doyle had been among the newspaper men H.B. Clarke's committee had interviewed in the summer of 1951. They had reportedly told Clarke that the newspapers did not want to 'hurt the whole welfare structure,' but they thought there was something wrong when $14,000 of donors' gifts were being paid by the chest to an inadequate agency.[99] Doyle's call in April 1952 meant that handling 'the situation' in secret was threatened.

Doyle's expression of the newspapers' interest in the CAS problem was couched in terms of the chest's accountability to its donors. It marks the entry of charitable matters into the realm of public criticism and debate – democratic public culture – in Halifax. The threat of publicity accomplished what Farquhar's more discreet insider tactics had not. Throughout years of starving the CAS for funds, the Halifax chest had been able to ignore protests and continue to present the CAS to the public falsely as successfully fulfilling the community's needs. Secrecy and discretion had allowed passivity to flourish in the face of problems.[100]

Outside observers of the Halifax chest in the 1940s found it exceptionally stagnant, with a cadre of board members who, for the most part, had been with the organization from the start. The executive secretary since 1925, Gwladys Kennedy, was perceived as running the board, who were grateful to be saved from doing any real work.[101] In public, Kennedy was a specialist in anodyne speeches praising the services of Halifax social agencies.[102] Campaign publicity was handled year after year by a prominent life insurance man, G. Raymond Smith, with the newspaper stories on agencies' work always emphasising the gratitude of the orphans, the blind, the friendless girls, and the aged.[103] To make any form of change was to risk hurting feelings among the dedicated folk who volunteered to administer and raise funds for these agencies. This prospect was especially troubling in a small city such as Halifax where individuals were linked by multiple business, family, and associational relationships.[104] Not surprisingly, a fear of criticism pervaded the chest culture.[105] In Halifax, as elsewhere, that fear was one reason labour representatives, who were perceived (accurately) as critics, were unwelcome as decision makers in the chest movement.[106] For this political culture to become more democratic, with agencies being held accountable to improved standards of service, there had to be some significant, relatively autonomous force brought to bear. Fred MacKinnon's position as an agent of governmental authority made it possible for him to act as that force.

The pressures brought to bear on the Community Chest and the CAS board by MacKinnon and his allies signalled a move to more democratic ways of doing things. Eight months after Lantz's ouster, the Community Chest's efficiently autocratic Gwladys Kennedy was removed, none too gently, from her key position. Lantz's main opponents – MacKinnon, Shand, and Farquhar – had targetted Kennedy, like Lantz, as a barrier to progress.[107] She was replaced by George Hart, a young man with expansive ideas, who quickly made it possible for the chest to meet doubled fundraising targets. Hart came to the chest from Fred MacKinnon's staff at the Division of Child Welfare.[108] This was one more sign that the crucial force in orchestrating the changes in Halifax welfare circles was Fred MacKinnon, a man empowered by the growing importance of welfare matters in government.

MacKinnon's personal qualities of intelligence and drive were significant in instigating the changes in Halifax, although arguably he was neither smarter nor more energetic than Gwendolyn Shand or Lillian Farquhar. He benefitted from such allies in the Welfare Council, with their commitment to professionalism and democratic process within social work. But what was most new in the structure of welfare practices was MacKinnon's ability to deploy power from an institutional funding base other than the chest's. This was what gave the necessary reinforcement to the campaign that women reformers had been fighting since the early 1940s. Once Lantz was gone, replaced by Thomas Blue, who brought to the CAS job a mix of CAS and civil service experience, the annual provincial grant to the Halifax CAS rose from $2,000 to almost $9,000.[109] Even Nova Scotia's unambitious welfare state had ample means to direct a 'private' agency. Public and private responsibilities in child welfare were becoming ever more thoroughly intermixed.

In the rationale for the role of private agencies that was developed in Canada through the 1940s and 1950s, it was sometimes claimed, in liberal terms, that privately funded agencies were valuable as 'a check on the welfare work of government agencies,' because the 'trained people' they employed were 'capable of appraising the work of public bodies.'[110] The Halifax story confirms that having two different kinds of funding base for welfare services did indeed help support necessary change. But in the case of the Halifax CAS, it was a government agency, equipped with new regulatory tools and apparently backed by partisan interests, that corrected, at least temporarily, the conservatism of the 'normal' way of doing welfare business in postwar Halifax. By introducing more effective regulation of the private CASs by a government agency, MacKinnon may have violated some liberal norms of government, but he also helped open channels of democratic political accountability into which more radical energies, such as the welfare rights movement of the 1960s, would ultimately flow. And Gwendolen Lantz lost her job in the process. She retired to Wolfville, Kings County, in 1954 and died there in 1960.[111]

NOTES

1 Shirley Tillotson, 'Class and Community in Canadian Welfare Work, 1933–1960,' *Journal of Canadian Studies* 32, 1 (1997): 63–92.
2 Originally named the Council of Social Agencies when it was founded in 1930, the organization changed its name to the Welfare Council in 1950. For stylistic reasons, I have used the later name throughout.
3 James Struthers, *No Fault of Their Own: Unemployment and the Canadian Welfare State, 1914–1941* (Toronto: University of Toronto Press, 1983), 149–50; Shirley Tillotson, 'Reason, Sentiment, and Citizenship in the Community Chest Movement, 1930–35,' paper presented to the Canadian Historical Association, St John's, 6–8 June 1997; Gale Wills, *A Marriage of Convenience: Business and Social Work in Toronto, 1918–1957* (Toronto: University of Toronto Press, 1995), 73.
4 Public Archives of Nova Scotia (PANS), Welfare Council Papers (hereafter WC Papers), vol. 208, file 10.1, minutes of the Halifax Conference on Child Welfare Standards, 8 Oct. 1948, including reference to a letter from Fred MacKinnon 'last spring' that brought 'forcibly' to the attention of the council the inadequacy of child welfare services in Halifax.
5 Unless otherwise noted, the biographical detail of Lantz's life before 1925 is from Judith Fingard Papers, Dalhousie University Archives, MS-2-713 (hereafter Fingard Papers), Dalhousie Women Graduates card file, Gwendolen Lantz card.
6 PANS, Records of the Halifax Relief Commission, MG 36, series E, file E.1, J.H.T. Falk to officials of Halifax Ladies' College, Acadia University, Truro Normal School, and St Francis Xavier University, 30 Jan. 1918, soliciting women volunteers for rehabilitation work; series E, file E.5, untitled list dated 29 Jan. 1918 [Lantz not on list]; J.H.T. Falk to Miss Lush, 26 Feb. 1918 [lists Lantz among the visitors supervised by Lush]; list entitled 'Personnel of Staff, April 15, 1918' [lists Lantz as a visitor]; and various lists of paid staff, showing non–Nova Scotian origins of most of the paid staff.
7 The McAlpine *Halifax City Directory* lists Lantz with her Halifax Relief Commission job in 1918, but not in 1919, and she is absent from the directory between 1920 and 1924, inclusive; on Falk's position in Montreal, see Marlene Shore, *The Science of Social Redemption: McGill, the Chicago School, and the Origins of Social Research in Canada* (Toronto: University of Toronto Press, 1987), 52.
8 On Falk's style of criticism and his emphasis on 'up-to-date' and 'modern' methods, see City of Vancouver Archives, Records of United Way of the Lower Mainland, Add. MSS 849, box 1, file 2, F. Ivor Jackson, *History of the*

Community Chest and Council of the Greater Vancouver Area, typescript, March 1960, 11, 22, 33–34; Shore, *Science of Social Redemption*, 62–3, and P.T. Rooke and R.L. Schnell, *No Bleeding Heart: Charlotte Whitton, a Feminist on the Right* (Vancouver: UBC Press, 1987), 74. Lantz's style is best appreciated by comparing her annual reports to the provincial director of child welfare to those submitted by other CAS agents around the province. Hers are lectures, offering analysis and prescription rather than data, while most others are plainer description. The reports are sprinkled with forthright assertions such as 'The axiom with which we start, no matter what the individual problem, is that social case work offers the only sound approach.' Nova Scotia, *Journals of the House of Assembly*, 1939, pt. 2, Appendix 23, p. 57; see also 1931, Appendix 23, p. 48; 1932, Appendix 23, p. 40; 1928, Appendix 28, p. 40; and 1928, Appendix 28, p. 30. The most similar ones are those for societies where the agent was a clergyman, although these reports also tended to include analysis. But Lantz's language, while not exclusively secular (for example, she calls for foster homes where there is 'spiritual unity'), includes more terms such as 'modern and efficient' than do these clergyman-agents' reports. More laborious to demonstrate, but an inescapable impression, is that her tone is less emollient than that of her equally educated counterparts. For Lantz's style, see also the discussion, below, of her response to the 1951 Child Welfare survey.

9 A master of this kind of language was the province's first superintendent of child welfare, E.H. Blois, and the phrase quoted here is one he used to mark one of his rare departures into a more critical tone. *Journals*, 1926, pt. 2, Appendix 28, p. 7.

10 WC Papers, vol. 415, file 9, executive committee minutes, 12 Sept. 1952, 2; National Archives of Canada (NAC), Papers of the Canadian Council on Social Development, MG 28, I 10 (hereafter CCSD Papers), vol. 227, file 227-6, K.M. Jackson to Phyllis Burns, 8 April 1948; memo by K.M. Jackson, quoting Miss Torrey, vol. 227, file 227-24, 1 April 1948; an incident of Lantz's publicly contradicting findings of Halifax policewoman May Virtue is described in Renée de Gannes, 'Better Suited to Deal with Women and Children: Pioneer Policewomen in Halifax, Nova Scotia' (MA thesis, Dalhousie University, 1999), 72–4.

11 WC Papers, vol. 415, file 9, executive committee minutes, 9 Oct. 1951, 2.

12 Falk's itinerant social work career is outlined in Shore, *Science of Social Redemption*, 52–3. The contribution of his difficult personality to his frequent moves is clear in the Vancouver case, described in my 'Reason, Sentiment, and Citizenship.' Falk's successor in Vancouver, George Davidson, who went on to head the Canadian Welfare Council, warned Lillian Farqu-

har in 1948 against taking tactical advice from Falk because of Falk's tendency to 'rush headlong into battle ... [while forgetting] about the necessity of having an army to take along into battle with him.' CCSD Papers, vol. 228, file 228-16, Davidson to Farquhar, 28 March 1948.

13 PANS, Papers of the United Way of Halifax-Dartmouth, MG 20 (hereafter UW Papers), vol. 1713, executive committee minutes, 22 Jan. 1926. (The Infants' Home was an institution for unwed mothers and their children.)
14 *Journals*, 1927, pt. 2, Appendix 28, p. 40.
15 UW Papers, minutes of a meeting of representatives of the Halifax Welfare Bureau and Children's Aid Society, 1 Dec. 1927; executive committee minutes, 21 Dec. 1927, report by Alex Craigie.
16 WC Papers, vol. 415, file 9, executive committee minutes, 12 Sept. 1952, 2; 9 Oct. 1951, 1.
17 James Struthers, *The Limits of Affluence: Welfare in Ontario, 1920–1970* (Toronto: University of Toronto Press, 1994), 150–1; Struthers, *No Fault of Their Own*, 49–50.
18 *Journals*, 1930, 1934, and 1939, pt. 2, Appendix 23, statistical reports of the Children's Aid Society of Halifax. I have calculated the number of wards requiring supervision by subtracting from the total number of wards those whose 'condition' was listed as had died or had reached the age of majority, or who were in other categories where they were beyond the need of supervision.
19 CCSD Papers, vol. 227, file 227-26, 'Memo for Halifax [CAS] file' [by Nora Lea], Feb. 1944; WC Papers, vol. 415, file 9, executive committee minutes, 2; vol. 408, file 10, document 10.15, F.R. MacKinnon, 'Report for committee of the Welfare Council of Halifax,' 12 June 1951, 4.
20 Miriam Jacobson, 'A Better Deal for Children: An Historical Study of the Children's Aid Society of Halifax – A Half Century of Service, 1920–1970' (unpublished manuscript, 1971, held in the PANS), 30. Jacobson's study does not include any documentation of its sources. The anecdote about Lantz's protest gesture thus has no provenance; contextual detail suggests it may have taken place in the summer of 1938.
21 *Journals*, 1939, pt. 2, Appendix 23, p. 59.
22 The arguments in favour of this position had been advanced by J.J. Kelso in the 1890s: Andrew Jones and Leonard Rutman, *In the Children's Aid: J.J. Kelso and Child Welfare in Ontario* (Toronto: University of Toronto Press, 1983), 81–3; for Lantz's agreement with these views, see *Journals*, 1931, pt. 2, Appendix 23, p. 50.
23 CCSD Papers, vol. 227, file 227-26, John Pembroke (chairman, Dependents' Board of Trustees) to George Davidson, 19 June 1942; Davidson to Lantz, 2 July 1942; Lantz to Davidson, 10 July 1942.

24 Dalhousie University Archives, Papers of the Maritime School of Social
    Work, MS-1 22, file A 588, 'Opening of School.'
25 CCSD Papers, vol. 227, file 227-26, 'Memo for Halifax [CAS] file' [by Nora
    Lea], Feb. 1944.
26 Ibid., vol. 228, file 228-16, memo 'Re: Halifax Chest,' 8 April 1945; WC
    Papers, vol. 411, files 3 and 4, Speakers' Committee calendars, 1942–1957.
27 CCSD Papers, vol. 228, file 228-16, CWC Cross Reference Sheet, 2 April
    1943, Correspondence from Mrs Charles Monroe, Association of the Junior
    Leagues of America, New York, to Nora Lea, original dated 1 April 1943.
28 Ibid., vol. 227, file 227-6, K.M. Jackson to Phyllis Burns, 8 April 1948.
29 WC Papers, vol. 415, file 1, council minutes, 3 Feb. 1944; on the body of
    social work opinion opposed to family allowances, see Brigitte Kitchen,
    'The Introduction of Family Allowances in Canada,' in A. Moscovitch and
    J. Albert, eds., *The Benevolent State? The Growth of Welfare in Canada* (Tor-
    onto: Garamond, 1987), 229–31.
30 For Lantz's views on the private agency's role in shaping the welfare state,
    see *Journals*, 1950, pt. 2, Appendix 23, p. 54. For the various policy currents
    of the 1940s, see Dennis Guest, *The Emergence of Social Security in Canada*,
    3rd ed. (Vancouver: UBC Press, 1997), 109–17.
31 CCSD Papers, vol. 227, file 227-6, K.M. Jackson to Phyllis Burns, 8 April
    1948; vol. 227, file 227-26, 'Memo for Halifax [CAS] file' [by Nora Lea], Feb.
    1944.
32 WC Papers, vol. 415, file 9, executive committee minutes, 9 Oct. 1951, 1.
33 Ibid., 2; WC Papers, vol. 415, files 2-6, and file 9, executive committee min-
    utes, 12 Sept. 1952, 2; PANS, Papers of the Business and Professional
    Women's Club of Halifax, MG 20, vol. 713, files 43 and 43a, member lists;
    vol. 711, file 3, minutes, comment about charter members with lapsed
    memberships, 2 May 1940.
34 McAlpine's *Halifax City Directory*, entries for Gwendolen Lantz, 1925 to
    1952. Lantz shared an apartment with another woman social worker
    between 1927 and 1929, and stayed on in the same building until 1936,
    when she moved into a house owned by Mary Fegan, a bookkeeper. Fegan
    had lived at that address since 1933, apparently without a lodger or room-
    mate, if the city directory is accurate. When Lantz left Halifax in 1952, so
    did Mary Fegan. The house the two women shared on Victoria Road had
    new owners in 1953.
35 Whitton's contribution to Canadian social work and social policy is
    described in Rooke and Schnell, *No Bleeding Heart*, and James Struthers, 'A
    Profession in Crisis: Charlotte Whitton and Canadian Social Work in the
    1930s,' in Moscovitch and Albert, eds., *The Benevolent State*, 111–25. For
    Falk, see Shore, *Science of Social Redemption*, 52–3. Falk's service as a mentor

to Whitton has not been itself the subject of scholarly study, but is mentioned in Rooke and Schnell, *No Bleeding Heart*, 74. I noted Falk's relationship with Whitton in Whitton's papers, in the files dealing with her role in organizing Ottawa's Council of Social Agencies and Community Chest: CCSD Papers, vol. 43, file 214, Whitton to Falk, 28 March 1932; Falk to Whitton, 16 March 1932; Whitton to Falk, 8 Dec. 1931; Falk to Whitton, 14 Dec. 1931.

36 Peter N. Stearns, 'Men, Boys and Anger in American Society, 1860–1940,' in J.A. Mangan and James Walvin, eds., *Manliness and Morality: Middle Class Masculinity in Britain and America, 1800–1940* (Manchester: Manchester University Press, 1987), 83, 87. On Falk's propensity to righteous anger, see notes 8 and 12, above. On Whitton's 'fiery temper,' see Struthers, 'A Profession in Crisis,' 114.

37 On Falk's successes in the early 1930s, see my 'Reason, Sentiment, and Citizenship,' and for Whitton's 'successes' see Struthers's 'A Profession in Crisis.'

38 UW Papers, executive committee minutes, 16 Dec. 1930, 10 Oct. 1931, and 23 Nov. 1932; minutes of annual meetings, 22 Feb. 1932, 21 Feb. 1934, and 14 Feb. 1935; CCSD Papers, vol. 228, file 228-16, Memorandum to Marjorie Bradford Re Halifax Community Chest, by Charlotte Whitton, 11 Jan. 1939.

39 WC Papers, vol. 416, no. 5, G. Shand to B. Touzel, 19 Nov. 1938.

40 'Veteran Welfare Worker to End 21 Years Service,' *Halifax Mail-Star*, 12 Nov. 1959, 3.

41 Rooke and Schnell, *No Bleeding Heart*, 68, cite Lantz's salary in 1928 (of $1,800 per annum) as an example of the low end of social work and academic salaries in the period. On Lantz's pension, see WC Papers, vol. 415, file 9, executive committee minutes, 19 Nov. 1952. Her pension was to be $50 per month, $10 more than the poverty-level pension paid 65- to 69-year olds under the means-tested federal-provincial old age security program after 1951. On old age pension rates in the period 1951–7, see Donald Creighton, *The Forked Road: Canada, 1939–1957* (Toronto: McClelland and Stewart, 1976), 207, 289. On the problem of providing pensions for older social workers who were being forced into retirement in the early 1950s, see a parallel case in the records of the United Way of Ottawa-Carleton (hereafter OC United Way) held at the United Way office, joint executive committee minutes, 8 Aug. 1951, and special retirement committee, 7 June 1954; for a list of a whole cohort of older social service workers in Ottawa with little or no resources for retirement, see OC United Way, minutes books, 1954 vol., pt. 2, 'Report of the Committee on Special Retirement – Staff Separation Problems.' On the gender composition of the social work

profession in the late 1930s, see 'Report on Questionnaire on the Composition of the Staff of Agencies in Social Work in Canada,' *Social Worker* 8, 4 (1940): 21–5. Schools of social work and the Canadian Association of Social Workers organized this survey, and replies were received from a variety of social service agencies in English Quebec, Saskatchewan, Manitoba, and Ontario. Some public welfare departments were represented, but the majority of responding agencies were private ones such as Montreal's Society for the Protection of Women and Children or Hamilton's Neighbourhood House. On self-sacrifice as part of the occupational ethos of social work during Lantz's years in Halifax, see James Struthers, '"Lord Give Us Men": Women and Social Work in English Canada, 1918–53,' in Moscovitch and Albert, eds., *The Benevolent State*, 133.

42 For an example of the image of social workers as either 'women in flat heels' or clergymen, see City of Vancouver Archives, J.S. Matthews clippings files, Vancouver Welfare Federation fiche, 'Join Them in Welfare Work,' unidentified newspaper, circa 1937. For the perception that social work pay should be minimal, see J.H.T. Falk, 'The Future of Social Work in Canada,' *Dalhousie Review* 1 (July 1921): 185, as quoted in Shore, *Science of Social Redemption*, 56–7.

43 Doug Owram, *The Government Generation: Canadian Intellectuals and the State, 1900–1945* (Toronto: University of Toronto Press, 1986), 124–5, 148; Struthers, '"Lord Give Us Men,"' 136–8.

44 'Community Service Groups Honor Gwendolyn Shand,' *Halifax Mail-Star*, 9 Dec. 1959, 3; 'Veteran Welfare Worker to End 21 Years Service,' *Halifax Mail-Star*, 12 Nov. 1959, 3.

45 Gwendolyn V. Shand, *A Brief History of the Welfare Council of Halifax, Nova Scotia, 1930–1960* (Halifax: Welfare Council, n.d. [1960?]), 8, 15; CCSD Papers, vol. 227, file 227-26, 'Memo for Halifax [CAS] file' [by Nora Lea], Feb. 1944.

46 'Relationship of Employment Offices to Administration of Unemployment Insurance,' *Labour Gazette* 45, 10 (1945): 1550; F.R. MacKinnon, *Biographical Sketches of Ministers of Public Welfare* (Halifax: Ministry of Public Welfare, 1971), 3; Dominique Marshall, *Aux origines sociales de l'état-providence* (Montreal: Les Presses de l'Université de Montréal, 1998), 114–15.

47 'Community Service Groups Honor Gwendolyn Shand,' *Halifax Mail-Star*, 9 Dec. 1959, 3.

48 'Time to Look at 21 Years with the Junior League,' publicity pamphlet for the Halifax Junior League, 1954, PANS, vertical file, vol. 128, no. 27; 'Annual Reports of the President,' a publication of the Halifax Junior League, loaned to the project by the Junior League president; *V Is for Volun-*

teer, a film jointly produced by Canadian Welfare Council and Junior Leagues of America in 1952; Florence Bird, *Anne Francis: An Autobiography* (Toronto: Clarke, Irwin, 1974), 149–50.

49 Wills, *A Marriage of Convenience*, 133; Struthers, '"Lord Give Us Men,"' 133–9; Judith Trolander, *Professionalism and Social Change* (New York: Columbia University Press, 1987), 51; Harold Wilensky, *Industrial Society and Social Welfare* (New York: Free Press, 1958), 323.

50 NAC, National Council of Women Collection, MG 28, I 25, vol. 101, file 7, Gwendolyn Shand and Alice Haverstock, 'Social Status of Women in Nova Scotia,' report presented to the Provincial Council of Women of Nova Scotia, 26 April 1955.

51 OC United Way, minutes, joint executive committee, 25 June 1945; minutes of a special committee to consider the appointment of an executive director for the chests and an executive secretary of the council, 4 Jan. 1946; City of Vancouver Archives, Records of United Way of the Lower Mainland, Add. MSS 849-2 (hereafter UW Vancouver records), box 617-A-5, Board of Directors minutes, 2 Oct. 1945; CCSD papers, vol. 254, file 254-5, C. Romer to G. Davidson, 29 Aug. 1944.

52 Struthers, '"Lord Give Us Men,"' 136–7; Rooke and Schnell, *No Bleeding Heart*, 100–2, 106–8. Whitton's MA was not actually a post-graduate degree but rather the designation given at Queen's in the early twentieth century for undergraduates achieving 'full honours in two subjects and a double first' (Rooke and Schnell, *No Bleeding Heart*, 17).

53 WC Papers, vol. 411, file 6, document 6.52; *Journals*, 1949, Appendix 23, p. 2; MacKinnon, *Biographical Sketches*, 2; *Journals*, 1942, Appendix 23, p. 11 (first mention of an assistant director, presumably MacKinnon, is made in Blois's report for 1941); *Journals*, 1946, Appendix 23 (MacKinnon's first report as director of child welfare).

54 WC Papers, vol. 208, file 10.1, minutes of the Halifax Conference on Child Welfare Standards, 8 Oct. 1948.

55 CCSD Papers, vol. 227, file 227-6, K.M. Jackson to Phyllis Burns, 8 April 1948.

56 Long-time social work volunteer Marjorie Bell affirmed at a key 1951 meeting that not just the Division of Child Welfare but all the children's institutions were 'equally strong in the dissatisfaction with the work of the Children's Aid Society': WC papers, vol. 415, file 9, executive committee minutes, 9 Oct. 1951.

57 *Journals*, 1952, Appendix 23, p. 10; WC Papers, vol. 408, file 10, document 10.15, 'Report for Committee of the Welfare Council of Halifax,' 12 June 1951, 1.

58 WC Papers, vol. 408, file 10, document 10.15, 'Report for Committee of the Welfare Council of Halifax,' 12 June 1951, 2.

59 WC Papers, vol. 408, file 10, minutes of the Halifax Conference on Child Welfare Standards, 8 Oct. 1948.

60 Ibid., minutes of the Round Table conference, 28 March 1951, 1; 18 April 1951, 1.

61 Ibid., minutes of the Round Table Conference, 8 March 1951, 28 March 1951, 18 April 1951, 18 May 1951.

62 Ibid., document 10.15, 'Report for Committee of the Welfare Council of Halifax,' 12 June 1951, 'Exhibit A.'

63 Until 1942 four or five child-caring institutions paid most of Lantz's salary. WC Papers, vol. 408, file 10, minutes of the Round Table Conference, 8 March 1951, 1; 18 April 1951, 3; Report from Children's Aid Society by Miss Gwendolen Lantz, 29 May 1951, 9.

64 WC Papers, vol. 415, file 9, executive committee minutes, 12 Sept. 1952, 2.

65 Ibid., vol. 408, file 10, minutes of the Round Table Conference, 18 April 1951, 2.

66 Ibid., minutes of the Round Table Conference, 8 March 1951, 3; MacKinnon, 'Report,' 12 June 1951.

67 WC Papers, vol. 408, file 10, minutes of the Round Table Conference, 18 April 1951, 3.

68 Ibid., Report from Children's Aid Society by Miss Gwendolen Lantz, 29 May 1951, 7; minutes of Child Welfare Division of Halifax Welfare Council, 29 May 1951, final page of minutes.

69 For Clarke's obituary see *Halifax Chronicle-Herald*, 3 May 1958, 4.

70 WC Papers, vol. 408, file 10, minutes of the Child Welfare Division, 29 May 1951; vol. 415, file 9, executive committee minutes, 22 June 1951, 25 Sept. 1951, 9 Oct. 1951.

71 'Liberal Sweep in Halifax,' *Halifax Chronicle-Herald*, 10 June 1949, 3; Shirley B. Elliott, ed., *The Legislative Assembly of Nova Scotia: A Biographical Directory* (Halifax: Province of Nova Scotia, 1984), 59–60; E.D. Haliburton, *My Years with Stanfield* (Windsor, NS: Lancelot Press, 1972), 9, 24; John Hawkins, *The Life and Times of Angus L.* (Windsor, NS: Lancelot Press, 1969), 240.

72 *Nova Scotia Royal Gazette*, 7 May 1952, 868.

73 WC Papers, vol. 415, file 9, executive committee minutes, 12 May 1952; 12 Sept. 1952 (including transcript of Touzel letter of 8 July 1952 saying 'no survey could be successful while the Executive Secretary at present at the Children's Aid Society, remained in office.')

74 Ibid., executive committee minutes, 29 Feb. 1952, 8 April 1952, 7 May 1952, 12 Sept. 1952.

75 Ibid., executive committee minutes, 12 Sept. 1952, reference to meeting on 8 Sept. 1952.

76 UW Papers, vol. 1713, executive committee minutes, 28 May 1952.

77 CCSD Papers, vol. 228, file 228-17, 'Report of Field Trip to Halifax,' by Henry Stubbins, 6 and 7 Feb. 1952.

78 The departmental and ministerial records at PANS for this period are minimal, so direct evidence of this knowledge may be unobtainable.

79 WC Papers, vol. 415, file 9, report of meeting between Donahoe and representatives from the Community Chest and Welfare Council, 7 May 1952.

80 Wills, *A Marriage of Convenience*, 72.

81 *Journals*, 1946, pt. 2, Appendix 23, p. 9; PANS, Angus L. Macdonald Papers, MG 2, vol. 1087, file '1953 Health,' Hon. Harold Connolly, 'Report on Welfare,' clipping from *Richmond County*, 1 Jan. 1953.

82 *Journals*, 1952, pt. 2, Appendix 23, p. 8; *Statutes of Nova Scotia*, 1950, c. 2, Child Welfare Act.

83 WC Papers, vol. 415, file 9, executive committee minutes, 8 April 1952.

84 City of Vancouver Archives, Add. Mss. 300, Board of Trade Papers, vol. 146, report of Special Committee to study the Community Chest system (J. Pitcairn Hogg, chairman), 26 June 1923, at 43–4; vol. 48, minutes of a special meeting of the council of the Vancouver Board of Trade, 'Report of the executive re Community Chest,' 8 Nov. 1928, 487; OC United Way Records, minutes of executive committee meeting with the Board of Directors of the Ottawa Branch of the Canadian Cancer Society, 11 Feb. 1954; 'Confidential minutes of meeting with Welfare Council directors on agencies not already invited to join the Chests,' 23 March 1953; Wills, *A Marriage of Convenience*, 44, 64, 126.

85 UW Vancouver records, box 617-A-3, file 8, minutes of Board of Directors, 10 April 1952, 137; box 617-A-4, minutes of Board of Directors, 11 March 1943, 119, and 4 Jan. 1944, 124; 'Disabled Veterans Protest Welfare Federation Ouster,' *Vancouver Province*, 4 March 1943, 7.

86 UW Vancouver records, box 617-B-1, minutes of Board of Directors, 61.

87 H.R.W. Allan, 'Public Reaction to More Campaigns?' *Canadian Welfare* (Sept. 1950): 16–17; 'Too Costly – and Too Many?' *Financial Post*, 5 May 1951, 11; C. Reinke, 'The Unholy Mess of the Good Works: How Charity Suffers from Too Many Campaigns,' *Financial Post*, 26 April 1952, 9; UW Papers, vol. 1713, executive committee minutes, 26 March 1952.

88 UW Papers, vol. 1713, annual meeting minutes, 27 Feb. 1936; Dalhousie University Archives, S.R. Balcom Papers, MSS-2-128, Halifax Community Chest file, various circular letters from chest to member agencies, soliciting publicity material, e.g., Gwladys Kennedy to President of Halifax Visiting Dispensary, 15 May 1948; CCSD Papers, vol. 228, file 228-16, memo 'Re:

Halifax Chest,' 8 April 1945, expressing Kennedy's unhappiness at the CAS's refusal to participate in publicity work; 'Visits Reveal Work of Social Agencies,' *Vancouver Sun*, 31 Oct. 1934, 5; UW Vancouver records, vol. 617-A-3, file 1, Memo on Vancouver Welfare Federation and Council, by J.H.T. Falk, July 1935; description of agencies' role in public relations in the 1940s provided by Mrs Walter (Alma Gale) Mowatt, 'History of the Community Chest and Councils of the Greater Vancouver Area,' typescript, 1951 (original held in the office of the United Way of the Lower Mainland), 48.

89   On the effect of the Halifax Children's Hospital's attempts to manipulate the chest or to raise more money on their own by dropping out, see UW Papers, vol. 1713, executive committee minutes, 13 Sept. 1937, 13 Dec. 1937, 23 June 1938, 8 March 1949. For similar developments in relation to the Vancouver Children's Hospital, see UW Vancouver Records, box 617-A-5, Report of the Executive Director, 30 April 1946, 75. The threat of withdrawal became a bargaining chip for large 'illness' charities when they became chest members in the 1950s. See, for example, the withdrawal of the Heart Fund from the Vancouver Welfare Federation in 1960, and the issues around it, described in CCSD Papers, vol. 254, file 254-9, 'Dear Subscriber' letter by Ross Wilson, president of the Community Chests and Councils of Greater Vancouver.

90   Wills, *A Marriage of Convenience*, 102–3, 108–9, 114, 119; UW Vancouver records, Board minutes, vol. 617-A-5, 1 May 1945, 43, and 23 May 1946, 79; 617-B-1, 6 Aug. 1951, 98; 617-B-2, 31 March 1953, 51; OC United Way, minutes binder, 'Interim Report on Personnel Practices at the Ottawa Welfare Bureau,' 15 Feb. 1954, and D. Longmire (Ottawa Welfare Bureau) to the Board of Directors, 19 Feb. 1954.

91   Wills, *A Marriage of Convenience*, 103, 124, 130; WC Papers, vol. 416a, file 3, Gwendolyn Shand, 'More or Less Confidential Material, 1948'; UW Vancouver records, minutes of annual general meeting, motion from agency representative for more equitable distribution of funds, 27 Feb. 1950.

92   Wills, *A Marriage of Convenience*, 124; WC Papers, vol. 416a, file 3, document 3.5, 'Information from Community Chests and Councils N.Y. January 1948'; CCSD papers, vol. 254, file 254-6, Nora Lea to Hazeldine Bishop, 21 Aug. 1946, describing tensions between council/agency social workers and chest fundraisers, referring to 'dirty work at the crossroads' and the 'unsocial process' by which chest and council relations had fallen into a bad state; CCSD Papers, vol. 254, file 254-4, Hugh Allan (executive director of Vancouver Chest and Council) to Eurith Goold (CWC staff member), commenting acerbically on the 'theory' that needs should not be subordinated to budgetary constraints, 27 Dec. 1945.

93 CCSD Papers, vol. 228, file 228-16, 11 Jan. 1939, Memorandum to Miss
    Bradford Re Halifax Community Chest by Charlotte Whitton; Personal,
    Lillian M. Farquhar to George Davidson, 20 March 1944.
94 Ibid., CWC Cross Reference Sheet, 2 April 1943, Correspondence from
    Mrs Charles Monroe, Association of the Junior Leagues of America, New
    York, to Nora Lea, original dated 1 April 1943.
95 'Annual Reports from the President,' a publication of the Halifax Junior
    League, 1949–50 report; CCSD Papers, vol. 228, file 228-16; undated [circa
    1942] Confidential Memo to Dr Davidson, Re: Halifax, by EG (Eurith
    Goold); Nan T. Pierpont (Mrs Donald W.), Consultant, Community Ser-
    vice Staff, Association of Junior Leagues of America, to Miss Nora Lea,
    Canadian Welfare Council, 16 Feb. 1943; Eurith Goold to Mrs James G.
    Farquhar, 10 Feb. 1945; memo 'Re: Halifax Chest,' 8 April 1945; Farquhar
    to R.E.G. Davis, 6 June 1945; vol. 228, file 228-17, Report of field visit by
    Henry Stubbins, 31 May 1950; vol. 228, file 228-14, G. Shand to H. Stub-
    bins, 16 Oct. 1950.
96 WC Papers, vol. 415, file 9, report of meeting between Donahoe and repre-
    sentatives from the chest and council, 7 May 1952.
97 UW Papers, vol. 1713, executive committee minutes, 28 May 1952.
98 WC Papers, vol. 415, file 9, executive committee minutes, 8 April 1952.
99 Ibid., executive committee minutes, 8 April 1952; file 9, 9 Oct. 1951.
100 Ibid., vol. 416A, file 3.5, G. Shand to B. Touzel, 23 Sept. 1948.
101 CCSD Papers, vol. 228, file 228-16, memo 'Re: Halifax Chest,' 8 April 1945;
    CWC Cross Reference Sheet, 2 April 1943, Correspondence from Mrs
    Charles Monroe, Association of the Junior Leagues of America, to Nora
    Lea, Canadian Welfare Council, original dated 1 April 1943.
102 An unusually complete text of one her annual meeting speeches may be
    found in the CCSD Papers, vol. 228, file 228-16, report of Gwladys
    Kennedy, 28 Feb. 1938. References to the themes of her speeches are
    reported in the minutes of the annual general meetings: e.g., UW papers,
    vol. 1713, 27 Jan. 1930, 20 Feb. 1931, 22 Feb. 1932, 23 Feb. 1933, 21 Feb.
    1934, 14 Feb. 1935, 27 Feb. 1936, 14 Feb. 1940, 21 Feb. 1941, 17 Feb. 1942.
103 Two campaigns that I chose for close examination because they took place
    during especially challenging years for charitable fundraising were the
    campaigns of 1933 and 1941. The agency stories for those years may be
    found in the Halifax Mail at the following dates and page numbers: for 1933
    – 19 Oct., 17; 21 Oct., 2; 1 Nov., 8; for 1941 – 16 Sept., 3; 17 Sept., 3; 18 Sept.,
    3; 19 Sept., 3; 20 Sept., 3; 23 Sept., 3; 24 Sept., 3; 25 Sept., 3; 26 Sept., 3.
104 CCSD Papers, vol. 228, file 228-16, Nan T. Pierpont (Mrs Donald W.), Con-
    sultant, Community Service Staff, Association of Junior Leagues of Amer-

ica, to Miss Nora Lea, Canadian Welfare Council, 16 Feb. 1943; Eurith Goold to Mrs J.G. Farquhar, 13 June 1946.

105 Some examples from Vancouver, Ottawa, and Halifax of chest attempts in the interwar years and 1940s to deal with threats to fundraising posed by critics may be found in UW Papers, vol. 1713, executive meeting, 7 Oct. 1929; OC United Way, minutes binder, meeting of Board of Directors (Protestant) with YMCA representatives, 10 May 1935; UW Vancouver Papers, vol. 617-A-2, executive committee minutes, 22 and 26 June 1934 and 10 July 1934; CVA, Mayors' Papers, series 483, file 33-D-6-1, 1937 Welfare Federation canvasser's pamphlet; UW Vancouver Papers, vol. 617-A-4, Directors' minutes, 27 Oct. 1942. A Toronto chest director's repressive reaction to criticism by social workers of the business practices of potential donors is described in Struthers, *Limits of Affluence*, 139–40.

106 Tillotson, 'Class and Community,' 80.

107 CCSD Papers, vol. 228, file 228-17, 'Report of Field Trip to Halifax,' by Henry Stubbins, February 1952; file 228-16, 'Confidential. Memo to Dr. Davidson. Re: Halifax. By EG [Eurith Goold],' undated [circa 1942]; file 228-16, CWC Cross Reference Sheet, Correspondence from Mrs Charles Monroe, Association of the Junior Leagues of America, New York, to Nora Lea, CWC, original dated 1 April 1943; WC Papers, vol. 408, document 10.7, minutes of Round Table Conference on Child Welfare, 9 May 1951. In this meeting of the round table, MacKinnon called on social agencies to pressure the chest to increase the CAS grant. While not a direct criticism of Gwladys Kennedy, his remarks imply at least some dissatisfaction with her, given the important role she was acknowledged to have in determining chest priorities.

108 UW papers, vol. 1713, executive committee minutes, 26 May 1953.

109 WC Papers, vol. 411, file 6, document 6.1; *Journals*, 1954, pt. 2, Appendix 23, CAS Halifax financial report.

110 CCSD Papers, vol. 77, file 564 'Labour and Welfare Services, 1946–57,' Toronto and Lakeshore Labour Council, 'Report of the Special Committee on Welfare.' More gently expressed, 'The private agency may draw public attention to unmet needs and to shortcomings in both public and private services': vol. 79, file 591, Bessie Touzel, 'Some Factors Affecting Public-Private Relationships in Social Work,' 4. The role of private agencies as sources of pressure on government was urged by Harry Cassidy in 'The Dilemma of the Chests,' *Canadian Welfare* 24, 4 (1948): 6.

111 Fingard Papers, Dalhousie women graduates card file, Gwendolen Lantz card.

Managing the Unmarried Mother 'Problem': Halifax Maternity Homes

SUZANNE MORTON

Although Nova Scotia had the dubious distinction of being the province with the highest illegitimacy rate in Canada, local social service agencies were slow to respond to this remarkable and as yet unexplained demographic phenomenon. Before 1950 Nova Scotians did not amend the punitive contents of the bastardy law (only its name was changed to the more modern Illegitimate Children's Act in 1905), reform the inadequate paternal support provisions of the Poor Law, or extend state support to single mothers. As a result, outsiders were openly critical. In 1933, Charlotte Whitton, executive secretary of the Canadian Welfare Council, drew national attention to the paradox that the province with the highest illegitimacy rate was the only province that had not amended or improved its bastardy legislation.[1] Her successor, George Davidson, in his 1944 *Report on Public Welfare Services*, claimed that the provision for illegitimate children was 'the greatest weakness in the entire chain of protective services for children in the Province.'[2]

While contemporary social reformers focused on the children, particularly getting them out of institutions, the unmarried mothers were also a cause for concern. This paper examines the residential facilities available for unmarried, pregnant women in Halifax in the first thirty years following the Second World War. These facilities were an important example of private and public cooperation, both philanthropic and governmental. Moreover, they represented a largely female world. With the exception of high-level provincial bureaucrats such as the deputy minister of welfare, and some financial advisers within the Salvation Army, the volunteer board members, the managers, and the employees (both professionals and support staff) were all women.

Although a handful of very small private maternity homes existed in the province after 1947, larger philanthropic homes for unmarried mothers operated only in Halifax and industrial Cape Breton. The largest of these homes were in Halifax, where local unmarried pregnant women joined others drawn from rural areas and small towns throughout the Atlantic region in using these specialized facilities before and after their confinement. Between 1945 and 1960 three institutions, the Halifax Infants' Home, the Home of the Guardian Angel, and – after 1955 – the Salvation Army Home for Girls (later the Bethany Home) served this group of women. After the Halifax Infants' Home closed in 1960, Bethany Home continued to cater to Protestant women until 1996, and the Catholic Home of the Guardian Angel still continues to help mothers in need of support. Although the original three institutions were ostensibly 'private' – operated by specific religious denominations or, in the case of the Halifax Infants' Home, a coalition within the Halifax Protestant community – the homes were also at least partially supported by municipal and provincial grants and annual public solicitations. Increasingly they were integrated into and regulated by an emerging welfare state bureaucracy.

The Halifax institutions challenge any assumptions that make a clear distinction between private and public facilities, and between religious and 'professional,' or secular, social work. If there ever was a dichotomy between religious and professional social work, it did not exist in Halifax after the war.[3] Even then, the provision of welfare services to unmarried mothers in the city was not entirely secular, and important denominational differences existed between 'Protestant,' Salvation Army, and Roman Catholic facilities.

Maternity homes served women and infants who were among the most vulnerable in a society that harshly judged women who contravened sexual respectability, provided women with few opportunities for adequate self-support, and allocated to them full responsibility for child rearing. Yet women who ended up in these houses represented a small minority of those who gave birth outside of marriage. We need to remain aware that most unmarried mothers depended on private networks, especially their own families.[4] While this paper offers a view of the small number of women who were literally hidden from society in maternity homes, it tells us nothing about the majority of unmarried mothers who gave birth unaided by, and often unknown to, public and private agencies.[5]

Our knowledge of the women who turned to maternity homes for help is incomplete. In part, this is the result of the women's own efforts to keep their pregnancies secret. As a result, these women are largely invisible, but glimpses of their experience can be seen through government statistics and the para-private institutions that sought to assist them. The rates of birth to non-married mothers in Nova Scotia ranged from 8 per cent in the mid-1940s to 10 per cent in the late 1960s and then continued to climb sharply throughout the seventies, eighties, and nineties to the present level of more than 30 per cent of all births.[6] Until the late 1940s and 1950s, most single women giving birth in Nova Scotia were in their late teens and early twenties, often having left home for waged employment before they became pregnant.[7] During the period from the 1950s to the early 1980s, teenagers were the largest cohort of new single mothers. The absolute number of births to teenage unmarried mothers declined after the late 1980s, presumably the result of accessible birth control and legal abortions, while the number of births to unmarried women over nineteen increased.[8] Unmarried mothers came from all backgrounds. The diverse social backgrounds of the women served by the Home of the Guardian Angel immediately after the war were apparent in one report that described the home's residents as 'nurses, teachers, stenographers, domestics, waitresses, school children, college graduates and illiterates.'[9]

At the end of the war, both the Protestant Halifax Infants' Home and the Catholic Home of the Guardian Angel insisted on six months' compulsory residence after confinement, which was thought to have the dual benefit of promoting infant health through breastfeeding and cementing a strong emotional bond between mother and child. The goal was to create (or reinforce) in the new mother a sense of responsibility for the infant and to redeem the wayward woman through the power of mother-love. Compulsory residence also provided a permanent, if ever changing, roster of workers to care for the large number of demanding infants.[10] The attitude in both homes was that the mother should take responsibility for the care of the child, even if it meant boarding him or her while she returned to work. Within a short period following the war, the residency structure at both institutions was inverted: the emphasis was placed on expectant mothers entering the facility before delivery, and leaving within two weeks of birth. The change in practice stemmed from a change in attitude: the best interest of the child was now believed to be served by severing the bonds between mother and child through infant adoption. Redemption for past transgressions might best be achieved through a mother's unselfish act of handing over her child to a deserving, 'normal' family.

Although both institutions changed their practices to emphasize adoption, which was becoming the prescribed social practice across North America, their approaches to care began to diverge. The Home of the Guardian Angel, operated by the Sisters of Charity, was in the vanguard of international secular standards and practices, while the Protestant Infants' Home remained the preserve of the conservative 'amateur.'[11] After 1960 a third model of care for unmarried mothers, represented by the Salvation Army's Bethany Home for Girls, combined professional expertise with a religious conservative ethos. Collectively these homes remind us of the complexity of public/private/professional/religious distinctions, and all provide compelling examples of the social construction of the problem of unmarried mothers.[12]

Unmarried mothers in Nova Scotia had few legal options for gaining financial support for themselves and their children. Before 1951 the Illegitimate Children's Act was designed to protect local communities from the expense of maintaining the mother and child. As Janet Guildford discusses in her chapter on welfare reform in this volume, until 1958 Nova Scotia retained a form of the Poor Law, which held poor districts – small local communities – responsible for the support of individuals who had acquired settlement rights. These districts had the potentially conflicting responsibility of providing for those in need and keeping expenses as low as possible. One way of reducing expenses was for the Poor Law district to initiate action against the putative father, a right ensured under the Illegitimate Children's Act. However, if the district initiated such an action to cover its expenses, the mother's right to do so herself was permanently forfeited. In any case, the publicity involved in making a claim before a magistrate led to very few mothers taking such action. It also became less common for most poor districts themselves to proceed after the First World War.

Under the Poor Law, a woman had the settlement of her father until she married, and any child born out of wedlock had the settlement of his or her mother. Thus, it was clearly in the economic interest of local districts to send pregnant women back to their home communities, a strategy frequently attempted in Halifax through the auspices of the Children's Aid Society.[13] Gwendolen Lantz, the secretary of the Halifax Children's Aid Society (who is discussed more fully in Shirley Tillotson's essay in this volume), explained the influx of pregnant 'girls' to her city as stemming from the woman's need to escape her family's and community's censure, her attempt to follow the alleged father in the hope of marrying, the lack of facilities for care in her home district, and the concentration of services in Halifax. Although it was her responsibility to send the women home before birth, Lantz noted in 1945 that pregnant women made their own plans and 'several girls have refused to leave Halifax at this time.'[14] In such cases, Halifax, the poor district burdened with the expense of the mother and child, could sue for costs the district where the woman had settlement. These refunds may have assisted the public purse, but they did nothing for the mother and child. Even if the mother received support from the putative father, authorities working in the field recognized that unless the woman had relatives or friends to give her a home, the amount collected was insufficient for the maintenance of mother and child.[15]

The 1950s brought changes in the legal position of unmarried women and their children. The most important was amendment of the Illegitimate Children's Act, which became the Children of Unmarried Parents Act in 1951. This revised act placed the mother's interest first in the collection of payments from the putative father, increased the sum that could be collected, and closed court proceedings to the public. The legislation gave the provincial director of child welfare the authority, if he believed it was in the best interest of the mother and child, to lay information against the putative father and follow with a court order that would demand payment. In cases where an admission of paternity existed, the director of child welfare could make an agreement with the father about maintenance. The 1951 act transferred responsibility from the local overseers of the poor to the provincial Division of Child Welfare, and converted the law from a 'quasi criminal' to a civil process.[16]

Another postwar legal change was the extension of income support from the provincial government to all unmarried mothers. When the Nova Scotia Mothers' Allowance Act was introduced in 1930, all illegitimate children were specifically excluded from its provisions. The 1956 Social Assistance Act extended the first provincial payments to certain unmarried women and their children. This act recognized common-law relationships of over five years and provided payments to common-law widows when one or more children was registered in the deceased 'husband's' name. Other unmarried mothers accessed provincial funds through foster support programs, leaving their children with their grandparents, who were entitled to payment. Although, by 1961, provincial bureaucrats in the Department of Public Welfare expressed approval for extending payments to all unmarried mothers over eighteen who maintained their own home as long as the home was 'suitable' and they had made efforts to collect from the father, no such reform occurred until Ottawa intervened.[17] In 1966, when federal matching funds became available to the province through the Canada Assistance Plan, social assistance was extended to these mothers. Beginning in 1975, women no longer had to maintain their own homes in order to receive benefits.

The provincial government's tardiness in extending such benefits contrasts sharply with the self-depicted modernity of the Halifax residential maternity homes. Halifax institutions in the 1920s saw themselves at the forefront of modern North American institutional care for unmarried mothers, particularly because the child-care institutions were able to overcome important confessional divisions and work through the secular Children's Aid Society (CAS) to coordinate all applications for admission and discharge.[18] Generally, assistance to unmarried mothers was constructed as relief for their children, who bore no responsibility for their origins. The vulnerability of these children was seen in the high rates of institutionalization they faced. The 1941 census records that 511 of the 2,329 children living in Nova Scotian institutions were illegitimate, a higher proportion than in the general population.[19] Yet, there was often little indication in the policies of the provincial government, quasi-government agencies such as the CAS, and philanthropic organizations that the mothers were entitled to assistance. Many of the mothers themselves clearly expressed a sense of entitlement to respectful assistance. Significantly, it was a member of the older cohort of professional social workers, Gwendolen Lantz, the much criticized director of the Halifax CAS, who most clearly acknowledged that non-married mothers had rights. Lantz believed that the mother was personally accountable for her actions and therefore she had the 'right to make her own decision.' In her address to the annual meeting of the Halifax Infants' Home in 1946, Lantz expressed concern about the trend to regard adoption as 'the only solution' and urged that 'the mother be given time to make her decision and without pressure.'[20]

There is a great deal of evidence of mothers making decisions about their own lives even when their options were obviously limited. Pregnant women from Newfoundland who came to Halifax simply refused to return home, although their own welfare department was willing to care for them.[21] Women also complained about the level of services they received. During a survey of child welfare facilities conducted in 1958, clients were vocal in their complaints against the CAS, which they claimed offered no assistance, not even a recommendation to the religious refuges.[22] Finally, for the nineteen years of its operation, between 1928 and 1947, the private Ideal Maternity Home in Chester, fifty kilometres southwest of Halifax, was the facility pregnant women themselves chose, even if it meant bearing the cost of high fees. Despite its infamy, many unmarried pregnant women who had or could borrow the money took advantage of its services. In his wartime report on welfare services in Nova Scotia, George Davidson described the Ideal Maternity Home as 'the main resource in the Province for the care of the unmarried mother.'[23] That home was not only the preferred choice for pregnant unmarried women but, according to the Halifax Infants' Home in 1945, it secured 'most of the available homes' for local adoption, causing the Halifax home to have difficulties in placing its infants.[24] A campaign mounted by the provincial welfare bureaucrats against the Ideal Maternity Home reduced the choices for women and eliminated a problematic institution that women themselves had seen as the best option.

Other than the religious refuges and other small private maternity homes, unmarried pregnant women who, for whatever reason, could not return to their family had few choices. The Halifax City Home – a poorhouse – was one; the Halifax County Home and Mental Hospital was another. In the only extant register of the Halifax City Home inmates dating between 1929 and 1938, at least twenty-three women spent the last months, weeks, or days of their pregnancy as inmates and, after birth in the city's maternity hospital, often returned with their infants.[25] In 1942 the Halifax County clerk acknowledged the problem of an expectant mother who was sent to the County Home by her local overseer of the poor, and noted that presumably after the birth 'both she and the child will be removed from the institution as soon as she is able to go.'[26] In her chapter in this volume on the end of the Poor Law, Janet Guildford describes conditions in such institutions. That women who had no other means of support were forced to depend on these poorhouses is the real scandal of Nova Scotian maternity care.

The Halifax Infants' Home

The Halifax Infants' Home was founded in 1875 as a Protestant reform response to the problem of 'baby farms' and their high rates of infant mortality. The creation of the home met with opposition from those who believed its facilities 'would encourage vice.'[27] With the opening of the Grace Maternity Hospital in 1922, all deliveries were transferred to that facility, and, until 1947, women returned to the home for a required stay of six months after the birth.[28] After the Second World War, the Halifax Infants' Home and the Salvation Army Girls' Home in Sydney were the only Protestant institutions for the care of unmarried mothers and their children in the Maritimes.[29] Although the home adopted a policy of racial integration in 1945, the women it assisted were almost exclusively white. Few women of colour used its services, and when they did their race was specifically noted.[30]

As the name would suggest, the Halifax Infants' Home placed the interests of the children first and the mothers second.[31] The lengthy compulsory residence reduced the number of places available for new cases. Indeed, given this policy, the home was able to assist only twenty-two unmarried mothers in 1946 and sixteen in 1947. The liberalization of the compulsory residency requirement, just after the closure of the Ideal Maternity Home in 1947, made more beds available and may have made the institution more appealing to potential clients. As the post-delivery stay was reduced to six and, eventually, two weeks, the number of women the home assisted rose to forty-eight in 1948 and peaked at sixty-one in 1956. The shortened stay was somewhat counter-balanced by encouraging women to enter the home in their sixth or seventh month of pregnancy. In 1954 the superintendent noted that the future mothers should arrive at the beginning of their seventh month, since few had had prenatal or dental care at this point. Stress was placed on a nourishing diet and contact with CAS social workers.[32]

The Halifax Infants' Home had very limited programming and, although it appears to have hired its own social worker in the 1920s, it provided virtually no casework after the Second World War. Periodically various matrons organized sewing, cooking, or home-nursing courses to promote appropriate and practical feminine skills.[33] Organized recreation was also haphazard, with seasonal parties (Valentine's Day may have been the most delicate for young women who had been abandoned by their lovers; Christmas was the greatest celebration), occasional films and travelogues from the provincial film library, singsongs, and bingo.[34] Women in local Protestant congregations donated subscriptions to respectable women's magazines such as *Ladies' Home Journal* and *McCall's*.[35] The acquisition of a television in 1956 must have been a great relief for the young women.[36] Smoking was another key pastime of the pregnant women and one for which the home maintained a special room. The general importance of smoking in maternity home culture was supported by the evidence of the sister superior of the Home of the Guardian Angel, who included a cigarette allowance in the list of expenses a resident might anticipate.[37]

The residents of the Halifax Infants' Home remain largely invisible to the historian, especially as this institution adopted professional notions of confidentiality. An even earlier inclination towards secrecy meant that provincial bureaucrats were concerned about such basic issues as poor record-keeping.[38] But glimpses of the women do exist. A 1947 provincial inspection report at first appears almost superficial, as the investigator focused on the cheerless nature of the home and the lack of an evening lunch.[39] But the Department of Public Welfare social worker also included specific complaints expressed by some mothers during an interview. They reported their intense frustration with the long delays in adopting out their infants. In the words of one mother, she had 'served her time' – an allusion that linked compulsory residency with imprisonment. The seriousness of the delay in arranging timely adoptions was compounded, in the opinion of the social worker, by the inferior care infants and young children received while in residence. The inspector concluded that children living in the Halifax Infants' Home had none of the 'meticulous care' and 'nursery school enrichment' given to those who were wards at the Home of the Guardian Angel.

The unusually critical tone of this report followed an initiative taken by the mothers themselves. They had written a letter directly to the minister of public welfare under the name of 'Home Girls,' outlining a litany of complaints such as overwork, isolation, lack of leisure time and evening food and drink, and an inadequate adoption procedure. These women leap out of obscurity by demanding 'a little more freedom and better treatment.'[40] Their efforts also seemed to produce at least some symbolic results. Shortly thereafter, for example, the residents started receiving an evening snack.[41] By 1954 the women had a 10:00 p.m. curfew and were permitted to have unlimited visits from local relatives. However, pregnant women were still not permitted to leave the premises after their eighth month.[42]

The clearest indication of management problems at the Halifax Infants' Home was the decision of its volunteer executive to fire its superintendent in 1950. At the time of this action, the board expressed its hope that the next director would be a 'trained social worker.'[43] Concerns about professional standards were evident earlier, in the unanimous 1948 decision that no detail of cases or individuals should be given to the board by the case committee.[44] Despite the direction indicated by the board, it appears that the home was unable to move in the direction of professionalization. The delayed arrival of the new superintendent, Minnie L. Peers, almost a full year following the decision to remove the former matron, suggests there was difficulty in finding qualified help, a reflection perhaps of poor wages. Minnie Peers was not a social worker but had the credential of being a former director of the Nova Scotia Training School, the provincial residential facility for mentally challenged children.[47] That this institutional experience was presumed to be relevant speaks to the vision of the home as a refuge for young women who could not manage their own lives. While previous superintendents had boasted nursing qualifications, reflecting concerns about children's health, Peers brought new approaches, if not professional social work skills. Peers, in fact, clearly rejected the social work model when she explained in a conflict with the Children's Aid Society in 1951 that the home was not a social agency but a refuge offering shelter, care, and privacy.[46]

The difficulty of sustaining a focused policy direction was connected in part to the power of a generally conservative all-female volunteer board of managers. In 1941 a matron complained vehemently to provincial government bureaucrats about the composition of the board and the ability of a few members to dominate policy. This superintendent described the president of the board as a 'reactionary' who directly interfered with the home's operation. The extent of the difference between this matron and her board was evident in her decision to smuggle psychological tests into the home against the direct wishes of the board's president.[47] When, in 1948, the board of managers attempted to ban admission to the home by recidivists, the provincial deputy minister responsible for child welfare intervened and argued that the Halifax Infants' Home should be open to 'second and even third offenders.'[48] The board was responsible for the religious orientation of the home, and began its meetings with prayers, but it lacked the power to do much more than offer occasional optional Sunday services for residents. Such services were not well attended. The special nature of Sunday was marked instead by the decision in 1941 to continue the ice cream treat on that day, despite financial difficulties.[49]

The early 1950s were difficult times at the Halifax Infants' Home. A chronic staff shortage meant that, occasionally, unmarried mothers who were residents had to be hired as domestics and nursery helpers.[50] As women's stays in the home grew shorter, more infants were left in its care. In March 1952, the superintendent's report drew attention to the shortage of space, noting the need for boarding facilities for babies who were ill, deserted, or awaiting suitable foster homes. The problem of unpaid fees for women who left the home and continued boarding their infants was ongoing, and the superintendent admitted that few unmarried mothers could really 'afford to pay the board required as their wages are small.'[51] The result was that a large number of babies, who arrived from the maternity hospital when they were eight days old, remained until arrangements were made for adoption, legal guardianship was determined, foster homes were found, or non-institutional boarding was arranged by their mothers, or until they reached the age of four years and were moved to another facility.

In 1953 the home boasted that while it could not accept any further infants at that time, no pregnant woman had been refused admission, even if she turned up without notice.[52] Superintendent Peers touted the personal flexibility of the Halifax Infants' Home and contrasted it to the rigidity of the Home of the Guardian Angel, which admitted only those women who had made previous arrangements. The superintendent stated that 'quite frequently' women unexpectedly appeared at the Halifax Infants' Home in 'an upset, hysterical state' and required immediate attention.[53]

Despite the flexible admission policy, it is clear that even the managers of the Halifax Infants' Home understood that it was not a popular choice. Peers explained that she had many calls from young women who were looking for help but who looked elsewhere when they discovered that they must remain in the home until plans were made for their babies.[54] The contentious issues continued to be compulsory residency and mandatory labour. The presence of a large number of infants and young children who stayed long after their mothers had left meant that the home was dependent on the unpaid labour of the ever changing workforce of mothers. The tension between the mothers as both clients and a necessary source of labour led the superintendent to condemn women anxious to leave the home as 'transients' with little interest in the children. On the other hand, in February 1950, a field worker for the Canadian Welfare Council drew attention to another perspective on the complications related to hiring clients as labour in the nursery after a board member complained about the use of unmarried mothers as hired help. Although 'the institution paid them wages ... they were being kept as cheap labour, when they should be encouraged to return to the community.' However, the Ottawa social worker concluded that it was the 'girls' who 'asked to stay and did not seem to want to leave the institution.' Rather than casting them as transients, this perspective suggests women stayed in the home as a strategy for remaining with their children.[55]

But the home could not always depend on the free labour of the unmarried mothers; expenses increased as more paid labour was engaged. The Halifax Infants' Home, perhaps incorrectly, believed that the Home of the Guardian Angel refused to admit any infants without their mothers and was therefore free from the 'help' problem.[56] Budget problems at the Infants' Home were alleviated somewhat in 1950, when it began receiving a grant from the provincial government of $5 a week for each unmarried mother.[57] This grant provided a more stable stream of revenue than the income from the few women who were able to pay their board.[58]

But income was always insufficient to cover the labour-intensive work of caring for infants, and it is not surprising that work remained a matter of contention between the home and its residents. Clients of the home complained to external social workers about the amount of work expected of them. Although these complaints were passed along to provincial bureaucrats, who were generally unsympathetic to the home's practices, the same bureaucrats dismissed the women's concerns, claiming it was 'better for these girls to be occupied than to be idle and have their minds constantly on their troubles.'[59] The home again changed its residency policy in November 1953, when it was decided that if mothers stayed for six weeks after birth, they should be paid $5 a week for five of the six weeks, as long as they worked. An earlier decision not to employ on a permanent basis as nurse maids women who had been in the care of the home was amended; the board decided that such decisions would be made on an individual basis.[60]

By 1956 the board's greatest challenge no longer came from rebellious residents or tense relations with the Children's Aid Society. Rather, the opening of a Salvation Army Home for Girls drew clients away from the Halifax Infants' Home, thereby depriving the home of unpaid labour for its nursery.[61] Mounting costs and the loss of a significant number of its Protestant clientele led the management board of the Halifax Infants' Home to begin to assess its future. It looked at moving out of the care of unmarried mothers and their children and explored the possibility of becoming a boarding home for children of unmarried or working mothers or providing temporary care for children whose mothers needed hospitalization as a result of serious diseases such as polio or tuberculosis. Others envisaged the home as an institution for physically or mentally challenged children.[62] The self-examination and the awareness of the home's vulnerable future became even more acute when the United Appeal intimated that its $16,000 grant might not be continued indefinitely.[63] A report on child welfare institutions in the City of Halifax conducted by the Canadian Welfare Council in 1958 concluded that the superintendent of the home was 'unsatisfactory,' that the 'unmarried [mothers] are most unhappy,' and that although numbers were up slightly this was the result of a publicity campaign aimed at young women from outside of the city.[64] In fact, the Halifax Infants' Home was described by the child welfare survey as the last 'Infants Home' in Canada at a time when all child welfare authorities agreed that children under three years old should not be in an institution.[65]

The home closed on 31 March 1960, the loss of clientele linked specifically to competition from by the Salvation Army. Two months later it was announced that the Salvation Army itself would buy the facilities at a low price on the understanding that the institution would be used for unmarried mothers.[66]

The Salvation Army's Bethany Home

If the Halifax Infants' Home was run by a group of conservative but well-meaning 'amateurs,' the Salvation Army provided religious professionals for unwed mother care in Canada. The Salvation Army specialized in care for unmarried mothers and had established thirteen residential facilities across Canada with the policy of admitting clients 'regardless of religion, race or other considerations.' In Halifax, the Salvation Army originally established a maternity home and children's refuge in the early 1890s, but after the opening of the Grace Maternity Hospital in 1922, its work among unmarried mothers continued only in Sydney.[67] Halifax operations resumed in 1955, when the Salvation Army rented a boarding house on Seymour Street near the Grace Hospital. In 1960 it opened a new facility in the former Halifax Infants' Home, where it remained until June 1996.

In 1946, during his campaign to shut down the Ideal Maternity Home, provincial director of child welfare Fred MacKinnon had approached the Salvation Army about the possibility of establishing a home on the mainland of Nova Scotia. MacKinnon claimed that there was a 'definite need' for a charitable home that would combine the 'moral and religious training' lacking in the private home with 'the most modern accepted methods and standard of social treatment of unmarried mothers.'[68] There is no indication that this plea had any effect. The unusually late establishment of a Halifax home by the Salvation Army instead coincided with efforts by a Pentecostal group to establish its own operations in the city. This Pentecostal plan faced the opposition of local social workers, who sought to expand and modernize the Halifax Infants' Home rather than enter into what they somewhat self-servingly called 'wasteful duplication.'[69] Faced with a new religious institution as competition, a social worker from Ottawa reported that the Salvation Army 'settled on the plan to open the Home here, and nothing would have deflected their purpose.'[70]

The Bethany Home offered prenatal and limited postnatal service to unmarried mothers with the understanding that no infant would be cared for without the mother being in residence and that care should not exceed a period of six weeks after delivery. The operations were governed from the national Women's Services Department in Toronto, with no local input. In 1958, the home claimed to have assisted seventy-five 'girls,' half of whom were in their teens, with an average of twelve or thirteen women in residence at any one time. (After the move to the Halifax Infants' Home facilities on Tower Road its capacity would increase to thirty residents.) Residents were expected to contribute an hour and a half of domestic labour every day, with alternative arrangements made for those taking school courses. The domestic regimen was very strict, with a wake-up call at 7:30 a.m. and lights out at 10:30 p.m. Residents were free to leave the home as they wished but had an 8 p.m. curfew. Visitors other than the putative father were received at any time. Fathers had visiting privileges only by arrangement with the Children's Aid Society or the Department of Public Welfare. Unlike the Halifax Infants' Home and the Home of the Guardian Angel, residents were not permitted to smoke. Religion was an explicit aspect of the program, with compulsory chapel service on Friday. Residents were also encouraged to attend morning and evening prayers. Admission in the sixth or seventh month of pregnancy was encouraged, but exceptions were made to admit younger women earlier in their pregnancies. After delivery at the Salvation Army Grace Maternity Hospital, the mothers were expected to return to the home for a minimum of one week, which could be extended to as many as six.[71] There is little evidence of the origins of the mothers, but in 1970 less than a third of the clients came from Halifax and the average age of the residents was sixteen.[72]

Like the Halifax Infants' Home, until the 1970s the superintendent of the Bethany Home had a background in nursing rather than social work. An exposé in 1971 by the independent weekly *The 4th Estate* reported that counselling was inadequate and that there was no follow-up once the residents left the facility. The report described an ethos of 'Victorian morality' and an atmosphere of 'guilt and tension' pervading the residence. Although the Salvation Army engaged a social worker in 1971, her presence did not appear to alter the established approach.[73] One gains a sense of the philosophy behind the home in an early 1960s press release. This release stressed the importance of 'positive living,' described as 'consistent, balanced meals, regular times for sleep, exercise and work.' The redemption offered by the Salvation Army was a religious salvation – the hope that, through her time at the home, an unmarried mother would experience 'the strength that comes from God to those who seek to find Him.' This mission was blended with modern rhetoric: *The 4th Estate* report also stressed that the Salvation Army officers were 'trained' and cooperated with all levels of government for 'the highest possible standard of efficiency.'[74]

Although the Salvation Army rejected modern social work approaches, it mixed traditional religious language with contemporary psychological insights. An undated national pamphlet described the background of the mothers as ranging from the lowest to the top levels of intelligence and as often having had unsatisfactory family relationships. It explained their 'illicit conduct [as] indicative of deep-seated needs.' What the young women needed was spiritual and physical correction of a 'behaviour pattern.' While the diagnosis was psychological, the solution was to be found in a nineteenth-century faith in the 'dedicated women who love and "mother" the girls' and the therapeutic impact of a Christian influence. The 'all-important' goal was no longer viewed as responsibility, accountability, or material care of the infant but rather as preventing another mistake.[75]

The Salvation Army home was contrasted with the Home of the Guardian Angel, which the same 1971 article in *The 4th Estate* posited as 'a brighter alternative.' The director of the Catholic home, Sister John Elizabeth, was a professionally trained social worker and the home engaged an additional caseworker. The atmosphere at the Catholic home was described as 'pretty well unstructured,' with the use of group discussions to address governance issues.[76] While the Home of the Guardian Angel was clearly influenced by contemporary social work practices, rules and operations at the Bethany Home remained rigid even into the 1980s and 1990s. A 1980s brochure explained that late leaves until 10 p.m. were granted twice weekly and that weekend passes were at the discretion of the resident's parents, guardian, or the administrator of the home.[77]

Like the Halifax Infants' Home, the Salvation Army home faced financial difficulties. Until 1965 its budget was derived from the financial contributions of residents and a modest grant from the municipality for the care of local women; the balance was made up by the Salvation Army, including local contributions to the annual Red Shield campaign.[78] Beginning in 1963, Salvation Army officials at the national office in Toronto began intensive lobbying for a provincial government per diem subsidy; however, provincial bureaucrats found it difficult to justify supporting residential care and not the out-client counselling and foster care undertaken by the Children's Aid Society and the Home of the Guardian Angel.[79] In 1965, the provincial government introduced a modest per diem grant to the Bethany Home at a rate of 50 cents a day for the three months prior to delivery and for the two weeks immediately following.[80] The willingness of the province to support the Salvation Army home in this way provides a good example of how the government could shape institutional practices and conformity through its granting policies: the structure of the grant entrenched the residency pattern of the clients. The success of a modest grant opened the door for increased spending, and the Salvation Army continued to campaign hard for increased funding, arguing that practically every other province contributed an annual grant to this work and that Ontario paid 75 per cent of the cost of care.[81] By 1974 the provincial share had increased so that the province paid 50 per cent of the actual costs, or $4.24 per day per resident.[82] Correspondence between the Salvation Army and the province suggests that the government was much more willing to offer one-time infrastructure grants to improve facilities than to undertake ongoing commitments.[83]

Home of the Guardian Angel

If the Salvation Army was the charitable organization with the greatest specialized experience in dealing with unmarried mothers, then the Sisters of Charity's Home of the Guardian Angel was the institution that consistently received the most praise from provincial government bureaucrats and national welfare experts. Established in the late 1880s, the Home of the Guardian Angel offered residential prenatal and post-natal care for unmarried mothers and care for their infant children.[84] The home was operated by the Sisters of Charity of Saint Vincent de Paul, Halifax, primarily a teaching order working out of its mother-house at Mount Saint Vincent. The success of their home for single mothers was a result of the order's secular professionalism, and, ironically, the marginal position of the home within the order's mission. The Home of the Guardian Angel was burdened with neither the non-professionals of the Halifax Infants' Home nor the Salvation Army professionals who specialized in serving 'fallen women.' Like the Salvation Army, the Sisters of Charity had an institutional financial base behind its operations, and provincial bureaucrats described the Catholic home as well staffed. In addition, the home had remarkable physical flexibility, with the option of sharing resources with other Catholic institutions.[85] For example, after early adoption reduced the number of infants in residence, between 1955 and 1973 the much smaller Home of the Guardian Angel was located in a wing of St Joseph's Orphanage.[86] When the number of young women desiring assistance expanded in the mid-1970s, the home was able to create an annex in the nearby St Thomas Aquinas convent.[87]

The sisters at the Home of the Guardian Angel brought to their work not only professional qualifications and training, but also experience in community work and as teachers and professors of 'non-delinquent' young women. Even at the home, their world was never completely isolated from 'normal' young women. Sisters working at the Home of the Guardian Angel in the 1960s shared living quarters with nuns teaching at nearby St Patrick's High School. In contrast to preconceptions about the cloistered lives of nuns, the Sisters of Charity brought a breadth of experience not evident in the backgrounds of staff at the Halifax Infants' Home and the Salvation Army Home. Catholic attitudes about working with unmarried mothers may also have been distinct from Protestant ones. Linda Gordon, in a study of American Catholic orphans before the First World War, notes that the sisters, who were also Sisters of Charity, 'enacted and symbolized a gender system that did not place women's highest aspirations into the frame of marriage, motherhood, and family.' Irish Catholic nuns did not view the roles of wife and mother as the pinnacle of achievement for women, and they indulged far less than Protestants in characterizing single mothers as 'fallen.' Instead, the sisters dedicated themselves to rescuing poor mothers by providing opportunities for them to shed the burden of a baby with relatively little humiliation, or by offering a chance to surrender a child only temporarily.[88] Gordon's portrayal of these nuns as sensitive and skilled reflects the perception of professional civil servants in Nova Scotia, but is very much at odds with the findings of Andrée Lévesque in her study of the Sisters of Miséricorde in Montreal, who specialized in caring for unmarried mothers and their children.[89]

The sisters put in charge of the Home of the Guardian Angel were a remarkable group of talented women. The sister superior between 1943 and 1949, Sister Miriam de Lourdes, née Elizabeth Scully, had experience as a teacher and educational administrator before she came to the Home of the Guardian Angel. She brought not only a diploma in social work but also the community credentials of working with Father James J. Tompkins in Reserve Mines, Cape Breton, and at the Star of the Sea community development experiment in Terrence Bay, Halifax County.[90] In 1946, when she addressed the Canadian Conference on Social Work, she became the first member of a female religious order to appear on the program of this biennial gathering. In her paper, Sister Miriam employed the insights of casework, which stressed the individuality of each 'girl's' situation and argued that the clients of the Home of the Guardian Angel were 'average girls ... "more sinned against than sinning."'[91]

Three years later, in 1949, Sister Mary Clare Flanagan, who became the dominant force in the life of the Home of the Guardian Angel in the postwar period, replaced Sister Miriam. An American, she also began her career with the Sisters of Charity teaching school and working with Father Tompkins in establishing the famous People's Library. Social work was her second career; she graduated from the Maritime School of Social Work in 1950. Sister Mary Clare pioneered infant adoption in Nova Scotia as part of a new policy to move infants out of institutions. Before the Second World War, social workers believed it was preferable to keep children in institutional care until they were at least two years old. In 1954, Sister Mary Clare and her eventual successor in charge of the Home of the Guardian Angel, Sister John Elizabeth, attended the Washington conference of the Council of Social Work Education in the company of the director and assistant director of the Maritime School of Social Work, and the two women remained closely connected.[92] After leaving the home in 1969, Sister Mary Clare served as staff training and development officer in the Department of Social Services until 1979. She was not only the first president of the Nova Scotia Association of Child Caring Institutions[93] but also served as president of the Mainland Nova Scotia Branch of the Canadian Association of Social Workers, and in this capacity she was active at the national level.[94] Her education did not stop with her social work training: she continued to keep abreast of currents in welfare policy through attendance at international conferences.

Sister Mary Clare mentored Sister John Elizabeth, née Honora Teresa Joyce, who joined the staff of the Home of the Guardian Angel in 1961. Sister John Elizabeth's professional credentials included a BA from Dalhousie, an MA from the Catholic University of America, and experience working as a social worker in Cape Breton and teaching at the Maritime School of Social Work and at Mount Saint Vincent College, where for ten years she taught sociology and served as dean of students.[95] In 1962 Sister John Elizabeth became the executive director (not sister superior) of the Home of the Guardian Angel. She held this position until her death in 1976.

Even before it enjoyed this distinguished leadership in the postwar years, the Home of the Guardian Angel received glowing reports from all inspections and tours. Child welfare reformers typically praised 'the cleanliness and happiness of the children' and its very low mortality rates.[96] One slightly critical report in February 1950 pointed to the institutionalized atmosphere, but noted that 'although the Sisters are aware of this they seem unable to do anything about it.'[97] This small detraction stands alone in a series of praising reports by professional social workers and government bureaucrats of the home's direction under Sisters Miriam de Lourdes, Mary Clare, and John Elizabeth. A 1958 report commissioned by the local welfare council drew attention to the quality of the casework made available to both the unmarried mother and putative father, noting that the Home of the Guardian Angel went 'beyond the usual role of a maternity home and offers a very complete service in the unmarried parents field ... in accordance with high standards of practice.' The home provided integrated psychiatric referral services, child-care training for those who would keep their infants, and home studies and adoption placements for those giving up their children. With regret, the outside expert noted that there was no real counterpart to these services in the non-Catholic community, even within the Children's Aid Society. Significantly, the Home of the Guardian Angel framed adoption as an alternative that could be in the best interest of both the mother and the child rather than primarily for the child's welfare.[98] As a result, the home actively developed a professional approach to infant adoption, and foster care in the province and from the early 1950s worked to move infants out of the institution. It also pioneered non-residential support for unmarried mothers in the province; by the reporting year 1964–5 over half of the women it assisted never lived in residence.[99]

Before provincial funding became available in 1965, an annual municipal grant, the United Appeal, and the Halifax Archdiocese supported the Home of the Guardian Angel. Those 'girls' who were in a position to pay were charged a weekly fee which was, in fact, also the case in the other institutions.[100] In response to an inquiry about the full costs of residency and delivery through the Home of the Guardian Angel in 1960, a total of just under $300 was required as the fee for anyone accepting ward care. This included two months' board for the expectant mother, spending money for cigarettes, transportation, prenatal medical expenses at the Dalhousie Public Health Clinic, expenses of the birth, and ten weeks of infant boarding until adoption.[101] No woman was accepted before her sixth month of pregnancy and all had to work in the nursery before confinement. Counselling was offered in the form of a weekly interview with a social worker.[102]

Although there was a concern for the protection of the young women's privacy – the institution's record keeping was done using only the expectant mother's initials – there was also a conscious attempt not to isolate the residents. A 1946 report by Sister Miriam de Lourdes noted that some women in residence had obtained good day employment. Leisure concerns were similar to those at the Halifax Infants' Home. Sister Miriam's report informed the child welfare committee that a second social room had been created complete with radio, piano, and reading material. In 1953 the home opened a television room, where residents could smoke. Provisions for school-aged girls were made for correspondence courses from Quebec, Boston, and New York.[103]

In 1949, in addition to the superintendent, the Home of the Guardian Angel employed one lay registered nurse, ten sisters (three of whom were registered nurses), one lay social worker in charge of adoption, and two domestics in the laundry. The residents were involved in what was described as 'light housekeeping' and the care of the children. Unlike the Halifax Infants' Home and the Bethany Home, the Home of the Guardian Angel had no specific residency guidelines. A Department of Public Welfare inspector concluded that residents themselves decided 'when they will or will not leave.' The same inspector noted that although there were no planned recreational activities, the residents were free to do as they wished every evening until the 10 p.m. curfew.[104]

The relationship between the provincial bureaucrats in the child welfare division and the Sisters of Charity at the Home of the Guardian Angel was characterized by mutual admiration and occasionally even special treatment. In 1956 provincial director of child welfare Fred MacKinnon wrote to Sister Mary Clare that, in light of his high regard for 'the quality of leadership' at the home, he had attempted, albeit unsuccessfully, to secure Department of Health funds for additional equipment.[105] Indeed, the sisters were lauded by various levels of provincial bureaucrats as efficient and, the ultimate compliment, 'progressive.'[106] Despite the favour of provincial bureaucrats, there are suggestions that the quasi-governmental Children's Aid Society favoured the Salvation Army home, an issue that may have become more critical once the province started paying a per diem rate for residents. In 1966 Sister John Elizabeth complained that unless a woman approaching the Children's Aid Society explicitly stated she was Catholic, she was sent to the Bethany Home for Girls.[107]

The high opinion of bureaucrats reflected the fact that the policies of the Home of the Guardian Angel were at the forefront of modern secular practice. Sister Mary Clare's notion of prenatal care in the early 1950s included educating expectant mothers about childbirth itself, as 'many of the women in the Home have little or no accurate knowledge in this regard, a fact which can lead to very detrimental effects on both mothers and infants.'[108] In 1956 she unsuccessfully attempted to introduce a preparation course in the home, but the original cooperation of the Victorian Order of Nurses (VON) cooled as a result of jurisdictional problems with the Dalhousie Public Health Clinic. The resulting compromise saw the VON giving medical instruction to individual residents of the Home of the Guardian Angel, classes at the health clinic, and tours of the Grace Hospital to which women from the Halifax Infants' Home and the Bethany Home were also invited.[109]

After the Home of the Guardian Angel moved to the east wing of St Joseph's Orphanage in 1956, there was living accommodation for only nine or ten residents. This relatively small capacity may have encouraged the development of casework services, and after 1959 the home stressed counselling over residential facilities. Women in residence were expected to help with housekeeping chores, but the deinstitutionalization of infants through early placing in adoptive homes or foster care lessened labour needs.[110] The purpose of casework in 1963 was 'to help the mother in reaching a decision on the future of both the infant and herself.' The process was acknowledged as a difficult one in which the mother often changed her mind, but emphasis was placed on the belief that the ultimate decision was 'entirely the mother's.' The residential facility was presented not as a place to escape from society but as an alternative for women who wished a 'group experience.' The benefits of casework were vaunted as having long-term 'enormous psychological value.'[111] A September 1973 newspaper interview with Sister John Elizabeth emphasized the home's commitment to prenatal casework and the importance placed on giving the mother 'freedom from stress and anxiety.' The influence of contemporary psychology was evident in the emphasis on the individual self-esteem of the mother, but counselling was also available to the putative father and, if the mother planned to return home, to her parents so that they had 'a different appreciation of what she is going through.' Residents in school were strongly encouraged to continue their studies by attending class or taking advantage of volunteers and visiting teachers. Sister John Elizabeth directly addressed the issue of keeping unmarried pregnant women in seclusion, stating that 'this idea is being changed through the efforts of trained social workers and a more enlightened attitude on the part of the public.'[112]

The success of the home is evident in the number of women it served and its ability to adapt to change. In 1970 the Home of the Guardian Angel helped 140 unmarried mothers, provided residential facilities for 41 women, and placed 48 infants for adoption.[113] In 1972 it assisted 125 women, 45 women of whom used the residence, and placed 50 infants, usually under one month of age, for adoption. New initiatives to serve its non-residential clientele included the establishment in 1966 of the first resource centre for single mothers in the province. The centre was located in Spryfield, a Halifax suburb, where the sisters perceived a need for such a service.[114] The expanding role and importance of the provincial government was clear by 1972. In that year the home's funding came primarily from four sources: the largest grant by far was the $30,725 provided by the provincial government. In addition, $11,300 was given by Catholic Social Services and another $10,000 came from the annual United Appeal. The City of Halifax's contribution of $3,500 remained remarkably constant throughout the period.[115]

A 1970 study of maternity homes by the newly formed Halifax Women's Bureau, an early manifestation of second-wave feminism in Halifax, signalled a change in attitudes towards unmarried mothers and introduced a new interest group. The study – which adopted the term 'single mother' in order to include widowed and divorced mothers – represented a departure from past practices and interpretations in two important ways. First, it was conducted by feminist activists, not social welfare professionals or religious reformers. Second, it emphasized the needs of the mothers rather than their children and explored the support networks available to the women. In this report, services were completely 'mother defined,' inverting early reformers' exclusive concern about the infants. For this study, researchers designed questionnaires for residents of the Home of the Guardian Angel and the Bethany Home and clients of the Children's Aid Society. Although permission to conduct the survey had been received from the Salvation Army home, the questionnaires were never seen by the residents and were mailed back blank by the brigadier in charge of the home. It is therefore not surprising, that the Bethany Home received much criticism. Indeed, it was described as a Dickensian, Victorian institution. In contrast, the report noted that the atmosphere at the Home of the Guardian Angel was much more 'relaxed,' with the general belief 'that the girls should be encouraged to help themselves and go out into the community.'[116] However, the report described both homes as 'still in the bleak stereotypes of the first of the century when they were established as shelters for wayward girls. Religious and punitive overtones stressing their "sin" predominate [sic] the atmosphere, rather than constructive programmes in sex education and family planning.' While it is hardly surprising that neither the Salvation Army nor the Sisters of Charity conducted counselling in the area of sexual relations (other than chastity), this report was a harbinger of things to come. The needs and expectations of non-married mothers were changing, although stereotypes remained. The report's author admitted that alternatives such as 'living alone, in an apartment with friends, or at home have their advantages, but these too pose problems of lonliness [sic], finances and family reactions respectively ... The road of the single mother is not an easy one and the stigma society attaches to the single mother has prevented the exchange of information about methods of handling the problems.'[117] The report concluded with an extended discussion of the need for welfare reform, social assistance, infant daycare, and income support for women raising children outside an established family unit. Such demands foreshadowed the direction that public policy would follow: the eventual implementation of government welfare programs brought about the end of most maternity homes.

Between 1940 and 1975, the three major institutions offering residential assistance to unmarried mothers in the Halifax area provide very different models of care. Although the Halifax Infants' Home closed in 1960, the Home of the Guardian Angel continues to operate a residence and community resource centre for 'lone parent mothers.' The Salvation Army closed its last Nova Scotia operation in 1996, a casualty of women's preference for independent accommodation available in public housing. Driven by similar attitudes about infant care and the women who contravened dominant sexual mores, these institutions nonetheless demonstrated considerable variations in their responses. The two institutions that survived into the 1960s – the Home of the Guardian Angel and the Bethany Home – combined religious professional social work with state support. While the Catholic home was characterized by its innovations, the Salvation Army home embodied traditional approaches.

Collectively, the homes encourage us to think about the important and sometimes difficult relations between philanthropic, quasi-governmental, and private agencies and provincial bureaucrats, and to keep in mind a vision of welfare provision that was not state centred. There is nothing new about the privatized welfare services we face today, and it would be well to remember why past attempts to offer such did not always succeed. Finally, the maternity homes provide a glimpse into an area of welfare services that was completely female-based, with women simultaneously serving and regulating other women. The clients of these homes posed a threat to the core definition of 'good women' by illicitly entering motherhood through extramarital sexual relations and thereby overturning religious, economic, and political mores. The women who sat on volunteer boards or worked as professionals in the homes often felt more comfortable focusing on the services to the children than to the mothers. But, despite their judgmental, punishing, and often self-righteous stance, they did provide assistance to that minority of the province's non-married mothers who may have had no other option.

NOTES

1 Charlotte Whitton, 'Some Social Factors in the Treatment of Illegitimacy,' address given at the meeting of the Committee on Illegitimacy, Toronto, Child Welfare Council, 6 Dec. 1933, *Child Welfare* 9, 5 (1934): 17.
2 Royal Commission on Provincial Development and Rehabilitation, George

Davidson, *Report on Public Welfare Services* (Halifax: King's Printer, 1944), 153.

3 Regina Kunzel, *Fallen Women, Problem Girls: Unmarried Mothers and the Professionalization of Social Work, 1840–1945* (New Haven, CT: Yale University Press, 1993).

4 The importance of informal assistance is discussed in Suzanne Morton, 'Nova Scotia and Its Unmarried Mothers, 1945–1975,' in Nancy Christie and Michael Gauvreau, eds., *Mapping the Margins: The Family and Social Discipline in Canada, 1700–1975.* (Montreal and Kingston: McGill-Queen's University Press, 2004), 327–48.

5 Marian J. Morton, *And Sin No More: Social Policy and Unwed Mothers in Cleveland, 1855–1990* (Columbus: Ohio State University Press, 1993), 10.

6 *Canada Year Book* (Ottawa: Dominion Bureau of Statistics, 1945–1980).

7 This trend is evident in the records of the Halifax Infants' Home, although Bette Cahill in her study of the Ideal Maternity Home claims that the average age of unmarried mothers was seventeen. *Butterbox Babies: Baby Sales, Baby Deaths – The Scandalous Story of the Ideal Maternity Home* (Toronto: McClelland-Bantam, 1992).

8 Nova Scotia, *Women in Nova Scotia: A Statistical Handbook*, 2nd ed. (Halifax: Women's Directorate, 1995), 5–9. The decline in births to non-married teenage mothers is probably connected to the availability of abortions, while the increase in births to older non-married mothers probably reflects the increased number of women in common-law relationships.

9 Ibid., Public Archives of Nova Scotia (PANS), MG 20, vol. 408, Minutes of Halifax Council of Social Agencies – Child Welfare, 9 April 1948.

10 Many of these ideas were first articulated in Crittenton Homes in the United States. See Katherine G. Aiken, *Harnessing the Power of Motherhood: The National Florence Crittenton Mission, 1883–1925* (Knoxville: University of Tennessee Press, 1998).

11 See Rickie Solinger, *Beggars and Choosers: How the Politics of Choice Shapes Adoption, Abortion and Welfare in the United States* (New York: Hill and Wang, 2001).

12 This historian's understanding of the three homes is also shaped by the kind of records available. While all homes appear in the records of the provincial department responsible for public welfare and in the research of the Canadian Welfare Council, the Halifax Infants' Home also left the minutes of the volunteer board and its general annual meeting. The involvement of a local volunteer board was unique to this institution, and it often overshadowed even the home's superintendent.

13 *Nova Scotia Journal of House of Assembly (JHA)*, 1916, no. 28, Office of the Superintendent of Neglected Children, 34.

14 Ibid., 1945, no. 23, Child Welfare, re: Halifax Children's Aid Society, 63.

15 Ibid., 1941, no. 23, Child Welfare, Cape Breton Children's Aid Society, 21.

16 PANS, MG 20, vol. 408, Minutes of Halifax Council of Social Agencies – Child Welfare, 6 Feb. 1948, Unmarried Children Act.

17 PANS, RG 72, Department of Community Services, vol. 19, no. 12, Unmarried Mothers 1961–66.

18 'The Halifax Children's Aid Society,' *Child Welfare News* 5, 2 (1928): 30.

19 PANS, MG 20, vol. 408, Halifax Welfare Council, 5.29, Report on Public Welfare Services made by George F. Davidson – Dawson Report on Provincial Development and Rehabilitation.

20 Halifax Infants' Home (HIH), *Annual Report*, 1946, 70, Gwendolen Lantz, Halifax Children's Aid Society.

21 *JHA*, 1947, Child Welfare, Appendix 23, p. 53, Gwendolen Lantz, Halifax Children's Aid Society.

22 PANS, MG 20, vol. 408, Halifax Welfare Council, 5.23, Child Welfare Survey Letter 1957–8.

23 Ibid., Halifax Welfare Council, 5.29, Report on Public Welfare Services made by George F. Davidson – Dawson Report on Provincial Development and Rehabilitation, 157.

24 PANS, MG 177, HIH, Minute Book, 14 Feb. 1945.

25 PANS, RG 35-102, Series 33A, 40, Halifax City Home – Admissions and Discharges 1929–38. It is possible to identify and trace individual women from the City Home who were released to or admitted from the Grace Maternity Hospital.

26 PANS, RG 25, Series E, 7, 5. Martin Archibald, Clerk, to Rev. H.H. Walsh, Chairman, Hospital's Board of Visitors, 7 Oct. 1942.

27 *Halifax Daily Echo*, 11 March 1911, 7.

28 HIH, 72nd *Annual Report*, 1946, 7.

29 PANS, MG 177, HIH Minute Book, 22 Feb. 1945, Annual Meeting.

30 Ibid., 10 Dec. 1947, 9 Feb. 1949, 14 Sept. 1949.

31 HIH, *Annual Meeting*, 1949.

32 HIH, *Annual Report*, 1954, superintendent's report.

33 PANS, MG 177, HIH Minute Book, 17 Sept. 1941, 15 April 1942, 27 May 1942.

34 Ibid., 8 Oct. 1947, 12 Nov. 1947, 9 Feb. 1949, 21 Feb. 1942; RG 72, Department of Community Services, vol. 199, no. 7, Halifax Infants' Home, 1940–60, Correspondence to F.R. MacKinnon, Deputy Minister, from M.J. Britten, President HIH Board, 23 Feb. 1955.

35 PANS, MG 177, HIH Minute Book, 12 April 1950.
36 HIH, *Annual Report* 1956, president's report: 9.
37 National Archives of Canada (NAC), MG 28, I10, vol. 228, no. 11, Canadian Welfare Council/Canadian Council on Social Development, Home of the Guardian Angel, Correspondence, 21 Nov. 1960.
38 PANS, RG 72, vol. 199. 7, Department of Community Services, Halifax Infants' Home, 1940–60, Report of the visit to HIH, 31 Jan. 1958.
39 Ibid., Halifax Infants' Home, 1940–60, visit report, 4 March 1947.
40 Ibid., handwritten letter, 15 Feb. 1947.
41 Ibid., 8 July 1949.
42 Ibid., inspection tour, 5 Nov. 1954.
43 PANS, MG 177, HIH Minute Book, 6 June 1950; Minutes executive meeting, 19 June 1950.
44 Ibid., HIH Minute Book, 14 July 1948.
45 Ibid., HIH Minute Book, executive meeting, 18 May 1951.
46 PANS, MG 20, vol. 408, 5.27 Correspondence re HIH and Children's Aid Society, 15 Feb. 1951.
47 Ibid., Report of Visit, Jan. 1941.
48 PANS, MG 177, HIH Minute Book, 11 Feb. 1948.
49 Ibid., 22 Oct. 1941, 18 Nov. 1942.
50 Ibid., 14 Nov. 1951.
51 Ibid., 13 Feb. 1952.
52 Ibid., 8 Oct. 1952.
53 Ibid., Aug. 1953.
54 Ibid.
55 NAC, MG 28, I 10, Canadian Welfare Council/Council on Social Development, 216, 13, NS Dept. of Public Welfare, Notes Field trip to Hfx, Feb. 1950.
56 PANS, MG 177, HIH Minute Book, Oct. 1953. This was contradicted in the 1958 Child Welfare Service Survey by Eric Smit, which claimed that the Home of the Guardian Angel was willing to take infants without their mothers. NAC, MG 28, I 10, vol. 228, Canadian Council on Social Development, 2, Halifax (NS) Child Welfare Service Survey (1958). The biggest labour advantage the Home of the Guardian Angel had over the Halifax Infants' Home was the labour of the Sisters of Charity.
57 PANS, MG 177, HIH Minute Book, 8 March 1950.
58 HIH, 75th *Annual Report*, 1949, President's Report, 5.
59 PANS, RG 72, Department of Community Services, vol. 199.7, Halifax Infants' Home, 1940–60, Report of the department visit to HIH, 31 Jan. 1958.

60 PANS, MG 177, HIH Minute Book, November 1953. The money was to provide a means of securing decent room and board once they left the home.

61 HIH, *Annual Report*, 1956, President's Report, 6; NAC, MG 28, I 10, Canadian Welfare Council, vol. 228, 8, HIH correspondence to Eric Smit from Gwendolyn Shand, 18 Feb. 1959.

62 HIH, *Annual Report*, 1958, Report of President, 1 April 1957 to 31 March 1958.

63 NAC MG 28, I 10, Canadian Welfare Council, vol. 228, 8, HIH correspondence to Eric Smit from Gwendolyn Shand, 18 Feb. 1959.

64 Ibid., to Eric Smit from Gwendolyn Shand, 4 Feb. 1959.

65 PANS, MG 20, vol. 411, Halifax Welfare Council, 9.16, Child Welfare Survey, 18 Nov. 1958.

66 *Halifax Mail-Star*, 11 Dec. 1959, 31, 'To Close Infants Home'; ibid., 4 May 1960, 1.

67 *JHA*, 1917, no. 28, Office of the Superintendent of Neglected Children, 57. In her book, *The Dark Side of Life in Victorian Halifax* (Porters Lake, NS: Pottersfield Press, 1989), 149, Judith Fingard dates the founding of this work to 1894.

68 PANS, RG 72, Department of Community Services, vol. 9, no. 14, Salvation Army, 1946–59, Correspondence from F.R. MacKinnon to Col. W.J. Carruthers, 22 Aug. 1946.

69 NAC, MG 28, I 10, vol. 228, Canadian Welfare Council/Canadian Council on Social Development, 15, Field Visit Report, Peter Stanne, 6 June 1955; PANS, MG 20, Halifax Welfare Council, vol. 415, 11.16, 3 Nov. 1954.

70 NAC, MG 28, I 10, vol. 228, Canadian Welfare Council/Canadian Council on Social Development, 5; Correspondence, to Eric Smit from Gwendolyn Shand, 28 April 1958.

71 NAC, MG 28, I 10, vol. 228, Canadian Welfare Council/Council on Social Development, vol. 228, 2 Hfx (NS) Child Welfare Service Survey (1958), Eric Smit – draft.

72 Pauline Janitch, 'Bethany Home: Victorian Morality, Guilt Plague Unwed Mothers,' *The 4th Estate* (Halifax), 19 Aug. 1971, 12–14.

73 Ibid. The troubles at the home are also suggested by Department of Social Services correspondence, PANS, RG 72, Department of Community Services, vol. 108 15, Homes – Bethany 1974, to Fred R. MacKinnon from D.H. Johnson RSW, 12 July 1974.

74 PANS, RG 72, Department of Community Services, vol. 38, no. 12, Homes – Bethany Girls Home, 1963–66, the Salvation Army – Public Relations Department, *Unmarried Mothers Homes*, n.d.

75 Ibid.

76 Janitch, 'Bethany Home.'
77 Salvation Army Heritage Centre, Toronto, Halifax Bethany Home File, Brochure, n.d.
78 Janitch, 'Bethany Home'; PANS, RG 72, Department of Community Services, vol. 38, no. 12, Homes – Bethany Girls Home, 1963–6.
79 PANS, RG 72, Department of Community Services, vol. 38, no. 12, to Mjr Sidney Tuck, Public Relations and Finance, from W.S. Kennedy Jones, Minister of Public Welfare, 24 Dec. 1963.
80 Ibid., to James Harding, Minister of Public Welfare, from Carman A. Jerry, Chair Salvation Army Finance Committee, 4 March 1965.
81 Ibid., to James Harding from Carman A. Jerry, 14 Oct. 1965.
82 Ibid., vol. 108. 15, Homes – Bethany 1974, to Fred R. MacKinnon from D.H. Johnson RSW, 12 July 1974.
83 Ibid., vol. 38, 12, Homes – Bethany Girls Home, 1963–6, Program 'Re-Opening and Service of Dedication.'
84 NAC, MG 28, I 10, vol. 228, 2, Canadian Council on Social Development Halifax (NS) Child Welfare Service Survey (1958), by Eric Smit, gives the founding date of the Home of the Guardian Angel as 1887. In her 1956 study, Sister Maura *The Sisters of Charity Halifax* (Toronto: Ryerson Press, 1956), 177, dates the origins as 1888.
85 PANS, MG 20, vol. 408, Halifax Welfare Council, 5.23 Child Welfare Survey Letter 1957–58, Nov. 1957.
86 *Halifax Mail-Star*, 27 Sept. 1974, 4.
87 Mary Olga McKenna, *Charity Alive: Sisters of Charity of St Vincent de Paul, Halifax, 1950-1980* (Lanham, MD: University Press of America, 1998), 125. After a short stay on Parker Street, in May 1973 the Home of the Guardian Angel moved to facilities on Coburg Road. *Halifax Mail-Star*, 27 Sept. 1974, 4; 15 March 1973, 8.
88 Linda Gordon, *The Great Arizona Orphan Abduction* (Cambridge: Harvard University Press, 1999): 15.
89 Andrée Lévesque, 'Deviants Anonymous: Single Mothers at the Hôpital de la Miséricorde in Montreal, 1929–1939,' Canadian Historical Association *Historical Papers* (1984): 168–84; Anne Petrie, *Gone to Aunt's: Remembering Canada's Homes for Unwed Mothers* (Toronto: McClelland and Stewart, 1998).
90 *Halifax Mail-Star*, 10 April 1987, obituary, notes from Mount Saint Vincent Motherhouse archives, Halifax. The People's Library was an early manifestation of the Antigonish Movement, spearheaded by Catholic priests of St Francis Xavier University.
91 Sister Miriam de Lourdes, 'Home of the Guardian Angel,' *Proceedings of the 10th Biennial Meeting of the Canadian Conference on Social Work*, Halifax 1946, 72–4.

92 MSV Motherhouse archives; *Halifax Mail-Star*, 15 July 1987, 40.
93 NAC, MG 28, I 441, Canadian Association of Social Workers, 6, 5, Board of Directors – Gen Cor (1) 1950–53, 7 Jan. 1954, telegram from Sister Mary Clare to Joy Maines, Director, re death of Frances L. Montgomery's father.
94 Ibid., 32, 17, NS Mainland Branch, 1948–50, 15 Jan. 1954, to Joy Maines, Director, from Sister Mary Clare. Both Sister Mary Clare and Sister John Elizabeth had also attended the 1946 Canadian Conference on Social Work in Halifax. *Proceedings*, 231.
95 *Halifax Mail-Star*, 31 March 1976, 48; notes from MSV Motherhouse archives.
96 PANS, MG 20, vol. 408, Minutes of Halifax Council of Social Agencies – Child Welfare, 26 February 1935. It is interesting to note that Superior Rev. Sister Christina of the Home of the Guardian Angel published an article in *Child Welfare News* in 1928 that indicated a scientific approach to nutrition and knowledge of the professional literature. 'The Health of Children in Institutions,' *Child Welfare News* 4, A (15 Feb. 1928): 42.
97 NAC, MG 28, I 10, Canadian Welfare Council/Council on Social Development, 216, 13, NS Dept. of Public Welfare, Notes Field trip to Halifax, Feb. 1950.
98 This is clearly a matter of subsequent debate. See, for example, Solinger, *Beggars and Choosers*.
99 PANS, RG 72, Department of Community Services, vol. 25. 2, Homes – Guardian Angel, 1966–67, File Notes.
100 NAC, MG 28, I 10, vol. 228, Canadian Welfare Council/Canadian Council on Social Development, 2 Halifax (NS) Child Welfare Service Survey (1958), Eric Smit – draft.
101 Ibid., 11 Home of the Guardian Angel, correspondence, 21 Nov. 1960, response re inquiry for admitting Ontario girl. Those wishing a private doctor and private room in the hospital could expect to pay $500.
102 PANS, MG 20, vol. 408, Halifax Council of Social Agencies, Child Welfare, 9.10 Summer 1953.
103 Ibid.; also vol 415, 2.6, 1946 Child Welfare.
104 Ibid., 17 May 1949 visit.
105 PANS, RG 72, Department of Community Services, vol. 119, no. 9, Guardian Angel, 1952, to Sr Mary Clare, from Fred MacKinnon, 23 May 1956.
106 Ibid., to F.R. MacKinnon from E.L. Eagles re Feb. visit, 17 Feb. 1955.
107 Ibid., vol. 25, no. 2, Homes – Guardian Angel, 1966–67, file notes.
108 Ibid., vol. 199, no. 9, Guardian Angel, 1952–58, correspondence to Allan Morton Halifax Commission of Health, from Fred R. MacKinnon, 23 Feb. 1956.

109 Ibid., to F.R. MacKinnon from F.R. Langin, Deputy Assistant, Department of Public Works, 18 May 1956.
110 *Halifax Mail-Star*, 16 Jan. 1970, 1, 8.
111 Ibid., 9 Nov. 1963, 36.
112 Ibid., 17 Sept. 1973, 17.
113 Ibid., 17 March 1971, 24.
114 PANS, RG 72, vol. 25, no. 2, Homes – Guardian Angel, 1966–67, Correspondence, Timothy T. Daly, Antigonish Diocesan Services, to F.R. MacKinnon, 16 March 1966.
115 Ibid.,15 March 1973.
116 NAC, RG 127, Pt 1, file 2101-C-45, Urban Affairs, 'Single Mothers' by Anne Chaldecott.
117 Ibid.

The 'Right Kind' of Single Mothers: Nova Scotia's Regulation of Women on Social Assistance, 1956–1977

JEANNE FAY

Nova Scotia's new Employment Support and Income Assistance Act, proclaimed on 1 August 2001, eliminated impoverished maternity as a cause of need for social assistance. This disentitlement posed immediate and serious financial consequences for all state-assisted single mothers: an average 10 per cent lower benefit rate; loss of a higher proportion of their earnings from paid employment; further restrictions on transportation, dental coverage, child care, and postsecondary education; and cessation of a dedicated allowance for their children. The non-financial consequences were as drastic: monthly monitoring; mandatory employment assessments and programs with only passing reference to maternity and child care as barriers to employment; and job searches for new mothers.[1] Like the cutbacks to welfare in Ontario, these changes signal yet another post–Canada Assistance Plan retreat from social security for single mothers. In Nova Scotia, from the introduction of the mothers' allowance, first paid in 1930, until the 2001 legislation, mothers were entitled to income assistance because they were performing the socially valued work of raising their children. This recognition by the state gave them a certain legitimacy and moral authority that has now been lost.[2] This is disheartening, but not surprising.

The ideological struggle for social security in liberal welfare states, such as Canada, has always been framed by moral debates, and the moral worthiness of single mothers has always been problematic.[3] This was particularly true if they were not the 'right kind' of single mother.[4] The politics of selling social assistance programs to the electorate has been to separate the deserving from the undeserving poor.[5] In the case of women on social assistance, this calibration of worthiness has articulated 'hierarchies of motherhood' based on race, class, and marital status.[6] In order to promote public acceptance of income assistance programs for needy mothers, some of these women had to be rescued from 'the stigma of pauperism and the poorhouse.'[7] This process of redefinition has been the primary ideological project of the welfare state everywhere, including Nova Scotia.

The movement for mothers' allowances in Canada was based on a maternalist ideology that, from today's perspective, contains several contradictory messages. On the positive side, maternalism cast worthy mothers as citizens who were entitled to public assistance, and maternalists argued that fulfilling the concrete, human needs of mothers and children was a public responsibility, making personal needs political in the best feminist tradition.[8] As heirs to this legacy, welfare rights activists have been able to argue that people in poverty, and women and children in particular, have a right to self-respect and the right to maintain 'some culturally determined standard of living,'[9] regardless of their participation in the labour force. Single mothers today claim the right to raise their children on their own, partly because of this legacy.[10] Beginning in the 1960s, grassroots groups of single mothers have relied on the idea of entitled motherhood when they claim adequate benefits for themselves and their children.

On the negative side, maternalism reinforced socio-economic inequalities based on class, gender, and race. The needs of women in poverty were defined from the perspective of the Protestant work ethic, charity, patriotism, and British chauvinism.[11] Maternalists sought reasons for welfare dependency not only in desperate circumstances, but also in ethnicity.[12] Borrowing heavily from the social purity movement of the late nineteenth and early twentieth centuries, maternalists defined Canadian women in poverty and particularly immigrant women as needing cultural supervision and moral uplift.[13] This side of maternalist ideology created the image of the worthy widow, an icon of morally upright and self-sacrificing maternity against which all future impoverished single mothers were measured.

Nova Scotia's first income support for mothers was provided by the Mothers' Allowance Act of 1930. Entitlement to mothers' allowance – available only to widows – was based on a determination of whether the woman was suitable, fit, and proper to raise her children. Annual *Mothers' Allowance Reports* bristle with morally framed discourse, particularly concerning the distinction between the 'right kind' of mothers and those who had fallen into moral delinquencies or whose low mental and moral qualities meant they could not provide a proper home for their children.[14] The test of maternal worthiness included an inquiry into a mother's character, competence, education, occupation, relations, family traditions, ideals, and possessions.[15] Home visitors supervised homemaking and cleanliness, household budgets, child hygiene and school attendance, mental health, and morality.[16]

Yet, the worthy widow ideal did not shield entitled women from economic privation. As with all programs based on Poor Law ideology, mothers' allowance never provided adequate assistance.[17] The women deemed entitled did not escape their lives of toil and anxiety. They cobbled together livings by taking in laundry and boarders, by doing shift work or piecework, by sending their older children to work.[18] Nor did the emphasis on maternal worthiness actually advance social policy for the women themselves. The allowances were for the *children* – and only for the *younger children*. The mothers – as members of the working class, as members of ethnic, racial, and cultural minorities, and, as women – continued to be defined by Poor Law ideology, which blamed them for their poverty.

Until unmarried mothers in Nova Scotia became entitled for social assistance in 1966, maternalist discourse held sway, emphasizing the need of widows in the context of their worthiness as mothers and the innocence of their children. Between 1930 and 1966, worthy widows were *the* moral standard for women seeking social assistance. Others did become eligible during this time, however, including the wives of disabled husbands (1942), and common-law widows and deserted wives (1956). They were defined as worthy because they had lost or been deserted by male providers. Once unmarried mothers became recipients, the hierarchy of motherhood was complete. Unmarried mothers' need for public assistance was defined as pathological, in contrast to the 'genuine need' of widows and deserted mothers.[19] This new definition of pathology spread to all single mothers on social assistance, whether their children were born in or out of wedlock. All became stigmatized for their dependence on social assistance and the taxpayer.[20] The Nova Scotia Family Benefits Act of 1977 attempted to dispel this stigma by changing the name of social assistance for single mothers and persons with disabilities but it did not change any of the punitive regulations already in place.[21]

This chapter assesses the dramatic changes in discourse relating to single mothers between 1956 and 1977. The first section analyses the impact of the provincial government's termination of the Poor Law in the late 1950s and the official discourse that accompanied the changes in liberal welfare policy in the late 1960s. The discussion then shifts to the bureaucratic discourse evidenced by the policies of the provincial Department of Public Welfare. The section concludes with an examination of the role of civil and welfare rights movements in the same period. The second section parallels the first by analysing, for the post-1970 period, official, bureaucratic, and advocacy discourses: the government's view of the amendments to the Social Assistance Act between 1970 and 1974, the measures adopted from 1970 to 1977 by the Department of Public Welfare (which became Social Services in 1973), and the influence of the women's rights movement in the 1970s. A brief third section discusses the legislative regulations relevant to single mothers between 1975 and 1977, which remained in effect until 2001.

Creating New Income Assistance Programs for Single Mothers

In 1956 the Liberal government of Henry Hicks created provincial social assistance (PSA) in Nova Scotia with the introduction of the Social Assistance Act. The act extended eligibility for PSA to deserted wives, common-law widows, and the wives of prisoners. The new program retained the moral supervision found in the Mothers Allowance Act: assistance was granted only when a committee appointed by the minister found the applicant financially needy and suitable to raise her children. The groundwork for expanding social assistance programs had been laid in the previous decade. Inspired by Britain's Beveridge Report (1942), Canadian social planners proposed a Charter of Social Services, which promised social security and full employment.[22] More importantly, the federal government had raised expectations with the Unemployment Assistance Act of 1956. The Hicks government hoped that extending eligibility to new categories of women and children would attract much-needed federal dollars to Nova Scotia coffers.[23] There were compelling economic reasons for extending assistance in the mid-1950s. The dramatic loss of jobs in primary industries had forced 82,000 people to emigrate from the Maritimes in that decade.[24] The appalling conditions in outdated municipal poorhouses cited by the Canadian Welfare Council in a 1949 report singled out Atlantic Canada as a social-service backwater.[25] A severe downturn in the economy during the winter of 1955 pushed municipalities beyond their capacity to provide local relief and forced men to desert their families so that the women and children could get assistance.[26]

None of this was mentioned in the legislative debates. When the subject of social assistance was mentioned at all, it was within the strict maternalist framework of deserving women and children. When the 1956 social assistance bill was introduced, the minister of public welfare commented briefly that 'Legislation has been enacted for the payment of social assistance to *certain families which have been deserted.'*[27] The opposition responded equally briefly, expressing pleasure that the government was making 'some provision for *children of deserted parents and children of parents who may be serving a penitentiary term*,' and called upon the government to add 'illegitimate children' to the list of those entitled.[28] The minister replied that they would be part of the proposed legislation.[29] Since the 1956 Social Assistance Act did not, in fact, mention 'illegitimate children,' the minister was presumably referring to the children of common-law widows, who did become eligible.

Robert Stanfield's Progressive Conservatives ended twenty-three years of Liberal rule when they were elected on 30 October 1956. Taking advantage of the changes made to the Unemployment Assistance Act by the newly elected Diefenbaker Conservatives in Ottawa, Stanfield revolutionized Nova Scotia's social assistance system by adopting a new regime in 1958. The Social Assistance Act was combined with the Poor Relief Act to create Nova Scotia's two-tiered social assistance system. Part I of the act addressed PSA, adopted in 1956 by the Hicks government for widows (including common-law widow), deserted wives, and wives of disabled men and wives of prisoners.[30] Part II established municipal social assistance (MSA) and infused provincial dollars into municipally administered poor relief to able-bodied single or married men, single women, and others not entitled to assistance under Part I. For the first time municipalities were required to provide assistance in the form of food, shelter, fuel, clothing, medical care, or other necessities. The new act allowed municipalities to meet the obligation to provide assistance by admitting adults without children into a municipal home. The 'haunting spectre' of the poorhouse was ended, at least for families with children.[31]

Most of the debate during the second reading of the bill, 29 April 1958, focused on the creation of the new social assistance system. The minister of public welfare said the language had changed to take some of the sting out of poor relief.[32] He noted a changed public attitude towards state-provided entitlements – a *social consciousness* wrought by the two world wars and the Great Depression.[33] With the advent of federal unemployment insurance in 1940 and improved veterans' and old age pensions after the war, Canadians had come increasingly to expect government to provide assistance. The minister's acknowledgment of these social changes did not, however, extend to a change in the maternalist ideology governing the provision of social assistance to single mothers. As Part I of the 1958 Social Assistance Act makes clear, only worthy women who had some claim to respectability because of desertion, disability, or widowhood were entitled to assistance.

The election of Lester Pearson's Liberal minority government in Ottawa in April 1963 – with Tommy Douglas and his New Democratic Party holding the balance of power – signalled new welfare initiatives. This political realignment significantly changed the social policy landscape of Canada. Bills liberalizing several laws were introduced by Justice Minister Pierre Trudeau in 1967; they were enacted when he became prime minister in 1968. Two of these changes had a profound effect on the lives of women. First, the Divorce Act of 1968 resulted in significant increases in the divorce rate.[34] The legal termination of marriage became accessible to women and men in relationships that had broken down, and to people in poverty, who could not afford the expensive litigation required under the old law. This led to an increased reliance on social assistance by women and children who suffered the negative economic consequences of divorce.[35] Second, birth control became available legally in Canada in 1969 through amendments to the Criminal Code. Therapeutic abortion was decriminalized at the same time.

The Pearson Liberals also initiated a crusade against poverty in 1965, which changed the nature of the discourse. When Canadians rediscovered poverty in the middle of the affluent 1960s, people in poverty were recast from villains who were the authors of their own misfortune to victims who were trapped by unemployment, lack of skills and education, disability, infirmity, and single parenthood. As the 1960s ended, a widespread socio-political consensus developed about the national disgrace of one in five Canadians living in poverty. 'Doing something about poverty' became politically popular.[36] Reflecting a move to the left by the federal Liberal Party, in part as a conscious effort to contain the NDP, this consensus engendered a period of social policy innovation in Canada.[37]

The resulting federal–provincial negotiations about poverty began with pressure from the provinces, especially Quebec, for more control over social policy, and culminated in 1966 with the adoption of the Canada Assistance Plan (CAP). CAP was a watershed in the development of Canadian social security.[38] Besides eliminating earlier categorical programs based on demographics or special designations (the elderly, the blind, etc.),[39] CAP extended the idea of meeting need regardless of cause, a principle first introduced by the Unemployment Assistance Act.[40] It clearly established the federal role in sharing the cost of assistance to mother-headed families.[41] Because it included 'loss of principal family provider' in the causes of need, CAP made an additional two hundred thousand families, who had previously been excluded under the Unemployment Assistance Act, eligible for benefits.[42] The goal of Canada's version of the war on poverty was the rehabilitation of people in poverty and their communities through adequate social assistance, extended social services and programs such as labour mobility and training, the Area Development Program, rural development, and the Company of Young Canadians.

In contrast to the excitement caused by CAP, Nova Scotia's Social Assistance Act of 1966 was enacted without fanfare. Introduced during the last year of Robert Stanfield's tenure as premier of Nova Scotia, it aligned provincial social assistance programs with CAP requirements. One result was to entitle unmarried mothers. Following the tradition of the previous decade, however, there was no legislative debate on this major shift in social policy. When James Harding, the minister of public welfare, moved second reading on 16 March 1966 with no question or debate from the opposition, he noted that the bill brought Nova Scotia's legislation in line with CAP in order to take advantage of federal cost-sharing. He mentioned that it dealt with mothers' allowances, without elaboration on this point.[43]

Why was there no debate or public comment when unmarried mothers became entitled to provincial social assistance? The negligible numbers of women who became entitled – eighty-one in the first year – may have made their inclusion seem like a non-issue.[44] A newspaper article in June 1966 suggested another reason: the public was more concerned about the alleged abuse of municipal assistance by male recipients who drank and gambled.[45] It may also have been that unmarried mothers would be subject to strict regulation and supervision. When the minister reported that the province had assumed responsibility for several categories of mother-headed families, including unmarried mothers, he said child welfare casework supervision would be extended to these women.[46] Progressive Conservatives may not have had to defend their welfare programs: the public trusted they would assist only the worthy, in the best maternalist tradition of the day.

Within the Department of Public Welfare, however, the eligibility of unmarried mothers and deserted wives whose husbands' whereabouts were known raised a pressing moral and economic issue: the obligation of fathers to support their children. Entitling unmarried mothers to assistance in 1966–7 prompted a maintenance-enforcement provision to appear for the first time as a condition of eligibility. In order to receive assistance, the mother had to prove the father was unable, had failed, or had refused to support his children. Defining the eligibility of women and children on the basis of the physical absence of the father did not always work in the case of unmarried mothers. It became necessary for the women to prove these men were deadbeats. The Halifax Family Court, which opened in January 1967, would see thousands of these women forced to apply to the court for child support in order to be granted social assistance.

The Department of Public Welfare's Problem Mothers, 1966–1969

While the politicians barely mentioned only the most deserving women, bureaucrats often portrayed single mothers as problems. Welfare administrators and bureaucrats resisted the new social security view of poverty because it undermined their practice of defining clients as deficient and in need of supervision. Between 1966 and 1969, during the height of the federal Liberals' war on poverty, the Nova Scotia Department of Public Welfare's in-house publication, *Welfare News*, defined problem mothers in several ways.[47] First, mothers in poverty were compared unfavourably to others more worthy. Two new images of mothers appeared in 1967. The foster mother was rhapsodized in a poem as 'angel-queen,' most deserving of praise because she took in children from the goodness of her heart, in contrast to the 'someone' who 'selfishly allowed a baby to live alone.'[48] Then, a visit to Antigonish by the Queen Mother occasioned the choice of a five-year-old ward of the state to give her a bouquet. The selfless sacrifice of the foster mother and the noblesse oblige of the Queen Mother implicitly condemned women who were not able to raise their own children.

Second, poor people in general and poor women in particular were characterized as socially and culturally deprived. In a 1967 article, families in poverty were described as victims of intergenerational poverty.[49] A year later, two articles examined the cycle of poverty and defined families in poverty as culturally defective and socio-politically alienated. The first article redefined 'disabled' to include not only physical and mental, but also social, vocational, and economic disability: the unemployed could not be cured simply with a job, because they were also socially and culturally deprived.[50] In the second article, social assistance recipients were framed as socially and politically alienated by the conditions of their lives, by their cultural values and personal deficiencies.[51] The alienation motif promoted a warning – in language that conjured up the spectre of the social unrest convulsing African-American neighbourhoods throughout the late 1960s – that poor people were apt to be apathetic, and/or deviant, and/or to engage in destructive group behaviour. George Matthews, director of social development, labelled as 'disadvantaged' African–Nova Scotian communities on the outskirts of Halifax and Dartmouth.[52] Casting racial and ethnic groups as 'deprived' created the ideological conditions for the destruction of their communities, as happened in and to the Black community of Africville during this period.[53]

Third, women in poverty were held up to ridicule. In 1968 *Welfare News* published a piece written by Brigadier W.W. Reid, then deputy minister of public welfare in Prince Edward Island, which contained excerpts of letters from women on assistance. Each excerpt was obviously chosen for the comic value resulting from the woman's poor syntax and bad grammar. Most were offensive: 'In accordance with your instructions, I have given birth to twins in the enclosed envelope.' Some contained sexual innuendo: 'Mrs. Jones has not had any clothes for a year and has been visited regularly by the clergy.' Others ridiculed the woman's claims to morality: 'I am very much annoyed to find you have branded my son illiterate. This is a dirty lie as I was married a week before he was born.' Still others belittled the women, making light of great personal tragedies: 'I am forwarding my marriage certificate and six children. I had seven but one died which was baptised on a half sheet of paper.'[54] The casual cruelty of ridiculing these women's attempts to communicate the desperate conditions of their lives is breathtaking – a cruelty born of a paternalistic view of these women as being from 'the other side' – ignorant, childlike, and pathetic – far removed from the educated sophistication of the professional bureaucrat.

Finally, 'backlash' pieces warned people in poverty that to be worthy they had to be docile and grateful and accept their betters' view of what was in their best interest. For example, F.R. MacKinnon, then deputy minister, displayed his displeasure at activist single mothers who disrupted the 1969 annual meeting of the Canadian Welfare Council. Calling them 'a pressure group of angry, aggressive women, self-chosen and self-appointed,' MacKinnon lamented the misguided thinking that led the women to believe their actions represented anything that was 'Canadian or truly client-centred.'[55]

Civil and Welfare Rights, 1966–1970

Outside of the Legislative Assembly and the Department of Public Welfare, civil rights and welfare rights groups were changing the subject of poverty discourse. The Nova Scotia Project in Halifax's North End, a community with a large population of African Canadians, was the first such group. It was the first local community action supported by the Company of Young Canadians (CYC). CYC volunteer Joan Jones, an African Canadian from Oakville, Ontario, who worked on the Nova Scotia Project, was the first CYC worker in Canada. She and her Nova Scotia–born husband at the time, Burnley ('Rocky') Jones, moved to Halifax, inspired to become activists by the civil rights movement in the United States.[56] They talked openly of a system that denied education and jobs to Black youth,[57] of a history of oppression by white people that, unless improved, could lead to confrontation.[58] Although the term 'racism' was not used, this discourse reframed the problem and changed the analysis. Renaming the problem as racial discrimination and racial prejudice shifted the focus: no longer were Black people the problem, rather white society was being held accountable for denying equality to African Nova Scotians.[59]

The ideological shift that the Joneses and other young African Canadians brought to Nova Scotia in the mid-1960s recast Black people from downtrodden, powerless victims to proud bearers of human rights, impatient for full citizenship. When that bearer of human rights was embodied, however, the image invoked was male. At a human rights conference held in Halifax in early December 1968, the impediments to full citizenship identified were educational inequality, substandard housing, and lack of jobs and job training.[60] In this analysis, neither the injustices nor the solutions envisaged the lives of women as separate or distinct. Nonetheless, the voices of women were heard and respected in the Nova Scotia Project. Although the men usually took the public roles, the women carried out much of the community development work.[61] Women worked with mothers on Creighton and Maynard Streets to organize a 'tot-lot' playground. The mothers supervised the playground as volunteers. When the Nova Scotia Project organized the tenants on Creighton Street to oppose rezoning, women went door-to-door and were successful in convincing the City of Halifax to develop low-density public housing, which was two decades ahead of its time.[62]

The Halifax Neighbourhood Centre opened its doors on 1 November 1966 in the Hawkins House at 2421 Brunswick Street in the North End. By abandoning the casework approach to individual problems in favour of a community development approach, the Neighbourhood Centre made significant changes to working with people in poverty.[63] Community organizers worked with residents to help them meet their social and economic needs.[64] A shift in discourse accompanied the shift in approach. Parallelling civil rights discourse, the terms 'disadvantaged' and 'multi-problem families' were replaced in Neighbourhood Centre documents with 'community residents' and 'citizens' by 1970.[65] Casework labels used by the social workers were abandoned.[66] Also, as with civil rights, the political focus of Neighbourhood Centre work shifted from individuals with problems to the institutions oppressing people, such as slum landlords.[67]

The Neighbourhood Centre did not address women's issues explicitly. Yet, the focus on families and community issues engaged women directly in political activity, as had happened in the Nova Scotia Project. In the first community action organized by the Neighbourhood Centre – the St Patrick's School mobilization – women played prominent roles. Jackie Barkley, an experienced community development worker from the United States, was an organizer.[68] Two local women emerged as community leaders and went to all the meetings with the politicians and the school board and reported on these activities.[69] The Artz Street action for a crosswalk was also initiated and implemented by women: women and men walked back and forth across Artz Street during rush hour, tying up traffic to the south end of Barrington Street in the heart of downtown Halifax.[70] Meetings held by Neighbourhood Centre outreach workers in the North End public housing development, Uniacke Square, to revive a tenants' association inspired a number of women to take direct action and picket the offices of the Halifax Housing Authority for two days.[71] *The 4th Estate*'s coverage of the demonstration included a picture of a Black woman leading the demonstration and called the action 'marching by the mothers.'[72]

The Welfare Rights Committee, organized by the outreach workers of the Neighbourhood Centre in the spring and summer of 1970, followed the same pattern.[73] A corps of women was active in the group, although women's issues as such were not articulated. Welfare Rights used the discourse of the welfare rights movement in the United States to cast its members as 'human beings ... with the same needs and desires and hopes as everyone else [who is entitled to] the same full freedoms, rights and respect as all Halifax Citizens.'[74] Welfare Rights promoted 'people power' as the solution to poverty: recipients were urged to unite to fight for dignity and adequate income.[75] Welfare Rights also relied heavily on the social security discourse emerging from Canada's war on poverty.[76] Statistics were cited to prove that welfare recipients were not responsible for their poverty: men were unemployable because of lack of training or health-related problems; women received assistance because of lack of a male breadwinner.[77]

Although men held key positions in the formal structure of Welfare Rights and were quoted by the media most often, North End resident Sevilla Zinck emerged as the people's favourite because she stood up for their individual rights. A white woman on social assistance with a disabled husband and children, she was the first chair of Welfare Rights and one of the group's most tireless advocates.[78] When Elmer Briand, a group member and amateur cartoonist, depicted a confrontation between a man on social assistance and a male caseworker, Zinck's prowess as an advocate dominated the discourse. She hangs over the top of the cartoon frame scowling while the welfare recipient invokes her name and the caseworker says 'Not her please. Don't send her here. She is a hard woman to do business with. She always wins.'[79]

This advocacy was heady stuff for people who felt stigmatized by local welfare officials. It was also a key political consequence of welfare rights discourse. Rather than conceptualizing the system as a remote and complicated interrelationship between the economy and the state, the people who lived daily with this treatment resisted by confronting local welfare officials. Welfare Rights articulated this resistance by creating a morality play in which the genuinely needy were victimized by cruel welfare officials. The villainy of welfare officials lay in how they stigmatized people. To attack the villainy, however, welfare recipients had to be worthy. Members of a welfare rights group in Yarmouth, for example, cast themselves as legitimate welfare recipients because they were not lazy but disabled and concerned parents.[80]

The worthy/unworthy dichotomy extended to women specifically. Welfare Rights used maternalism to define mothers as entitled to assistance. This definition, however, was not based on the middle-class maternalist distinction between married and unmarried women, which singled out unmarried mothers as 'lower than the rest.'[81] People in the community made little differentiation between legally married and common-law couples. 'Mrs' was a sign of respect used in the community to address any woman with children. People resented the fact that caseworkers used it only for legally married women. A second class-based difference in the married/unmarried distinction concerned the support of the children. The economic reality for families in the North End in 1970 sent the men outside the area, sometimes outside of the province, to find work. When that happened, the women applied for assistance as single mothers, if they were not married, or as deserted wives, if they were. The community attached no stigma to receiving aid, because there were children to support. Rather, the stigma came from middle-class social workers labelling men in the community as 'lazy bums who should have taken any job.' If the men returned without work, social assistance rules prohibited them from living with their families. Welfare Rights fought to protect these relationships by ensuring that caseworkers did not visit women unannounced and terminate their assistance because there was a man in the house.[82]

Amendments to the Social Assistance Act, 1970–1974

Discourse in the period after 1970 again reflected both change and continuity among all those concerned with the policy process. The silence in the Legislative Assembly concerning social assistance ended when Gerald Regan's Liberals took power in October 1970. In the next sitting of the Legislature, two newly elected NDP members, Jeremy Akerman and Paul MacEwan, both from Cape Breton ridings, significantly changed the tenor of social welfare debates.[83] The debates became wide-ranging, long-winded, often raucous, and firmly rooted in the hierarchy of motherhood. Akerman and MacEwan introduced the nefarious 'welfare warlord' into the cast of villains and recast worthy widows as heroic victims who were their friends and constituents.[84] No one on any side of the House mentioned divorced women or unmarried mothers. When teen mothers became entitled to public assistance in 1974, the legislative debates were again almost silent.

So rarely were any women – other than the most pitiful and worthy – mentioned that a speech by an MLA on 10 June 1974 stands out as unique. He described 'ladies who are drawing social assistance who would, if they could, go out and do a half a day's or a day's work, house work or what have you.'[85] The use of the term 'ladies' rather than 'widows' or 'deserted mothers' signalled that the women in question might not have been the deserted wives or widows usually invoked. Was the MLA thinking about unmarried mothers, as opposed to widows or deserted wives? Does the reference to 'day's work' provide a rare clue as to the race of the women he, and presumably the other MLAs, might have had in mind when they used such terms? African-Canadian women from the rural communities surrounding Halifax and Dartmouth, discussed in more detail by Wanda Thomas Bernard and Judith Fingard in this collection, continued to be disproportionately represented among women doing domestic work – often called 'day's work' – in 1974.[86] Except for these comments, one would have no idea, from reading the legislative debates, that there were almost 2,000 deserted and divorced women on PSA at this time, as well as over 500 unmarried mothers. That the MLAs did not refer to them suggests it was not politic to do so. To deflect controversy about expanding social assistance entitlements, they mentioned only the least controversial beneficiaries.

Social Services' Problem Mothers, 1970–1977

After Nova Scotia's Department of Public Welfare changed its name to the Department of Social Services in 1973, bureaucrats continued their sparse but negative portrayals of women in the also renamed *Social Service News*. Undisguised elitism framed an article in 1973: a poverty-stricken housewife with her 'brood of dirty, hungry children' was visited by an immaculate, virginal social worker.[87] The piece was meant to be humorous. Instead of being envious of the social worker, the housewife – whose marriage to a drunken brute has brought her and her children nothing but poverty and deprivation – commiserated with the social worker about her unmarried state. 'How dreadful dearie,' the housewife was portrayed as saying. 'Ain't it hell to be an old maid?' The humour was meant to lie in the irony of the destitute housewife feeling pity for the professional social worker. At a deeper level was the sexual innuendo in the portrayal of a woman who stayed with a brutish husband and continued to have children, the implication being that she was allowing her base nature to rule her wretched life. This ridicule of women in poverty was bolstered by jokes belittling women in general: as little better than high-class prostitutes;[88] as being too stupid to diet; as daughters disgusted with their 'big' mothers;[89] as a working mother so indifferent to her child that she had forgotten his name.[90]

Single mothers began to appear more regularly in the *Social Service News* in 1973, less than a year before the Social Assistance Act was amended to entitle teen mothers. Unmarried mothers were portrayed as infantile and disturbed, morally and socially suspect. J.A. MacKenzie, director of social research and planning, revealed his angst about unmarried mothers in a book review of research on unwed mothers as parents.[91] His anxiety led him to commission *Vulnerable Mothers, Vulnerable Children* in 1978, a study of unmarried mothers and their children.[92] The study was designed to address the fear expressed by social services and child welfare staff that unmarried mothers were unprepared for motherhood and had a high potential for child neglect and abuse.[93]

According to *Vulnerable Mothers*, changes to the Social Assistance Act in 1970 and again in 1974 were responsible for the growth in the provincial case load of unmarried mothers.[94] This increase compelled social workers to adjust their practice to accommodate these women as clients. In two pieces on staff training in late 1973 and 1974, social workers were encouraged to stop thinking about unmarried mothers as 'problems' and start thinking of them as clients in need of expanded services.[95] The difficulty child welfare workers were having in changing their thinking was raised again in 1974.[96] At a Children's Aid conference in Ontario, child welfare workers exposed their stereotypical views by expressing their surprise that unmarried mothers were only a small portion of mothers raising children alone. The idea that all single mothers were unmarried was strong enough, however, that even after the figures were provided, the discussion continued to focus on whether child welfare workers should offer services to unmarried parents.

The child welfare perspective on single parents – that only unmarried mothers were of concern, because of their potential as bad parents – had dominated departmental thinking for many years, despite the increasing public assistance case load of deserted and divorced wives. In a brief history of the Halifax Children's Aid Society (CAS), Karl Marshall, then administrator of the CAS, expressed it succinctly: 'In 1975 we are concerned about the U.M. (unmarried mother) keeping her child although potentially unprepared. Fifty years ago the problem was trying to find the mother who just walked out of the maternity home deserting the infant.'[97] Even though unmarried mothers were no longer framed as morally depraved individuals capable of abandoning their children, social workers still thought of single-parent families as inadequate. An article in 1975 challenged child welfare workers to revise their thinking and recognize that poverty, not parental deficiency, was at the root of the problems faced by poor children. The article also, for the first time, collapsed the categories of single mother, no longer distinguishing among them on the basis of their marital status.[98]

After this article, single mothers were not discussed again in the *Social Service News* in the period covered by this study. In 1977, when the family benefits program was established, the silence in the *Social Service News* was resounding. The dominance of welfarist ideology and child welfare practices seems a primary reason for this silence: caseworkers could not envisage what services unmarried mothers might need, other than maternity homes and adoptions: the child was the focus of casework concern and policy development. As well, Deputy Minister F.R. MacKinnon's disdain for activist single mothers must have had a chilling effect on any progressive definitions.

Women's Rights, 1970–1976

It was not until women's rights groups changed the subject from the (male) citizens to women that the single mother as a political construction began to emerge in poverty rights discourse in Nova Scotia. The Halifax-Dartmouth Local Council of Women announced in June 1971 that it was organizing an 'active study' of the *Report of the Royal Commission on the Status of Women*. The spokeswoman said the group wanted 'to make a special effort to reach *women in low-income groups* who might not otherwise become familiar with the *Report*'s recommendations.'[99] That same summer, the Halifax Women's Bureau received funding from the Opportunities for Youth Program, which enabled several young women – mostly white university students – to conduct a study of women's issues in the Halifax-Dartmouth area.[100] The resulting report cast women in three distinct roles: as workers, as unmarried mothers, and as single heads of families.[101] In addressing the issues of working women, the Women's Bureau report used Marxist language to criticize both the Department of Labour and unions for not protecting waitresses from unfair labour practices.[102] The solutions were direct action and union organizing. In the case of unmarried mothers, however, the Women's Bureau drew upon the child welfare perspective to define them as 'girls' who needed proper sex education to prevent pregnancy, clearly implying that unmarried motherhood was inappropriate. Solutions aimed at rehabilitation and self-help, reflecting the postwar view that white unmarried mothers were treatable neurotics rather than fallen women.[103] The report recommended establishing small cooperative living groups for unwed mothers as an alternative to the 'homes' where many of them lived waiting for their children to be born. (See Suzanne Morton's chapter on Halifax's maternity homes in the volume for a description of these institutions.)

At about this same time, Welfare Rights was talking about setting up a house 'in the community where young girls could live together and bring up their babies as long as they met certain conditions such as going back to school.'[104] The strength of the race and class divide prevented the Women's Bureau and Welfare Rights from connecting to work on this project together. Both class and race differences were encoded in Welfare Rights activist Agatha Patterson's use of the phrase 'in the community.' Not only did it signal the working-class concern that the extension of social assistance to teen mothers allowed them to flaunt parental authority, but also the reality that homes for unwed mothers were located outside of the North End and controlled by the white-dominated Salvation Army (Bethany Home) and the Sisters of Charity (Home of the Guardian Angel).[105]

Finally, the Women's Bureau acted on the issues of single parents by promoting the One Parent Association in July 1971.[106] The involvement of men in the association probably minimized the importance of the maintenance-enforcement issue, which had brought the original group together in 1969.[107] The group took a gender-neutral stance on single parenthood.[108] This perspective would be formalized five years later in the report of the Nova Scotia Task Force on the Status of Women.

In most parts of its 1976 report, the task force replaced maternalist terms like 'unmarried mothers' and 'deserted wives' with 'single parent.' At first blush, the gender-neutral term 'parent' seems odd. It makes sense, however, in the context of liberal social policy and gender politics of the day. Liberal feminists focused on formal equality between men and women and eschewed women's maternal role: the Nova Scotia report debunked what it called the 'romanticized picture of the mother-child relationship,' which erroneously assumed that all women were equally suited to parenthood and that all fathers were not. The argument that traditional roles of mother/homemaker and father/breadwinner sold both women and men short was not unexpected from a task force composed almost entirely of career women.[109] The Nova Scotia Task Force proposed a guaranteed annual income for single parents because it was 'unthinkable that these people are made to feel the effects of the "welfare stigma."' In a quite radical stance, the task force specified that the guaranteed annual income was to be considered 'payment for work performed.'[110] It reverted to maternalist language and images, however, in a section entitled 'Women on Welfare.' Single parents were identified as deserted wives and mothers on welfare who deserved more credit than they received for shouldering their 'special burden.'[111]

In 1971 women living in poverty in Halifax began articulating an issue of their own: wife abuse. Agatha Patterson noted that women in the North End were using PSA as a source of income not only when their men went away to look for work, but also to flee violent relationships.[112] According to the Halifax Transition House Committee's brief to the Nova Scotia Task Force, the Women's Bureau first came into contact with women leaving abusive relationships during its survey in the summer of 1971: women in crisis asked for assistance in finding housing and employment. Then, the Halifax Help Line 'began referring women who wished to leave their homes and had no place to go, no financial resources to support themselves and their children.'[113] The brief focused on social assistance regulations that compelled women to file for divorce and seek maintenance before qualifying for financial help. By connecting their poverty to conditions affecting them as women, women in poverty had been successful in attracting the attention of feminists. Bryony House, a transition house for battered women, opened in Halifax in 1978.

Regulating Single Mothers, 1975–1977

In 1975, a year after teen mothers became entitled to social assistance, major regulatory changes were made to PSA, in effect establishing the regulation of single mothers until August 2001.[114] The man-in-the-house rule appeared for the first time: 'dependent mothers' were formally barred from cohabiting with a male person. Unearned income was defined for the first time to include maintenance payments. As a condition of eligibility, all single mothers were obliged to seek and enforce maintenance. It is ironic that these regulations came into effect during International Women's Year, given that they have been a source of pain, humiliation, and fear for thousands of single mothers in Nova Scotia. The man-in-the-house rule has subjected women to unreasonable invasions of privacy and loss of personal dignity, the terror of having benefits terminated with little warning, and punitively high rates of recovery of benefits 'improperly paid' when there was a man in the house. At the same time, these provisions did mark an advancement from negative maternalist and child welfare ideologies.

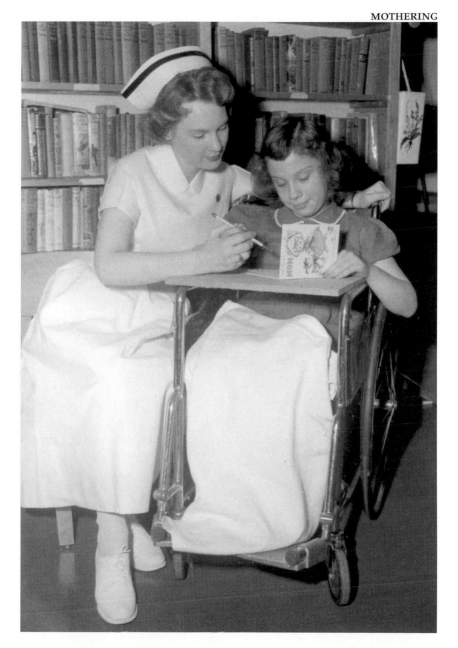

A young patient at the Children's Hospital, 1956, making a Mother's Day card.

Sisters of Charity nursing sister with Sister John Elizabeth in the nursery of the Home of the Guardian Angel in the early 1960s.

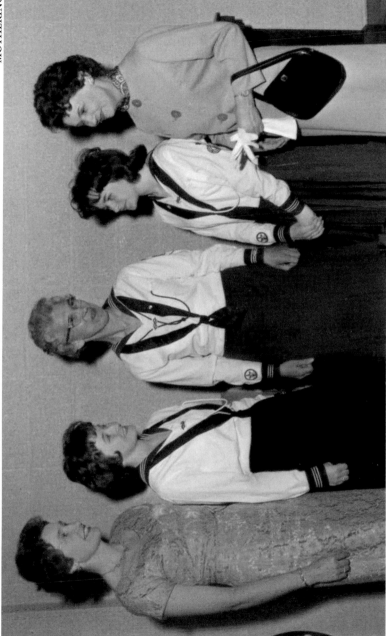

A Canadian Girls in Training (CGIT) mother-and-daughter banquet at St Andrew's United Church, 1963.

Mother and daughter, White Cross volunteers, delivering Christmas gifts at the Halifax Mental Hospital, 1963.

Bride and attendants, 1948.

The Halifax Coloured Citizens Improvement League Queen, 1965, attests to the enduring interest in beauty pageants.

The Debutantes' Charity Ball, 1965, when 'coming out' had an altogether different meaning.

Mount Saint Vincent University students and faculty enjoying a traditional women's tea, 1965.

Researcher at the Atlantic Fisheries Experimental Station, 1947.

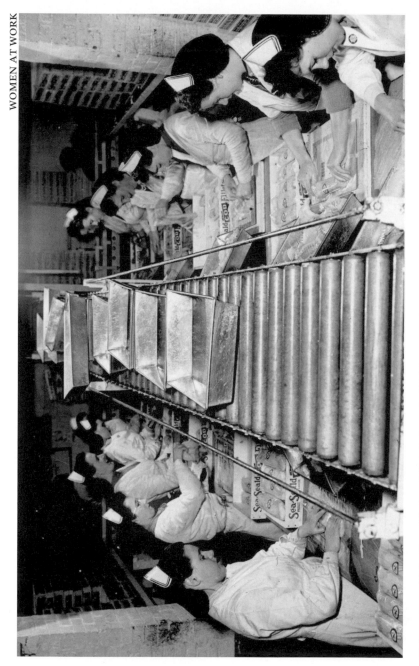

Fish packers at Maritime National Fish Ltd on the Halifax waterfront, 1949.

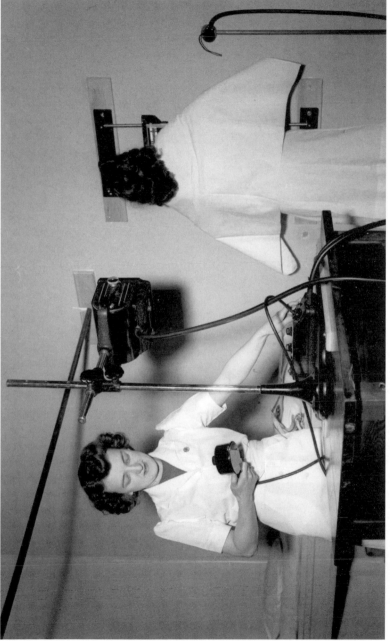

Technician giving a chest X-ray at the Dalhousie University Medical School, 1947.

A pioneer female taxi driver, 1965.

A woman shopping at the Dominion Store, 1948, one of the first supermarkets in the city.

African–Nova Scotian women, such as this pussy willow seller in 1953, were regular vendors at the Halifax City Market.

Retail clerk serving customers in the children's wear department at Saks Ltd. on Gottingen Street, 1949.

The Junior League's Bargain Box, a second-hand clothing store, 1962.

City Councillor Abbie Lane turning the sod for the North Branch of the Halifax City Library, 1965.

African–Nova Scotian civil rights leader Perleen Oliver at the CBC Radio studio, 1967.

National Voice of Women president Muriel Duckworth presenting the dark clothing 'Voices' knitted for North Vietnamese children.

Institute of Women of the African United Baptist Association meeting at Cornwallis Street Baptist, 1963.

Recognition for St John Ambulance Home Nursing Brigade members, 1964.

Baking for the Hadassah Fair, 1966.

Celebrating diversity: Indian Night at the YMCA, 1967.

Participants in the 'Women and Work' workshop, August 1975.

Debi Forsyth Smith, President of the Nova Scotia Advisory Council on the Status of Women (second from left on the balcony), celebrating International Women's Day in 1988 at Province House.

No longer were single mothers categorically disentitled for receiving child-support payments, although the numerous trips to Family Court to enforce unenforceable maintenance orders caused much hardship. No longer was the mere suspicion of sexual relations with a man enough to disqualify them, although it took another fifteen years for the Department of Community Services to write clear guidelines about relations with men.

In what was to be the last year of its mandate, the Liberal government of Gerald Regan introduced the Family Benefits Act in 1977. The length of the legislative debate is unprecedented during this period: it fills forty-four pages.[115] All parties spent considerable effort defining the right kind of recipients: disabled men who wished they could work, the unfortunate widow, the deserted wife/mother. The language ranged from general comments such as 'those unfortunate people in our society who require assistance from their government through no fault of their own' to specific circumstances, such as the young, depressed widow who wanted to go to university.[116]

The debates also identified bad men and women. Foremost among these were the husbands who had deserted their wives and children. These men were portrayed as wilfully refusing to support their families, as alcoholics, as irresponsible for heading to Ontario and Alberta and abandoning their families to be supported by the state.[117] Juxtaposed against the deserting husband's 'dissipation and irresponsibility,' his wife was a long-suffering martyr. The MLAs also expressed uneasiness about other women who might collude with their men to take advantage of the system. Progressive Conservatives asked whether the act prevented a man from deserting his wife just so she could get assistance, criticized social laws for favouring 'the unmarried state,' and told a story about a woman who deliberately misunderstood the meaning of separated until she was caught by the caseworker.[118] The uneasiness ultimately erupted in a joke about wife-swapping that was greeted with laughter and applause by all sides of the Assembly.[119]

Finally, the 1977 debates exposed the tension between the newly defined worthy mothers on family benefits, who were not expected to work, and the Poor Law idea that people in poverty needed to be rehabilitated and put to work. NDP MLA Paul MacEwan chided the government for not providing training programs for widows, who became 'useless' when their children were grown. He expressed doubt about whether single mothers and the disabled should be defined as unemployable and thus not be expected to take a full, active role in society.[120]

Unmarried mothers were mentioned only once, in the context of an employment project in Truro designed to train them so they could be 'put out into the community in employment.'[121] Clearly, there was ambivalence about relieving single mothers of the onus of 'working for a living' so that they could stay home and raise their children, an ambivalence that resurfaced in the Employment Support and Income Assistance Act of 2001.

Conclusion

The Family Benefits Act (1977) represented a watershed in social welfare policy in Nova Scotia, not because it was a significant departure from the more revolutionary Social Assistance Acts adopted in 1956, 1958, and 1967, but because it separated assistance for those who were not expected to work – persons with disabilities and single mothers – from municipal assistance for persons deemed to be employable.[122] In the best maternalist tradition, family benefits recognized single mothers' needs as a public responsibility: regardless of their marital status, all impoverished single mothers became entitled to this social assistance program designed especially for them and persons with disabilities.

Yet, the rehabilitation from unworthy to worthy was more apparent than real for single mothers. Liberal feminists and social security reformers relied on the negative elements of maternalist and welfarist ideology when it came to women on social assistance; so had the more judgmental advocacy movements. None succeeded in reframing the issue to non-stigmatized entitlement to social assistance. The hierarchy of motherhood was transferred to the Family Benefits Act. Several other provisions carried over from previous regulations reproduced the punitive and coercive code of earlier statutory regimes: cancellation of assistance if a man and woman separated to qualify for benefits, if a recipient refused employment or training, if non-disclosure of fact caused assistance to be improperly paid. Caseworkers were required to contact child welfare authorities to assess the suitability of every unmarried mother prior to benefits being granted. On the front lines, maternalist concern over suitability translated into welfarist supervision: the child welfare perspective continued to govern the policy and bureaucratic practices of social assistance programs for single mothers.

The man-in-the-house rule and the obligation to seek and enforce maintenance were also retained, encoding the ideology of female dependency in the family benefits regime. This element of social assistance legislation has received much attention from feminists, especially Brenda Thompson in her 1991 manual for single mothers.[123] Equally relevant, however, and seldom mentioned is the elitism that also frames the man-in-the-house rule and gives modern expression to the middle-class bias against the common-law marital arrangements of people in poverty. In order for women and children to qualify for benefits, couples were forced to separate. In order to continue to receive those benefits, women have had to hide intimate relationships with men. Economically marginal heterosexual couples in Nova Scotia were prohibited from receiving assistance under the Family Benefits Act. It also banned able-bodied men from the ranks of the worthy poor. If the men were able-bodied, then Nova Scotian social policy required that they feel 'the sting of the whip of privation' in order to spur them on to support their families.[124] Because the family benefits program was mired in the worst maternalist traditions of class, race, and gender bias, it confirmed maternalist contradictions. At the same time as it created single mothers worthy of assistance, the program regulated their relationships, disparaged their sexuality, threatened their children with child welfare supervision, and consigned such women, their children, and their men to continuing poverty.

NOTES

1 When an infant reaches three months, the mother must begin job searches if she has 'suitable' child care. There is no definition of suitable child care, although a government publication announces proudly that child-care funds (available for full-time work only) will no longer be tied to licensed daycare facilities: women can now pay neighbours and family members to care for their children.

2 Margaret Hillyard-Little, 'The Limits of Canadian Democracy: The Citizenship Rights of Poor Women,' *Canadian Review of Social Policy* 43 (Spring 1999): 60.

3 See Nancy Christie, *Engendering the Welfare State: Family, Work, and Welfare in Canada* (Toronto: University of Toronto Press, 2000), especially ch. 3; Margaret Jane Little, *'No Car, No Radio, No Liquor Permit': The Moral Regulation of Single Mothers in Ontario, 1920–1997* (Toronto: University of Toronto Press, 1998); James Struthers, *The Limits of Affluence: Welfare in Ontario, 1920–1970* (Toronto: University of Toronto Press, 1995); and Gosta Esping-Andersen, *The Three Worlds of Welfare Capitalism* (Princeton, NJ: Princeton University Press, 1990).

4 Linda Gordon notes that maternalists in the United States decided to

exclude deserted and unmarried mothers from early mothers' allowance programs because including them would promote the 'wrong kind' of motherhood. See *Pitied but Not Entitled: Single Mothers and the History of Welfare, 1890–1935* (New York: Free Press, 1994), 281. Little, '*No car,*' makes this point for Ontario as well.

5   Michael B. Katz, *The Undeserving Poor: From the War on Poverty to the War on Welfare* (New York: Pantheon Books, 1989), 5; Struthers, *The Limits of Affluence.*

6   Gwendolyn Mink, 'Welfare Reform in Historical Perspective,' *Social Justice* 21, 1 (1994): 114–31. Margaret Hillyard Little, 'Claiming a Unique Place: The Introduction of Mothers' Pensions in British Columbia,' in Veronica Strong Boag, Mona Gleason, and Adele Perry, eds., *Rethinking Canada: The Promise of Women's History,* 4th ed. (Toronto: Oxford University Press, 2002), 187–202, points out that although British Columbia included unmarried mothers in its mothers' pensions in the 1920s, it excluded women of Asian descent.

7   Gordon, *Pitied but Not Entitled,* 38.

8   Ibid., 40, 161; Little, '*No Car.*'

9   William H. Simon, 'The Invention and Reinvention of Welfare Rights,' *Maryland Law Review* 44, no. 1 (1985): 16.

10 Linda Gordon, 'The New Feminist Scholarship on the Welfare State,' in Linda Gordon, ed., *Women, the State and Welfare* (Madison: University of Wisconsin Press, 1990), 30.

11 Thelma McCormack, *Politics and the Hidden Injuries of Gender: Feminism and the Making of the Welfare State* (Toronto: CRIAW, paper no. 28 1991), 11–12.

12 Veronica Strong-Boag, '"Wages for Housework": Mothers' Allowances and the Beginnings of Social Security in Canada,' *Journal of Canadian Studies* 14, 1 (1979): 24.

13 Gwendolyn Mink, 'The Lady and the Tramp: Gender, Race and the Origins of the American Welfare State' in Gordon, ed., *Women, the State and Welfare*; Little, '*No Car.*'

14 Nova Scotia Minister of Public Works and Mines, *Eighth Annual Report of the Director Administering the Mothers' Allowance Act for the Year Ending November 30, 1937* (Halifax: King's Printer, 1938), 3.

15 Nova Scotia Minister of Public Works and Mines, *First Annual Report of the Director Administering the Mothers' Allowance Act* (Halifax: King's Printer, 1931), 13–14.

16 Nova Scotia Minister of Public Works and Mines, *Seventh Annual Report of the Director Administering the Mothers' Allowance Act for the Year Ending November 30, 1936* (Halifax: King's Printer, 1937), 9.

17 Little, 'No Car.'
18 For the situation in Halifax, which acts as a good introduction to the 1930s, see Suzanne Morton, *Ideal Surroundings: Domestic Life in a Working Class Suburb in the 1920s* (Toronto: University of Toronto Press, 1995).
19 Little, 'No Car'; Mink, 'Welfare Reform'; Gordon, *Pitied but Not Entitled.*
20 Little, 'No Car'; Mink, 'Welfare Reform.'
21 Most laws give authority to the minister or the governor-in-council (the cabinet) to make regulations pursuant to the act. In the case of the Family Benefits Act, most of the rules that affected people's daily lives were in the regulations. The act had under thirty sections, in contrast to others that have over one hundred. This gives more power to departmental officials and takes away an important democratic process from people in poverty.
22 Rodney Haddow, *Poverty Reform in Canada, 1958–1979: State and Class Influences in Policy Making* (Montreal: McGill-Queen's University Press, 1993).
23 While the Unemployment Assistance Act committed federal dollars to cost-sharing with the provinces for a wide range of 'unemployables,' it is not clear whether this included single mothers. Dennis Guest in *The Emergence of Social Security in Canada*, 2nd ed. (Vancouver: University of British Columbia Press, 1985) implies that it did. Christopher Leman in *The Collapse of Welfare Reform: Political Institutions, Policy and the Poor in Canada and the United States* (Cambridge: MIT Press, 1980) disagrees: he says aid to mother-led families was still not cost shared. Given that 1956 marks the first Nova Scotia legislation requiring the province, as opposed to municipalities, to provide social assistance for specific categories of single mothers, it seems that the Unemployment Assistance Act, whether it actually provided cost sharing for them, did create an incentive to extend benefits to them. See also Janet Guildford, 'The End of the Poor Law: Public Welfare Reform in Nova Scotia before the Canada Assistance Plan' in this volume.
24 Margaret Conrad, 'The 1950s: The Decade of Development,' in E.R. Forbes and D.A. Muise, eds., *The Atlantic Provinces in Confederation* (Toronto: University of Toronto Press, 1993), 382.
25 Ibid., 393.
26 James Struthers, 'Shadows from the Thirties: The Federal Government and Unemployment Assistance, 1941–1956' in Jacqueline Ismael, ed., *The Canadian Welfare State Evolution and Transition* (Edmonton: University of Alberta Press, 1987), 19.
27 *Debates of the Nova Scotia House of Assembly* (1956), 1: 223. Emphasis added.
28 Ibid., 1: 61. Emphasis added.
29 Ibid.
30 Disabled individuals eighteen years or over were added in 1961. Jeanne

Fay, 'From Welfare Bum to Single Mum: The Political Construction of Women on Social Assistance in Nova Scotia' (MSW thesis, Dalhousie University, 1997), Appendix B.
31 Conrad, 'The 1950s,' 389.
32 *Debates of the Nova Scotia House of Assembly* (1958), 5: 2360.
33 Ibid., 5: 2260.
34 Mary Jane Mossman and Morag MacLean, 'Family Law and Social Welfare: Toward a New Equality,' *Canadian Journal of Family Law* 5, no. 1 (1986): 46.
35 Ibid., 44.
36 Leonard Shifrin, 'Income Security: The Rise and Stall of the Federal Role,' in Jacqueline S. Ismael, ed., *Canadian Welfare Policy* (Kingston and Montreal: McGill-Queen's University Press, 1985), 26.
37 Besides CAP, Parliament adopted the Canada Pension Plan (1966), Guaranteed Income Supplement (1967), and Medical Care Act (1968), and made significant improvements to the Unemployment Insurance Act (1971). Rodney Haddow, *Poverty Reform in Canada*, 84.
38 Struthers, 'Shadows from the Thirties'; Shifrin, 'Income Security'; and Derek P.J. Hum, *Federalism and the Poor: A Review of the Canada Assistance Plan* (Toronto: Ontario Economic Council, 1983).
39 Hum, *Federalism and the Poor*, 4.
40 Guest, *The Emergence of Social Security*, 156.
41 Leman, *The Collapse of Welfare Reform*, 37.
42 Ibid.
43 *Debates of the Nova Scotia House of Assembly* (1966), 1: 98–103.
44 *Welfare Services in Nova Scotia 1967* and *1968* (Halifax: Department of Public Welfare).
45 Sheila Urquhart, 'Only Small Amount Spent on Drink, Betting,' *Halifax Mail-Star*, 28 June 1966, 39.
46 James Harding, 'Minister Explains Changes in Welfare Act,' *Halifax Mail-Star*, 23 July 1966, 8.
47 Published as a newsletter for staff of the Department of Public Welfare beginning in July 1950 as *Child Welfare News*, it became the *Welfare News* in the spring of 1951 and the *Social Services News* twenty-two years later in the spring of 1973.
48 *Welfare News* 18, 1 (1967).
49 Ibid., 41.
50 *Welfare News* 19, 1 (1968): 5–8.
51 *Welfare News* 19, 6 (1969): 3.
52 *Welfare News* 18, 1 (1967): 22–4.
53 Africville was an African–Nova Scotian settlement at the northernmost end

of the Halifax peninsula. Rather than provide services and financial assistance to the residents to upgrade the community, the City of Halifax forced the residents to move and razed their houses in the late 1960s, in the name of urban renewal. The controversy surrounding the destruction of Africville as politically and financially motivated by the value of the land as a container pier, and the determination of the residents and their descendants to remember the community and not let 'another Africville' happen, live on in Nova Scotia.

54 *Welfare News* 19, 3 (1968): 42.
55 *Welfare News* 19, 5 (1969): 56–8.
56 Joan Jones, interviews by the author, 20 January and 9 February 1994, Halifax, Nova Scotia. A transcript of the tape recording is in the collection of the author, Mahone Bay, Nova Scotia.
57 Ibid.
58 'No Plans to Disrupt Conference – Jones,' *Halifax Chronicle-Herald*, 6 Dec. 1968, 2.
59 Joan Jones interview.
60 Sheila Urquhart and Jim Robson, 'Never Before – Wedderburn,' *Halifax Chronicle-Herald*, 9 Dec. 1968, 14.
61 Burnley Jones, Notes to the author, June 1997, Halifax; interview with Joan Jones.
62 Interview with Joan Jones.
63 *Halifax Neighbourhood Centre: Executive Director's Summary Report, August 15, 1970* (Halifax), 2, collection of the author.
64 Halifax Welfare Council, *Neighbourhood Centre Proposal* (Halifax, 1965), 13, collection of the author.
65 *Halifax Neighbourhood Centre: Executive Director's Summary Report*, 5 and 15.
66 Michael Barkley, interview by the author, 26 July 1995, Halifax. A transcript of the tape recording is in the collection of the author.
67 Ibid.
68 In April 1970 parents in the community began meeting about the desperate condition of the St Patrick's School building. Evidently, the need to replace it had been recognized for years. The residents were promised a new building two years earlier, but nothing had been done. The mobilization began with small kitchen-meetings, a meeting of 150 people in St Patrick's Church to explain the history and background of the broken promises, a larger meeting at the North Branch Public Library attended by local and provincial politicians, and several meetings between a committee of twenty residents and government officials. A call for tenders on the construction of the new building went out on 10 July 1970: reported in *Halifax Neighbourhood*

Centre: Executive Director's Summary Report; 'New School?!' *Speak Out!* 1, 1
(1970): 1 and 'It's Coming Down At Last!' *Speak Out!* 1, 3 (1970): 2, collection of the author. Jacqueline Barkley and her husband, Michael, were
white community organizers from the United States hired by the Neighbourhood Centre board to implement the community development
approach to poverty.

69 The women are identified as Mrs Clyde Mannett and Mrs Carmen
    Johnstone in 'New School?!' 1.
70 Jacqueline Barkley, interview by the author, 23 June 1995, Halifax. A tran-
    script of the tape recording is in the collection of the author.
71 *Neighbourhood Centre: Executive Director's Summary Report*, 14.
72 Steve Kimber, 'Living with Big Brother: Tenants Rights Denied by Housing
    Authority,' *The 4th Estate* (Halifax), 18 July 1970, 15.
73 *Neighbourhood Centre: Executive Director's Summary Report*, 13.
74 'Welfare Rights Committee Starts,' *Speak Out!* 1, 4 (1970): 1 and 3, collection
    of the author.
75 'Letter to the Editor,' *Speak Out!* 1, 5 (1970): 5, collection of the author.
76 Pauline Janitch, 'People on Welfare Want a Better Deal: The Poor Are Just
    Starting to Fight; Must Defeat the Fallacy That They're Lazy,' *The 4th Estate*,
    22 Oct. 1970, 10.
77 Ibid.
78 'Welfare Rights Committee Starts.'
79 'He Better Give Him Some Welfare,' *Speak Out!* 1, 8(1971): 3, collection of
    the author.
80 'Yarmouth Group Seeks Social Justice,' *The 4th Estate*, 17 Sept. 1970, 22.
81 Agatha Patterson, outreach worker with the Halifax Neighbourhood Cen-
    tre, and president of Welfare Rights, practical nurse and indigenous Afri-
    can Nova Scotian, interviews by the author, 24 May, 30 May, and 3 August
    1995, Halifax. Transcript of notes are in the collection of the author.
82 Ibid.
83 The Co-operative Commonwealth Federation (which became the NDP in
    1961) was represented in the Nova Scotia Legislative Assembly by at least
    one member between 1939 and 1963. At one point in the 1940s the CCF had
    three sitting members: all MacDonalds, all coal miners and union activists
    from Cape Breton.
84 These 'warlords' were municipal welfare officers, particularly in Cape Bre-
    ton, who had earned MacEwan's displeasure for the manner in which they
    were treating his constituents. *Debates and Proceedings of the Nova Scotia
    House of Assembly* (1970–1) 1: 778–9.
85 *Debates and Proceedings of the Nova Scotia House of Assembly* (1974), 1: 485.

86 Dionne Brand, 'We Weren't Allowed to Go into Factory Work until Hitler Started the War: The 1920s to the 1940s,' in Peggy Bristow et al., eds., *'We're Rooted Here and They Can't Pull Us Up': Essays in African Canadian Women's History* (Toronto: University of Toronto Press, 1994), 190.
87 Nova Scotia Department of Social Services, *Social Services News* 23, 2 (1973): 12.
88 *Welfare News* 20, 2 (1970): 41.
89 *Welfare News* 22, 1 (1972): 45.
90 *Welfare News* 22, 2 (1972): 43.
91 *Social Service News* 23, 1 (1973): 32.
92 Susan MacDonnell, *Vulnerable Mothers, Vulnerable Children: A Follow-up Study of Unmarried Mothers Who Kept Their Children* (Halifax: Policy, Planning and Research Division, Nova Scotia Department of Social Services, 1981).
93 Ibid.
94 Ibid.
95 *Social Service News* 24, 1 (1974): 15; 24, 2 (1974): 21–4.
96 *Social Service News* 24, 2 (1974): 36–7.
97 *Social Service News* 25, 3 (1975): 51.
98 *Social Service News* 25, 1 (1975): 33.
99 'Groups Will Study Status of Women Report,' *The 4th Estate*, 21 June 1971, 2. Emphasis added.
100 Susan Perly, 'Bureau Has 4 Major Projects: Helping Women Achieve Equal Rights in Nova Scotia,' *The 4th Estate*, 22 July 1971, 3.
101 National Archives of Canada, RG 127, Pt 1, file 2101-C-45, Urban Affairs, 'Single Mothers' by Anne Chaldecott.
102 Pauline Janitch, 'Labour Dept., Unions Rapped: Waitresses "Wage Slaves Without Any Protection,"' *The 4th Estate*, 9 Sept. 1971, 15.
103 Rickie Solinger, *Wake Up Little Suzie: Single Pregnancy and Race before Roe v. Wade* (New York: Routledge, 1992).
104 Interview with Agatha Patterson.
105 Ibid.
106 Perly, 'Bureau Has 4 Major Projects.'
107 According to a study done in Canada in the 1970s, the membership of One Parent Associations was a ratio of three women to two men. The male membership level was significantly higher than in any other single-parent group. Benjamin Schlesinger, *Poverty in Canada and the United States: Overview and Annotated Bibliography* (Toronto: University of Toronto Press, 1979), 103.
108 Perly, 'Bureau Has 4 Major Projects.'

109 Nova Scotia Task Force on the Status of Women, *Herself/Elle-Meme* (Halifax: Nova Scotia Department of Social Services, 1976), 7.
110 Ibid., 41.
111 Ibid., 58.
112 Interview with Agatha Patterson.
113 Public Archives of Nova Scotia, Nova Scotia Task Force on the Status of Women, vol. 117 no. 2, Brief 2.
114 Regulatory changes ended family benefits entitlement for new applicants in May 2000. Those single parents and persons with disabilities already on family benefits remained entitled until August 2001, when the Family Benefits Act was repealed by the Employment Support and Income Assistance Act, implemented late in 2001.
115 *Debates and Proceedings of the Nova Scotia House of Assembly* (1977), 2: 1284–1322.
116 Ibid., 2: 1309, 1286.
117 Ibid., 2: 131, 1239, 1296, 1309, 1296, 1294.
118 Ibid., 2: 1298, 1284, 1288.
119 Ibid., 2: 1285, 1286.
120 Ibid.
121 Ibid., 2: 1321.
122 Ibid., 2: 1280.
123 Brenda Thompson (see the Introduction pp. 6–7), for example, in *The Single Mothers' Survival Guide* (Halifax: Dal-PIRG [Dalhousie Public Interest Research Group], 1991), suggests that the 'man-in-the-house' provisions cast as prostitutes those women on social assistance who are having sex with a man, since the rule assumes that if a woman is having sex with a man, then he must be supporting her financially.
124 *Debates and Proceedings of the Nova Scotia House of Assembly* (1974), 1: 119.

From Infant Homes to Daycare: Child Care in Halifax

SUZANNE MORTON

The 2000 Nova Scotia budget dealt severe reductions to many areas of social spending, including education, hospitals, and social assistance. In the midst of $192 million worth of cuts, one of the few areas where spending actually increased was daycare, with the addition of one hundred new subsidized spaces created to help parents – read mothers – 'get back to work.'[1] In a time of restraint and cutback, the government's decision to support daycare is in keeping with its objectives of the last thirty years and conforms to a longer tradition of institutional support to keep women and their children off public relief. Since the involvement of the Nova Scotia government in the field of public daycare in the 1960s, government has almost universally regarded it as a welfare service rather than an educational or labour program. In fact, there were significant ideological and institutional links between Halifax daycare centres of the 1970s and older philanthropic, religious, and charitable institutions. Nineteenth-century child-care institutions, such as St Joseph's Orphanage, the Home of the Guardian Angel, the Halifax Infants' Home, and the Protestant Orphans' Home – and, after 1910, the Jost Mission – regarded at least part of their service mandate as child care to free mothers to work. Infant homes and orphanages, like the later public daycare centres, were used by a minority of women who did not use or have access to family or community support for their child-care needs. When St Joseph's Orphanage closed in the 1960s, it transformed itself into the St Joseph's Children's Centre, a daycare facility. This was an option also explored by the Halifax Infants' Home before it shut its doors in 1960 and by the Protestant Orphans' Home in 1970. Space sharing with a daycare delayed the closure of the Salvation Army's Bethany Home for Girls in the 1990s. The Jost Mission Daycare has a direct institutional line to the present.[2]

Child-care institutions, whether orphanages, infant homes, or day-care centres, have served similar client groups and have shared common sources of financial support, although their similarities should not be exaggerated. While their objectives have been remarkably alike, the role of women clients in the older philanthropic child-care institutions and modern daycare centres was completely different. Unlike the almost invisible and silent women who used the services of infant homes and orphanages to care for their children before 1950, by the 1970s visible and vocal lobby groups composed of an alliance of clients, middle-class feminist activists, and professional child-care workers organized to exert pressure on facilities, politicians, and bureaucrats. While these activists used a language of entitlement, the one persuasive argument politicians and provincial bureaucrats always heard and often responded to was that government-supported daycare had the potential to reduce spending on social assistance, as it permitted mothers to accept paid work and therefore stabilized family income.

The argument presented here is not about a direct devolution from children's homes to public daycare. Only the case of St Joseph's would support such a claim. Rather, the point is that the public daycare system that emerged in the late 1960s and early 1970s was descended from a long 'charitable tradition.' This legacy is not unique to Nova Scotia. In the postwar period, everywhere in Canada daycare was more likely to be seen as part of a charitable or welfare tradition rather than as a provision that assisted mothers with their reproductive duties and permitted them equal access to paid labour. Scholars have noted this disjuncture. In her 2001 book on the federal government's approach to female labour, Annis May Timpson identifies a policy direction that did not connect employment programs and child care.[3]

Various historians have examined daycare over the last twenty years from a variety of perspectives. Some studies, such as those by Alvin Finkel and Rianne Mahon, have taken a national or federal perspective to explore the place of child care in debates about the welfare state. In doing so they have alerted us to the importance of feminism and the labour movement to the evolution of policy.[4] Christina Simmons has done a similar service for an earlier period by focusing on the Jost Mission in Halifax.[5] Like Simmons, Wendy Atkin focused on a particular facility, the University of Toronto Campus and Community Cooperative Day Care Centre, to explore the themes specific to a time and place.[6] Donna Varga approached the issue more from an interest in a historical understanding of child development.[7] Not surprisingly, these different approaches have highlighted different aspects of the subject. For example, Mahon's national approach obscures provincial and local motivations for daycare. She argues that while Canadian bureaucrats in the 1960s were influenced by American policy developments, 'the issue of getting mothers off social assistance and into the labour market did not share the same urgency' in Canada as in the United States.[8] While it may generally have been the case for federal policy advisors, this conclusion did not necessarily reflect the interests of provincial bureaucrats, who were faced with rising costs for social assistance even when federal money was available. This study of daycare in twentieth-century Halifax highlights the interest of provincial bureaucrats and lobbyists in the development of a publicly supported system. It builds on and agrees with the work of Sue Wolstenholme, who argues in her study of Nova Scotia daycare that both the provincial and federal governments conceptualized government supported daycare as serving a welfare need.[9]

During the Second World War, in contrast to Toronto or Montreal, Halifax missed out on government support for daycare. Indeed, given the massive impact of the war on the city, Ottawa officials were surprised at local claims of lack of demand. In response to a query from Ottawa, Ernest H. Blois, the Nova Scotia director of child welfare, dismissed any need for a state-supported child-care program. He expressed his belief that such a program would only cater to those women who 'because of the dullness and wearisome features of home-life would be glad to escape even to go out to work in a factory for a short time, but I do not believe that should be encouraged by making it easier.' Blois felt that state-supported daycare would disturb 'the most vital part of our national existence, namely, the individual family.'[10] The secretary of the Halifax Welfare Council, Gwendolyn Shand, also refuted the need for public wartime daycares in Halifax because the booming economy had brought an end to depression-era male unemployment, and thus fewer married women were now seeking either paid work or child care.[11]

Neither Blois nor Shand considered women without male breadwinners as being among those who might need child care, nor did they acknowledge existing facilities. During the war, a chapter of the Imperial Order Daughters of the Empire (IODE) operated a nursery school program two mornings a week out of the North End City Mission with the purpose of promoting health and enriching child development.[12]

Children were taught to sing and to play with clay and were plied with cod liver oil, tomato juice, and a hot lunch. A local social worker observed that the children who attended had to be 'taught to eat vegetables' and that before the program they knew no 'stories, hymns or nursery rhymes.'[13] Another child-care facility in Halifax, the Jost Mission Nursery, was less interested in child development. It was organized specifically to provide care for 'otherwise destitute mothers' combining child care with a domestic employment agency so that these mothers could earn a living for themselves and their children.[14] By the 1940s, the clients were not only involved in domestic service by the day but were employed also in clerical, retail, and service occupations, although the nursery's hours of operation – Monday to Friday 7:30 a.m. to 4:30 p.m. – continued to reflect its day's work origins.[15]

During the war the local Women's Voluntary Service (WVS) explored the possibility of opening a day nursery for the children of war workers, despite the dissuasions of the Jost Mission, which did not think it was necessary.[16] Significantly, the impetus here was not women workers requesting help. Rather the WVS was acting on what it described as the 'complaints being voiced' that women were volunteering for war work and leaving their children without 'proper care and supervision.' While the WVS provided training for volunteers who augmented the staff at the Jost Mission, it does not seem to have been successful at launching its own nursery school at the Protestant orphanage.[17]

In the first ten years that followed the war there was no public discussion of daycare, although a survey of classified advertisements in the local *Chronicle-Herald* suggests an increasing number of women looking for child care and offering to 'mind' children in their homes. This public silence was broken in the mid-1950s; thereafter local and national welfare experts periodically identified the need for daycare in Halifax. In 1955 daycare emerged as an issue for the welfare community after officials from the federal Department of Health and Welfare contacted Gwendolyn Shand of the Halifax Welfare Council concerning the lack of child-care facilities in the city. The department reported that in the previous two months, there had been ten or twelve cases where a mother could not find care for her child while she was at work. In addition to noting the existence of these working mothers without access to assistance, the department also expressed a belief that there was a need for child care among women whose husbands were alcoholic and out of work. It was thought that these women would seek temporary work if they could find child care. The department's interest in this issue was clear in this inquiry's concluding line: 'many women would seek temporary employment if they had a place to leave their children and they would not need to come to our office for relief.'[18]

In response to the department's concerns, Shand contacted other Halifax welfare agencies to solicit their views. The superintendent of the Dalhousie Public Health Clinic expressed the opinion that the lack of child-care facilities meant that 'women and children are lacking medical care because there is no one to look after the family while the mother is attending clinic herself, or bringing a child to the clinic.'[19] The director of Home Services for the Red Cross replied that it received about ten calls a month from women looking for child-care placements and that the number of advertisements in local papers for 'help wanted' in 'minding' children was increasing. This agency suggested that the need was seasonal, with a particular demand around Christmas, when mothers took advantage of employment opportunities, not 'to buy luxuries but just to ease the burden of household finances.'[20] Although the Red Cross homemaker program may have taken the need for mothers' employment seriously, Judith Fingard has noted that this agency was very conservative in its expectation that working husbands should support their wives and that mothers' allowance should support those without a male breadwinner.[21] While the Halifax Welfare Bureau claimed it had 'not noticed any particular increases in working mothers,' the proprietress of the city's only private babysitting agency acknowledged a need for additional day nurseries in the city.[22] In response to these concerns, the Child Welfare Committee of the Halifax Welfare Council organized a meeting on daycare in November 1955, but no specific action was taken and the issue disappeared from its agenda for another two years.[23]

In 1957 Gwendolyn Shand replied to another external inquiry about daycare in Halifax, this time from the federal Women's Bureau. Shand explained the lack of day nurseries in Nova Scotia as a reflection of the local economic structure, which saw relatively few women in 'industrial employment.' As a result, Nova Scotia had fewer 'working mothers' than other places, and Shand saw no evidence that child-care needs were not being met. Women's 'industrial employment' was no doubt a red herring here, as Halifax women in the paid workforce, like women elsewhere in Canada, were more likely to be found in service and clerical areas such as typing, cleaning, teaching, and selling. However, Shand's impression of the labour patterns of married women, or at least women who had been married at some point, was in keeping with the 1961 census. It indicates that 44.02 per cent of the female workforce resident in the City of Halifax fell into the categories of married, widowed, and divorced, compared to the national urban average of 56.43 per cent. Of Canadian cities, only the other older ones – Quebec City, Montreal, and St John's – had fewer married or once-married women employed outside the home. But the percentage of 64.4 for the new City of Dartmouth, where many Halifax workers lived, was in line with Calgary, Hamilton, Kitchener, and London, which had the highest participation rates in Canada.[24]

Shand may have been correct that daycare needs in peninsular Halifax were being met by several small private agencies. Most Halifax mothers seemed to have made personal arrangements with relatives or friends. Research undertaken by students enrolled at the Maritime School of Social Work in 1956 as part of the federal Department of Labour's study on married women in paid labour confirmed that family, especially grandmothers, played a crucial role in providing child care for preschool children. The Halifax women surveyed by the students, like women in other Canadian cities, regarded day nurseries as useful to working mothers but dismissed any personal need for such a service.[25] This prejudice against daycare for their own children may have indicated concern about the cost of the service or reflected the welfare stigma associated with institutional preschool daycare. While private arrangements served the majority, others argued that the unmarried mother was 'handicapped' by the lack of public facilities.[26]

A similar ambivalence characterized the Women's Bureau in Ottawa. Rianne Mahon has noted that while Marion Royce, the director of the Women's Bureau, recognized the need for childcare, she was not at all certain that daycare lay within the jurisdiction of the bureau, linking the issue to family and social services rather than to women and work. Indeed, in the early 1960s, the Women's Bureau discreetly lobbied the Family and Child Welfare Division of the federal Department of Health and Welfare to explore the need for daycare. By transferring responsibility to welfare, the bureau avoided defining child care as a labour issue.[27]

In Halifax, local welfare officials had already been considering the issue of child care. The 1958 Halifax survey on child welfare commissioned by the provincial Department of Welfare pointed to the need to expand daycare services. Yet the Halifax Welfare Council again failed to press the issue.[28] In November 1959, the council reported 'rumours' that women were unable to find places to care for their children and expressed concern that neither the board nor superintendent at the Jost Mission felt that its crèche was 'part of the community "welfare" picture.'[29] At this point, the Jost Mission was the only day nursery in Halifax, serving about thirty children. Children using the services of this facility had to be two years of age, toilet-trained, and 'clean.'[30]

Despite regular calls for action, no new not-for-profit daycare programs were established in Halifax until the 1960s. The first new ones were influenced by the 'war on poverty' ideals rather than the need to provide child care for women who wanted paid work. In 1964 the Halifax Junior League, a woman's volunteer service organization described more fully by Judith Firgard in the chapter on women's organizations, began a daycare program in conjunction with the Neighbourhood Centre Project.[31] The program was originally offered only part-time and, like the Second World War–era IODE project, it was aimed at socially and educationally enriching the lives of underprivileged children. By 1966 this program had developed into a full daycare program and moved to the YWCA on Barrington Street. Their direct involvement in daycare meant that members of the Junior League were among those most critical of the lack of regulatory legislation and the poor quality of informal private care.[32] A member of the Junior League was appointed to the first Minister's Advisory Committee on Day Care Services in 1966, along with provincial bureaucrats and representatives from Catholic Social Services and the Halifax Welfare Council.

Meanwhile, 1964 saw the initiation of another type of 'head-start' program consciously modelled on American racial integrationist programs and aimed at educationally enriching preschool children so that they could adjust and meet social norms once they began school. A preschool program designed to promote racial tolerance, organized out of the Cornwallis Street Baptist Church and the Brunswick Street United Church and funded as a research site through a private foundation, was among the first day nurseries to receive provincial funding from the Department of Public Welfare.[33] Describing such projects as 'interracial programs especially for Negroes,' and praising their 'human rights' benefits, Deputy Minister of Public Welfare Fred MacKinnon approved lump sum grants to other head-start projects conducted through daycare programs across the province.[34] Even though the objective of head-start programs was educational, the fact that these programs were being funded by the Department of Public Welfare and targeted specific disadvantaged groups placed them within the welfare network. In addition to their integrationist agenda, head-start programs were established in the belief that some mothers lacked maternal skills, and this patronizing attitude continued to shape daycare policy in Nova Scotia.

By the 1960s the number of young children needing care during the day was increasing beyond the population served by charity or head-start programs. D.H. Johnson, provincial director of child welfare, acknowledged that there were a 'fairly large number of daycare facilities in operation' and 'a good many private individuals' took children by the day into their home.[35] By the fall of 1969, in addition to ten publicly supported head-start enrichment programs for underprivileged children, there were nine daycare centres in Halifax, two in Dartmouth, and five in Halifax County, serving a total of 474 children, along with thirty-six private nursery schools.[36]

The initial provincial financial contribution to daycare followed the establishment in 1966 of the Minister's Advisory Committee on Day Care Services. The composition of this appointed committee – bureaucrats; welfare professionals, both religious and secular; and members of middle-class women's service organizations – reflected its welfare impetus and orientation.[37] The mandate of the advisory committee was to survey existing facilities, especially in the Halifax area, as they related to local needs. In addition, it was to examine the financing of existing programs to determine how they provided 'for the children of needy families' and to investigate how the Canada Assistance Plan (CAP) funding might play a role. The final task was to prepare recommendations concerning the role of the Child Welfare Division of the provincial Department of Public Welfare in program direction and finances.[38] Three of the four responsibilities of the division were directly connected to provincial welfare policies and welfare expenditures. The committee oversaw the introduction of the 1967 Nova Scotia Day Nurseries Act, a rushed piece of legislation based on that of Ontario. It was almost immediately subject to criticism. Even Fred MacKinnon admitted that there was 'basis for criticism,' as Nova Scotia bureaucrats had no experience in the area and depended heavily on Ontario's twenty-year record in this field.[39]

Significantly, like the Mothers' Allowance Act, the Nova Scotia Day Nurseries Act required that each daycare supervisor be, in that familiar welfare phrase, a 'fit and proper' person. As scholars such as Margaret Little have reminded us, welfare not only has economic implications but also carries with it concern for moral regulation.[40] Among the critics of the welfare orientation of the committee and the act was the second-year class at the Maritime School of Social Work. In a statement presented to the committee by student Alexa McDonough (later the leader of both the provincial and federal New Demoncrats), the students noted that the committee was focused on the need for daycare only among the children of poor working mothers.[41] The social work students unsuccessfully attempted to cast daycare in a broader context that might include child development, early education, or respite care for full-time homemakers.

The linkage between daycare and welfare increased after 1967, when the possibilities for provincial funding of daycare increased as federal funds became available under the CAP. This program provided for federal cost-sharing with the provinces and municipalities through financial assistance to all persons in need or who were likely to find themselves in need.[42] The potential to employ CAP funds in such a manner placed daycare programs firmly within a provincial welfare context. It is interesting to note that although the *Report of the Royal Commission on the Status of Women* of 1970 heightened public awareness of daycare, and other feminists unsuccessfully tried to unhook the public and bureaucratic association between daycare and welfare, this link remained intact.[43]

The problem in part was that the welfare arguments were very effective in increasing the amount of government funds available for child care. The Rev. Colin Campbell, executive director of Catholic Social Services in Halifax, pointed out that without government funding for the experimental St Joseph's Day Care Centre, its clients would need social assistance. St Joseph's Day Care was opened in March 1968 on the understanding that the City of Halifax would assist in financing and subsidizing children whose families were on municipal assistance.[44] In 1969 Campbell noted that the typical client of the centre was a deserted mother with two children, earning $60 a week as a bank teller. In a request for increased levels of subsidization, Campbell argued to the deputy minister of welfare that 'obviously the solution is much better for all than having the mother in receipt of public assistance. This mother presently is able to pay but a small fraction of the true cost of care.'[45] Similarly, politicians exploring the public acceptance of tax dollars going to daycare stressed that it 'would enable many mothers, widows, deserted wives to obtain a job.'[46] Although the rhetoric seemed to stress economic considerations, the moral value of mothers working to support their children is implicit in their attitudes.

The effectiveness of emphasizing this type of clientele was also obvious to daycare activists. In 1970, before permanent provincial funds were made available, St Joseph's Day Care Centre issued a public statement noting that many of its clients were 'heads of fatherless homes' or working because the husband was either unemployed or earning too little to 'meet essential family needs.' The statement concluded that 'even with both parents at work, many families still experience poverty.' Although the facility was receiving some money from the Halifax Welfare Department through subsidies for individual families, the centre complained that it was being shunted between the municipal and provincial governments in its request for further funding. Meanwhile, its finances were in crisis, as grants from the Catholic Church were being withdrawn and the majority of the families using the daycare could not meet the full cost of $5.50 per child per day. In a public brief, the centre argued that without its services, working mothers would stay at home and go on welfare or, if they chose to remain in the paid workforce, they would have to leave the children unsupervised or place them in foster homes. The implicit argument behind this explanation was that the provincial and municipal governments would end up spending money on these families, whereas there was federal money available to support daycare through the CAP program. The frustration of St Joseph's board was clear in its conclusion that 'everyone feels deeply for the courageous working mother struggling to keep off welfare and pay her own way, but government agencies will not help here – and this in spite of the fact that the federal Government will match any funds expended for such a person for Day Care service for her children.'[47] The city's largest daycare facility placed its argument for government funding completely within the context of welfare.

When the Halifax Protestant Orphans' Home considered its future, it also explored the possibility of entering the daycare field. In 1969, in an ultimately unsuccessful overture to the Halifax Social Planning Office, its board proposed transforming the orphanage into a daycare centre, presenting a welfare-based case. The argument held that one-parent families with preschool children were barred from the labour force because of child-care concerns. The proposal also identified a need for daycare among two-parent families 'undergoing severe financial difficulty,' to enable the mother to take paid employment.[48] Once again, there is no mention of child development, early childhood education, or creating options for individual women who might wish to be free of primary child-care responsibility.

Even the provincial legislation reflected this welfare orientation. In the 1970 provincial election campaign, one of the Liberal Party's planks was support for daycare. When Premier Gerald Regan introduced the Day Care Services Act in 1971, which permitted the first cost-sharing subsidization of non-profit daycare spaces, he emphasized that the primary objective for the government program was assisting 'poor and low income families in respect to employment opportunities and thus adding to family income where such is most needed.' A secondary object was to enrich the social development of underprivileged children and to contribute to the well-being of large families.[49] These priorities were echoed in the House in February 1971, when A.E. Sullivan, minister of public welfare, introduced the legislation. According to the minister, the primary objective of the bill was to assist families where the mother was the sole wage earner or, secondarily, where the mother's income was needed to supplement a 'marginal income of the father or to meet unusual financial burdens.'[50]

The tension that the emphasis on the welfare aspects of daycare created was identified by a 1972 national study conducted by the Canadian Council on Social Development. This report defined the origins of daycare as 'custodial service for children of families suffering from economic deprivation or some form of social maladjustment' but attempted to present a 'modern view,' which addressed the 'education and development of all children.'[51] Provincial bureaucrats did not accept that daycare had an educative and developmental value for all children, and the fact that daycare was under the purview of the Department of Public Welfare rather than Education is significant.

Given the provincial government's welfare orientation towards child care, it was preoccupied with evaluating who was using daycare. There was, no doubt, considerable disapproval about the results of a 1969 study that suggested the majority of women using facilities were married women bringing in a second income. When the daycare debate resurfaced in 1972, after federal funding to daycare centres through the Local Initiative Program (LIP) of Canada Manpower and Immigration ended, it was again conducted in terms of the value of the social investment of providing enrichment for at-risk children. Once again, however, the campaign demonstrated the economic importance of daycare services, especially for single mothers. The impact of closing the four LIP daycare projects was measured in terms of the number of single-parent families using its facilities (38 per cent). It was noted that twenty-one mothers had become employed since their children were enrolled in the day care, and that four mothers had gone off social assistance.[52] Similarly, attention was paid to the increased proportion of single mothers using public daycare services in the Halifax/ Dartmouth area, which had grown so that by 1973 women headed 141 of the 233 families with children in daycare. By April 1975, 254 of the 353 children (72 per cent) receiving a complete subsidy for daycare in Halifax-Dartmouth came from families headed by women.[53]

After the 1972 legislation, the bureaucrats in the Department of Public Welfare painted themselves as at the forefront of child-care policy in Canada. A federal civil servant with the Department of National Health and Welfare complimented the deputy minister on 'developing one of the most desirable comprehensive programs' in the country. MacKinnon reported that 'whether it is for "off or on the record" we drew from her that we in Nova Scotia stand out front in day care.' The explanation behind this brief period of bravado seems to have been the willingness of Nova Scotia, in May 1972, to assume the costs not covered by CAP of daycare facilities that had been established under the federal LIP.[54]

By 1974 it was clear that expenditures were growing at a much faster rate than had been anticipated. Lobby groups and daycare activists put pressure on the government for even more funds. In 1970–1 the government spent no money in this area; by 1973–4 the costs had risen to $561,350 and there was no end in sight with regard to further demands.[55] Daycare support emerged as a campaign issue in the 1974 provincial election, with the Liberals promising a new maximum subsidization rate of $6 a day, subject to cost-of-living increases. But along with the new rate came new guidelines that, according to a reporter at The 4th Estate, took 'day care out of the field of education and places it in the field of social welfare.'[56] Activists complained about the 'welfare interpretation' of daycare, which meant that every parent who applied for a subsidy had to be screened by a provincial social assistance worker. Critics argued that this process implied mistrust of both the daycare centre's ability to obtain accurate financial information and the parents' honesty in divulging this information. Time and money were being spent on administrative apparatus instead of on daycare centres. A similar complaint was launched by Brian Flemming, president of the St Joseph's Children's Centre's board. Flemming, who had impeccable Liberal connections, felt that the department's questioning of parents was invasive and 'demeaning.' The response of the activists and Flemming is a good example of how standard welfare practice was not seen to be appropriate for all citizens, especially by middle-class clients. The Citizens' Day Care Action Committee, founded in 1971, concluded that such procedures fostered a 'welfare attitude toward daycare which stigmatizes those who use the service and discourages others who would benefit from it.'[57] Parents for Better Day Care, a group formed to fight new guidelines that 'harassed' low-income families when they applied for daycare subsidization, joined with the older committee to agitate for change.[58]

Underpaid daycare workers at St Joseph's Children's Centre added their voices to the campaign for more resources for daycare. They formed the first daycare workers' union in Atlantic Canada, the Canadian Union of Public Employees (CUPE) Local 1747, during the summer of 1974.[59] On 3 December, the Coalition for Better Day Care, a new organization that resulted from the amalgamation of five daycare groups, sponsored a large public meeting that was boycotted by elected officials and senior provincial bureaucrats. The administrator of the provincial Welfare Department's Child and Family Welfare Division attended and reported back to MacKinnon that the coalition was a 'small group of astute and experienced political agitators.' The civil servant claimed that complaints were not coming from parents. Rather, it was 'a hard core of malcontents, agitators, professionals, aided by CUPE who are moving in to organize the personnel at daycare centres.' The leadership was largely 'professional social workers and sociologists,' 'professional LIP and OFY [Opportunities for Youth] types,' 'professional political agitators who are anti-government and anti-establishment,' and 'representatives of CUPE who were called in and were the main backers of the meeting.'[60] The next day a demonstration was called at Province House that brought out four hundred protestors demanding provincial capital cost grants, such as were available in British Columbia, Alberta, Saskatchewan, and Ontario, and an expanded range of parents who might qualify for subsidized rates.[61]

A memorandum sent to the premier by the minister of social services was incredibly dismissive of these aspirations. Written in a style a great deal like that of Deputy Minister Fred MacKinnon, the memorandum stated that there was no need for sympathy since the 'uproar is largely from middle class professionals [and] ... those at the YWCA meeting last night know very little about poverty and hardship.' Acknowledging the welfare connection, the minister pointed out that there was no agitation from those on provincial or municipal social assistance against personal investigations and 'there is no argument for treating daycare users differently from the users of provincial social assistance.' The memorandum continued to map out the future political strategy of the Liberal government.

> If concessions and conciliation would bring about peace and satisfaction, we would aggressively push for a solution. We believe, however, that concessions will only whet the appetite for more and more greater demands. We believe anything we offer or give, at this stage, will be called mean, small and picayune by the agitators and the media.
>
> If we take a firm stand, the storm and agitation will play itself out and pass, if for no other reason than the fact that the principals and the agitators will have found some other target for attack.[62]

The result was a complete breakdown in relations and communications between the nascent daycare movement and the provincial government.

Three months later, in March 1975, the province cut $100,000 from daycare budgets. Thus, it is hardly surprising that an April meeting between Premier Regan and representatives of the Coalition for Better Day Care was described as 'stormy.'[63] Representatives of the coalition claimed that the premier was 'very rude, insulting and threatening': his behaviour amounted to a 'temper tantrum.'[64] The small increase offered by the government did not even cover the mandatory increase in the minimum wage, which most child-care workers were paid.

The Department of Social Services' enthusiasm for daycare had clearly dissipated by May 1975, when the government was faced with recession, spiraling costs related to inflation, wage and price restraints, and revisions to CAP, which had expanded the number of children eligible for support. At that point MacKinnon described daycare as a 'middle priority or low priority social service' and claimed that, with current government financial restraint, there would be no money for expansion. In a memorandum to the minister, MacKinnon explicitly rejected the ideal of universality and regretted the course of development of daycare provision in the province since the 1971 act, stating that the municipalities should have played a much more important role in financing, as they did in Ontario. He characterized daycare as 'a preventive community social service' but noted that the department had many other more pressing demands. MacKinnon also took the opportunity to vent at daycare professionals and activists who 'instead of beating on the doors of government should be beating on the doors of public opinion if they want public support.' A request by the daycare lobby to have responsibility transferred away from the Department of Social Services had been rejected by various commissions and the Department of Education itself. MacKinnon went on to explain that 'some daycare specialists feel Education would lend a degree of respect and prestige to daycare which is not available in Social Services. We are, like Lil' Abner, there is a "sartin" air about us. And obviously the air is not good in the eyes of daycare specialists.'[65] MacKinnon's observation that some daycare professionals sought to distance themselves from welfare reflected their difficult position. A welfare emphasis on daycare was what had encouraged public spending in the area. At the same time, the welfare orientation stigmatized daycare and limited arguments about its potential for child development and equality for women. Moreover, as a welfare program, it had to vie with a range of competing demands, especially after 1975, when governments had begun to look for ways to cut welfare spending.

A dramatic reversal occurred a year later. MacKinnon met with a group whom he referred to as 'the daycare people,' who 'forcibly brought' to his attention the fact 'that a very large percentage of the children in daycare centres were the children of one-parent families.' MacKinnon wrote 'when it is observed that almost 60 per cent of the families using daycare are in this category, it becomes very obvious that daycare is not the horrible rip-off that some of us – and I include myself – thought it to be. One cannot help but ask the question, what would happen if we didn't have it?'[66] Single mothers' use of daycare was increasing: by March 1977, 71 per cent of the 567 children registered in the seven Halifax area daycare centres had single parents.[67] Once again, the welfare arguments appear to have been persuasive, and once again they placed daycare firmly within the welfare orbit. Unfortunately, even the welfare argument did not result in further funds; the freeze on new subsidized spaces lasted from 1976 to 1979.[68]

A study emphasizing the welfare orientation of daycare reminds us that attitudes towards mothers working outside the home were complex. Women's responsibility for child rearing and their need to support themselves and their children were not new. There is a thread of philanthropic and welfare state thought that sought to create opportunities for women with children to participate in the workplace by assisting with child care. Provincial welfare programs such as the early mothers' allowance, which in Nova Scotia was open only to mothers with more than one child, on the assumption that a woman should be able to support one child, were insufficient to support a family. Unmarried women with children were not eligible for any social assistance until 1967, and then they had to maintain their own home to qualify for payment. Mothers with no or an inadequate male breadwinner and who needed paid employment had used a variety of strategies for child care, such as an informal network of family members, and public, philanthropic, or private-care facilities. The orphanages and infant homes established in the nineteenth century held women responsible for the financial support of their children but recognized that they needed help. These institutions sought to assist women at the same time as they instilled values of self-sufficiency. Self-sufficiency and an individual work ethic were also present in the assumption of the late 1960s and early 1970s that women should pay some portion of their child-care expenses. It is clear that the Nova Scotia government held these values as it entered the field of daycare subsidization as a means to support women and their families in order to avoid their complete dependence on the public purse. The policy choice of subsidizing daycare also meant that there was no need to insist that employers pay women sufficient wages to pay for child care or provide flexible working hours to balance family and income responsibilities. As a result, today, at a time of government retrenchment, when cost cutting shapes the direction of social policy, amid the myriad of cuts, government spending on daycare subsidization actually increases. Daycare, like its philanthropic antecedents, is a welfare program aimed at promoting self-sufficiency and preventing pauperization. Although feminists and early childhood educators can dress it up in the rhetoric of women's equality or child development, daycare receives budget appropriations because the Nova Scotia government ultimately sees it as a means to reduce social assistance costs and welfare dependency.

NOTES

1 *Halifax Chronicle-Herald*, 12 April 2000, A1-2.
2 Public Archives of Nova Scotia (PANS), RG 72, vol. 62, no. 7, Halifax Protestant Orphanage 1969–70, 'Project Proposal submitted by the Social Planning Office, City of Halifax for Consideration of the Board of Trustees of the Halifax Protestant Orphan's Home,' Sept. 1969; RG 72, vol. 21, no. 22, Day Care Committee 1967, to James Harding, Minister of Welfare from Sis-

ter Mary Clare, 14 Dec. 1967; 'President's Report,' Halifax Infants' Home, *Annual Report*, 1958; *Halifax Daily News*, 12 Aug. 1997, 7.

3 Annis May Timpson, *Driven Apart: Women's Employment Equality and Child Care in Canadian Public Policy* (Vancouver: UBC Press, 2001).

4 Alvin Finkel, 'Even the Little Children Cooperated: Family Strategies, Child Care Discourse and Social Welfare Debates, 1945–1975,' *Labour/Le Travail* 36 (1995): 91–118; Rianne Mahon, 'The Never-Ending Story: The Struggle for Universal Child Care Policy in the 1970s,' *Canadian Historical Review* 81, 4 (2000): 582–615.

5 Christina Simmons, '"Helping the Poorer Sisters": The Women of the Jost Mission, Halifax, 1905–1945,' *Acadiensis* 14, 1 (1984): 3–27.

6 Wendy Atkin, '"Babies of the World Unite": The Early Day-Care Movement and Family Formation in the 1970s,' in Lori Chambers and Edgar-Andre Montigny, eds., *Family Matters: Papers in Post-Confederation Canadian Family History* (Toronto: Canadian Scholars Press, 1998), 57–70.

7 Donna Varga, *Constructing the Child: A History of Canadian Day Care* (Toronto: James Lorimer, 1997).

8 Mahon, 'Never-Ending Story,' 595–6.

9 Sue Wolstenholme, 'Development of Day Care in Nova Scotia: A Socio-Political Analysis' (master of education thesis, Dalhousie University and Atlantic Institute of Education, 1984), 133. This is an especially interesting piece of scholarship, as Wolstenholme has been one of the key activist professionals in the Nova Scotia daycare movement.

10 National Archives of Canada (NAC), MG 28, I, 10, vol. 283, Canadian Council on Social Development, vol. 49, no. 448, Day Nurseries Question, to Mrs Parker from E.H. Blois, 14 March 1942.

11 Ibid., to Mrs Parker from Gwendolyn V. Shand, 11 March 1942.

12 Judith Fingard, 'The North End City Mission: Building Use in the Old North End,' *Royal Nova Scotia Historical Society Journal* 3 (2000): 14.

13 PANS, MG 20, vol. 407, Halifax Welfare Council, no. 1.4, 8 Jan. 1940.

14 Simmons, '"Helping the Poorer Sisters"'; *Halifax Mail-Star*, 14 Dec. 1957, 13. Renée Lafferty, '"A Very Special Service": Day Care, Welfare and Child Development, Jost Mission Day Nursery, Halifax, 1920–1955' (MA thesis, Dalhousie University, 1998).

15 PANS, MG 20, vol. 408, Minutes of Halifax Council of Social Agencies, Child Welfare, no. 4, 10 Dec. 1948.

16 PANS, MG 20, Local Council of Women, vol. 535, no. 13, Executive Meeting, 14 Oct. 1943.

17 Ibid., Local Council of Women, vol. 536, no. 9, Reports, Women's Voluntary Service, 21 March 1946, 19 April 1945, 21 Dec. 1944.

18 Ibid., vol. 408, Halifax Welfare Council, no. 6.8, to G.V. Shand from Assistant Deputy Minister, Department of Public Health and Welfare, 4 Oct. 1955.

19 Ibid., no. 6.9, Florence Fraser, Superintendent, Dalhousie Public Health Clinic, 4 Oct. 1955.

20 Ibid., no. 6.10, Director, Home Services, Red Cross, 4 Oct. 1955.

21 Judith Fingard, 'Marriage and Race in Women's Employment Patterns in Post-War Halifax' (paper presented to the Atlantic Canada Workshop, Halifax, 1997).

22 PANS, MG 20, vol. 408, Halifax Welfare Council, no. 6.14, 17 Oct. 1955, Halifax Welfare Bureau, 6.15, Day Nursery Care Halifax, Oct. 1955.

23 Ibid., vol. 411, Halifax Welfare Council, no. 9.25, 28 Nov. 1955, meeting 'Day Care for Children in Halifax'; ibid., no. 3.13, Annual Report, 26 March 1956.

24 See Fingard, 'Marriage and Race.' Canada, *1961 Census, Labour Force, Bulletin 3.1-7*, Labour force 15 years and older, by marital status, schooling, class of worker, and sex for incorporated cities, towns, and villages of 10,000 population and over; Canada, *Married Women Working for Pay in Eight Canadian Cities* (Ottawa: Department of Labour, 1958).

25 Henry Bourgeois, 'A Report of the Survey of Married Women Who Are Working for Pay in Halifax' (MSW thesis, Maritime School of Social Work, 1956), 15, 20; Mary E. Rand, 'Implications When Grandmothers Assume Responsibility for the Care of Children Whose Mothers Are Working for Pay' (MSW thesis, Maritime School of Social Work, 1956).

26 PANS, MG 20, vol. 408, Halifax Welfare Council, no. 6.22, 6 Sept. 1957; ibid., no. 6.21.

27 Mahon, 'The Never Ending Story'; Timpson, *Driven Apart*, 19–20.

28 NAC, MG 28, I 10, vol. 228, no. 2, Canadian Welfare Council/Canadian Council on Social Development, Halifax (NS) Child Welfare Service Survey (1958), Eric Smit – draft, 8.

29 PANS, MG 20, vol. 408, Halifax Welfare Council, no. 6.26, Nov. 1959.

30 Ibid., no. 6.32, 16 Nov. 1959.

31 PANS, RG 72, vol. 21, no. 22, Committee Day Care, surveys of four facilities, 24 Aug. 1967.

32 Ibid., vol. 17, no. 7, Day Care Nursery Junior League 1966, 5 April 1966.

33 Ibid., vol. 20, no. 16, Brunswick St United Church (preschool grant), 1967, 29 Nov. 1967; vol. 21, no. 22, Committee Day Care 1967, meeting minutes, 10 Jan. 1967.

34 Ibid., vol. 47, no. 8, Day Care, 1968, to Percy Gaum from Fred R. MacKinnon, 26 Nov. 1968.

35 Ibid., vol. 16, no. 21, Committee Day Care 1966, to Director of Child Welfare, Federal Public Welfare, from D.H. Johnson, 15 Sept. 1966.
36 Ibid., vol. 50, no. 1, Day Care Committee 1969, to J.H. Clarke, executive assistant to Premier from Gordon A. Tidman, 15 Oct. 1969.
37 Ibid., vol. 21, no. 22, Committee Day Care 1967, Minister's Advisory Committee on Day Care Services, 4 April 1967.
38 Ibid., Minutes 14 Nov. 1966.
39 PANS, RG 72, vol. 47, no. 8, Day Care, 1968, to J. Harding, Minister of Public Welfare, from Fred R. MacKinnon, 25 Jan. 1968.
40 Margaret Little, 'No Car, No Radio, No Liquor Permit': The Moral Regulation of Single Mothers in Ontario, 1920–1997 (Toronto: Oxford University Press, 1998).
41 PANS, RG 72, vol. 21, no. 22, Committee Day Care 1967, Minister's Advisory Committee on Day Care Services meeting, 4 April 1967. The brief also noted that insufficient consideration had been given to rural areas of Nova Scotia.
42 Rodney Haddow, Poverty Reform in Canada, 1958–1978: State and Class Influences on Policy Matters (Montreal: McGill-Queen's University Press, 1993), 27.
43 PANS, RG 72, vol. 49, no. 25, Committee Day Care 1969, Janice Tyrwhitt, 'Why the Hell Can't We Provide Day Care for Working Mothers' Kids?' Star Weekly, n.d.
44 Ibid., vol. 21, no. 22, Committee Day Care 1967, to James Harding, Minister of Public Welfare, from Sister Mary Clare, 14 Dec. 1967; to D. Johnston – Director Child Welfare, from H. Bond Jones, Welfare Administrator Halifax, 8 Sept. 1967.
45 Ibid., vol. 50, no. 27, Day Care Centres St Joseph 1968–9, to Fred R. MacKinnon from Colin Campbell, Executive Director Catholic Social Service Committee, 25 April 1969.
46 Ibid., vol. 87, no. 6, Day Care 1971, to Allan Sullivan from Ron Wallace, 8 Feb. 1971.
47 Ibid., vol. 61, no. 1, St Joseph 1970, Public Statement re Day Care Services August 1970 – St Joseph's Children's Centre.
48 Ibid., vol. 62, no. 7, Halifax Protestant Orphanage, 1969–70.
49 Ibid., vol 81, no. 17, Day Care Act, 1970–71.
50 Ibid., Text to be used by Hon. A.E. Sullivan in Speaking on Behalf of the Day Care Services Act, 25 Feb. 1971.
51 NAC, MG 28, I 10, vol. 283, Canadian Council on Social Development, no. 23, Day Care – Report of a National Study, 1972.
52 PANS, RG 72, vol. 68, no. 13, Day Care General, 1971–72, notes on introduction of Day Care Services Act, Feb. 1971.

53 Ibid., vol. 81, no. 18, John Sears 1971, Margaret MacDonald, 'Study Profile on Day Care Services (Registered) June 1973'; vol. 116, no. 14, Day Care – General, 1974–75, Report, 23 Jan. 1975, by Social Research and Planning Division, Department of Social Services.
54 Ibid., vol. 68, no. 11, Day Care Centres, 1971–72, to D.H. Johnson from Stewart Brown, 24 May 1972.
55 Ibid., vol. 105, no. 19, Day Care Coordinating Committee, 1974, to Priscilla Schmid, Chair, Day Care Coordinating Committee, from Harold Husklison, Minister of Social Services, 13 March 1974. See also vol. 93, no. 3, Day Care Correspondence Community 1973, to Priscilla Schmid, Chairman of the Day Care Coordinating Committee, from William Gillis (Minister of Public Welfare), 26 Feb. 1973. In 1973, the Nova Scotia Department of Public Welfare was renamed the Department of Social Services. It adopted the name Community Services in 1987.
56 The 4th Estate (Halifax), 1 Aug. 1974, 6.
57 PANS, RG 72, vol. 105, no. 27, Day Care rates 1974, Day Care Subsidization: Who Pays? Brief from Citizen's Day Care Action Committee, Oct. 1974; vol. 105, no. 27, Day Care rates 1974, to Harold Husklison from Brian Flemming, 7 Oct. 1974.
58 The 4th Estate, 24 Oct. 1974, 1, 15.
59 The 4th Estate, 15 Aug. 1974, 3.
60 PANS, RG 72, vol. 105, no. 12, Day Care General 2, 1974, to Gerald A. Regan from Fred MacKinnon, D.H. Johnson, Admin, Family and Child Welfare Division attended the public meeting last night, 4 Dec. 1974.
61 The 4th Estate, 12 Dec. 1974, 2; 23 Jan. 1975, 5.
62 PANS, RG 72, vol. 105, no. 12, Day Care General 2, 1974, Memo to Gerald Regan from Harold Husklison, 4 Dec. 1974.
63 The 4th Estate, 12 March 1975, 6.
64 The 4th Estate, 30 April 1975, 1.
65 PANS, RG 72, vol. 145, no. 22, Day Care General 1976, Draft – Background information re daycare and Mrs Shirley Bradshaw's letter of 28 April 1976 to the Hon. William MacEachern, Minister of Social Services, 11 May 1976.
66 Ibid., to Bill MacEachern, Minister of Social Services, from Fred R. MacKinnon, 18 June 1976.
67 Ibid., no. 21, Day Care General 1977, Day Care Facts March 1977.
68 Wolstenholme, 'Development of Day Care,' 69.

Black Women at Work: Race, Family, and Community in Greater Halifax

WANDA THOMAS BERNARD AND
JUDITH FINGARD

After the Second World War, a common scene at the Halifax-Dart-mouth ferry terminals was a group of Black women socializing as they waited to cross the harbour or for a ride to take them home. They were working women from eastern Halifax County, making the long journey to and from their employment as domestics. In order to understand their experiences and those of their co-workers to the west of the Halifax peninsula, we interviewed a dozen older women who had earned their living for varying lengths of time as day cleaners.[1] When most of them started work in the 1940s and 1950s, their opportunities were severely restricted by systemic and overt racism, inadequate community services, and lack of self-confidence. They left their employment in the 1960s or later in the midst of progressive reforms that expanded their options in both the paid and voluntary sectors and transformed their daughters' prospects beyond their wildest dreams.

Our interviewees resided in various locations in what is now the Halifax Regional Municipality, which was home to 20 per cent of all African Canadians in the mid-twentieth century. Although Blacks constituted only about 3 per cent of the total population of the area, numbering some 7,000 people in the mid-1960s, their families had dwelt in the area for generations. The Black population lived in urban Halifax and Dartmouth, including Africville on the northern fringe of the Halifax peninsula; the Preston area east of Dartmouth, made up of the settlements of Cherrybrook/Lake Loon, East Preston, and North Preston; and a cluster of more scattered settlements outside Halifax – Beechville west of the city, Hammonds Plains to the northwest, and Cobequid Road, Lucasville, and Middle Sackville, all northwest of the town of Bedford, which lay just north of Halifax. In terms of the size of the Black population, the Prestons ranked first. About two and one-half times as many Black residents made their homes in rural as in urban areas. Because all the rural Black settlements were within a twenty-kilometre radius of Halifax-Dartmouth and came increasingly to depend on that close proximity, sociologists in the 1960s began to refer to them as 'urban-fringe' communities.[2]

Each of the communities had distinctive characteristics and a strong sense of social cohesion, although in the 1940s and 1950s most rural residents shared a persistent and worsening poverty.[3] North Preston (also known as New Road) was noted for its large families and high welfare rates.[4] Hammonds Plains experienced severe economic dislocation with the demise of the coopering industry and overt hostility from nearby white residents.[5] Africville had the reputation for being something of a transitional residence for Black Nova Scotians making their way to central Canada.[6] Besides occasional family ties, contacts between the various communities were confined largely to church events. In the City of Halifax itself socio-economic conditions were mixed. Unlike the county, some class differentiation could be found. A small middle class of professionals, skilled artisans, and service workers, as well as members of old families that had seen better days before the Great Depression, valiantly pursued self-improvement. Some of them actively promoted racial uplift, an activism that culminated in the formation in 1945 of the Nova Scotia Association for the Advancement of Coloured People (NSAACP).

Using the interview data as our central focus, this paper addresses four topics: postwar job opportunities for Black women, Black women's experiences as domestics, reforms in the fields of human rights and community development, and the impact of social change on Black domestics and their families. Except for a small number of recent master's theses, there has been little scholarly analysis of Black women's lives in twentieth-century Nova Scotia.[7] Moreover, the myriad of Canadian studies on the postwar domestic labour market deal exclusively with foreign contract labour and the problems immigrant minority women in the large cities have encountered in their quest for better jobs, permanent residence, and social justice.[8] In contrast, this study attempts to explain the importance of domestic work for women of a local minority resident in Halifax for two hundred years.

Black Women and the Postwar Job Market

Descriptions of Black women's paid occupations, such as those contained in W.P. Oliver's account of African–Nova Scotian communities in 1964, might mislead us into thinking that cleaning was the only job for Black women.[9] Although domestic employment was indeed the topic of our interviews, we were aware that even in the immediate post-war period some Black women secured other jobs. A handful of Black women, including Sydney native Gertrude Tynes, one of the women featured in the introduction to this volume, taught school in the segregated schools of the predominately Black communities. Standard normal college qualifications did not secure them jobs in urban schools and did not protect them from substandard working conditions in the rural settlements. They taught in badly equipped and overcrowded school buildings where split morning and afternoon sessions were common. Teachers who lived in the communities in which they taught encountered inadequate housing and poor roads.[10] Other occupations also depended on Black clients. Black beauticians were trained in Viola Desmond's School of Beauty Culture in Halifax to provide a service that their white counterparts refused or did badly.[11] Some talented musicians acquired conservatory training and gave private lessons to their neighbours' children.[12]

In a more competitive job market such as health care, the struggle for access to jobs culminated after the war, when nurses' training programs – beginning in the Halifax area with the Children's Hospital – started to accept Black applicants and subsequently to employ them.[13] By the 1950s Black women were beginning to challenge the gatekeepers of the higher professions in the health field. Haligonian Doris Marshall took an undergraduate degree at McGill and decided, on her return to Halifax, to pursue studies in dentistry. Her supportive mother interviewed the dean of dentistry at Dalhousie University. Although he advised her that Doris would probably find the training very uncomfortable, he did not discourage her application. She applied, was admitted, and graduated in 1956.[14] The fact that she then went to Ontario to practise speaks to the lack of prospects for Black women in a male profession in Halifax and to the continued brain drain, which deprived the local Black community of much-needed talent among both its young women and men.[15]

For the majority of ambitious Black women – that is, those with some high school education and perhaps a business course – the 1940s and 1950s provided few new opportunities. Retail stores would not hire them, except for a few token variety store jobs, and clerical training was not a passport to an office job. Businessmen or their personnel managers claimed either that their white employees would not work with Blacks or that their clients or customers would not agree to be served by Black women. Even if some whites were sympathetic, they displayed a singular lack of initiative, claiming that they did not want to be the first to hire Blacks, that they had no desire to be the pioneers in the field of fair employment practices that were introduced to the private sector in Nova Scotia in 1956.[16]

This racism meant that many of Halifax's Black women were trapped in a domestic service ghetto. A late 1950s report of Dalhousie University's Institute of Public Affairs on the condition of the Blacks in the City of Halifax found that 67 of 130 (51.5 per cent) employed Black women living on Maynard and Creighton Streets, a deteriorating mixed-race area where the majority of the city's Black population resided, worked in dead-end, underremunerated jobs as charwomen. They did not engage in this employment because they preferred it to other work; they did it because they lacked the alternatives available to white women. One woman, who firmly believed that a good education was the key to advancement, had achieved a junior matriculation high school certificate. She was bitterly disappointed when she could not find a better job than work as a char. Another woman reached the point where she was unwilling to apply for any position other than domestic work because of the repeated and demoralizing refusals she experienced.[17]

The worst forms of racial discrimination in the general job market were experienced by women with the darkest skin. While restaurants in Halifax would not hire Black waitresses, one of our informants spoke of her sister, who was successful in securing a job at the Green Lantern, Halifax's best-known eatery, because she was fair-skinned and passed for 'French.'[18] Many of Halifax's middle-class Blacks in the 1940s and 1950s were light-skinned and admitted to encountering less discrimination in the job market, which suggests a hierarchy of racism, based on skin colour, familiar to historians of the Black experience in the United States.[19] But attitude was also important. Doris Marshall, the dentist, did not have light skin but she did have the encouragement of determined parents, born and raised in the West Indies, who believed 'that opportunities are there for Negroes if they will only take advantage of them.'[20]

Admittedly, the limited range of job opportunities helps us to appreciate the importance of domestic work for the women of Doris Marshall's generation and the frustrations that held back most women who tried to move beyond the confines of the cleaning industry in the 1940s and 1950s. Until the reforms of the civil rights period, cleaning was one of the few remunerative activities that Black women were permitted to do for the white majority.

Although Black women had always been part of the domestic workforce in Nova Scotia, they came increasingly in the postwar period to meet the demand that had once been supplied through British immigration schemes, recruitment of white farmers' daughters, and the rehabilitation of local delinquent or mentally disabled women and girls.[21] They met little competition after the war from displaced, southern European and Third World women recruited under the federal domestic servant schemes, because such women tended to pass Nova Scotia by.[22]

This is not to suggest that Halifax's white matrons were necessarily eager to turn to Black houseworkers, although 'the servant question' itself remained of utmost concern to them. The middle-class members of the Local Council of Women (LCW), which was comprised exclusively of white women's organizations till the 1960s, gradually came to the realization that there was 'little or no hope of drawing from ex-service girls for domestics' and that young, single women were 'going down the road' to Ontario in search of well-paid industrial work. This seemed to leave for consideration middle-aged women who might be enticed into the workforce partly as a result of their positive experience as workers during the war.[23] The council's representation on the local advisory committee of the National Employment Service of the Unemployment Service Commission enabled it to monitor supply and demand issues relating to domestic work. In 1952 the LCW's representative reported that 'casual workers were in demand and many have been established in various houses "by the day" through the unskilled and semi-skilled section' of the local office of the National Employment Service.[24] Two years later she reported that, as usual, 'the demand for domestics is constant' and that 'employment of the older worker is much to the fore.'[25] Race was not mentioned in council documents until a 'Social Status of Women in Nova Scotia' report in 1955 suggested that some employers of domestic workers would not hire Black women because they considered them to be incompetent. Nonetheless, the trend towards work by the day and participation in the workforce of older women implicitly favoured married Black women.[26]

Over a decade later, in 1969, the Nova Scotia Home Economics Association, a racially integrated organization, concluded, on the basis of a survey, that most employers preferred mature, experienced women as 'home maintenance' workers and that there was a 'desperate lack of good service people with an increasing need for the same.'[27] Although race did not enter into the home economists' discussions, that same year journalist Nancy Lubka, a Voice of Women and human rights stalwart, raised the issue in *The 4th Estate*. She suggested that household workers should organize to improve their working conditions, noting that a considerable proportion of houseworkers were Black women.[28] Between the 1940s and the 1960s, therefore, a significant shift occurred towards hiring Black household help.

For married Black women, the pull of the labour market was accompanied by the push of the changing rural economy. Until the postwar period few married women outside the urban area had been able to pursue regular paid employment. They married young and concentrated on the reproduction of labour in its two traditional forms – caring for husbands and raising children. Some of them also participated seasonally in the economic activities that helped to supply the farmer's market or Halifax-Dartmouth homes more directly by peddling door-to-door. These activities centred on their market gardening, their berry and flower picking, and their handicrafts.[29] While ample evidence of this rurality still existed in the late 1940s, the men were becoming dependent on wage labour in town. The problem with the urban labour market was its seasonality. The resulting bouts of unemployment propelled the women into the workforce, the great advantage of domestic work being its regularity and reliability. In 1963 social worker George Brand surveyed the Black communities outside the City of Halifax proper; he found a greater dependence on domestic labour among Black women there than was the case in the old North End studied by the Institute of Public Affairs. In Africville and Dartmouth, 83 per cent of the 65 employed women worked as domestics either steadily or occasionally. In the urban-fringe communities east of the City of Dartmouth and west and north of the City of Halifax, the figure was 85 per cent of 127 women who worked for wages.[30]

Women's Experiences of Domestic Labour

The Black women who entered the postwar domestic labour market were not a homogeneous group. Their experiences varied according to a number of factors. Place of residence was one distinguishing feature. The women who lived in the city yearned for better opportunities than cleaning because they knew such opportunities were available to some women and because they considered char work to be a low-status occupation. One woman described the challenges that she faced when she worked as a cleaner during daytime hours in a business setting. She was embarrassed to clean in a shop while the customers came and went. She experienced the work as demeaning. For her, work in a private home had the comforting advantage of relative anonymity.[31]

Black women who continued to live in the urban-fringe communities had a more tolerant, even positive, attitude towards cleaning work. In their own communities economic opportunities were extremely limited and access to paid employment requiring formal education was negligible. The segregated schools went only to Grade 8 and secondary education was prevented by the prohibitive cost of attending city high schools, which charged fees and required local boarding arrangements, or by the unsympathetic attitude of fathers towards prolonged schooling. When arrangements to attend school in town were made, as occasionally happened, fate could intervene. One woman, who finished Grade 8 at Partridge River School in East Preston, began her Grade 9 at the new Bicentennial Junior High School in Dartmouth in the early 1950s only to find that the second instalment of fees could not be paid because of her father's hospitalization.[32]

In these circumstances, cleaning work in the city must have seemed like a good opportunity to these women, not only as short-term employment before marriage but as a lifelong possibility.[33] They were the first generation of married women to work outside the home on a continuing basis in any significant number. In addition to the essential cash that cleaning provided, it gave women the opportunity to travel to the city, meet different people, and learn about an enhanced standard of living.[34] Hence their attitude towards working as charwomen or domestics was different from that of city women.

The significance of the income derived from cleaning was another feature that varied from one woman to another. Since most of the men were seasonally employed, a wife's earnings were particularly important during times of hardship, such as the harsh winter months. A number of the women in our study indicated that their wages were indeed used to supplement the family income.[35] Others claimed that their income was used to buy little 'extras' for their children, extras that might seem like essentials today.[36] However, when, as a result of separation or death, a woman became a single parent and sole supporter of her family, her ability to work and earn a living wage was essential. One woman spoke of working part-time before her husband died but then needing to work full-time in order to make ends meet.[37] Some women with large families talked of being separated from their husbands and of the need to work to make sure their children stayed together.[38]

Women's experience also differed by age of entry into the workforce and patterns of employment. Some women did housework as young, single, live-in servants.[39] Our informants who had worked in that capacity had been more content than studies of immigrant domestics in central Canada, such as that by Audrey Macklin, would lead us to expect.[40] For example, being a live-in worker provided one teenager with a home when she had no other and gave another girl the chance to overcome her sickliness through good care provided by her employer and surgery in a hospital.[41] For married women, however, live-in work was another matter altogether. Only the most desperate need could encourage a Black mother to abandon her family for days at a time to reside in her employer's household. Like township women in apartheid South Africa, such employment 'illustrates the cruel paradox of a situation that drives a black mother to seek employment to support her family, and then neglect her family in the process.'[42] One such woman, the mother of an interviewee, had at least been able to make an arrangement whereby she returned on weekends to her community, where her farmer-husband and eldest children maintained the household for the rest of the week.[43]

A number of our informants who had worked as teenagers did not continue to work after marriage. Some preferred to stay at home while their children were young. One woman said she began to do day's work only when her youngest child went to school, as a way of getting out of the house and occupying her time. Another woman entered the workforce as a way of relieving the monotony after her youngest child was grown. At the other end of the spectrum, after their children had grown up, several of the women indicated that they continued to work well into their senior years for something to do. Working was a pastime that provided them with some structure to their week, a break in the routine of their home life, and an opportunity to get into the city and socialize with other women.[44]

Family size helps to explain working patterns. Although not all the women in our sample had several children, large families were certainly the norm in the Black community before, during, and immediately after the war. Before the 1960s, childbirth was in the hands of midwives, who were accessible in the local communities. These community-based midwives were specialists in their field but did not know about modern methods of birth control. Medical care was not available in the urban-fringe communities; women had to travel to the city to see a doctor at least until the opening of the first local clinic in the late

1960s. Before the establishment of family planning programs, even medical practitioners could be unhelpful in this regard. One woman stated that she asked her doctor about birth control after she had borne her nineteenth child. He advised her that her husband would have to give his permission. As a result of sexist policies and practices, she was denied birth control and went on to have yet another child.[45]

In addition to their own large families, Black women often took in other children in times of need. The informal adoption practice was quite prevalent: homes were open to grandchildren, godchildren, or any community child in need. This openness in rural communities to taking in the children of other women was a common practice for Black women throughout the diaspora. In *Black Feminist Thought*, Patricia Hill Collins says that even when relationships were not those of kin or fictive kin, African-American community norms traditionally were such that neighbours cared for one another's children.[46] Indeed, Wanda Thomas Bernard and Candace Bernard state that the helping tradition of the Black community has been central to its collective survival.[47] This has been most evident in the provision of assistance with child rearing. This willingness to take in children is rooted in the African principles of community connectedness and caring for each other.[48] Historically in Nova Scotia, the community concern for children is most visible in the development of the Nova Scotia Home for Coloured Children (NSHCC), established at the end of the First World War.[49] The home's proximity to the Prestons had a significant impact on those communities, as it provided much-needed employment for men and women from the area. Women were hired as cleaners, childcare providers, teachers, and cooks.[50] In addition, the children who were raised in the NSHCC, many of whom came from communities outside Halifax County, formed kin and love relationships with residents of the Preston communities. The NSHCC also provided local residents with many opportunities to be involved in volunteer work and social action.[51] Local women opened their homes on weekends and during the summer to the residents of the NSHCC. As a local resource rather than yet another Halifax city institution, the NSHCC reflected local interest in children, nurturing, family, and education, elements that were pervasive in the Black communities.

Although the NSHCC provided some employment for women in the Prestons, only the lucky few could work close to their own community. For the others, the transition to live-out work increased the opportunities for domestic service in private homes in the urban areas, but getting to work on a regular basis constituted a problem. Workers had to contend with inadequate – sometimes non-existent – bus service; unpaved roads; rides with neighbours, which occurred according to the work schedule of the driver, not the passenger; and long delays in town waiting for a drive home after work. When the uncomfortable but convenient ride in the open back of a truck failed, women had to walk to town from such communities as East Preston, about ten kilometres from Dartmouth.[52] Few contemplated moving their families closer to town as a solution to the remote location; they enjoyed home ownership or its equivalent in the outlying communities, and they benefited from their kitchen gardens and from the support of neighbouring kinfolk.[53] More often than not, removal to town denoted a decline in status, such as the loss of a husband through death or separation.[54]

While poor transportation was a unique local problem, the ambiguous labour status of domestic service was national and even international. Although the occupation remained, even as late as 1961, a major one for women in the Halifax region, Nova Scotia, and Canada as a whole, domestic workers were excluded from the protection of labour legislation.[55] Their work was consistently enumerated as an exception to the minimum wage requirements for women, which first came into effect in Nova Scotia in 1930. That this was the case everywhere in Canada can be explained by the widespread belief, except among progressive women, that domestic workers simply could not be covered by a minimum wage.[56] With the decline of live-in service, domestic workers in private homes became even further removed from the reach of labour standards and fringe benefits, because of the prevalence of part-time work. Houseworkers were part of an informal economy. The state knew of its existence but completely ignored the impact on the welfare of its workers. Female employers were very willing to collude with their domestics to hide their work in the informal economy. They understood that employees were sometimes trying 'to supplement a family income which is not supposed to exceed a fixed amount' and therefore wanted to avoid declaring 'their salary for purposes of CPP, income tax, or unemployment insurance.' Unofficial employment enabled them to 'take home a sum of money with no strings attached.'[57] Even though they might have appreciated the uncomplicated wage system, the overrepresentation of Blacks in domestic service meant that African–Nova Scotian women were disproportionately affected by the exclusion of their work from the protection of the state.[58]

The accounts of former day's workers themselves, contained in the interviews, help to identify some of the common features of their employment between the 1940s and 1970s. For one thing, although we were interested in them mainly for their experience as day's workers in private homes, most of them worked in other low-paid jobs either before or during the period of their domestic employment. One woman started off in commercial laundry work, supplemented her day's work with other cleaning jobs in shops and offices, moved on to employment as a presser with a dry cleaning firm, and then took several jobs in restaurant and hospital food services. Another went to Montreal for a spell, where Black women were not barred from retail sales positions as they were in Halifax, and worked in the ladies fashion department of Holt Renfrew. Two of the younger women in our sample started off, as teenagers on leaving school, in institutional cleaning in one of the city's large hospitals. So much cleaning was available that those with the energy and the need could work morning, afternoon, and night. One interviewee cleaned offices at night and did domestic work during the day. She later exchanged her housework for cleaning first in a hospital and later in a shopping mall. Experience was sometimes a passport to better-status domestic work. The competence of three of our women resulted in a transition to more desirable housekeeping jobs, one in a private home attached to a small business and the others in charge of housekeeping in hotels.[59]

When it came to finding day's work in private homes, few seem to have resorted to employment offices, though several answered 'help wanted' advertisements in the newspaper. The women's networks for securing positions were largely familial. Their day's work in the houses of white women coincided with similar work done by their mothers, aunts, and sisters. One woman, who did not work outside her home until she was in her forties, got her first referrals from her two eldest daughters.

Most long-time domestic workers saw their working conditions change considerably over the course of their employment. Postwar workers were participants in a household revolution as new household technology and furnishings, as well as commercial goods and services, gradually reduced the time that was needed to complete domestic chores. Within a period of a couple of decades, work that had once taken two or three days (such as the hated polishing of hardwood floors) could be completed in one day (such as vacuuming wall-to-wall carpet). Women who did not take up day's work until the 1970s found that easier work and higher wages in the more vibrant economy made half-day employment an option.[60]

The flexibility of char work was attractive to married Black women because it enabled them to continue to perform domestic labour for their own families. Although it meant a gruelling double day, the daily routine of work in the marketplace and work in the home enabled day's workers to keep an eye on the results of the child care and household work assigned to their children during their absence.[61] However, daytime arrangements for children were seldom ideal. Far removed from their homes for eight to ten hours a day, Black women worried greatly about the care their children were receiving and generally distrusted adolescent babysitters who were not their own children. Even at mid-century some of the Black communities were still completely devoid of telephone service, which made matters worse.[62] The day's worker sometimes had to forego much-needed income in order to stay home and attend to the needs of her children in times of sickness or other crises. Some city women had access to the interracial Brunswick Cornwallis Pre-School in the 1960s, but public daycare centres were not opened in the urban-fringe communities until the 1970s, far too late for workers with young children in the 1940s, 1950s and 1960s.[63]

While most charwomen who had experience in other types of employment, including institutional cleaning, preferred them to domestic cleaning, day's work did, when judged on its own terms, provide a number of frequently noted satisfactions. One was the cash paid every day. Without the same access to credit as whites, and with their men frequently subject to periods of unemployment, Black women thereby had the wherewithal to provide for the day-to-day expenses of family life. Even those who initially worked in the city's hospitals as single women expected wages to be paid daily so that they could take the money home to help their parents and siblings.[64] Another positive feature of private housework was the quiet, solitary work routine.[65] Instead of finding domestic work isolating and lonely, Black women cherished the calm of an empty house, where they could work according to their personal preferences. Certainly the day's worker resented having to provide company for the middle-class housewife if her chat interfered with the work schedule and delayed her beyond her accustomed quitting time.[66] Moreover, rather than expressing concern over the lack of contracts and benefits, the Black cleaner identified the flexibility inherent in employment based on trust as an asset. She enjoyed being her own boss; it was tantamount to self-employment.[67] 'Quality' employers inspired confidence. Why did she need a contract, commented one woman, when she worked for 'a religious family?'[68] Hours that could be negotiated to allow her to be home in time to prepare the evening meal or to deal with a family crisis suited the Black charwoman more than an ironclad contractual arrangement would have. Moreover, when their personal circumstances permitted, many women preferred to work part-time, which meant two or three days in other women's homes rather than five or six.[69] Although sick pay was seldom given, time off for illness was understood: the job was still there when the worker returned. Admittedly, not all work settings were so benign. Employer callousness was at its most extreme in the case of Mrs B.E., who broke her leg on the job. Her employer left the matter of transport to hospital to the woman's family and made no enquiries as to her well-being after the accident.[70]

In circumstances where employment became unbearable, the day's worker could simply quit. She did not need to give notice, and if she had a score to settle she could refuse to recommend a replacement, which might create a real hardship for the errant employer.[71] This assertive approach was possible in circumstances where domestic help was always in demand. Noting that the housewives of Africville seldom participated in the urban job market, one of the interminable studies of Nova Scotian Black communities of the 1950s and 1960s claimed that they would 'take day work erratically when the urgent need arises,' and 'that such unemployment as exists among women is voluntary, for they do not appear to have much difficulty getting domestic day-work on a year-round basis.'[72]

Self-reported wages are difficult to interpret, but if a Black domestic making $4 a day, a high-end rate in 1961, worked full-time, she would have taken home roughly the same amount (about $1,000) reported in census tables as average earnings for women in the personal service industry in Halifax, and more than the $713 reported for Dartmouth.[73] Although former day's workers claim that the employer set the rate, the informal network of Black cleaners could improve the pay scales, which rose rapidly in the 1970s. Shared travel to jobs in Halifax provided collective opportunities for swapping stories with sister workers, unloading frustrations, and plotting work strategies.[74] Mrs C.E., who entered domestic service only after the youngest of her twenty children went to school in the 1970s, was one of a group of South End Halifax houseworkers who set out to secure an increase in the daily rate of pay. On more than one occasion these women threatened to quit if their employers did not comply with their demands.[75]

The going rate was so low that certain expectations for supplementation prevailed. This might take the form of bus fare or car rides by the employer.[76] Above all, day's workers expected the provision of a midday meal; only when hourly work at a number of different houses in the same day became the norm did this expectation change. The nature of that meal could arouse strong feelings. In households where the day's worker was more of a housekeeper than a charwoman, she prepared her own lunch, often along with the children's. In most cases, however, food preparation was not a regular part of the work, and the lunch was prepared by the employer. If members of the employer's family were also dining, the worker did not think much of being fobbed off with leftovers while the family ate fresh.[77] The venue of the meal was just as important. Some workers felt the weight of their class and race when they were relegated to the kitchen while the family meal was being taken in the dining room.[78] Others accepted their status as 'servant' or preferred to eat alone out of shyness.[79]

The standard of treatment that was appreciated and always held up as the ideal was the employer who made the domestic feel at home.[80] The courtesies of the employer-employee relationship remain in the memory of these women – the special gifts (even from the dog at Christmas), the concern shown for the worker's children, the bonuses at holiday time, the invitations to family weddings and other celebrations, the legal advice in times of crisis, the friendly encounters long after the employment ceased.[81] Although the employer and employee lived in two different worlds defined by both class and race, their relationship was not shaped by the excesses of master-servant arrangements, inescapable in live-in work, or the tensions characteristic of the employment of contract immigrant labour.[82] Long-time employment in the same household could produce forms of interdependence and mutual respect. In an exceptional acknowledgment of a job well done, Mrs F.D. was presented with a retirement cheque for $14,000 from one employer.[83] When Mrs P.M.'s first husband died, she found that her five daily employers provided her with more tangible support than did the people in her community.[84] In order to promote amicable working relations, degrees of employer paternalism were tolerated by Black women, as was the demeaning but customary ritual of money deliberately left lying around to test the honesty of the new houseworker.[85]

The nature of day's work itself varied widely, depending on the needs of the employer and the attitudes of the employee. Mrs J.R., who worked for nine years exclusively for the one family – a family engaged in a demanding small business – had an unusual degree of responsibility, including access to her employer's safe. Since her job was akin to a housekeeper's rather than a charwoman's, she never did, and never was expected to do, heavy work: instead men were employed for seasonal housecleaning.[86] Mrs F.D. too developed close relationships with her employers, which raised the status of her job in her eyes and theirs. The strong bond meant that she was often given a key and asked to keep an eye on the employer's house when the family was away.[87]

The regular work of most charwomen fifty years ago was extremely laborious, and most workers believed that the workday was done when the enumerated tasks were completed. In this they sometimes did not see eye-to-eye with the employer, who was eager to devise other tasks at the end of the day to round out the time, even if quitting time was 4:00 p.m. and the worker was finished by 3:45 p.m.[88] Other women found that they had free run of the house as far as the work routine was concerned and prided themselves on never having to be told what to do.[89]

With respect to the identity of the employers themselves, a disproportionately large number of employers of Black women in metropolitan Halifax-Dartmouth were Jewish, as Judith Rollins found to be the case in Boston in a more recent period.[90] Exactly what this means is unclear, but there is no reason to think that Jews were more wealthy or more accustomed to servants than Christian matrons. It may mean that Jews were less prejudiced and therefore more willing to employ Blacks at a time when they too suffered many racist indignities in smug, white, Christian Halifax.[91] Black workers had an ambivalent relationship with their Jewish employers. There is no doubt that they felt the cultural distance. They regarded Jewish rituals for high holidays as bizarre at the same time as they appreciated well-paid extra work preparing for and serving at the celebrations.[92] One woman who complained bitterly about how hard her Jewish employers made her work nonetheless pointed out that the highlight of her working life was the ten years she spent as a day's worker with a young Jewish family, during which time her own children 'were treated like part of the family.'[93] Another who also thought that Jewish women were too demanding of their employees believed that she understood the reason for their obsessiveness: they had 'come up the hard way [in the old country] and felt you could never do enough.'[94]

While at one level, Black women interacted with Jewish women as their cleaners, at another level human rights activists in the postwar period, led by Jewish organizations, worried about the discrimination encountered by racial minorities and discovered that Black Nova Scotians were especially disadvantaged by racism. In the late 1940s, Carrie Best's pioneering Black newspaper, the *Clarion*, included examples of the bond against racism shared by the Jews and Blacks of Nova Scotia.[95] The Jewish Labour Committee of Canada and the Human Rights Committee of the Canadian Labour Congress, staffed by Jewish lawyers, turned their attention to Nova Scotia's human rights scene in the mid-1950s and continued to monitor it through reports from the Halifax Human Rights Advisory Committee until the early 1970s, by which time the provincial government's Human Rights Commission, watched over by a citizens' human rights federation, was well established.[96]

Employment, Human Rights, and Community Development

Racial discrimination and inequality found many critics in Nova Scotia at the end of the Second World War. By the mid-1950s the human rights momentum had escalated under the encouragement of the central Jewish Labour Committee and a number of Halifax-based interracial initiatives, including the NSAACP. For our purposes, the story of the human rights movement and the simultaneous community-development movement is significant because of the prominence they gave to employment reform. In the course of promoting an expansion in the employment opportunities for African Nova Scotians, human rights activists broadened the prospects for our interviewees and their families.

The first target of the reformers was employment in the private sector in the 1950s. The evidence for discrimination in private employment was overwhelming. Young Black women with suitable qualifications applied for jobs advertised in stores and offices, only to be told when they arrived for interviews that the jobs were filled or cancelled. While large retail outlets like Simpson's would not put Black saleswomen on the floor, in 1960 a Dartmouth Jewish clothier, Jacobson's, responded to the growing exposure of job discrimination by hiring a young, Black high school graduate for its dress department. The *Dartmouth Free Press* commented favourably in 1962 on this pioneering form of tokenism: 'Far from any criticism, many of their patrons went out of their way to express their satisfaction that the girl had been given a chance.'[97] Too often the tokenism of the 1960s meant that unofficial quotas prevailed – very low quotas, where one Black employee was normally considered enough.

The concern for increasing job opportunities by removing the colour bar grew in the early 1960s. As Frances Early notes in her study of the Voice of Women in this volume, women played a prominent role in forming the Halifax Interracial Council in 1961. It conducted a survey of Halifax businesses that employed a total of three thousand male and female workers and discovered that only nine Blacks were included in that number, all of whom worked in maintenance jobs. The Inter-Racial Council also collaborated with the NSAACP to mount a program aimed at improving job prospects for high school students. The NSAACP itself undertook educational and employment projects, including career counselling, ad hoc employment agency work, and the provision of university scholarships.[98]

Other initiatives occurred at the level of the provincial government. An interdepartmental government committee on human rights was struck in 1962 under Premier Robert Stanfield 'to find ways and means of improving the lot' of Blacks in Nova Scotia.[99] In 1965 it established an educational fund for African Nova Scotians – an important incentive system for keeping young people in school – and in 1966 appointed two employment officers in the new social development division of the Department of Public Welfare to take over the NSAACP employment work.[100] After the provincial Human Rights Commission, established in 1967, became operational with the appointment of its first director in 1969, the first sixteen formal complaints were job-related ones involving Blacks from the Halifax area.[101]

Meanwhile, the City of Halifax put its efforts into student employment, sponsoring in 1968 and again in 1969 a Negro Employment Committee to find summer jobs for Black students. The voices of the young female job-seekers, quoted in the report for the summer of 1968, reveal their frustration and demand for a more militant approach. An eighteen-year-old commented, 'The last employer I went to see told me I had the job, and said he would phone me in a couple of days to let me know when I'm to start working. I never heard from him. I called him about this, and you know what he said, "I lost your phone number." I slammed the damn phone in his ear.' Another woman, who applied for five sales positions, reported: 'I never heard from any of them ... Maybe what the man [employer] needs is a threat – like hire me or else.' Even when they did get the job, some Black women felt they were expected to work harder than their white colleagues. One woman blamed her own community for the lack of progress by criticizing the defeatism of her elders, who continued to subscribe to a policy of gradualism, cooperation, subordination. She complained that the adults told her 'we can do nothing, so leave it alone.'[102]

Although the human rights movement was crucial for the children of Black domestics, the women themselves probably benefited more from the concurrent community-development movement. Community development for urban-fringe communities began with adult education courses developed as a result of pressure from the NSAACP. The first programs were initiated in Hammonds Plains in 1946. Many of the Black schoolteachers were encouraged to deliver these programs, which began with very basic literacy skills, local problem solving, household economy training, and instruction in how to fill out forms.[103] Although school upgrading soon became a focus, Halifax's most experienced social worker, Gwendolyn Shand, came to the conclusion in 1961 that the program had not 'so far contributed appreciably to raising the employment status of the coloured people.'[104]

Public awareness of the lack of services in the urban-fringe communities was heightened between the mid-50s and mid-60s for a number of reasons, including graphic journalistic depictions of the poor quality of life in North Preston splashed across the country in *Macleans's* magazine in 1956.[105] The provincial government reacted – although none too rapidly – to the adverse publicity of the period by appointing W.P. Oliver in 1964 as adult education liaison in the Department of Education for work in the Black communities. It also established in 1965 the social development division of the Department of Public Welfare 'to work in the disadvantaged or economically deprived communities in Nova Scotia, which, in the initial phases, were mainly Negro communities,' with an emphasis on housing, education, and employment in Hammonds Plains and the Prestons.[106]

Oliver's appointment opened up new job prospects for women in the urban-fringe communities. For instance, one of our interviewees took a job as Oliver's adult education coordinator for East Preston.[107] The activities of the Social Development Division also provided opportunities for local women. Its head-start programs for preschool children in two Black communities in the summer of 1966 meant more new job opportunities in the communities themselves. Although there were not a large number of jobs, the head-start programs led to the demand for permanent daycare facilities, as did the medical clinic started in North Preston in 1968. First in North Preston and then in East Preston, permanent daycare centres opened in 1972 and 1974, respectively.[108] Some of our informants were involved in these facilities, took the training in early childhood education that was made available by extension in cooperation with the Nova Scotia Teachers College, and staffed the new centres.[109]

Perhaps because of the emphasis on the relocation of Africville in the 1960s, the story of community development in the urban-fringe communities has yet to be fully explored. Yet, it is clear that, through the strengthening of the institutions of community life, some women could combine their need for employment with the improvement of opportunities for their children, their neighbours' children, and their children's children. Similarly community development for the old North End neighbourhood in the city of Halifax was occurring in the 1960s and 1970s. Our interviewees, some of whom lived from time to time in the city, have helped us to understand the incredible expansion in Black women's unwaged, volunteer work both in the cities and the county communities – work of great social value.[110]

The Impact of Social Change on Black Domestics and Their Families

Domestic work provided rural women with goals and inspiration for improving their prospects, and more especially those of their children. Self-help organizations and government policies helped to supply the wherewithal to enable their daughters to move beyond the limited prospects encountered by their mothers. Most of the interviewees claimed that if given the opportunity for further education in their youth, they would have become schoolteachers. Teaching would have been the only other occupation besides domestic work that they saw performed by Black women, and this limited experience shaped their vision of what was possible. The more significant point is that none of these women wanted their daughters to do domestic work as a permanent occupation.[111] While it was alright for them – they appreciated their domestic work, took their jobs seriously, and worked to the best of their ability – they had dreams and hopes for their daughters that would see them enjoying other types of work that would more fully match their potential and give them greater opportunities for advancement. In the difficult postwar years, when there were few social benefits and the standard of living and educational prospects in the Black settlements continued to decline, Black women who worked in the homes of white families broadened their awareness of the range of possibilities in wider society. Yet they were also painfully aware that few, if any, of these opportunities would be available to their children without far-reaching reforms.

They therefore welcomed the changes that came in the 1960s, changes that they helped to determine. Their own provincial organization for promoting improvement in the conditions experienced by Black citizens, the NSAACP, challenged racist hiring practices in Halifax and Dartmouth businesses and fostered reform. The NSAACP used test cases to make changes in employment and other conditions that discriminated against the Black community. Later in the decade the government's community-development initiatives in the urban-fringe communities focused largely on youth. Young people were encouraged to continue in school and to think in terms of postsecondary education. Financial support came from the NSAACP, which established a bursary fund, the African Baptist Church, which also provided much-needed moral support, and the Black Incentive Fund established by the provincial Department of Education. While the women in our study were not candidates for the youth programs, they took advantage of the literacy-enhancement initiatives. The commitment of a mother who attended night school classes after the long working day made a positive impression on the children for whom most of the new programs were designed.

The changes that resulted from a combination of the ambitions of working mothers, the human rights movement, and the community-development initiatives can be illustrated by the shift in employment patterns in the Thomas and Bernard families. Co-author Wanda Thomas Bernard draws on the experiences of the two families she knows best to chart the impact of the most significant period of reform in the history of the Black Halifax community. In fact, her mother and mother-in-law were two of the interviewees for this study. The following section is a critical reflection on personal stories of two families that helps us to understand the change in Black women's work patterns in greater Halifax.

I begin with my birth family, the Thomas clan of East Preston. My parents married during the Second World War when they were in their late teens. My mother had ten birth children, one of whom was raised by her parents. She also raised two of her own grandchildren, for a total of eleven children in our home, five boys and six girls. My father worked as a labourer and was seasonally employed. He was killed in a tragic accident in 1965, when he was forty years old, leaving my mother with the eleven children aged eighteen years to eighteen months. My mother had always worked part-time to supplement the family income, but went to work full-time as a domestic after my father died. My mother recalls that when she applied for widows' allowance, she was informed that she would not be eligible until she had exhausted her husband's life insurance. She says she had no choice but to work full-time, as she knew that, with such a large family, the $10,000 life insurance would not last very long, and she felt very uncertain about whether the state would actually help her when the money was gone. Clearly the rejection and the insensitivity were not something that my mother wanted to risk again, and so she was determined to provide for her children to the best of her ability.

Working full-time meant long days in the homes of other women and little time to attend to her own family's needs. I recall that she travelled into the city by car pool in the mornings and took the Eastern Shore bus home at night, which meant that she arrived home after 6:30 p.m. She relied on neighbours to care for the younger children during the day and my older sister and I provided the after-school care. Mother later went to work as an industrial cleaner in a hotel that was owned by one of her earlier employers. This meant that she had a steady income with some security and benefits such as unemployment insurance and sick pay. However, the wages were not very high, and she did have to rely on income assistance after she had exhausted the insurance money. Living in the urban-fringe community of East Preston gave her access to fruit, vegetables, and meat from neighbours' farms, but once we moved to the City of Dartmouth in the early 1970s, the cost of living was significantly higher. I believe that we survived because of the helping tradition in our family and community. The older siblings assisted the younger ones. Things were difficult but we managed and we were not really aware of the financial hardships. There was always enough food to go around and there was also an opportunity to share. For example, I recall my mother taking in one of her godchildren when both parents died. Any visitor who was present during mealtime was invited to share in that meal. My mother remembers one of her employers buying Christmas gifts for all of the children one year. Employers helped in many other ways as well, giving gifts of clothing and furniture and providing information and advice on various issues. Two community-development workers were particularly helpful with respect to housing issues during the late 1960s. When mother's efforts to build a new house in East Preston through the cooperative housing program failed, they assisted her in the move to the city and in getting established there.[112]

That we survived is amazing; however, even more amazing is that we are all successful and productive citizens in society. Every girl went into one of the 'helping professions'; and of the five boys, three went into industrial labour, one worked in a helping profession, and one in the service industry. None of the girls worked as domestics, even temporarily. In the early 1960s my eldest sister was one of the first Black women to work in a business in Dartmouth, an opportunity that came about because of the work of the NSAACP. She was later the first Black telephone operator at the Maritime Telephone & Telegraph Company, as a result of another initiative of the NSAACP. Other women in our family were encouraged by these changes in women's prospects, and higher education became the goal for many of us. All of the women in my family went to university, and four of us have completed two or more degrees, for a total of ten degrees. Interestingly, like other working-class families in the twentieth century, only the women sought higher education, although the new opportunities were available to all of us. The helping professions we entered were nursing, education, social work, child care, and law.[113]

The experiences in my family by marriage, the Bernard clan of Cherrybrook/Lake Loon, have many similarities, but also some significant differences. The Bernards also married young. They had eight birth children (six girls and two boys) and raised one granddaughter. My father-in-law, who was born in 1916, grew up in the Nova Scotia Home for Coloured Children with his four sisters after their mother died. He was one of those residents of the home who spent a lot of time in the neighbouring communities and married a woman from Cherrybrook/Lake Loon. He worked in a coal yard and later in a fuel company as a driver. He ended his employment as a furnace technician for a large oil company. He always had steady employment and was able to provide well for his family.[114] My mother-in-law went to work later in life, when her last child went to school, ostensibly as a way of making extra money for the family, but it was more likely because she was bored and wanted something to occupy her time. She worked as a domestic for only a few years and was then able to take advantage of employment opportunities in the community when a daycare centre opened in the mid-1970s.

The Bernard children were also able to take advantage of new career opportunities. The eldest daughter became a nurse's aid at a time when few Black women were entering the nursing field. Another daughter became a registered nurse, later taking a degree in nursing and pursuing graduate studies in business administration. Two are social workers, one studied education, and the other worked in pink-collar occupations. One son became a labourer and the other studied at the Nova Scotia College of Art and Design before becoming a photographer. The Bernards are productive and successful citizens, some of whom are community activists as well. For example two members of the Bernard family – Delvina and Kim – were co-founders of Four the Moment, an acapella vocal quartet. As leader, Delvina claims that the group gave her the platform to say things that most women do not have the opportunity to articulate.[115]

There are similar patterns in both families: in the older generation, early marriages, large numbers of children, the rearing of grandchildren, domestic labour for the women, and labouring jobs for the men, often of a seasonal variety. The children in both families, mainly the girls, took advantage of the opportunities that became available because of initiatives by groups such as the NSAACP. In both cases, the mothers were the dominant parental figure. I describe them both as matriarchs and early feminists. They were strong survivors in every sense. Like the women studied by Patricia Hill Collins, they recognized the power of self-definition and passed this message on to their children, especially their daughters. They demonstrated a positive work ethic and sheer will and determination in their families. Like the women in Joyce Ladner's work on African-American adolescent mothers, my *mothers* have not only been shaped by their experiences of oppression, but have exerted their influence so as to alter some of those patterns in their children's generation.[116] There was a strong subliminal message to the girls that they should be fiercely independent, that they should prepare to provide for themselves in the future and to take care of themselves. When Black mothers prepare to pass the torch to their daughters, they teach them to deal with their oppression, to resist, survive, and be creative in their acts of empowerment and strategies to succeed in a world where they are caught at the intersection of race, class, and gender oppression.[117] Most of my sisters and sisters-in-law have continued this tradition of determination and activism.

In both the Thomas and Bernard families, the fact that the eldest girls had 'raised the bar' was quite significant to the future success of the other daughters in these families. They were important role models in breaking through the systemic barriers in employment for Black women. They represented the first generation of African–Nova Scotian women who were able to get jobs or enter occupations that were not cleaning or char work. This had a powerful impact on other women in the family, who could then envisage themselves working in other fields. Our sisters' success taught us that we could do more than dream, that we could have better opportunities. We were also the first generation who could take advantage of the opportunities opening up in education. My second oldest sister and I were the first in our families to go on to higher education. This set the standards for the younger Thomas girls to follow. A similar theme holds for the Bernard family, where all of the younger daughters went on to postsecondary education. In both families there were many visible and accessible role models and mentors, and the expectation of higher education soon became the norm rather than the exception.[118]

The cleaning women in our study had dreams deferred because their life chances were scripted by segregationist education policies that limited their career choices. Both my mother and mother-in-law were educated in segregated schools that went only to Grade 8. Neither was able to go to the city high school because of the cost and the lack of public transportation. But both women had dreams of successful careers. My mother's desire to be a teacher and my mother-in-law's to be a nurse were to be realized a generation later in the lives of their daughters. As a result of systemic racism and sexism, they did not have access to those fields, but they encouraged their daughters to break through the glass ceiling. They were able to dream big for their children largely as a result of what they saw in the homes and families of the women they worked for. Their lack of access to what others took for granted – television was not available; books and magazines were not an option – made the ideas derived from their work settings all the more important. Their dreams were not only for their own children but for the Black community at large, as evidenced by their involvement in church and community activities.

Other families in the urban-fringe communities of the Prestons were also able to benefit from the new employment that opened up in the 1960s and 1970s, but most women went into clerical jobs after completing business diplomas or secretarial programs at vocational school. One of the factors here is the issue of immediate versus delayed gratification. Although opportunities to go to university were there, they came with a big price tag and commitment of time. When a person lives in poverty, the assumption of a huge student loan debt can be a daunting undertaking. A one-year diploma may seem much more attractive than a three- or four-year degree program. Something must be said as well about the type of support and direction that was provided by the education sector. I recall that I was considered one of the brightest students in my high school, based on my placement in the highest academic stream, but the guidance counsellor and teachers never talked with me about university. If I was not encouraged to pursue higher education, then I assume that neither were my peers. As noted in the report of the Black Learners Advisory Committee, there have been systemic barriers in education for Black learners in all of Nova Scotia, and the Preston communities were no exception.[119] That any of us went on to postsecondary education is exceptional, for, even as late as the 1980s, access to university education was nothing more than a fantasy for many Black youth.[120] As the Human Rights Commission's affirmative action files indicate, many young Black women did not finish school and remained stuck in low-paying jobs, including employment by industrial cleaning companies.[121]

Conclusion: Black Women's Role in Effecting Social Change

Black domestic workers of the postwar period cleaned houses because they had no other options. Denied secondary education in the rural communities and discriminated against in the urban labour market, they worked in low-status jobs unprotected by labour standards. What they learned in those jobs was nonetheless valuable to them as mothers and community volunteers. When adult education and better prospects for their children came along, many of them were keen to take advantage of the changes. Edna Staebler, a well-known central Canadian journalist who wrote a controversial article for *Maclean's* about North Preston in 1956, quoted a mature, married woman, engaged in domestic work, whose views exemplified this positive outlook: 'I worked all my days, since I been twelve years old ... Scrubbin' an' waxin' for the people in Dartmouth. I believe if you want to git on you got to keep workin' ... If they have 'em this year I'm goin' to the night class to learn readin' and writin' ... I tells my five children "always take all the chances you got to learn."'[122]

The women in this study provide ample evidence of interest in the new opportunities in education that became available in the later 1950s and the 1960s. These women, who had left school when they finished all that the segregated community schools could offer them, ended up taking, as mature women, classes which gave them Grade 10, Grade 12, and a university certificate in social work; others pursued specialized training courses in nursing, early childhood education, and management.[123]

These women also found new opportunities for their talents as volunteers. Their work in the community and church was used as a platform to make changes at the local community level, such as starting a daycare centre, promoting the ethic of caring through membership in the Red Cross, and running a hot lunch program for children in the inner city.[124] Initiatives like these helped to build character, foster racial pride and self-esteem, and prepare youth for the future.

Daughters of postwar cleaners used the new access to education, jobs, and empowerment to enjoy a measure of social mobility that their mothers could not have imagined to be possible. The Thomas and Bernard families typify this trend. They were large, closely knit families that included highly motivated girls poised to make their way in the world just at the time when opportunities were opening up for the Black population. Their contribution to new patterns of education and employment, which resulted from the campaign against discrimination, owed an incalculable debt to their strong mothers – working women who had learned to take full advantage of the limited opportunities presented by cleaning the houses of urban white women.

NOTES

1 The interviews were conducted in 1999 and 2000 by Lana MacLean, a Master of Social Work student, using a structured questionnaire developed by the authors and approved by the Dalhousie University Ethics Committee. As interviewer, MacLean had the advantages of being from outside the community and at the same time known in the community as a church member and a social worker. The interviewees were identified by both Thomas Bernard and MacLean, the former using her close connections with African Nova Scotians in the Halifax Regional Municipality, the latter on the basis of her professional and congregational knowledge of elderly women in the Black community. All the interviews were taped and reviewed by both the authors. We have refrained from giving identifying information about these women in order to preserve the requisite degree of confidentiality. Below, interviewees are identified by fictitious initials.

2 For example, Donald H. Clairmont and Dennis W. Magill, *Nova Scotian Blacks: An Historical and Structural Overview* (Halifax: Institute of Public Affairs, Dalhousie University, 1970); Fred Wien and Joan Browne, 'A Report on Employment Patterns in the Black Communities of Nova Scotia: Marginal Work World Research Program,' Institute of Public Affairs, Dalhousie University, April 1981.

3 Frances Henry's research on the Prestons in the late 1960s, which contrib-

uted to her study of the attitudes and values of Black Nova Scotians, chron-
icles the antagonism between and among the three communities of
Cherrybrook/Lake Loon, East Preston, and North Preston. Frances Henry,
Forgotten Canadians: The Blacks of Nova Scotia (Don Mills, ON: Longman
Canada, 1973), 54–5. For the identification of Henry's 'Far Town' as Cherry-
brook, see Director's Report to the Nova Scotia Human Rights Commis-
sion, 26 May 1969, Jewish Labour Committee (JLC), National Archives of
Canada (NAC), MG 28, vol. 75, no. 41-1.

4 Sid Blum's notes on his visit to Halifax, 1–3 Sept. 1957, JLC, NAC, MG 28,
vol. 75, no. 40-8, Blum visited the Maritimes in his capacity as director of
the Standing Committee on Human Rights of the Canadian Labour Congress. Schiff to Wilson Head, 26 Sept. 1969, Human Rights Commission
(HRC), Public Archives of Nova Scotia (PANS), RG 85, 605-14. Regretably,
since this paper was completed, PANS has deaccessioned or reorganized
beyond recognition the original RG 85 collection. On Blum's early work for
the Jewish Labour Committee, see Ross Lambertson, '"The Dresden Story":
Racism, Human Rights, and the Jewish Labour Committee of Canada,'
Labour/LeTravail 47 (Spring 2001): 71–8.

5 C.R. Brookbank, 'Afro-Canadian Communities in Halifax County, Nova
Scotia: A Preliminary Sociological Survey' (M.A. thesis, University of Toronto, 1949).

6 Although they dismiss transience as an Africville myth promulgated by
Brookbank, Clairmont and Magill contradict themselves by acknowledging
the mobility in and out of the community and the growing diversity after
the war. See Brookbank, 'Afro-Canadian Communities in Halifax County';
Donald H. Clairmont and Dennis William Magill, *Africville: The Life and
Death of a Canadian Black Community* (Toronto: McClelland and Stewart,
1974), 39, 65–70.

7 Notable in the published literature is Constance Backhouse's study of Viola
Desmond's experience of racism in 1946, placed within the context of her
life as a whole. See Backhouse, *Colour-Coded: A Legal History of Racism in
Canada, 1900–1950* (Toronto: University of Toronto Press for the Osgoode
Society for Canadian Legal History, 1999), ch. 7. For theses, see Barbara-
Ann G. Hamilton, 'What Is the Leisure Experience of Older African Nova
Scotian Women?' (M.A. thesis, Dalhousie University, 1998); Susan Marion-
Jean Precious, 'The Women of Africville: Race and Gender in Postwar Hali-
fax' (M.A. thesis, Queen's University, 1999); Sylvia Hamilton, 'African Bap-
tist Women as Activists and Advocates in Adult Education in Nova Scotia'
(M.A. thesis, Mount Saint Vincent University, 2000).

8 Still a matter for debate, there is a considerable literature on policies affect-

ing immigrant domestics since the Second World War. See Franca Iacov-
etta, 'Primitive Villagers and Uneducated Girls: Canada Recruits
Domestics from Italy, 1951-52', *Canadian Woman Studies* 7, 4 (1986): 14–18;
Patricia Daenzer, *Regulating Class Privilege: Immigrant Servants in Canada,
1940s–1990s* (Toronto: Canadian Scholars' Press, 1993); Abigail B. Bakan
and Daiva Stasiulis, eds., *Not One of the Family: Foreign Domestic Workers in
Canada* (Toronto: University of Toronto Press, 1997); Agnes Calliste, 'Can-
ada's Immigration Policy and Domestics from the Caribbean: The Second
Domestic Scheme,' in Jesse Vorst et al., eds., *Race, Class, Gender: Bonds and
Barriers*, rev. ed. (Toronto: Garamond Press for the Society for Socialist
Studies, 1991), 136–68; Vic Satzewich, 'Racism and Canadian Immigration
Policy: The Government's View of Caribbean Migration, 1962–1966,' *Cana-
dian Ethnic Studies* 21,1 (1989): 77–97; Linda Carty, 'African Canadian
Women and the State: "Labour Only, Please,"' in Peggy Bristow et al.,
*'We're Rooted Here and They Can't Pull Is Up': Essays in African Canadian
Women's History* (Toronto: University of Toronto Press, 1994), 193–229. For
a different regional focus, see Rachel Epstein, 'Domestic Workers: The
Experience in B.C.,' in Linda Briskin and Lynda Yanz, eds., *Union Sisters:
Women in the Labour Movement* (Toronto: Women's Press, 1983), 222–37.
  9 W.P. Oliver, Brief Summary of Nova Scotia Negro Communities, March
1964, JLC, NAC, MG 28, vol. 75, no. 40-19.
10 *Clarion* (New Glasgow), 27 Sept. 1947, 6. Roy Brookbank noted during his
graduate fieldwork in 1949 that in the little brick schoolhouse in Hammonds Plains, 'children of the Fourth grade and below attend school in the
afternoon and those above Fourth grade receive instruction in the morning.' Brookbank's field notes in the PANS copy of his thesis, 'Afro-Canadian Communities in Halifax County, Nova Scotia: A Preliminary
Sociological Survey.' For Irene Reddick's experience as a teacher in North
Preston, beginning in 1949, see *Dartmouth Free Press*, 5 Sept. 1963, 1, 12. See
also Doris Evans and Gertrude Tynes, *Telling the Truth. Reflections: Segregated Schools in Nova Scotia* (Hantsport, NS: Lancelot Press, 1995).
11 *Clarion*, 15 Feb. 1947; 15 April 1947, 4; 2 July 1947, 2; Backhouse, *Colour-
Coded*, 234–43.
12 *Clarion*, 15 June 1948, 3. For the identification of the first Black female students at the conservatory see *Atlantic Advocate* (Halifax) 1, 1 (April 1915):
14. The *Atlantic Advocate* was the first Black periodical in Nova Scotia.
13 *Clarion*, Jan. 1947; 1 April 1947, 5; 1–15 May, and 1 June 1947 (three in one
issue), 4; 6 Oct. 1947, 1; 24 Nov. 1948, 6; 12 Jan. 1949, 1.
14 Sid Blum's notes on his visit to Halifax, 2 Sept. 1957, JLC, NAC, MG 28, vol.
75, 40-8; Dalhousie University *Calendars*, 1953–4, 241; 1954–5, 245; 1955–6,
254; 1956–7, 261; Dalhousie *Yearbook*, 1956, 49.

15 The loss of role models through the continued outmigration of the brightest young Blacks is deplored in an address given to the Rotary Club of New Glasgow, on 9 December 1963, by W.S. Kennedy Jones, chair of the Nova Scotian government's interdepartmental committee on human rights, Attorney General (AG), PANS, RG 10, E 288A-2.

16 See clipping from the Port Arthur *News Chronicle*, 21 Nov. 1957, describing Sid Blum's visit to the Maritimes, JLC, NAC, MG 28, vol. 75, no. 40–7.

17 Jean Beverly Ross, 'The Effects of Racial Attitudes and Prejudices on the Colored People of Halifax' (MSW thesis, Maritime School of Social Work, 1959), 32, 39; *The Condition of the Negroes of Halifax City, Nova Scotia* (Halifax: Institute of Public Affairs, Dalhousie University, 1962), 9–12.

18 Taped interview with U.E.

19 See Betty Wangenheim, 'The Negroes of Halifax County,' JLC, NAC, MG 28, vol. 75, no. 40–17, 31; Willard B. Gatewood, *Aristocrats of Color: The Black Elite, 1880–1920* (Bloomington: Indiana University Press, 1990). The JLC copy of Wangenheim's manuscript has lost its identification but that can be verified by the quotation on page 20 of *The Condition of the Negroes of Halifax City, Nova Scotia* which is taken from page 125 of the manuscript. Winks also had access to the manuscript. See Robin W. Winks, *The Blacks in Canada: A History* (Montreal: McGill-Queen's University Press, 1971), 453. Wangenheim's analysis is heavily reliant on the notes she borrowed from Sid Blum.

20 As a student she had been the first Black woman to get summer work as a city playground supervisor. In this capacity she found the white children accepted her. According to a family anecdote, the only adverse comment she reported was that of a Black child who said: 'Humph, they must be scraping the bottom of the barrel because they hired you, a nigger playground supervisor.' Notes of Sid Blum's visit to Halifax, 2 Sept. 1957, JLC, NAC, MG 28, vol. 75, no. 40-8.

21 Marilyn Barber, *Immigrant Domestic Servants in Canada* (Ottawa: Canadian Historical Association, 1991); on the rural-to-urban migration, as well as out-migration of women from the Maritimes, see Betsy Beattie, *Obligation and Opportunity: Single Maritime Women in Boston, 1870–1930* (Montreal and Kingston: McGill-Queen's University Press, 2000), esp. ch. 3; for references to the work placements of girls from the Nova Scotia Training School, see Minutes, 1 April 1937, Local Council of Women of Halifax (LCW), PANS, MG 20, 535-11. For an earlier period, the employment of immigrant and delinquent women is discussed in Magda Fahrni, '"Ruffled" Mistresses and "Discontented" Maids: Respectability and the Case of Domestic Service, 1880–1914,' *Labour/Le Travail* 39 (Spring 1996): 69–97. For Black women see Suzanne Morton, 'Separate Spheres in a Separate World:

African–Nova Scotian Women in Late-19th-Century Halifax County,' in Janet Guildford and Suzanne Morton, eds., *Separate Spheres: Women's Worlds in the 19th-Century Maritimes* (Fredericton: Acadiensis Press, 1994), 185–210.

22 Halifax had some experience of female displaced persons (DPs) from the refugee camps of Europe. In 1949, of 108 DP women in the city, 34 were reported to be employed in domestic work, some presumably in private homes. Report of the Employment for Women Committee for 1949, Annual General Meeting, 16 March 1950, LCW, PANS, MG 20, 536-1.

23 Minutes, 21 March 1946, LCW, PANS, MG 20, 535-13 (quotation); Employment for Women Committee Report for 1947, Annual General Meeting, 18 March 1948, LCW, PANS, MG 20, 536-1. For analysis of the failure of the federal government to build up the industrial potential of the Maritimes during the Second World War, see Ernest R. Forbes, 'Consolidating Disparity: The Maritimes and the Industrialization of Canada during the Second World War,' *Acadiensis* 15, 2 (1986): 3–27. Black women in Nova Scotia, such as Carrie Best, later a journalist, and Irene Reddick, later a teacher, were among those who gained confidence through war work.

24 Employment for Women Committee Report for 1951, Annual General Meeting, 20 March 1952, LCW, PANS, MG 20, 536-1.

25 Employment for Women Committee Report for 1953, Annual General Meeting, 18 March 1954, LCW, PANS, MG 20, 536-2.

26 Gwendolyn Shand and Alice Haverstock, 'Social Status of Women in Nova Scotia,' 1955, National Council of Women (NCW), NAC, MG 228, I25, 101-7.

27 Home Services Questionnaires and Penny Annand's Report, Home Maintenance Committee Files, Nova Scotia Home Economics Association (NSHEA), PANS MG 20, 709-10.

28 Nancy Lubka, 'Household Workers Should Organize,' *The 4th Estate* (Halifax), 13 Nov. 1969.

29 For evidence of rural Black women's farming, craft, market, and peddling activities see the synopses of interviews conducted in the 1980s with people born at the beginning of the twentieth century, including Amelia Brown, Hattie Colley, and Susanna Smith in volume 1 and Rita Brooks, Edith Clayton, Lavinia Ewing, and Kathleen Riley in volume 2 of *Traditional Lifetime Stories: A Collection of Black Memories* (Dartmouth: Black Cultural Centre for Nova Scotia, 1987, 1990).

30 Brand did not identify marital status. 'Survey of Negro Population of Halifax County including Africville but not the remainder of the City, under the terms of reference laid down by Inter-Departmental Committee on

Human Rights,' 8 Aug. 1963, PANS, Acc.No 1992-178/001, Human Rights Minutes and Records 1962–3.

31 Taped interview with U.E.

32 Taped interview with R.L.; Judith Fingard, 'Race, Gender and Domestic Service in Post-War Halifax,' paper presented to the Canadian Historical Association, Edmonton, 2000.

33 Taped interviews with R.J., R.L., P.M.

34 The theme of the domestic workplace as a learning environment is noted in the case of another ethnic group in Frieda Esau Klippenstein, 'Scattered but Not Lost: Mennonite Domestic Servants in Winnipeg, 1920s–50s,' in Catherine A. Cavanaugh and Randi R. Warne, eds., *Telling Tales: Essays in Western Women's History* (Vancouver: UBC Press, 2000), 226.

35 Taped interviews with F.D., P.M., R.L.

36 Taped interviews with J.R., R.J., B.E.

37 Taped interview with P.M.

38 Taped interviews with C.B., U.E., M.T.

39 Ample evidence of live-in service before marriage among Black women born a generation earlier than our interviewees can be found in *Traditional Lifetime Stories*, vols 1 and 2. For a similar experience in the United States, see Barbara Thornton Dill, *Across the Boundaries of Race and Class: An Exploration of Work and Family among Black Female Domestic Servants* (New York: Garland Publishing, 1994), 9.

40 Audrey Macklin, 'On the Inside Looking In: Foreign Domestic Workers in Canada', in Wenona Giles and Sedef Arat-Koc, eds., *Maid in the Market: Women's Paid Domestic Labour* (Halifax: Fernwood Publishing, 1994), 14–45.

41 Taped interviews with M.T., C.B.

42 Jacklyn Cock, *Maids and Madams: Domestic Workers under Apartheid* (London: Women's Press, 1989), 46.

43 Taped interview with C.E., who was prohibited from going into service as a girl by her mother, who had the live-in position described here. For an instructive discussion of the transition to day's work for Black women in the United States, see Elizabeth Clark-Lewis, *Living In, Living Out: African American Domestics in Washington, D.C., 1910–1940* (Washington: Smithsonian Institution Press, 1994), 140–72.

44 Hamilton, 'What Is the Leisure Experience of Older African Nova Scotian Women?'

45 Taped interview with C.E.

46 Patricia Hill Collins, *Black Feminist Thought* (New York and London: Routledge, 1990).

47 W.T. Bernard and C. Bernard, 'It Takes a Village: Building Networks of

Support for African Nova Scotian Families and Children,' in Marilyn Calla-
han and Sven Hessle with Susan Strega, eds., *Valuing the Field* (London:
Ashgate, 2000).

48 Wanda Thomas Bernard, Winnie Benton, and Rene Baptiste, 'Africentric
Perspectives,' unpublished Social Work Conference Proceedings, Halifax,
1999.

49 Charles Saunders, *Share and Care: The Story of the Nova Scotia Home for Colored Children* (Halifax: Nimbus, 1994).

50 Taped interview with G.M.; see also Elizabeth Johnston's recollections of
her mother's domestic work at the NSHCC, *Traditional Lifetime Stories*, 2: 53.

51 One of the former members of the board of directors fondly recalls that the
women of the communities and the African Baptist Association raised
funds for a new roof when the NSHCC was in dire need of repairs. Personal communication with Rev. Dr Donald E. Fairfax, former board member, NSHCC, Nov. 2000.

52 Taped interviews with C.B., P.M. Urban-fringe women shared the commut-
ing problem with township women in South Africa. See Cock, *Maids and
Madams*, 32–3.

53 Taped interview with J.R.

54 Taped interviews with U.E., M.T.

55 *1961 Census of Canada: General Review, The Canadian Labour Force*, Bulletin
7.1-12, especially table 8, and *Labour Force*, Bulletin 3.1-7, table 13; *Nineteenth Annual Report of the Unemployment Insurance Commission*, 1960, 19;
Twenty-Second Annual Report ... , 1963, 14; Sylvia Ostry, *The Occupational
Composition of the Canadian Labour Force* (Ottawa: Dominion Bureau of Statistics, 1967), 76; H. Monck, *Labour Force Participation in Canada, 1971 Census
of Canada*, vol. 4, pt. 2, Bulletin 5.2-1, 38–9; *1961 Census of Canada: General
Review, The Canadian Labour Force*, Bulletin 7.1-12, table 5; *Women at Work in
Nova Scotia* (Halifax: Halifax Women's Bureau, 1973), 8. Until the war,
housework had been the most readily available work for women, employ-
ing 'the single largest category of paid female workers in Canada from 1871
to 1941.' Judy Fudge, 'Little Victories and Big Defeats: The Rise and Fall of
Collective Bargaining Rights for Domestic Workers in Ontario,' in Bakan
and Stasiulis, eds., *Not One of the Family*, 121.

56 The extension of normal state employment regulations to domestic service
was advocated by the Subcommittee on the Post-War Problems of Women
(1943) and the Royal Commission on the Status of Women in Canada
(1970). See Gail Cuthbert Brandt, '"Pidgeon-Holed and Forgotten"': The
Work of the Subcommittee on the Post-War Problems of Women, 1943,'
Histoire sociale/Social History 15, 29 (1982): 249–50, 258.

57 Completed Home Services Questionnaire from a Halifax respondent, Home Maintenance Committee Files, NSHEA, PANS, MG 20, 709-10.

58 The unattractiveness of domestic service – especially with respect to wages, working conditions, and status – was noted by Ruth Hamilton, women's employment adviser, National Employment Service. Minutes, joint meeting of the National Employment Committee and the Maritime Regional Employment Committee, Saint John, 14, 15 April 1947, 11–14 passim, NAC, RG 50, vol. 62-33. The anomalous position of houseworkers, a large percentage of whom were Black, was a concern of the Halifax Women's Bureau, *The 4th Estate*, 9 Sept. 1971, 15.

59 Taped interviews with U.E., J.R., R.L., R.J., P.M., C.B.

60 Taped interviews with F.D., B.E., C.E., U.E., J.R., G.M., M.T.

61 Taped interview with R.L.

62 Brookbank's field notes in 1948 claim that there were no telephones at all in Cherrybrook, New Road (North Preston), or Lucasville.

63 Taped interviews with R.L. and R.J. On the Halifax experiment in interracial pre-schooling, see Barbara S. Clark, 'The Brunswick Cornwallis Pre-School: A Programme for Disadvantaged White and Negro Children,' *Child Study* 24, 3–4 (1967): 17–27; Judith Fingard, 'Town and Gown: Academic Women in Post-War Halifax,' paper presented to the Dalhousie-King's Reading Club, Sept. 2001.

64 Taped interviews with R.L. and R.J.

65 Taped interview with P.M.

66 Taped interview with F.D.

67 Taped interviews with C.B. and F.D.

68 Taped interview with J.R.

69 Taped interviews with B.E. and J.R.

70 Taped interview with B.E. For the desire of one domestic to sue her employer for injuries see *The 4th Estate*, 10 Feb. 1972, 2.

71 Taped interview with B.E. Some did not like to recommend replacements in case they were let down: taped interviews with F.D. and R.L.

72 Betty Wangenheim, 'The Negroes of Halifax County,' JLC, NAC, MG 28, vol. 75, 40-17, 23. J.R., who was raised in Africville, also commented that the (married) women of that community did not work outside the home in the prewar period.

73 Interviewees mention $2.00–2.25 as the immediate daily postwar rate (which was the amount reported to Simmons by a Jost Mission–placed worker for the late 1930s) and often mention $4, a figure that seems to apply to a period in the mid-late 1950s and into the 1961 census period. Young cleaners in an institutional setting in the mid-1950s started at $3 a

day. Taped interviews with U.E., F.D., C.B., R.L., R.J., P.M; *1961 Census of Canada: Labour Force, Earnings of Wage-Earners by Industry Divisions, Cities of 30,000 and Over*, Bulletin 3.3-12, table 34; Christina Simmons, '"Helping the Poorer Sisters": The Women of the Jost Mission, Halifax, 1905–1945,' *Acadiensis* 14, 1 (1984): 12. Average wages for working women in general in 1961 were about twice those of women in the domestic service sector.

74 Taped interviews with U.E., B.E., F.D.

75 Taped interview with C.E.

76 Taped interviews with U.E. and F.D.

77 Taped interview with B.E.

78 Taped interviews with U.E. and M.T.

79 Taped interview with G.M. F.D., who normally ate with the family, was unwilling to join them when they had guests, despite their invitation.

80 Taped interview with J.R.

81 Taped interviews with F.D., U.E., P.M., J.R.

82 On the horrendous experiences of domestics from the Caribbean, see Makeda Silvera, *Silenced* (Toronto: Sister Vision, 1983; reprinted 1989).

83 Taped interview with F.D.

84 Taped interview with P.M.

85 Taped interviews with G.M., F.D., C.E., P.M.

86 Taped interview with J.R.

87 Taped interview with F.D.

88 Taped interviews with U.E. and B.E.

89 Taped interviews with C.B. and P.M.

90 Judith Rollins, *Between Women: Domestics and their Employers* (Philadelphia: Temple University Press, 1985), 93–4, 149. Another useful American study on employer-employee relationships, which refers to a slightly earlier period than the current study, is Phyllis Palmer, *Domesticity and Dirt: Housewives and Domestic Servants in the United States, 1920–1945* (Philadelphia: Temple University Press, 1989).

91 In 1969 the first director of the Nova Scotia Human Rights Commission, himself a Jew, wrote to a Black consultant with respect to North Preston: 'I gather that some women work as domestics in Dartmouth, but lack of adequate transportation (and probably discrimination) bear heavily on their ability to find work.' Marvin Schiff to Wilson Head, 26 Sept. 1969, HRC, PANS, RG 85, 605-14.

92 Taped interviews with F.D. and M.T.

93 Taped interview with U.E.

94 Taped interview with F.D. P.M. left her live-in job with a Jewish family because she was asked to pluck chickens, a task that was too reminiscent of the semi-agrarian childhood in the county that she had just escaped.

95 *Clarion*, 28 Feb. 1947 (see advertisements of Jewish merchants on Gottingen St.); 1, 15 May, 1 June 1947 (one issue).

96 For many aspects of these developments, see Bridglal Pachai, ed. and compiler, *Nova Scotia Human Rights Commission 25th Anniversary, 1967–1992: A History* (Halifax: Nova Scotia Human Rights Commission, 1992). On the activities of the Jewish Labour Committee in postwar Ontario see Carmela Patrias and Ruth A. Frager, '"This Is Our Country, These Are Our Rights": Minorities and the Origins of Ontario's Human Rights Campaigns,' *Canadian Historical Review* 82, 1 (2001): 1–35.

97 *Dartmouth Free Press*, 4 Oct. 1962, 12. Frances Mansfield (later Harper) went on to have a successful career as a registered nurse. Her obituary nonetheless noted her employment at Jacobson's, clearly a landmark in her life and that of the Black community. *Halifax Mail-Star*, 4 March 2003, C15.

98 The major organizations that were working to combat racism are listed in a summary of human rights projects and activities by Donald Maclean, secretary, Halifax Human Rights Advisory Committee, 1965, JLC, NAC, MG 28, vol. 75, no. 40-14.

99 'Human Rights and Social Development,' an address given by J.M. Harding, Minister of Public Welfare, to Rotary Club of Truro, 16 Nov. 1964, AG, PANS, RG 10 E, 288A-2.

100 The interdepartmental committee on human rights met between 14 November 1962 and 9 August 1967. AG, PANS, RG 10 E, 288A-2.

101 See Pachai, *Nova Scotia Human Rights Commission 25th Anniversary.*

102 Final Report on the Problem of Unemployment for the Negro, submitted to the Negro Employment Interim Committee by J.R. Oliver, Executive Secretary, 14 Aug. 1968, JLC, NAC, MG 28, vol. 75, no. 40-19.

103 See *Clarion*, 28 Feb. 1948, 1.

104 Gwendolyn Shand, *Adult Education among the Negroes of Nova Scotia* (Halifax: Institute of Public Affairs, Dalhousie University, 1961), 13.

105 *Maclean's*, 12 May 1956.

106 List of accomplishments in the human rights field in province of Nova Scotia, HRC, PANS, RG 85, 604-20.

107 Taped interview with R.J.

108 Minutes of meeting of concerned people regarding establishment of daycare centre and medical clinic in North Preston, 26 Sept. 1969, and Report of Harry Adams, Welfare Officer, Halifax County re North Preston Day Care, 28 Oct. 1969, HRC, PANS, RG 85, 605-14; East Preston Day Care Centre, 1972–1979, HRC, PANS, RG 85, 602-2.

109 Taped interviews with R.L. and R.J.; *Dartmouth Free Press*, 23 Feb. 1972, 5.

110 Taped interviews with U.E., G.M., J.R., F.D., M.T., P.M.

111 Taped interviews with R.J., P.M., U.E., F.D., M.T.
112 Calvin Ruck and Eugene Williams were hired by the Department of Social
    Welfare in the late 1960s as community development workers in the Pre-
    ston area. The cooperative housing project was developed as a strategy to
    help bring housing in the area up to standard. On the housing projects, see
    Mohamed Abucar, *Struggle for Development: The Black Communities of North
    and East Preston and Cherry Brook, Nova Scotia, 1784–1987* (Halifax: the
    author, 1988), ch. 7.
113 Lawyers are regarded as advocates in many communities. Well-known
    activist lawyer Rocky Jones defines the legal profession as a vehicle for
    redressing systemic injustice for those who are marginalized by race or
    class or by some other form of oppression. Therefore we classify law as a
    helping profession in this context.
114 For George C. Bernard's reminiscences, see *Traditional Lifetime Stories*, 2:
    10–12.
115 The Knowledge Lab, 'Black Women and Community Leadership:
    Together Changing the World' (report produced by the Knowledge Lab, a
    Feminist Research Women's Collective in Montreal, 2001). Four the
    Moment not only had a political message in song but also significantly
    influenced and changed the arts culture in Nova Scotia by challenging
    local and regional arts organizations to be more inclusive while simulta-
    neously working to create alternative media for the presentation of Black
    arts and cultural traditions.
116 Joyce A. Ladner, *Tomorrow's Tomorrow: The Black Woman* (New York:
    Anchor Books, 1972), 265; Collins, *Black Feminist Thought*.
117 Wanda Thomas Bernard and Candace Bernard, 'Passing the Torch: A
    Mother and Daughter Reflect on Their Experience Across Generations,'
    Canadian Woman Studies 18, 2/3 (1998): 46–50.
118 However this journey has not been so smooth for the boys. For the racial
    aspects of their experiences of education and employment see Terry
    Symonds, 'Techniques on the Survival of the Black Family: From the Male
    Perspective, in Preserving the Black Family' (unpublished conference pro-
    ceedings, Association of Black Social Workers, Halifax, 1989); Wanda Tho-
    mas Bernard, Lydia Lucas White, and Dorothy Moore, 'Triple Jeopardy:
    Assessing Life Experiences of Black Nova Scotian Women from a Social
    Work Perspective,' *Canadian Social Work Review* 10, 2 (1993): 256–76;
    Wanda Thomas Bernard, 'Survival and Success: As Defined by Black Men
    in Sheffield, England and Halifax, Canada' (PhD thesis, University of
    Sheffield, 1996).
119 Black Learners Advisory Committee, *Report on Education, Redressing Ine-
    quality: Empowering Black Learners* (Halifax: Author, 1994).

120 A.W. MacKay, J. Eastman, A. Johnstone, J. Jones-Darrell, V. Robinson, and K.S. Wood, *Breaking Barriers: Report of the Task Force on Access for Black and Native People* (Halifax: Dalhousie University, 1989).
121 See affirmative action requests for employment, 1976–80, HRC, PANS, RG 85, 615-1.
122 Edna Staebler, 'Would You Change the Lives of These People?' *Maclean's*, 12 May 1956, 60.
123 Taped interviews with G.M., C.B., J.R., R.L., R.J., U.E., P.M. Similarly in Dartmouth, Adrienne Lucas Sehatzadeh noted that her mother, a resident after 1948 of the 'Black end' of Crichton Avenue, worked as a domestic once her children were school aged and then became a personal care-worker for sixteen years at Northwood Manor, Halifax's major eldercare facility. 'Survival of an African Nova Scotian Community: Up the Avenue, Revisited' (M.A. thesis, Dalhousie University, 1998), 135.
124 Taped interviews with R.J., P.M., U.E.

'Home Nursing Has Continued to Present Problems ...' The St John Ambulance Home Nursing Program in Nova Scotia

FRANCES GREGOR

In 1966 Margaret Hunter, chief nursing officer for the St John Ambulance Association and Brigade in Canada, visited Halifax to promote the association's program in home nursing. While in the city she declared, in an interview reported in the local press, '[we] need ... to teach the public to be able to look after themselves and know what to do when sickness strikes in a home.'[1] The members of the Nova Scotia Council of St John welcomed Hunter's visit and the profile her words gave the home nursing program.[2] Although St John Ambulance could take pride in a seventy-five-year record of training and service in the province, at the time of her visit the popularity of its home nursing program was flagging. In 1966 only 180 completion awards were made in the province in home nursing, in contrast to 2,791 made in first aid,[3] the association's major training program. Nationally, only 2,400 awards were made in home nursing, while 74,000 were made in first aid, indicating the country-wide problem of course participation.

The council's concern, however, was not only with the home nursing program; rather, the whole St John Ambulance movement appeared to be in decline. In 1966 membership in the St John Ambulance Brigade, the volunteer corps, was falling. Long-time members were aging and withdrawing from active service. Young members could not be recruited in the numbers needed to maintain brigade strength.[4] This problem, bad enough for the brigade, had consequences for the vitality of the training programs, especially home nursing. Never as popular with the public as the first aid program, the home nursing program could at least count on brigade nursing divisions to provide both new and recertifying participants, but as brigade enrolments declined so too did the numbers requiring training.

Persuading Nova Scotians to train in home nursing, whether or not they were brigade members,[5] had not always been the challenge it was in 1966. Program participation rates blossomed during the Second World War and reached a peak in 1942, when over 1,200 home nursing certificates were awarded. Rates remained steady in the 1950s even though they never again achieved wartime levels. In the mid to late 1960s, however, a gradual decline began to occur in both the number of persons taking the program and the programs offered. This decline could not be reversed despite the stalwart recruiting efforts of the soon-to-retire brigade nursing officer, Marion Grant. In his annual report of 25 June 1971, the president of the Nova Scotia Council, Harris Miller, declared 'Home Nursing has continued to present problems and with Mrs. Grant's immanent [sic] retirement we will have new problems. Mrs. Grant has laboured under considerable difficulties to encourage this training and it seems almost a losing battle.'[6] His words were prescient. By the mid-1970s, the traditional home nursing program – and Marion Grant – were gone, save for the occasional course offered by one of the brigade nursing divisions (themselves struggling for survival) or within a community adult education program.

This paper examines a twenty-five-year period, 1950–75, in the history of the St John Ambulance Association and Brigade in Nova Scotia to elucidate the reasons for the decline of the home nursing program. In its day, this program prepared voluntary aid detachment (VAD) nurses for service in two world wars and thousands of Nova Scotia women in the care of the sick. Its failure seems particularly relevent now that early discharge from hospital and care at home are such central health care practices. I argue that the gradual loss of the program's vitality is linked most directly to the changing and ultimately declining fortunes of the brigade in Nova Scotia. These, in turn, were influenced by developments in the world beyond the organization, developments in health care in Canada and in the lives of women who were the mainstay of the brigade in Nova Scotia. Ultimately, the masculine ethos of both the association and the brigade meant that they were unable to respond creatively to the challenges presented by these changes in social policy and social attitudes.

A brief history of these two organizations is essential to an understanding of the gendered nature of their approach. The St John Ambulance Association and the St John Ambulance Brigade are two foundations of the worldwide Order of St John of Jerusalem, established to serve citizens of the industrial towns and cities of late-nineteenth-century England. The association provided training programs for its volunteers in first aid and home nursing, while the brigade provided voluntary first aid and rescue services. Founded by the Order of St John in England in 1877 and 1887, respectively, these organizations quickly spread to Canada and other countries, while remaining under the control of the order.[7] In 1882 members of the St John Ambulance Association began giving courses in first aid in Quebec City and by 1892 had established twelve branches of the association across Canada.[8] Within twenty years the St John Ambulance Brigade formed sex-segregated divisions – ambulance divisions for men and nursing divisions for women – in many parts of the country.[9]

While these terms suggest a sex-segregated division of labour within the brigade (first aid service for men, home nursing for women), this was not entirely the case. From its inception, the primary function of the brigade was to maintain a corps of volunteers, both men and women, trained in first aid.[10] For female members, preparation in home nursing was an additional requirement. Women trained in home nursing and men trained in first aid were to be used in voluntary service at community events, within the home (in the case of home nursing), and to supplement regular rescue and hospital personnel in times of extraordinary need. Since the inception of the brigade in Canada over one hundred years ago, members have given thousands of hours of voluntary service in communities large and small, at home and overseas, and in both peace time and wartime.[11] The vast majority of this service has been in staffing first aid posts at community events.

A branch of the St John Ambulance Association was founded in Halifax on 24 June 1892; three years later a branch of the St John Ambulance Brigade was established. In the decades that followed, thousands of Nova Scotians were trained in first aid in courses taught at the St John Ambulance offices in Halifax, at work sites, and in community facilities and schools throughout the province. At the same time ambulance and nursing divisions of the brigade developed in Halifax and Dartmouth, and elsewhere.[12]

There is no record of when home nursing classes were first offered in Halifax or in the rest of the province but it seems likely that they were already established at the time of the Halifax Explosion in 1917. Members of the Halifax Central Nursing Division No. 17 of the St John Ambulance Brigade assisted doctors and nurses in caring for the injured in hospitals. Lady Divisional Superintendent Clara H. MacIntosh, the wife of a physician, and an active member of the Local Council of Women of Halifax, opened her house to the injured and also began the task of organizing the hundreds of men and women who volunteered for relief work. Further evidence for the availability of home nursing instruction in the early decades of the twentieth century is found in the records of the Victorian Order of Nurses (VON). A history of that organization notes that, at the time of the influenza pandemic of 1918, its executive council 'set aside normal regulations in order to permit [VON] branches to recruit and train assistants from the volunteer corps of the St John Ambulance Association.'[13] It is probable that, given the presence of a VON branch in Halifax at the time, volunteer recruits from St John Ambulance Brigade, trained in home nursing, assisted this visiting nurse service in the care of the sick.

In Nova Scotia during the 1950–75 period, the strength of the brigade was in the number and size of its nursing divisions. In the 1960s, when combined divisions began to emerge, joining previously existing (and struggling) ambulance and nursing divisions, nursing divisions consistently and significantly outnumbered both the combined divisions and separate ambulance divisions by a ratio of 2:1.[14]

Brigade divisions were quasi-military organizations.[15] Members wore uniforms, met regularly for drills, inspections, and competitions, and were awarded medals and other insignia for years of service. They were organized hierarchically by rank. The provincial nursing superintendent and the provincial nursing officer, headquartered in Halifax, oversaw the activities of all nursing divisions within the province. The provincial nursing superintendent made regular visits to each division to conduct inspections or competitions. The provincial nursing officer helped divisions recruit and train new members. This frequently involved the difficult task of finding registered nurses to teach the home nursing program.[16]

The association and brigade were administered through a volunteer board of management of the Nova Scotia Council of St John Ambulance, made up of Halifax-Dartmouth business leaders and physicians, the majority male. Despite the overwhelming preponderance of women in the divisions of the brigade, in neither organization during these years did women fill the role of president of the association or commissioner of the brigade. The provincial superintendent of nursing divisions was the most senior role filled by women. Dr. E. Pearl Hopgood, a psychiatrist, held the position during the 1950s until her sudden death in 1957. She was succeeded by Isobel MacAulay, who filled the role until her retirement in 1975. Hopgood and MacAulay reported on the activities of the nursing divisions at the regular meetings of the executive council and the annual meeting. Their reports, often lengthy, provided precise detail about the contribution made by the women of the nursing divisions. The report delivered in June 1965 by MacAulay shows the wide range of public events at which members of nursing divisions staffed a first aid post and lists their other work:

> The past year the Brigade Women worked in 62 separate events, such as Exhibitions – Fairs – Revivals – Crusades – Musical Rides – Swimming – First Aid Posts – Summer Camps – Band Concerts – Natal Day Celebrations – Picnics – Plays – Cruises – Lectures – Skating Sessions and Parties – Ice Capades – Clinics – Scottish Gatherings of the Clans – Festivals – Kermesse – Tract [sic] and Field Events – Transporting and escorting patients – Harbour Excursions – Lobster Carnivals, and taught Home Nursing and First Aid Classes, and helped with Save a Life Week. They gave 3606 voluntary hours, treating 760 casualties, and in so doing 679 appearances were made. Over 4000 hours Paid Nursing duties have been reported and over 500 Voluntary hours.[17]

The image of the St John Ambulance Brigade promoted to the public through promotional brochures of the 1950s suggested an organization of equal numbers of men and women. Men are shown in military-style uniforms in active, rescue situations.[18] Women are shown wearing a white linen head veil, bib, and apron, feeding a sick child or helping an elderly person get out of bed. These highly gendered images speak to the masculine and military ethos of the organization. The clear message they broadcast is that, within the brigade (the 'army' of St John Ambulance), saving lives under stressful conditions is what men do while women nurture the young and tend the frail within the safe environment of the home. These images from the 1950s reveal the brigade as an organization reproducing the gender order of the day within the familiar social form of military organization. They obscure the fact that, in Nova Scotia at least, by sheer dint of numbers, women 'were' the brigade. Women performed the majority of brigade first aid work, which, setting heroic images aside, was usually the mundane work of bandaging scrapes and wrapping sprains. A masculine ethos was present in the association as well as the brigade. Not only was the leadership of the association male, but more importantly the major training program, and source of revenue, was first aid, a program promoted as having a clearly masculine character.

The home nursing program was designed to teach women to provide rudimentary nursing care, both on their own and under the supervision of a professional nurse. The specific program objectives evolved over the years; changing objectives reflected changes in the social and health care conditions of the day. What did not change was the program's assumption that care in the home is the responsibility of women, and that deference is owed by the home nurse to the professional care provider, especially the physician. Change in the objectives but constancy in the regulation of trainee behaviour is revealed in instructional manuals issued in widely separated years.

The objective of the program of the 1930s was to prepare a home nurse to care for accident or illness in the home under the supervision of a doctor. Unlike succeeding programs, there is no evidence that it prepared one to perform one's maternal responsibilities more skilfully. The instructional manual published in 1932 described the personal qualities the home nurse must (and must not) possess, and provided clear direction on matters of personal hygiene and clothing.[19] The manual articulated the desired moral character (reliability, self-control, loyalty) and set a standard of behaviour that it appears to assume was absent in the women learning to be home nurses. It reads as a form of job training for working-class women, at that time the class of women who became nurses or domestic workers. While the 1932 manual was published in England, it was used in every country where St John Ambulance was established, including Canada. It is reasonable to assume that the financial hardship that affected many Canadian families in the economic depression of the 1930s may have led women to take the course with the view to seeking employment. In the period before medicare, families requiring the services of a home nurse but not able to afford a professionally trained one may well have turned to a St John Ambulance–prepared nurse for assistance.

The program of the 1950s differed from its predecessor of the 1930s in several respects. The objective shifted from training a woman to assist the doctor to training a mother and homemaker in the competent performance of simple nursing care. It introduced the notion that home nursing training was excellent preparation for voluntary service in the community and that it gave youth volunteers a taste of professional nursing as a career choice. Unlike the 1932 manual, which was silent on the issue of employment, the 1954 manual explicitly declared that the training was not intended as preparation for professional or paid nursing.[20] However, it seems likely that this directive did not have much force. Emma Dick, who joined the Halifax North Nursing Division in 1953 and rose to the rank of provincial nursing officer, remembers that some women who took the home nursing program found employment with their nursing skills.[21] Overall, the program of the mid-1950s was part of the postwar message to women that their proper place was in the home or in volunteer work in the community.

The objectives of the program of the 1950s were enlarged in 1957 when St John Ambulance and the Canadian Red Cross Society, as part of a national civil defence preparedness initiative by the federal government, agreed to take on the role of preparing a 'volunteer nursing auxiliary reserve force.' To the objective of competent home nurse and volunteer was added the objective of nursing auxiliary, a lay helper to work alongside doctors and nurses in treatment centres and hospitals, caring for the vast number of casualties a modern war was sure to bring. Responsibilities of the nursing auxiliary, too, went far beyond those of the home nurse to include, under professional supervision, 'controlling hemorrhage, immobilizing fractures and applying dressings to wounds and burns.'[22] To prepare the nursing auxiliary for the extended responsibilities she would face, a forty-four-hour supervised hospital training program was recommended by the civil defence authorities for 'selected trainees.'[23]

The addition of civil defence preparedness to the traditional objectives of the home nursing program had an enduring impact on the character of the course. Long after the threat of nuclear war had waned, the opportunity for home nursing enrollees to take the forty-four-hour hospital program remained. The majority of those who took the opportunity were members of the nursing divisions of the brigade. It is unclear why this additional training endured. There is no evidence that hospitals ever called upon the services of program graduates. Yet there is evidence in the annual reports of the provincial superintendent of nursing divisions that nursing division members performed both paid and voluntary service.[24] The nature of this paid work is unclear. Although there is no direct link in the records between paid service by nursing division members and the fulfillment of the forty-four-hour program, it is not unreasonable to assume that such service was rendered in nursing homes or other institutions of care. For those who were selected or applied for it, the forty-four-hour experience constituted a form of on-the-job training and would have increased the employability of those trained, whether as division members or as individuals. Another explanation for the endurance of the forty-four-hour program is that the brigade continued to believe there was a domain of action for the nursing divisions as a reserve army of home nurses, ready to respond to an unexpected demand on professional nursing services following local disaster. The memory of the Halifax Explosion of 1917 may have lingered in the collective consciousness of the brigade as a reminder of the need to be prepared, and at the highest possible level. The memory of St John Ambulance–trained VADs serving in two world wars may have acted as a further reminder of the value of having volunteers with extended training available for service. The home nursing program undoubtedly provided a highly professionalized course of instruction, prepared and presented by professionals. The forty-four-hour program, by taking the trainee into the hospital and placing her alongside professional nurses, was an opportunity to extend the professionalism of the training even further.

While training for participation in disaster relief remained a part of the home nursing program until the mid-1960s, it receded in importance and was eclipsed by preparing women for their essential role in caring for sick family members, which became the core objective of home nursing. But the requirement for such training became linked to changes in the state of Canada's health services, especially government-administered hospital insurance and the demand for hospital care. Women were urged to prepare in home nursing so that they could relieve the pressure on existing facilities, which, the training manual claimed, were expanding but still not adequate to meet demand. This message presaged the role the association hoped to play some ten years later when curtailment of hospital-sector growth raised the possibility of training women to participate in government-sponsored programs of care in the home.

The home nursing program of the mid-1960s used a 1965 Canadian text published by St John Ambulance, *Patient Care in the Home: A Textbook of Home Nursing*, prepared by leading nurse administrators.[25] The new manual was well received and became the standard text in home nursing across the country. In Halifax it was used for the first time in 1966 in home nursing classes taught at Camp Hill Hospital.[26] A unique aspect of this text was the emphasis on improvisation of sick room equipment not normally found in the home. Thus, in situations where the head of the bed needed raising, the manual suggested placing the top bed legs in juice cans filled with sand; where bed covers needed to be kept off frail legs, it showed how a cardboard carton could be fashioned into an attractive bed cradle.

The text was liberally illustrated with black and white drawings depicting typical examples of caregiving situations and equipment. Without exception the caregiver depicted is an adult female and the physician, when shown, is a male. In the chapter entitled 'Family Health Planning for Disaster,' 'father' is shown taking directions over the telephone from a male 'official' while 'children' gather up toys in the background. 'Mother' is nowhere to be seen! In 1969, a second, pocket book–sized text, *Home Nursing for Young Canadians* was produced for youth enrolled in the 'preliminary course in home nursing.' The very few illustrations depict young women in caregiving activities. The drawings in both these texts indicate that females were most certainly the intended audience for the home nursing program. For the girls and women who took the program, these manuals reinforced the notion that care of the sick is the responsibility of female members of society.

The approach to content presentation in the 1965 text was similar to the approach in basic 'nursing arts' texts for professional nursing students of the same era.[27] In its systematic approach to the care of the body and the maintenance of the sick room, the text imparted a professionalism to women's traditional caregiving tasks such as cleaning, bathing, and feeding, which contrasted sharply with the domestic images that filled these books. Having studied the text, having practised the various skills of observation and treatment, and having passed the examination, those who completed the program were deemed capable of becoming part of a team of professional care providers in the home care of the ill.

This text was the first St John Ambulance home nursing text to be used in Canada authored by nurses instead of physicians. The authority of these nurses to speak on home nursing derived from their qualifications and their leadership positions within Canadian nursing. Their authorship was also indicative of the connection between the St John Ambulance and the highest levels of the nursing profession in Canada. This connection was present at both the national and provincial levels. In 1959 both Christine Livingston and M. Pearl Stiver were members of the Priory Council of Canada, the national governing body of both the association and the brigade. In 1960 Jean Leask, RN, newly appointed executive director of the VON, replaced Livingston, and in 1963, Helen Mussalem, EdD, RN, the new executive director for the Canadian Nurses Association, replaced Stiver.[28] The nurses in these positions were recognized as Canada's 'first nurses' by the staff in the national association who had the responsibility for the home nursing program. They valued the prestige these nursing leaders lent to the program.

At the same time in Nova Scotia, nursing leaders were members of the governance structure of the Nova Scotia Council. In 1957 the Provincial Executive Committee of Council included Agnes Butler, RN, executive director, Victorian Order of Nurses; Florence Gass, RN, director of nursing, Victoria General Hospital; and Lillian Grady, RN, director of nursing education, Halifax Infirmary. While nursing leaders were appointed to influential committees within St John Ambulance in Nova Scotia, so too the provincial nursing officer of the brigade was invited to attend the annual meetings of the Registered Nurses Association of Nova Scotia, and during the period of civil defence preparedness, nursing division leaders attended a planning committee organized by the association.[29] The presence of nursing leaders on national and provincial governing bodies of St John Ambulance was significant for the credibility, perhaps even the survival, of the home nursing program. At the national level Mussalem remembers the struggle she and other nurses waged in the 1960s and 1970s to have the nursing component of the mission taken seriously by the Priory Council, which was made up almost entirely of men.[30] Mussalem is credited by her nursing peers at St John with initiating the creation of a professional advisory committee. This committee of physicians and nurses was formed after Mussalem made 'some very strong comments' about the lack of influence of nursing within the organization.[31] While home nursing had its nurse advocates at the national level, it is not clear that similar advocates were present among the nurses who served at the provincial level.

A further sign of the links between the program and the profession was the long-standing national policy that instructors be registered nurses and, if possible, experienced in teaching or supervision. Nursing divisions were advised to seek the assistance of the Registered Nurses Association of each province in finding nurses prepared to be home nursing instructors. However, this directive represented an ideal that over the years gave way to the reality of local conditions, especially where instructor qualifications were concerned. In Nova Scotia in 1970, for example, Marion Grant, provincial nursing officer, organized a training program for selected lay instructors to qualify them to instruct under the overall supervision of a registered nurse.[32]

Because they were not a permanent part of the St John organization, home nursing instructors were provided with teaching guides to ensure a uniform standard of delivery of the course. The 1960 guide describes in detail the organization of the program and the regulations the instructor was to enforce.[33] Like earlier program manuals, it emphasized the values of cleanliness, punctuality, and strict adherence to procedures and the doctor's orders. One participant in the home nursing program, in a letter to Margaret Matheson, RN, her instructor, indicated she had learned this lesson:

> This course has been most helpful to me – especially in seeing myself in relation to my two small daughters. It has given me a different feeling, also toward sick persons (young and old) – a much more tolerant one. Moreover, I would not hesitate to look after a patient although I would still rely on my doctor and my textbook I feel all people (men and women) would benefit from this course.[34]

It seems clear that the home nursing program prepared the graduate to become the eyes and ears of the professional, to see herself as their agent in the home and to feel the obligation of the professional care-giver. The requirement to employ registered nurses, where possible, as program instructors and to use a text authored by leading Canadian nurses, the presence on the St John Ambulance Provincial Executive Committee of local nursing leaders, and the attendance of the provincial nursing officer at annual meetings of the Registered Nurses Association of Nova Scotia, signalled more than a simple connection between the home nursing program and professional nursing. These elements conferred authority on the knowledge contained within the home nursing program, and ultimately on those who practised their skills as graduates of the program.

In the years I have examined, one motivation for women to enrol in the home nursing program was to join a nursing division within the St John Ambulance Brigade. Yet, classes were open to anyone who wanted the training, and this fact directs attention to other reasons for enrolling in the program. A history of public health insurance in Canada reveals a picture of both the health status of Canadians and the health care available to them at mid-century.[35] Two facts emerge of significance for the home nursing program. First, Canadians were not a healthy lot, and second, paying for both physician and hospital care was an individual responsibility.[36]

The Canadian Sickness Survey of 1950–1 was a year-long survey of a random sample of 40,000 Canadian households.[37] It found that 80 per cent of the total population reported a departure from good health, with an average of over two episodes in one year. Forty-eight per cent of the population reported a total of over 11,000,000 periods of bed

care, or an average of 5.5 bed days of care per person, during the survey year. (Some of these were in hospital.) Infections, ranging from
simple colds and influenza to rheumatic fever and tuberculosis, were
leading causes of illness. For some conditions, such as rheumatic fever,
prolonged bed rest was the prescribed treatment; for others such rest
was simply a measure taken by the sick person to manage illness-
related fatigue. Heart attack was a leading cause of hospitalization for
adult males, and rehabilitation of those who survived involved prolonged periods of rest.

The survey paints a picture of health and health care in which the
presence of a daughter, wife, or mother trained in home nursing
emerges as a distinct advantage, if not a necessity, when there was illness in the family. In a typical year most Nova Scotians, like most
Canadians, could expect to be ill and need a period of bed rest. Furthermore, for most of them, the cost of physician visits, hospitalization,
and medications had to be met through their own wages or savings.

The survey also obtained information on family expenditures on
health care. The report estimated that in the study year over $370 mil-
lion was spent by Canadian families on health care. The four top items
in terms of expenditures were prepayment plans for medical and hospital care, physicians' services, hospital care, and prescribed medi-
cines. Just 8.4 per cent of families surveyed reported contributing to
medical care prepayment plans and only 33.5 per cent of families made
payments to hospital care prepayment plans. The availability of both
medical and hospital plans varied from province to province. Maritime
Medical Care Incorporated, a non-profit organization founded by the
Nova Scotia Medical Society to offer prepaid medical insurance programs, came into effect in Nova Scotia only in 1948. By the end of 1950
British Columbia, Alberta, Saskatchewan, and Newfoundland were
the only provinces that had government hospital insurance programs
covering some portion of the population.[38]

While it seems reasonable to assume that fear of not being able to
afford medical help and hospital care led women to enrol in the program in the 1950s, records do not exist to confirm this. Yet it is likely at
a time when 'watchful waiting' and 'tender loving care' were still
among the most important tools of physicians and nurses that the
presence of a trained family member might influence the decision of
the doctor about the need for costly hospitalization. Perhaps the ill
child, husband, or grandmother might be cared for at home by a
female family member, under the supervision of a visiting nurse. If

hospitalization proved a necessity, perhaps the stay could be reduced if trained help were available at home. These considerations would have had special force for the physicians of poor or rural families. A further aspect of home nursing training that may have prompted enrolments was the emphasis on prevention of infection and the importance of good nutrition in maintaining health. At mid-century, communicable disease was a serious matter. Instruction in personal or household practices that could reduce or prevent the spread of infection would be beneficial on several counts: fewer visits to the doctor, fewer days lost to sick time for a wage earner or school child. It would not have been unreasonable for the local public health nurse or VON to encourage the taking of the home nursing program in a family where illness or the threat of infectious disease was present.

The records of St John do not distinguish between enrollees who were members of the brigade and those who were not, and so it is not possible to determine which was the more important reason for taking the home nursing program: brigade membership requirements or family sick care responsibilities. While the conditions of health and health care in the 1950s may have played a role in recruiting some women to the program, the small number of home nursing certificates awarded, in comparison to those awarded in first aid, suggest that it was membership in the brigade that attracted women.

The degree of motivation to train in home nursing to meet a family health care emergency started to erode in the mid-1950s, when Canadians began to experience changes in their health care because of federal government policy decisions.[39] These changes began with the post–Second World War entry of the federal government into the health domain. Although health care was traditionally the purview of the provinces, the national government, after considerable negotiation, embarked on what became a twenty-year project to establish state-sponsored hospital and medical care in Canada. In 1948 a program of national health grants was introduced which provided financial assistance to the provinces for hospital construction and professional training, among other allocations. In the first five years of that program 46,000 beds and 4,600 health care workers were added across the country, and these numbers grew significantly in the next five years. In April 1957 the Hospital Insurance and Diagnostic Services Act was passed. This provided, through a cost-sharing arrangement with the provinces, a basic level of care in acute, convalescent, and chronic-care hospitals (but not mental hospitals, TB sanatoria, nursing homes, and homes for the aged), regardless of a patient's sex, age, or physical condition. Nova Scotia began to participate in this program on 1 January 1959. In December 1966 the Medical Care Insurance Act was passed. In provinces that joined the program, the cost of physician services, both general practitioners and specialists, was funded under another cost-sharing arrangement. Nova Scotia entered this program on 1 April 1969. Within two decades, therefore, Canada went from being a country where a significant portion of illness care was centred in the home and paid for by the individual (insurance plans in certain provinces notwithstanding) to a country where institutional care for acute and some chronic conditions was widely available and funded through the public purse.

Challenges to enrolment in the home nursing program came from more than tax-supported hospital and medical care. The burgeoning of scientific and medical knowledge that began in the postwar years brought new drugs (antibiotics, anti-cancer drugs) and other therapies – open heart surgery, for example – to bear on previously debilitating diseases. Bed rest and immobility as the appropriate responses to illness began to give way to a philosophy of activity and the maximum possible physical independence. Yet more change was to come. The early 1970s saw the beginnings in Nova Scotia, as in the rest of the country, of an emphasis by government on health promotion. This was evident in the 1972 report of the Nova Scotia Council of Health and in the 1974 report of the Department of National Health and Welfare, the so-called Lalonde Report.[40] The message in both these documents was that citizens must take more responsibility for their own health and adopt practices that prevent illness and enhance well-being. Barbara Hart, RN, who was in 1971 the nursing officer in No. 481 Nursing Division in Dartmouth, appeared to understand the move towards health promotion and what it might mean for St John Ambulance's traditional instructional programs. She reported that she had added to the compulsory portion of the home nursing curriculum for a cadet division, 'a two hour session with Rev. Dennis Godley and Brian P. [sic] on the Use and Abuse of Drugs' and 'a showing of two films, Girl to Woman and Family Life, followed by a group discussion on the films and problems on sex in general.'[41] Hart's innovation suggests she saw that St John Ambulance could play a role in spreading the government message of health promotion to young people. Within a few years, however, as Judith Fingard notes in her essay in this collection, Hart became the first executive director of the Metro Area Family Planning

Association, which suggests she believed that St John Ambulance could not make the change to the new approach.

Changes in the health policy arena were matched during the twenty-five-year period under study by significant changes in the lives of Canadian women. They had fewer children and entered the labour force in larger numbers. Canadian social historians note that the economic depression of the 1930s and the sacrifices of the war years fuelled a postwar desire for material goods. To purchase the cars, furniture, and appliances that were heavily advertised in the 1950s as essential to modern life, women went out to work. In 1951, almost 25 per cent of all women, and nearly 10 per cent of married women, worked in the labour force. By 1971, these figures had grown to 39 per cent and 33 per cent, respectively, and would continue to rise in succeeding decades. In the 1950s married women in the workforce were likely to be those whose families had grown up. By 1975, women with children under sixteen years of age represented a significant and growing proportion of the female working population. The addition of full-time employment to the responsibilities of home and family affected the time and energy a working women had available for volunteer activities, such as staffing a first aid post at a community event.

Although the 1950s ushered in profound changes in health care and in the lives of women, these changes took some time to exert an effect on St John Ambulance. These were good years, marked by financial stability in the association and membership growth in the brigade. The militarism of the early postwar years, in concert with the continuing Cold War in the 1950s, made recruitment to the brigade a relatively easy matter, and several new divisions were opened in the province during these years. In 1956 and 1958 the work of St John Ambulance in the province was very high profile after it responded to the mining disasters in Springhill, Cumberland County.

While traditional first aid service at community events remained the bulk of the work of the divisions, other forms of voluntary service were added. In her report to the annual meeting of 25 June 1953, Provincial Superintendent of Nursing Divisions Pearl Hopgood noted that brigade members were assisting the Department of Psychiatry at the Victoria General Hospital by taking patients to the clinic and accompanying them to their homes after treatment. Six years later, her successor, Isobel MacAulay, called for the hiring of a provincial nursing officer, such was the intensity of the work of organizing the nursing divisions throughout the province. Shortly thereafter, Sharon Stacey, RN, was hired and set about her work, which included organizing home nursing classes. At the next Provincial Executive Committee meeting, this new staff member could report the formation of a provincial nursing advisory committee of eleven RNs and 'an upsurge of interest in Home Nursing training with some 22 classes completed or in progress, involving some 570 women.'[42]

The optimism found in the nursing divisions extended to the Nova Scotia Council of St John Ambulance as a whole. The council, while occupying cramped quarters above a commercial establishment on Barrington Street, could boast of a heathy financial position.[43] The future seemed to be assured if the right conditions, such as a better 'home' for St John Ambulance, could be put in place. At the 1957 annual meeting, the secretary to the Nova Scotia Council reported that 'from 1942-1957, some 51,500 persons have been trained by St. John in Nova Scotia. This is roughly one in every twelve, or one in every 2.5 families. This is not sufficient. There should be at least one in each family.'[44] The organization in Nova Scotia appeared well positioned to respond to the challenge these numbers presented.

The 1960s, however, saw a gradual reversal of fortunes in both organizations, as militarism declined and the fear of nuclear war receded. Association revenues failed to grow and financial appeals to the public and to the United Way Campaign, of which St John Ambulance was a member agency, were largely unsuccessful in improving the financial situation.[45] In 1960 class fees were instituted to cover costs associated with providing the training programs.[46] In 1966, President-Commissioner C. Beecher Weld, a member of the Faculty of Medicine at Dalhousie University, argued that home nursing enrolments declined because a similar home nursing course was offered without fee by the Canadian Red Cross Society. He believed that women who chose the Red Cross course failed to see that they actually did pay fees equivalent to St John Ambulance in the form of books and other costs. He was adamant that 'if these facts [were] more widely known, more groups of women would demand the St. John course.'[47]

Coincident with the association's financial difficulties in the 1960s, membership started to decline in both the nursing and ambulance divisions of the brigade. The problem was not confined to Nova Scotia. At the provincial executive meeting of 23 November 1960, Weld reported on a meeting of the Priory Council in Ottawa. The new chancellor of the Order of St. John, J.H. Molson, had expressed concern over the fact that 'new blood was not being infused into the Ambulance and Nursing

Divisions fast enough to replace older volunteers. Recruitment of younger men and women is desirable.' The problem of declining membership during these years concerned Provincial Superintendent of Nursing Divisions Isobel MacAulay. It seems clear that she understood that the changing lives of Canadian women affected their ability to participate in organizations such as the brigade, declaring in her report at the annual meeting of 1968, 'Ninety per cent of our members are in the workforce.' Yet in her 1970 report she identifies that the problem of recruiting new members is not only lack of time, but lack of interest: 'It becomes increasingly difficult to maintain strength in our Divisions. The majority of women are growing older like myself and we are not able to interest enough younger women to fill the gaps.'[48]

MacAulay herself represented the older image of the organization, which some saw as an obstacle to recruitment. She is remembered by one brigade member of the time as an individual with high standards regarding dress and deportment of nursing division members: 'She was adamant about the way you wore your hat, the way you wore your veil, in the former years. You had to have your skirt a certain length from the floor ... The shoes had to be spit and polished. It was very military things, that's what turned a lot of people off, I think.'[49] This member, with the perspective provided by thirty years, sees what MacAulay may not have seen, or wanted to see: the military as a form of social organization was losing ground; hierarchy was giving way to more egalitarian arrangements; and the consciousness of women, especially young women, about their place and contribution to society was changing.

Within the nursing divisions in Nova Scotia, the unexpected resignation in 1963 of Sharon Stacey, the provincial nursing officer, left a gap in this key position in the brigade at a time of declining membership. The gap was filled in 1965 with the appointment of Marion Grant.[50] The secretary of the Nova Scotia Council, in announcing Grant's appointment, informed the members of the provincial executive meeting that she had taught home nursing and done first aid duty during the war – she had been on duty at a first aid post during the magazine explosion of 1945. The meeting also heard what she was to do and what was hoped for from her work:

> Mrs. Grant will, of course, in addition to some administrative duties, concern herself mainly with the training of Brigade members as well as organizing Home Nursing classes throughout the province and maintaining a

close working liaison with members of the nursing profession in Nova Scotia ... The results of Mrs. Grant's work (when fully operative) might be reflected in more revenue.[51]

Grant served as provincial nursing officer until her retirement in 1973. Her yearly reports, delivered each June at the annual meeting of the council, reveal the attempts she made, working with members of the nursing divisions both in Halifax-Dartmouth and throughout the province, to increase enrolments in the home nursing program. The year 1967 was an especially busy one, and her report reflects the optimism of an individual pleased with the progress she was making towards the goal of increasing enrolments in home nursing. She reported nursing classes at the senior level through the adult education program at the Dartmouth High School; preliminary home nursing on a pilot basis to the Grade 7 class at the Cunard School in Jollimore; classes for students in the 'Auxiliary and Adjusted groups' at the Bicentennial Junior High School in Dartmouth; an agreement with the Girl Guides of Canada to offer both the preliminary and senior level courses; home nursing competitions organized between nursing divisions; and at least four provincial hospitals willing to accept home nursing graduates for the forty-four-hour hospital program.[52]

Each of Grant's reports illustrates the continuous effort that was required of the provincial nursing officer to find new students for the home nursing program, both within and outside the brigade. Her attempts at student recruitment took her beyond Halifax and into communities of people not previously involved. In 1970 she reported that 'classes for the Department of Indian Affairs were conducted at Afton, Whycocomagh and Nyanza. At St. Francis Xavier a class was given for the post graduate students of the Coady International Institute. There were 26 in the class, nine of whom were men. We also had three other men in our Home Nursing classes in this area during the winter.'[53] Despite her work to find new audiences among the school population and to reach out to groups not previously recruited, their connections to the home nursing program seldom lasted beyond one or two classes. It seemed a stable 'market' of home nursing attendees could not be established. Within the brigade, Grant faced the same challenge, frequently exhorting members through the newsletter to find new recruits among friends or family members, painting the nursing program as an essential skill for every household to call upon in the face of demands for caregiving.

Despite the pessimism of those around her, Grant's reports in the early 1970s were optimistic that the home care program recommended in the provincial Council of Health report of 1972 would turn the tables for the home nursing program.[54] She forecast a role for St John Ambulance in the training of family members to take over care in the hours when professional nurses would not be in the home. The cost of expansion in the hospital sector in the 1960s was difficult to absorb in a small province such as Nova Scotia despite arrangements with the federal government. In 1971 the Health Councils Act was passed in the provincial legislature, establishing the Nova Scotia Council of Health. The mandate of the council was to review the province's health care services and to recommend ways to improve their effectiveness and reduce their cost, which were seen to be rising at an unacceptable rate.

The Council of Health commissioned a study of 'home care,' a program operating in other provinces and the United States in which services and providers from many agencies were brought in a coordinated fashion to the patient in the home, as an alternative or extension to care in hospital.[55] The study report, when it appeared in 1972, included a brief from the Home Care Committee of the Halifax-Dartmouth Welfare Council. An advocate of this kind of service since the early 1960s, the Welfare Council had presented the brief to the minister of public health some two years earlier.[56] Marion Grant was a member of the Home Care Committee, having responded, on behalf of St John Ambulance, to a 1969 Welfare Council invitation to health and welfare agencies to attend a public meeting on home care and to form a steering committee.

At the same time as home care programs were being studied on behalf of the Council of Health, so too were voluntary health agencies. The purpose of the voluntary agencies study was 'to identify what new roles these agencies might play in a reorganized health system.'[57] A survey of twenty-three different voluntary health agencies was conducted and their activities categorized as either indirect or direct patient services. Agencies providing home care were identified within the category of direct service, a clear signal of the government's interest in this type of service delivery. While the Canadian Red Cross Society is listed as providing homemaker services, only St John Ambulance and the VON are identified as providing training in home nursing.[58] In fact, St John Ambulance was the only agency providing systematic instruction in home nursing, the VON's effort in this regard being limited to informal, bedside instruction of family members during routine visits.

The inclusion of Marion Grant on the Welfare Council Home Care Committee and the identification of St John Ambulance as an agency providing home nursing training suggests Grant kept herself informed of developments on the home care front, both in Halifax-Dartmouth and provincially. More than informed, she acted strategically in joining a committee with the capacity to command the minister of health's attention and to get the home nursing program 'counted in' when the inventory was taken of voluntary agencies with something to offer a government considering home care. Her actions are all the more remarkable given the absence of any deliberation by the Nova Scotia Council concerning the contribution that St John Ambulance, and specifically the home nursing program, might make in a reorganized health system. From 1968 until her retirement, Grant's annual reports to Nova Scotia Council of St John Ambulance informed them of impending changes in health care. In her 1973 report she stated: 'within the next year or so I would imagine that a Home Care program will be initiated in our Province. I am sure there would be a great need for St. John Home Nursing[,] for members of the family will be called upon to care for the patient for periods when the Home Care Team would not ordinarily be in attendance, e.g., the silent hours.'[59]

Despite Grant's repeated message of a new day dawning in health care, and the 1972 report of the provincial Council of Health recommending the establishment of a province-wide, government-funded home care program, the Nova Scotia Council of St John Ambulance did not seem to see any significance in this information. They did not encourage Grant to enlighten them further on developments within the province, nor did they direct her to think about a new future for home nursing. Grant herself did not elaborate on the significance of the government's proposed actions in much detail, thinking perhaps that the only change to be anticipated was increased enrolments to existing programs. The physicians on the Nova Scotia Council of St John Ambulance, and especially Harris Miller who would later serve as deputy minister of health for Nova Scotia, may have known that the intentions of the provincial Council of Health had little chance for implementation, given the existing funding arrangements that covered only in-hospital care. And it would have made little sense in an organization with the financial uncertainties of St John Ambulance to invest the resources to reinvigorate the home nursing program without a firm commitment from government to implement home care programs. Change was brewing in the world beyond St John Ambulance, but it was not at all clear if, when, and how it would benefit the home nursing program.

The widespread support in the province for the idea of comprehensive home care was evidenced by the number and type of organizations sending representatives to the Home Care Committee of the Halifax-Dartmouth Welfare Council.[60] The major stumbling block to change was the health service funding arrangements in place between the federal and provincial governments. The Hospital Insurance and Diagnostic Services Act of 1957, of significant benefit in the early days of state-sponsored health care, did not provide for coverage of program costs delivered outside of a narrow range of acute-care institutions. In the absence of government support, the costs would have to be born by individuals and families. A recommendation of this sort was clearly unacceptable. Thus, in some measure, the health policy improvements of the 1950s, long sought and highly valued, acted as impediments to change in the 1970s. A comprehensive home care program was not established in Nova Scotia. Health care remained firmly centred in the hospital. Indeed, in the two decades following the report of the Health Council, the number of hospitals beds in Nova Scotia actually increased and the problem of unsustainable costs continued to concern government.[61]

Grant retired in 1973. Her retirement was noted in the St John Ambulance *Newsletter* in words that point to the chronic problems of the home nursing program within the larger organization. 'Nursing is perhaps less glamourous than first aid but must on total review be equal to but slightly different from first aid. Mrs. Grant has worked hard and with ingenuity to make her work successful. She has had a fair measure of success and has also interested the younger generation in this important training.'[62]

Home nursing's struggle, and the retirement of Marion Grant, did not signal the end of the health care training effort by St John Ambulance or the nursing divisions. In an attempt to broaden the scope of training programs, and to attract more training 'customers,' a new approach was attempted. The position of nursing consultant was created within the association and, over the next fifteen years, several programs directed towards the elderly were implemented, generally under the aegis of a federal government initiative. Within the association these programs were seen as an opportunity to revive the field of health care training. The annual report of 1989 states, 'We are pleased to announce our new program Health and Independence in Later Life. Funding was made possible through the Federal Government's Seniors Independence Program. This is a very exciting opportunity for St. John Ambulance and represents an active role once again in the health care field.'[63] However, these programs proved no more sustainable than the home nursing program, and by 1991 the century-old tradition of health care training by the Nova Scotia St John Ambulance had come to an end.

The profound health and social policy developments in Canada in 1950–75 had serious consequences for the viability of the home nursing program. At the beginning of the period there was a tremendous expansion of the hospital sector, followed by the introduction in every province of government-funded hospital insurance and, ten years later, medical care insurance. These developments effectively established the hospital, instead of the home, as the centre of health care. Towards the end of the period, in the early 1970s, there was a 'rediscovery' of care in the home, and a new emphasis on health promotion, as government concern for rising health care costs led to curtailment of hospital-sector growth. These policy shifts might have led to a reinvigoration of the home nursing program, but existing health care funding arrangements effectively prevented the development of out-of-hospital government-supported programs of care.

During these years, Canadian women, who were the real targets of the home nursing program, began to enter the workforce in larger numbers. They had fewer children, and their families were more mobile than in earlier generations. The dynamics of women's participation in unpaid caregiving thus changed, and women's interest in and need to learn basic nursing skills also declined.

There is scant evidence that the St John Ambulance Nova Scotia Council, Association, or Brigade understood that the advent of state-sponsored health care in Canada, or the emergence of a philosophy of health promotion, would challenge program participation. Yet, for women who did not wish to join the brigade, the need to train in home nursing lost its urgency once state-sponsored hospital and medical insurance were in place. Women might have been recruited to a training program on the care of the aged, given that care in nursing homes was not funded by hospital insurance, or to programs with an explicit health promotion focus, given the emergence of 'lifestyle' concerns in the 1970s, but the curriculum of the home nursing program was not geared in either of those directions. It was organized to train a woman to provide care to the acutely ill under the supervision of a physician or nurse.

The program produced a kind of rudimentary professional nurse to serve, under the doctor's direction, in the home 'hospital.' But the hospital was no longer in the home, and the notion of how to respond to illness had evolved beyond a passive acceptance of rest and dependence on care administered by others.

In its heyday, the home nursing program imparted a degree of professionalism to women's traditional responsibilities of cleaning, bathing, and feeding ill family members. It raised this work out of the realm of the domestic and the intuitive and gave it meaning as skilled and valued work. At the same time it attempted to regulate women's behaviour in line with traditional nursing values of deference to authority. The program found an audience of women when health care delivery in Canada was still centred in the home and in the financial resources of individual Canadians, but the need for it, in its traditional form, waned in the 1960s and 1970s. The gradual loss of this program's vitality and value mirrors, if in a negative way, the emergence in Canada of a modern state-sponsored and hospital-focused health care system.

NOTES

1 *Halifax Mail-Star*, 11 Oct. 1966, 27.
2 Nova Scotia Council (NSC), St John Ambulance (SJA), *Annual Report 1967*, Secretary's Report, 2. After this paper was completed, I arranged for the papers of the NSC, SJA to be deposited in the Public Archives of Nova Scotia.
3 The Priory of Canada of the Most Venerable Order of the Hospital of St John of Jerusalem, St John Ambulance Association, St John Ambulance Brigade *Annual Report 1966*. (hereafter *Annual Report*).
4 NSC, SJA, *Newsletter* 2 (Feb.–March 1966). See message from C.B. Weld, K. St. J., President-Commissioner.
5 Records are not available that show the proportion of home nursing enrollees who were not brigade members. The program was usually organized and presented within a brigade division, and non-brigade 'students' were encouraged to join up once they completed their training.
6 NSC, SJA, *Annual Meeting, 25 June 1971*, President's Report, 1.
7 In 1946 the Canadian branch of the order was raised to the status of a priory. The Priory of Canada administers and controls the work of St John Ambulance across the country.
8 Strome Galloway, *The White Cross in Canada, 1883–1983* (Ottawa: St John Priory of Canada Properties, 1983).

9 Ibid.

10 St John Ambulance Brigade, *General Regulations of the St John Ambulance Brigade* (Ottawa: St John Ambulance Brigade, 1952). This document clearly establishes first aid training and service as the primary function of the brigade.

11 The value of brigade work was sometimes acknowledged in notes such as that written in 1969 by Estella Manchester, a member of the Women's Auxiliary of the Halifax Children's Hospital. She wrote: 'The members of the Women's Auxiliary of the Children's Hospital extend their sincere thanks to the ladies of your Nursing Divisions for assisting us the day of the Kermesse. We feel so very safe knowing they are on duty.' NSC, SJA, *Newsletter* 18 (June 1969). Brigade members aided regular emergency personnel in caring for the sick and injured at the Halifax Explosion of 1917, the Spanish Flu epidemic of 1918, and the Springhill mine disasters of 1956 and 1958. Members of Nursing Divisions served overseas as VADs, ambulance drivers, and welfare officers during the Second World War.

12 In 1969, nursing divisions were operating in Amherst, Springhill, Windsor, New Glasgow, Sydney, Northside (Cape Breton), Kentville, Dartmouth, and Halifax (three divisions).

13 Victorian Order of Nurses, *A Century of Caring, 1897–1997: The History of the Victorian Order of Nurses for Canada* (Ottawa: Victorian Order of Nurses, 1996), 5.

14 The total number of divisions varied over time, depending on the capacity of a division to maintain membership strength. In the twelve-year period from 1958 to 1969, there were, in any one year, an average of 10–11 nursing divisions and 2–5 ambulance divisions. In 1969, there were 11 nursing divisions, 4 ambulance divisions, and 5 combined divisions in Nova Scotia.

15 See St John Ambulance Brigade, *General Regulations*.

16 Under ideal circumstances each nursing division had its own nursing officer, but this was not the norm. In 1968, in the Dr E. Pearl Hopgood Nursing Division in Dartmouth, Barbara Hart, RN, was both the nursing officer for the division and a senior home-nursing instructor.

17 NSC, SJA, *Annual Meeting, 16 June 1965*, Report of the Provincial Superintendent of Nursing Divisions, 1.

18 Three promotional brochures for the years 1954, 1956, and 1958, each entitled 'For the Welfare of Mankind,' and declaring fundraising goals of $25,000, $35,000, and $50,000, respectively, are in the records of the Nova Scotia Council, St John Ambulance. An informational brochure, entitled 'St. John Ambulance. Dedicated to the relief of suffering' is also part of this collection.

19 St John Ambulance Association, *Home Nursing* (London: St John Ambulance Association, 1932).
20 The Priory of Canada, St John Ambulance, *Home Nursing* (Ottawa: Author, 1954).
21 Author's interview with Emma Dick, 9 Jan. 1999.
22 *What the Home Nursing Auxiliary Should Know about Civil Defence* (Ottawa: Department of National Health and Welfare, 1957), 25.
23 Ibid.
24 NSC, SJA, *Annual Meeting, 16 June 1965,* Report of the Provincial Superintendent of Nursing Divisions, 1.
25 The text was prepared by leading nurse administrators. M. Christine Livingston, BS, RN, a former executive director of the Victorian Order of Nurses for Canada, and M. Pearl Stiver, BS, RN, executive secretary of the Canadian Nurses Association, with some assistance from Evelyn Pepper, RN, RRC, nursing consultant, Emergency Health Services, Department of National Health and Welfare.
26 NSC, SJA, *Newsletter* 2 (Feb.–March 1966).
27 E.V. Fuerst and L.V. Wolff, *Fundamentals of Nursing: The Humanities and the Sciences in Nursing,* 2nd ed., (Philadelphia: J.B. Lippincott, 1959).
28 *Annual Report 1959*; ibid., 1960, 1963.
29 NSC, SJA, *Annual Meeting, 25 June 1971,* Report of the Provincial Nursing Officer.
30 Author's interview with Helen Mussalem, Ottawa, 10 June 1998.
31 Quote attributed to Marie Loyer, group interview with author, Ottawa, 10 June 1998.
32 NSC, SJA, *Newsletter* 22 (Sept. 1970).
33 The Priory of Canada, St John Ambulance, *Senior Home Nursing Course: Guide for Organizers and Instructors of Home Nursing Classes* ([Ottawa]: Author, 1960).
34 NSC, SJA, *Newsletter* 30 (Dec. 1972).
35 Malcolm G. Taylor, *Health Insurance and Canadian Public Policy: The Seven Decisions That Created the Canadian Health Insurance System* (Montreal: McGill-Queen's University Press, 1978).
36 In 1940, ten years before the Canadian Sickness Survey was undertaken, infant mortality rates in some provinces reached as high as 80 per 1,000. In the four eastern provinces of Canada, only 20 per cent of births occurred in hospital. Maternal mortality rates were still high, ranging from 2.9/1,000 in PEI to 4.8/1,000 in New Brunswick. Communicable disease was a significant cause of death. Tuberculosis was the most serious, with over 5,700 deaths, and influenza, with over 2,700.

37 Canada, Dominion Bureau of Statistics, *Illness and Health Care in Canada: Canadian Sickness Survey, 1950–51* (Ottawa: Dominion Bureau of Statistics, 1960).

38 Taylor, *Health Insurance.*

39 See Dennis Guest, *The Emergence of Social Security in Canada,* 2nd ed. (Vancouver: University of British Columbia Press, 1985).

40 Nova Scotia Council of Health, *Health Care in Nova Scotia: A New Direction for the Seventies* (Halifax: Author, 1972); Canada, Department of National Health and Welfare, *A New Perspective on the Health of Canadians* (Ottawa: Author, 1974).

41 NSC, SJA, *Newsletter* 24 (March 1971).

42 NSC, SJA, *Provincial Executive Committee Meeting, 23 November 1960,* Report of the Provincial Nursing Officer.

43 NSC, SJA, *Annual Meeting, 22 June 1955,* Report of the Provincial Secretary.

44 NSC, SJA, *Annual Meeting, 21 June 1957,* Report of the Provincial Secretary.

45 NSC, SJA, *Annual Meeting, 16 June 1965,* Report of the President-Commissioner; NSC, SJA, *Minutes, Provincial Executive Committee Meeting, 10 November 1965.*

46 NSC, SJA, *Minutes, Provincial Executive Committee Meeting, 23 November 1960.* No records remain of this course, which apparently was in competition with the St John Ambulance home nursing program. What knowledge can be gleaned of it is from references to it in the records of St John Ambulance.

47 NSC, SJA, *Newsletter* 2 (Feb. – March 1966).

48 NSC, SJA, *Annual Meeting, 24 June 1968, 29 May 1970,* Report of the Provincial Superintendent of Nursing Divisions.

49 Author's interview, 6 Jan. 2000. Identity protected.

50 NSC, SJA, *Minutes, Provincial Executive Meeting, 10 November 1965.*

51 Ibid.

52 NSC, SJA, *Annual Meeting, 22 June 1967,* Report of the Provincial Nursing Officer.

53 NSC, SJA, *Annual Meeting, 29 May 1970,* Report of the Provincial Nursing Officer.

54 Nova Scotia Council of Health, *Health Care in Nova Scotia.*

55 Nova Scotia Council of Health, *Home Care: A Report to the Nova Scotia Council of Health* (Halifax: Author, 1972).

56 Halifax-Dartmouth Welfare Council, *Co-ordinated Home Care Program: A Welfare Council Brief to the Minister of Public Health, November 30, 1970,* Public Archives of Nova Scotia, MG 20, vol. 766, no. 18.

57 Nova Scotia Council of Health, *Voluntary Health Agencies: A Report to the Nova Scotia Council of Health* (Halifax: Author, 1972), 1.

58 It appears that by 1972 the Canadian Red Cross Society in Nova Scotia no longer claimed to be offering training in home nursing. This was just six years after President-Commissioner Weld suggested they were luring potential trainees away from the St John Ambulance home nursing program.

59 NSC, SJA, *Annual Meeting, 22 June 1973,* Report of the Provincial Nursing Officer.

60 The membership of the Home Care Committee of the Halifax-Dartmouth Welfare Council included representatives from a wide range of health-related professional, academic, and service organizations.

61 Nova Scotia Royal Commission on Health Care, *Report of the Royal Commission on Health Care: Towards a New Strategy* (Halifax: Author, 1989), fig. 2.9.

62 NSC, SJA, *Newsletter* 32 (Sept. 1973).

63 NSC, SJA, *Annual Meeting, June 1989.*

'A Grandly Subversive Time': The Halifax Branch of the Voice of Women in the 1960s

FRANCES EARLY

When peace talks in Paris collapsed in the spring of 1960, and Cold War tensions between the United States and Soviet Union escalated, Lotta Dempsey, a columnist for the *Toronto Star*, had had enough. 'What can women do?' she asked. Would women not speak out about the threat of nuclear war? Heeding Dempsey's challenge, Canadian women deluged her desk with letters and even telephoned, asserting that they were ready to take action. Thinking along similar lines, the mixed-gender Toronto Committee for Disarmament (later a branch of Campaign for Nuclear Disarmament or CND), in which women played a key role, organized a meeting for 28 July at Toronto's Massey Hall; the enthusiastic attendees readily endorsed the idea of a Canadian women's peace movement. The Voice of Women (VOW) was launched that day, and Helen Tucker, a member of the Toronto Committee for Disarmament, became VOW's first president. Buoyed up on the rising tide of a worldwide 'ban the bomb' movement and a reviving peace movement in Canada and the United States, and aided initially by supportive media coverage, the fledgling organization grew rapidly; within a year, membership stood at 5,000 (10,000 received the newsletter) with over 100 local branches spread out across the country.[1]

During its first decade, the Voice of Women served as a lightning rod for women's discontent with Cold War politics, and the organization helped to bring into open debate women's marginalized civic role within the nation. Kay Macpherson and Meg Sears, two of VOW's early leaders, asserted that the association 'was born on a tidal wave of emotions – hope, fear and anger' and sought, above all, to combat 'the impression that nothing could prevent the drift to nuclear war.'[2] VOW members shared a generalized sense that men, who dominated politics, were responsible for nuclear brinkmanship, and that it was women's duty to set things straight. At its founding meeting and in its early statements, VOW sought legitimacy in the public arena by presenting its members as conventional housewives, who, while sincere in their desire to end the arms race, had no desire to challenge the male-controlled Canadian political system. VOW leaders, whose own public prominence took them well beyond the 'homemaker' appellation, recognized that simplified images of 'Voices' as serious-minded and mobilized mother-citizens would help them secure a public hearing for their views. This apparently transparent and non-threatening public identity of VOW members as civic-minded wives and mothers became part of an unbroken record of Canadian women's twentieth-century maternalist social reform and peace work and bolstered a readiness on the part of some concerned women to take a stand against the dangers of nuclear war and environmental radiation contamination.[3]

The heady moments of the Voice of Women's inception created the impetus for the development of self-determined and diverse local, provincial, and regional branches across the country, although a central council maintained formal control of the association's policies and projects at the national level. In urban centres such as Vancouver, Edmonton, Toronto, Montreal, and Halifax, VOW branches initiated creative programs that were sometimes taken up at the national association level. Voices also worked on their home turf to influence public policy in local settings with regard to specific issues connected either explicitly or implicitly to VOW's peace mission. Branches attracted talented, often fairly privileged women to the peace cause. Some had never engaged in social activism; others identified closely with and were immersed in women's, peace, and social justice groups in their own communities.

Although a comprehensive study of the Voice of Women has not yet been written, scholars have investigated aspects of the organization's history, and they agree that it served a bridging function between early-twentieth-century first-wave feminism and the second-wave feminist movement that emerged in the mid-to-late 1960s.[4] When VOW was founded as a 'women's peace movement' in 1960, its organizers chose not to define the group as feminist, preferring to unite women and to speak on their behalf solely on an antiwar platform. However, by virtue of grouping women together to change or eliminate male-dominant structures such as militarism and war making that they deemed to be oppressive to all women, Voices prefigured, at the same time as they set in motion, the development of theories and practices consistent with second-wave feminism(s).[5]

This essay takes up the history of one of the boldest and most hardworking local branches, VOW Halifax, in the tumultuous and politically innovative 1960s. An examination of the personalities and activities associated with VOW Halifax's first decade of existence helps us to comprehend the spirit and purpose that propelled some Canadian women into the international peace movement of the time. As well, studying how Voices in Halifax sought to reconceptualize peace so as to incorporate issues pertaining to human rights helps us recognize the theory-building component of VOW activism and throws needed light on a crucial chapter in peace and social justice coalition politics in Halifax. Finally, by elucidating the process through which VOW Halifax members chose to speak as one 'voice' for all women on matters relating to peace and human rights, we can identify a moment of inscription that heralded a new style of feminist politics: in the late 1960s, Halifax Voices, like their counterparts in other areas of the country, embraced second-wave feminism with verve and hopefulness.

By the fall of 1960, Peggy Hope-Simpson, a homemaker and mother of four, the youngest of whom was a toddler, had resided in Halifax for about a year. She and her British-born husband, David Hope-Simpson, had moved from the Vancouver area so that David could take up a position in the Geology Department at Saint Mary's University. In British Columbia the Hope-Simpsons had become involved in protests against the arms race, and they were members of the Canadian Committee for the Control of Radiation Hazards (CCCRH), founded in 1959.[6] CCCRH's members included leading scientists and academics, professionals, business executives, clergy, and representatives of women's groups. When David received some literature from the national VOW office by virtue of his position as chair of the Halifax CCCRH, he passed it on to his wife. In an interview conducted twenty years later, Peggy Hope-Simpson recalled: 'I was absolutely overwhelmed. It was an answer to what I was feeling.' She decided to form a Halifax branch of VOW. For help she turned to Muriel Duckworth. Duckworth had a public profile by virtue of her work in the Home and School Association, adult education, and the mental health field: 'I thought, she's always speaking out, and spouting off, so I'll phone her ... she responded immediately. We talked about it and then pulled together a first meeting, which took place in Muriel's home.'[7]

What motivated Hope-Simpson to move so quickly to organize a VOW group, and why did Duckworth react with such alacrity? Personal reasons interwove with a perception of grave danger to propel these individuals into action. Both women – in common with many other people in this era of heightened Cold War tensions – shared a sense of foreboding about the ominous implications of the nuclear arms race. Duckworth has commented that 'absolute terror galvanized VOW into being. There's no question that everybody was terrified about what was going to happen.'[8] For her part, Hope-Simpson remembers being haunted by the spectre of a nuclear holocaust, which caused a recurring nightmare: '[I was] in the water with [my] children, and I knew that I couldn't hold on to all of them, and always I would wake up just at the point when I was going to have to abandon one of them, and I would wake up in a sweat, just in terror.'[9]

On 23 November 1960, a few weeks after Hope-Simpson's decision to create a VOW group in Halifax, fifteen women, some of whom were strangers to each other, met at Muriel Duckworth's home. They wasted no time in committing themselves to take constructive action in concert with other women across the nation to 'achieve world peace.' Joan Marshall, a prominent radio commentator for the Canadian Broadcasting Company (CBC), chaired the meeting and outlined the purpose of the newly established national women's peace organization, the Voice of Women. Lillian Wainwright, a mother of two young boys and a geneticist with a PhD, who was employed part-time at Mount Saint Vincent University (and who knew Hope-Simpson through their work in nursery school development), served as secretary pro-tem. Also present was Pearleen Oliver, a greatly admired leader of the Nova Scotia civil rights movement. In 1944, she had almost single-handedly broken down the racial barrier preventing African-Canadian women from entering nursing training in hospitals in Halifax and elsewhere.[10] Others who attended included Marjorie Hatheway, the wife of CBC producer Harold Hatheway, and Sylvia Kaplan, a good friend of Lillian Wainwright's. Lillian and her husband, Stanley Wainwright, who had a position in the Biochemistry Department of Dalhousie University, were U.S. citizens. Sylvia Kaplan's husband, Gordin, who was appointed to Dalhousie University's Department of Physiology in 1952, had studied at the graduate level with Stanley Wainwright at Columbia University. Sylvia was British and had met Gordin during his wartime overseas service; she had travelled to the United States after the war to be with him. The Wainwrights and the Kaplans, like the Hope-Simpsons and Muriel Duckworth and her husband, Jack Duckworth, were members of the Halifax branch of the Canadian Committee for the Control of Radiation Hazards.[11]

The atmosphere at this first VOW meeting was charged with purpose. Hope-Simpson and Hatheway spoke briefly about their reasons for issuing a call to form a Halifax chapter of the Voice of Women, with Hope-Simpson declaring unambiguously that nuclear testing is 'one of the greatest deceptions of our age.' She also reiterated the national VOW's belief that women's maternal role and dedication to preserving life could cut through the 'deception' that nuclear weapons protected people. Women, Hope-Simpson insisted, need not be 'experts' to articulate their opinions about 'the survival of civilization,' but they did have to become well-informed citizens. Already cognizant of a wider international women's peace movement, she informed the group that in England women calling themselves 'Women Speaking' had as their motto 'The spirit of humanity cannot fly with only one wing.'[12]

Virtually everyone spoke her own mind at this founding meeting, and there was much agreement among these fifteen women about the need to create a separatist women's peace movement for the dark times in which they lived. Notable, too, was a commitment to study the issues. At their first meeting, Marge Hatheway read a report she had prepared on the widely read Canadian best-seller by CBC news correspondent James Minifie, *Peacemaker or Powder Monkey: Canada's Role in a Revolutionary World* (1960). Hatheway explained Minifie's nationalist argument that Canada should get out of NATO and NORAD in order to develop a neutral peacekeeping role in world politics, a position the national VOW would soon endorse, as would the Halifax branch.[13] In addition to deciding to call a public meeting to draw in additional members, plans to form a study group were entertained.

Two weeks later, on 7 December, VOW Halifax sponsored a well-attended public meeting at Sir Charles Tupper School auditorium in the West End of the city. Muriel Duckworth served as chair, and several speakers, including two men, pediatrician W.A. Cochran and David Hope-Simpson, urged Halifax women to embrace the women's peace movement. It was Lillian Wainwright, identified as 'Dr. Wainwright,' who repeated themes introduced at the founding meeting in November, thereby helping to set the tone and agenda for VOW Halifax's work in the months and years ahead. Her comments blended idealism and pragmatism with a shrewd understanding that some women were eager and prepared to challenge male-directed, sabre-rattling superpower politics. Wainwright first pointed out that the Cold War mentality encouraged people to conclude either that 'war is inevitable' or that 'peace is possible.' She suggested that the new thinking had to stress that 'peace is essential.' The VOW's only aim was 'anti-war.' Men had tried to end war and had failed. To date, women had 'not availed themselves of their political power and this they must do for peace.' Further, pressure had to be brought to bear on specific issues and, to become familiar with the problems, study groups had to be formed. 'Sanity and reason' had to create 'clarity in an unreasonable world.'[14]

Praxis followed theory at this meeting when Muriel Duckworth took up Wainwright's point about organizing around specific issues. As minute-taker Cora Greenaway put it, Duckworth, in a move that would become characteristic of her leadership style within VOW Halifax, 'explained that from time to time groups will have to take action on certain things. She said that a problem had arisen. This ... was the [proposed] dumping of radioactive waste material off the coast of Nova Scotia.'[15] VOW Halifax had its first 'issue,' and within just a few weeks the new Voices, in concert with the CCCRH, had mobilized such a groundswell of support against a U.S. private contractor's intention to dispose of radioactive waste in Canadian fishing waters that the plan was scotched. This initial peace movement victory in Halifax helped to increase the membership of VOW to about forty individuals and to bolster morale within the executive committee.

The women who directed VOW Halifax in its early years represented a diverse group, but they did share certain characteristics. The majority were in their thirties or forties and were wives and mothers. Most of those who composed the executive committee were also trained professionals, particularly in the fields of broadcasting and freelance journalism, education (including one university professor), social work, and nursing; two were artists, and one was training to be a child psychiatrist. A number of these women were homemakers and were not actively pursuing their vocations at the time they joined VOW, but some were fully engaged in building careers.[16] Community activism, frequently within women's organizations, informed the lives of most members of the VOW executive.

Interestingly, VOW Halifax leaders in the 1960s were most likely to be 'from away,' a phrase used by Maritimers for those who are not native to the region. While most in this group were Canadians, they had grown to adulthood in other regions, notably Ontario or Quebec.

A significant minority were British, a handful were American, and one woman, Cora Greenaway, was Dutch. A few in this 'from away' group were well-established residents in Halifax. Muriel Duckworth, for instance, had arrived from Montreal in 1947, when her husband accepted an invitation from the Halifax Young Men's Christian Association (YMCA) to become its general secretary. Others, such as Peggy Hope-Simpson, had been settled in the area for a year or less when the founding meeting took place. Regardless of their place of origin, all had been marked by their experiences as youths and adults during the Second World War and felt compelled to prevent another such catastrophe. For example, Hope-Simpson and Wainwright had lost their first husbands during the war, and Duckworth had lost a brother. Greenaway had served in the Dutch Resistance Movement and had put her life at risk to save the lives of Jewish friends; Kaplan had experienced the devastation of war first-hand in Britain. Several were war brides anxious to put war behind them.[17]

By early 1961, with several meetings under their belts, VOW members began to appreciate that their innovative separatist group constituted in some ways 'a society of outsiders.'[18] Not only were many of them newcomers to Halifax, they were also building a peace organization in a town dominated by the military. In 1960, one quarter of the city's labour force was dependent on employment associated with the military economy.[19] Casting doubt on the necessity of war as a legitimate instrument of foreign policy was perceived as audacious and ill-advised by many Halifax citizens, who were convinced that military readiness was essential to national security and the survival of the 'free world.' At times, Voices faced stiff public criticism and, upon occasion, ridicule. Belief in the worthiness of their peace mission, however, helped VOW Halifax maintain cohesiveness and a sense of higher purpose.

Despite VOW's unpopularity in many circles, mitigating forces reduced the organization's marginalization and helped its members secure a community-wide base for their insistent peace work. Nova Scotia–born members such as Pearleen Oliver and well-ensconced residents such as Muriel Duckworth were respected citizens in their communities. They and other VOW members held affiliation with progressive, reform-minded organizations such as the Home and School Association, the United Nations Association, and the Nova Scotia Association for the Advancement of Coloured People (NSAACP).[20]

The adept networking style of Oliver, Duckworth, and other members of VOW Halifax placed these individuals within a tradition of

Canadian women's public community work. The ability of Voices to find common ground with other associations extended to the Local Council of Women (LCW). This umbrella organization represented women's public service and other groups in the metropolitan area. Historian Judith Fingard has shown that in its heyday from the late nineteenth century to the mid-twentieth century, the council provided women with opportunity to grow as public citizens and as individuals and to work for the greater good of the community as conceptualized from a largely white, middle-class perspective. In the period between the two world wars, the LCW, in keeping with national developments, established a League of Nations committee, and in 1935 peace activists, including LCW members, established a Halifax Women's Study Group to explore the causes of war and to promote peace.[21] However, by 1960, the LCW had lost its cutting-edge leadership role and, in Fingard's words, had 'started to decline as the collective voice for women.'[22] Nonetheless, unlike most council groups in other parts of Canada, the LCW granted VOW Halifax affiliate membership status, and VOW delegates received a hearing for their views when they attended council meetings. VOW Halifax executive committee minutes and oral interviews reveal that the peace group understood the importance of maintaining a presence in the LCW, but that Voices did not feel particularly welcome at council gatherings.[23]

The networking skills of Voices were prodigious. The expansion of the university and medical systems and the establishment of a CBC office in Halifax in this era provided a growing pool of regional 'experts,' and VOW members did not hesitate to enlist their help as resource people and as speakers. Key individuals within the VOW Halifax leadership circle, such as Peggy Hope-Simpson and Sylvia Kaplan, were wives of academics or medical doctors who had secured positions in Halifax or Dartmouth during the 1950s, the 'decade of development' for Atlantic Canada. Moreover, a number of Voices, including Joan Marshall, Cora Greenaway, Fran Maclean, and Ella Manuel, were 'media people,' and the group benefited from their professional savvy.

The minutes of executive meetings reveal that during the 1960s the Halifax group kept in close contact with the central council of VOW, tailoring activities to dovetail with directives from the national office. In the early 1960s, Halifax branch members lobbied politicians about disarmament issues, especially the desirability of an independent 'nuclear-free' foreign policy for Canada, and took up fundraising activities on behalf of the newly established Canadian Peace Institute.[24] Educational work for projects conceived in relation to the United Nations' designation of 1965 as International Cooperation Year (ICY), an idea that originated with the Voice of Women, also took place.[25] In mid-decade, VOW Halifax tried to enlist the help of a local women's sorority, Beta Sigma Phi, in overseeing the collection of baby teeth for a VOW-supported University of Toronto study on the possible adverse effects to human health of low-level radiation from atmospheric nuclear weapons testing. Although its president, Shirley Duggan, initially agreed to help, she and her group later backed out of their commitment, and VOW Halifax had to take over the assignment.[26]

After the Partial Test-Ban Treaty was signed by the United States and the Soviet Union in 1963, VOW as a national body shifted much of its energy towards protesting the U.S. prosecution of the Vietnam War, and VOW Halifax followed suit. In one of VOW's most successful projects – knitting dark-coloured baby clothes for North Vietnamese children forced to live underground to avoid U.S. bombs – branches all over Canada, including the Halifax group (and supplemented by donations from U.S. women's peace groups), sent 30,000 pieces of clothing and blankets to Vietnam.[27] Members of the Halifax branch also welcomed visiting VOW speakers sent by the national office and sponsored high-profile public meetings that featured local experts speaking on specific issues such as 'war toys.'

The VOW Halifax branch's effectiveness in the 1960s was strengthened by the willingness of some of its members to assume important roles in the national VOW. Helen Cunningham, a physician and resident in psychiatry at Dalhousie University and a profound pacifist thinker, held the position of chair of the Research Committee of national VOW in the early 1960s. She brought a keen critical intelligence to her peace work and urged consistently that a key role for VOW was to nurture into being a climate permitting 'honest public discourse.'[28] Duckworth and Hope-Simpson have commented that Cunningham was their intellectual mentor, and Duckworth has attested to Cunningham's important contributions, at both local and national levels.[29] Other members of the Halifax branch helped out the national association by representing VOW at gatherings where the peace message could be communicated. In 1962, for instance, Sylvia Kaplan and a Quebec VOW charter member, Ghislaine Laurendeau, joined two thousand other delegates representing eighty-five organizations at a Canadian Conference on Education in Montreal. Back in Halifax, Kaplan reported that 'every contact we made there was a valuable one, both because of what we learned ourselves and perhaps even because of the ideas we passed on to others.' Nonetheless, Kaplan also admitted that at times 'we felt that we were ... wading through deep water with chains on our feet.'[30] As VOW expanded its networking work among peace-minded women around the globe, Duckworth and other Halifax Voices took leadership roles in organizing two successful VOW-sponsored international women's conferences held in 1962 and 1967.

A willingness to serve the national women's peace movement was epitomized by Muriel Duckworth's agreement to become national VOW president; she served with distinction for two terms, from 1967 to 1971. Her determination to build stronger bonds within the international women's peace movement helped to propel VOW onto the world stage, especially in the context of the organization's involvement in the North American protest movement against the continuation of the Vietnam War. During 1969, under Duckworth's leadership, VOW sponsored a visiting delegation of women from North and South Vietnam. With Duckworth accompanying them, the Vietnamese women toured Canada telling their stories, and U.S. women peace activists crossed the border into Canada on more than one occasion to meet with their nation's 'enemies.'[31] Despite her heavy workload as national president, Duckworth maintained a guiding role in the Halifax branch during the late 1960s, one that helped the local group maintain direction in a period of dramatic social upheaval.

Christine Ball's research on the founding and early years of VOW Canada demonstrates that women across the country channelled their well-founded 'mother rage' against the nuclear arms race and atmospheric nuclear testing – and, more obliquely, against the male politicians responsible for foreign policy – into a powerful political voice for disarmament. Members agreed on the need for nations to find alternatives to war and believed that ending war could not be accomplished without a thorough understanding of the causes of war. But no two branches were alike. The interplay of personality, personal history, and local context provided the framework for each group's organizational style, philosophical stand, and political agenda.[32]

VOW Halifax in the 1960s managed to maintain an active membership of between forty and sixty women, and during this time leaders emerged who possessed impressive organizational talents and the intellectual capacity to theorize creatively on war and peace issues.[33] Some core members were Quakers, including Duckworth, Hope-Simpson, Cunningham, and U.S. citizen Dorothy Norvell, a new resident of

Halifax. The Quaker-pacifist presence of these women constituted a decisive factor in the way VOW Halifax developed over the decade, notably with regard to the commitment of members to consensual decision-making processes.

According to Muriel Duckworth, Cunningham was the driving force behind VOW Halifax's early decision to establish study groups, a time-honoured practice among women's groups oriented towards public service and social change programs. As Peggy Hope-Simpson put it, 'We were constantly being driven by events ... Everything was classi-fied but we felt it was essential to have an informed public debate.'[34] At Cunningham's urging, a general study group was set up to educate Voices about the nature of the problems confronting them. The first book that members of the study group read was a Quaker pamphlet suggested by Cunningham, *Speak Truth to Power* (1955). This extended essay had been put together by concerned members of the American Friends Service Committee, a group that was founded in the United States in 1917 and that extended into Canada somewhat later. Scholars emphasize its importance in this era for North American peace activists.[35] The writers of *Speak Truth to Power*, in accordance with Quaker theology, accepted the presence of evil in the world. They also rejected violence (including war making) as a method of combating evil, arguing instead for the development of nonviolent resistance strategies in the pursuit of peace, along the lines propounded by Mohandas Gandhi in the Indian independence movement.[36]

Dorothy Norvell, another Quaker member of Halifax VOW, was the mother of an infant, and, like Cunningham, married to a medical doctor; her training was in education and social work. She was strongly rooted in the historic women's peace movement by virtue of her mother's and grandmother's membership in the U.S. section of the Women's International League for Peace and Freedom (WILPF). Norvell encouraged VOW members to reflect and act upon the notion of dedication to a higher cause that was embedded in the 'speak truth to power' philosophy. In language that echoed but also turned on its head the notion of 'just warriors' battling for a 'just war,' Norvell articulated a meaning for peace work that resembled the heroic and noble aspects of war making, a view that influenced other Voices. Writing to Liberal leader Lester Pearson in April 1962, at a time when he was still propounding a 'no nukes' position for Canada, Norvell averred that 'positive steps toward creating a peaceful world' could include Canada's support of peace research institutes and the United Nations

International Cooperation Year. She then asked Pearson to consider the notion of a peace army: 'For several years I have felt there was a need for a vast and varied effort for peace, something on the scale of the war effort in its utilization of all kinds of people and skills and in its appeal for devotion.'[37] Two years later, in a letter to a child psychiatrist who had spoken at a VOW meeting on the impact of television violence on child development, Norvell pursued this idea: 'Making peace probably needs to resemble making war more than it does that passive period between the wars. Wartime's sense of urgency and purpose, the willingness to sacrifice, and the need for research and discovery, for example, seem to be needed as much in making peace.'[38]

VOW members benefited from the theoretical bent of individuals such as Cunningham and Norvell, and they read widely on an array of topics and issues. Building on their already self-assured style, members of the General Study Group changed their name first to the Study-Action Group, and then to the Political Study Action Group. The summer 1962 reading list was daunting; titles included *The Rich Nations and the Poor Nations* by Barbara Ward, *The Rise and Fall of the Third Reich* by William L. Shirer, and *The Origins of World War II* by A.J.P. Taylor.

In November 1962, spurred on by renewed angst in the wake of the October Cuban Missile Crisis, which had brought the world to the brink of nuclear war, VOW Halifax, obviously influenced by the perspective articulated in *Speak Truth to Power*, announced that its members would be conducting a Vigil for Peace at the Sailors' War Memorial on Citadel Hill. The one-page statement attached to the announcement noted that both good and evil existed in all societies, making conflicts 'unavoidable'; nonetheless, peaceful solutions, many as yet undiscovered, were possible: 'We expect that these methods will require us to work for, and at times suffer for, our beliefs without inflicting suffering on others.'[39]

Ten days before the peace vigil, Halifax Voices sent a group to Ottawa to consult with External Affairs Minister Howard Green and to present him with a brief that argued against the acquisition of nuclear arms for Canada. The delegates were Peggy Hope-Simpson; Cora Greenaway, a historic preservation researcher, writer, and elementary school teacher who had served as a courier in the Second World War Dutch Resistance; and Dorothy Ellis, a young mother and artist from Prince Edward Island who, in common with other VOW mothers, felt strongly about the need to create a less violent world for the next generation. The *Halifax Chronicle-Herald* printed a photo of the three women in Ottawa and summarized Hope-Simpson's comments, including her statement critiquing the theory of deterrence. The pithy no-nonsense Hope-Simpson was quoted as saying: 'We Canadians have got to make it possible for our government to do some sensible things ... Maybe Canada could break the spell ... Everyone needs a dash of cold water in the face to wake them up.'[40]

Well before 1962 drew to a close, in line with the VOW women's determination to define peace broadly, two additional study groups, one on education, the other on human relations, had been formed. The establishment of an Education Study Group made sense within the parameters that the Voice of Women had set as a national body; its mandate underscored women's historic use of education and moral suasion as a means to creating a more humane world.[41] But it was the Human Relations Group that 'made history' during its two-year existence as a committee within VOW Halifax.

From its beginnings, a number of influential Halifax branch members had been convinced of the need to address issues relating to white racial discrimination and prejudice in their community, and they brought their concerns to VOW. Pearleen Oliver, an eloquent spokesperson for African-Canadian civil rights, had been a founding member of the NSAACP, and Muriel Duckworth was also a member of that group. Lillian Wainwright had strong convictions about the need to open up educational opportunities for African-Canadian young people. She helped to establish a tutoring system in the early 1960s so that African-Canadian students could finish high school and go on to university studies. Among Wainwright's associates in a group that came to be called the Inter-Racial Council was Fran Maclean, also a white woman. Maclean, a CBC journalist, had moved from Winnipeg to Halifax in 1953. She joined the Voice of Women shortly after its formation. Her commitment to work for racial understanding and equality of treatment for African Canadians was at the heart of her philosophy of peace, a perspective shaped by her affiliation with Bahaism, a religion with roots in Islamic theology that emphasizes tolerance and the worth of all religions.[42] It was her influence that drew into VOW's work two young African–Nova Scotian teachers, Maxine Gough and Elizabeth Reddick.

Maclean, with Wainwright's help, organized a study-action plan for the Human Relations Committee. In the spring of 1962 committee members read Gordon Allport's *The Nature of Prejudice*, and they discussed such topics as 'educating and freeing ourselves and our children from prejudice,' 'reaching the public,' and 'heightening our own and others' awareness of the corrosion developing from unchecked prejudice and discrimination.' As well, at this time, the committee, which consisted of three African–Nova Scotian women and six white women, was engaged in an investigation of the employment policies and practices of some Halifax companies, including Simpson's department store. The aim of the study was to put public pressure on business establishments to hire African Canadians for jobs for which they were qualified. This investigation became the focus of CBC radio and television coverage when it was revealed that the general consensus of businesses with regard to hiring African Canadians for any job that concerned 'meeting the public' revolved around the notion that whites would not tolerate being served by Black people. The Human Relations Committee worked closely with the NSAACP, organizing meetings on this issue. Shortly thereafter, hiring practices began to change and some African-Canadian young people were able to find jobs for which they had been trained.[43]

Maclean was pleased with the modest success, and she made a point of encouraging VOW to conceptualize peace as an active process of 'right living' with others. In a 1962 report on her committee's activities, Maclean stated:

> To some, concern with human relations may seem too far reaching past the present hour. Yet, it seems to us, that the very foundation of peace would crumble, for want of a solid base to build upon, if we do not take definite steps to eradicate fundamental injustices in our local communities. Injustice breeds resentment, ill-will, and generally, an uncooperative spirit, undesirable in a geographically one world.[44]

As evidenced by the work of the committee chaired by Maclean, VOW Halifax was moving in the early 1960s towards an expanded definition of peace activism that included the struggle for racial equality. The organization's first priority, however, remained nuclear disarmament and, for Canada, an independent foreign policy that rejected nuclear weapons as part of its military arsenal. In early 1963, newly elected prime minister Lester Pearson stunned VOW and the entire Canadian peace movement when he switched the Liberal Party policy on nuclear weapons and announced that Canada would acquire nuclear warheads. The Voice of Women was thrown into crisis, as its leaders grappled with how to respond to the government's abrupt change of course. Ultimately, the national executive chose a forthright political stance. Criticism of federal foreign policy led VOW away from its polite beginnings as a non-partisan and 'ladylike' women's pressure group into the politicized centre of the burgeoning North American peace movement. This new direction resulted in the loss of many members who rejected VOW's strong public stand against the federal government's decision to acquire nuclear weapons. Significantly, a large proportion of the defectors were members of the Liberal Party who felt that they had to respect Pearson's decision. A considerable number of those who remained with the organization, especially those at the national leadership level, were New Democrats, and their party was opposed to Canada's acquisition of nuclear weapons.

In Halifax, the majority of Voices, many of whom were members of the NDP, agreed with the political path charted by the national executive.[45] But, as was the case elsewhere, the group lost valued members, including most of the members of the Human Relations Committee. Letters of resignation were received from Fran Maclean, Maxine Gough, Elizabeth Reddick, and Catharine Verrall. Maclean's reasons for resigning help to shed light on the complex ethical and political dilemmas faced by social activists who were attempting to promote the interconnectedness of peace and racial equality in Halifax and elsewhere in this era:

> I have been quite willing, until recent months, to work side-by-side with the political action committee, but I do not wish to support the *present* 'ban-the-bomb' efforts of the local and national body ... VOW's nuclear stand has alienated many people who might well be involved in the more important issues of our ailing society. We wish to work with many of these people both directly and indirectly. But VOW's stand has already sent hands-off warnings to them, through its pronouncements.[46]

Reddick and Gough wrote a succinct joint resignation letter in which they stated that 'everyone is against Nuclear Armament, but we do not feel that Canada is in a position to abstain from the acquisition of Nuclear Armament.'[47] Catherine Verrall, a white woman who was active in interracial church work and whose husband was pastor of the Brunswick Street United Church, used stronger language:

> I cannot support the dogmatic stand which VOW is now taking on 'Nuclear Arms for Canada,' when the situation is so complex, with good and evil, reason and un-reason, on both sides. If it is wrong for Germany

or Russia to make decisions unilaterally, in terms of what the government considers 'right,' it may also be wrong for Canada to act as if we have the divine oracle ... The point is, I don't feel I could ever know enough to tell the government precisely what to do on this issue ... Although I respect the people who feel they must make a categorical stand on 'Nuclear Arms for Canada,' I cannot honestly remain joined to them.[48]

The executive committee accepted the loss of these members with regret. However, by 1963, VOW Halifax's commitment to racial justice, present from its beginnings, was firm. The group continued to co-sponsor public meetings with the NSAACP on topics relating to racial prejudice and discrimination after the VOW Human Relations Committee disbanded and became an independent Inter-Racial Council.[49] In 1965, amid the rise of a New Left and Black Power student protest movement in Canada, the executive committee of VOW Halifax invited members of the national umbrella group Student Union for Peace Action (SUPA) to one of its meetings. Afterwards, VOW lent support to SUPA-sponsored community-organizing projects in local neighbourhoods with significant African-Canadian populations. In 1966, Halifax Voices co-sponsored with the NSAACP a fundraising arts and crafts show at Dalhousie University that netted the civil rights group $325. In 1969, VOW member Nancy Lubka, an American freelance writer and mother of four who had moved to Halifax in 1967, published a well-written, authoritative, and insightful essay on the Black Freedom Movement in Nova Scotia with particular reference to the work of the recently established Nova Scotia Human Rights Commission. In the same year, when Pearleen Oliver and others founded the Black United Front, Halifax Voices stood squarely behind the separatist racial justice group.[50]

In the second half of the 1960s, VOW Halifax was drawn increasingly into the widening social protest movement that it had helped to bring into being. Especially important were the efforts VOW made to encourage the development of a strong and united local coalition against U.S. continuation of the Vietnam War. In this area of endeavour, VOW members were in their element. They had built many bridges with community action associations, organizations devoted to women's concerns such as the YWCA, and with religious bodies. In 1968, some Halifax Voices helped to initiate the establishment of the mixed-gender coalition group the Halifax Peace Action Committee. As a consequence of such assiduous networking, by the end of the decade, VOW found itself at the centre of the antiwar movement in Halifax.[51]

The main purpose of VOW Halifax remained 'antiwar,' but in this era such a stance took the group further afield as bonds with the flowering international women's peace movement strengthened. Halifax Voices, like their sister Voices in the Atlantic region and across Canada, felt a special kinship with the U.S. separatist peace group Women Strike for Peace (WSP), established one year after VOW's founding. WSPers (pronounced 'wispers') fostered a militant maternalist politics similar to that of VOW, and over the 1960s their activities and VOW's meshed at many points.[52] WSP members were among those who participated in VOW's international women's conference in Montreal in 1967, and WSP participated earlier in the decade in the children's clothing knitting project and sent members to Canada in 1969 to meet with the Vietnamese women's delegation. VOW and WSP activists met in many other settings, including Moscow in 1967, when invited delegates (including Muriel Duckworth) were the guests of the Soviet Women's Committee. As well, Dagmar Wilson, the founder of WSP, took time to visit Halifax for three days in April 1968. A VOW Halifax member reported that Wilson spoke at a number of meetings that were 'as usual ... attended almost exclusively by people who already agree with her views.' Despite negative public reaction to the inveterate peace activist, Voices soaked up her 'wonderful enthusiasm':

> Dagmar Wilson makes her way through an obstacle course of bigotry, apathy, despair, and even the House un-American Activities Committee with great energy and a splendid sense of humour. She willingly faces hostile opposition and – perhaps the greatest enemy – ridicule. Her refusal to compromise or disguise her beliefs is a characteristic that we should all try to develop.[53]

At the same time that VOW Halifax was being energized by an optimistic and increasingly influential international women's movement for peace, the stirrings of a 'new' feminist movement were beginning to churn up the waters closer to home. In January 1968, the executive committee broached the topic of the 'status of women' for the first time. It was agreed that two members would 'get more information on whether it would benefit working women to have child care expenses deductible.'[54] By their September meeting, the executive officers were congratulating Nancy Lubka for her 'fine job' in preparing the VOW Halifax Brief on the Status of Women. In that month, President Jo Shephard, like Lubka, a relative newcomer to the group, went before the Royal Commission on the Status of Women in Canada public hearings in Halifax to present the VOW Halifax brief.

Lubka, a regular contributor on women's issues for *The 4th Estate*, a Halifax weekly, produced a well-written and well-researched submission. It focused on the lack of opportunity for women in the paid dual-gender labour force and the low wages meted out to most female workers. The brief made the point that many women in the Maritimes were poorly educated and forced to seek low-paid employment to shore up family economies; the few women who were trained professionals and sought fulfillment in careers found 'their ambitions a contradiction of the prevailing status.' Lubka, in line with a feminist analysis already circulating in U.S. civil rights and New Left circles, made the case for an analogy between women's lot as a group and 'the conditions prevailing among the Negro population of this part of the country.' Continuing with this line of reasoning, Lubka noted: 'The traditional attitude of society toward women as a whole and also toward the minority Negro citizenry, has been one of low expectations, poor preparation for a working life, and the denial and waste of human potential. Negro women, therefore, suffer the double burden of two kinds of discrimination.'[55]

The brief's main recommendation to the federal government was that the cost of child care for working mothers become tax deductible. Easily accessible daycare centers and adequate maternity leave were included as suggestions. The brief also recommended that non-discrimination in job transfer and promotion become policy and included a general statement about the need to improve the overall economic condition of Nova Scotia and the Atlantic region.

Lubka was careful to tie VOW recommendations in this brief to the overall vision of her organization. She underlined that VOW did not hold that 'women are necessarily better equipped [than men] to deal with community, national, and international affairs.' But Lubka did reason that Voice of Women 'could achieve its purposes only with the participation of informed, concerned women who view themselves as effective, important members of society.' Lubka concluded the brief by insisting that 'vast changes must be made before women can make their optimum contribution to society.'[56]

In 1969, 'women's lib' appeared on the agenda of a VOW Halifax meeting. Further, a few young women with family backgrounds that included social-justice work had joined the group by this time. Elizabeth Mullaly, a young mother with a bachelor's degree from Mount

Saint Vincent University, became a member of VOW in 1968, and recalls the mentoring she received from Voices such as Muriel Duckworth and Ann Maxwell, a senior VOW leader who had close ties with Catholic social justice groups. While some young women at Dalhousie University founded the first women's liberation group in Halifax called the 1895 Feminist Revival Group (1969), neophyte VOW members such as Mullaly chose the women's peace group as a safe harbour from which to begin exploring the personal dimension of the new feminism. Mullaly and a group of eight or nine other young women formed a consciousness-raising group that she remembers as originating within the Voice of Women.

Thinking back to this period of her life, Elizabeth Mullaly recognizes, with hindsight, that the VOW experience 'stays with you.' A Dalhousie University Law School graduate, she holds a position with the Nova Scotia Department of Justice. Mullaly has a lifetime record of working on behalf of equity, civil liberties, and feminist issues, and she insists that her experience in VOW taught her how to speak in public, to march for social justice, and 'to put out there what your beliefs are.' Mullaly also underlines that 'the VOW way' combines a passion for peace and justice with analytical intellectual power and a hard-nosed realistic assessment of what is possible.[57]

It was not only the youth generation of women peace workers in the late 1960s who found their path to feminism illuminated by their involvement in the Voice of Women. Muriel Duckworth, who did not see herself as a feminist when VOW was founded, asserts that she 'came to the feminist movement through the peace movement.' Duckworth's public avowal of feminism came in 1970 during a week-long metropolitan public planning exercise, 'Encounter on Urban Environment.' In the course of one evening session, Duckworth, affronted by the all-male panel of experts, took the microphone and criticized the twelve-man committee for its gender exclusivity. Her testimony was captured on film by the National Film Board of Canada. Duckworth refers to this event as a turning point, the moment she chose 'to come out as a feminist.'[58]

The issues and debates swirling around a revived and youth-flavoured feminism in the latter part of the 1960s expanded VOW's already ambitious political agenda and influenced members to reframe their personal and public identities. But VOW had been incipiently feminist from its beginnings. The organization was linked in its separatist structure, strategies, and goals to a progressive social reform women's movement that had maintained a presence in Canadian society throughout the twentieth century. By taking as its purpose a foundational critique of male-controlled national security policies in order to find alternatives to militarism and war making, VOW ultimately helped to foment a rebellion among women in diverse circumstances against the Cold War domestic ideology that sought to constrict women's public civic role.[59] In this sense, Voices served as harbingers of second-wave feminism.

Voice of Women Halifax kept on course in the era that ushered in the new feminism. The group maintained its commitment to coalition politics, community organizing, educational work, and political lobbying. 'Everyone can do something' remained the credo of Halifax Voices, as they persisted in organizing women around an expansive concept of peace in the decades to follow. Ella Manual's reflections on VOW's purpose help us understand the key to the group's successful outreach style during the 1960s and beyond: 'We are a peace movement. We should ... keep two separate paths – not confuse our areas of interest – work on local problems through other groups or in the founding of other groups and hope that some of the women can be brought slowly to the acceptance of responsibility in "larger" issues, to the understanding that every single voice is important.'[60]

The theme of responsible citizenship resounds in the records of the Halifax branch of VOW. Paralleling a civic ethos of 'rationality and care' has been a self-conscious understanding on the part of Voices that they exist on the border of respectability in their communities. They accept that their 'rebel passion' earns them, at best, fitful public approbation. However, as compensation, active commitment to the cause has brought many Voices hope, lifelong friendships, and personal fulfillment. Muriel Duckworth has commented that working for peace 'on the left' has also been fun. As Ella Manual put it, VOW women have enjoyed 'a grandly subversive time.'[61]

NOTES

Thanks are extended to Margaret Conrad, Joan Sangster, and Veronica Strong-Boag for their thoughtful comments on an earlier version of this essay. I am deeply indebted to the Halifax Voices who spoke with me and wrote to me about their experiences in VOW and commented helpfully, as well, on my first-draft essay. Thank you Muriel Duckworth, Dorothy Ellis, Maxine Gough,

Cora Greenaway, Peggy Hope-Simpson, and Jo Shephard. I also appreciate having had the honour of interviewing the late Lillian Wainwright. A Social Sciences and Humanities Research Council of Canada Grant has helped cover costs associated with researching this paper.

1 Kay Macpherson and Meg Sears, 'The Voice of Women: A History,' in Gwen Matheson, ed., *Women and the Canadian Mosaic* (Toronto: Peter Martin, 1976), 71–2; Barbara Roberts, 'Women's Peace Activism in Canada,' in Linda Kealey and Joan Sangster, eds., *Beyond the Vote: Canadian Women and Politics* (Toronto: University of Toronto Press, 1989), 296–7; 'Voice of Women Dialogue,' *Atlantis* 6, 2 (1981): 168–9; and Lawrence S. Wittner, *Resisting the Bomb: A History of the World Nuclear Disarmament Movement, 1954–1970*, vol. 2 of *The Struggle against the Bomb* (Stanford: Stanford University Press, 1997), 198–99.
2 Macpherson and Sears, 'Voice of Women,' 71.
3 Insightful studies that examine the domestic ideology of the Cold War era are Veronica Strong-Boag, 'Home Dreams: Women and the Suburban Experiment in Canada, 1945–60,' *Canadian Historical Review* 72, 4 (1991): 471–504, and Elaine Tyler May, *Homeward Bound: American Families in the Cold War Era* (New York: Basic Books, 1988). For an overview discussion of Canadian women's historic progressive reform work and its persistence into the era following the Second World War, see Alison Prentice et al., *Canadian Women: A History* (Toronto: Harcourt Brace Jovanovich, 1988), esp. 333–42. On the social-reform and social-democratic context for the origins of women's peace work in the United States and Canada, see Frances Early, 'The Historic Roots of the Women's Peace Movement in North America,' *Canadian Woman Studies* 7, 4 (1986): 43–8. Also helpful for background on the context for a resurgent women's peace movement is Dee Garrison, '"Our Skirts Gave Them Courage": The Civil Defense Protest Movement in New York City, 1955–1961,' in Joanne Meyerowitz, ed., *Not June Cleaver: Women and Gender in Postwar America, 1945–1960* (Philadelphia: Temple University Press, 1994), 201–26. Garrison interprets the America of the 1950s as 'an era of muffled but rising rebellion' and credits women, many of whom were middle-class housewives, with reinvigorating a 'demoralized and scattered peace movement' (202).
4 See particularly Christine Ball, 'The History of the Voice of Women/La Voix des Femmes: The Early Years' (PhD diss., University of Toronto, 1994), and Jill Vickers, Pauline Rankin, and Christine Appelle, *Politics as if Women Mattered: A Political Analysis of the National Action Committee on the Status of Women* (Toronto: University of Toronto Press, 1993), esp. ch. 1,

'The Intellectual and Political Context for the Development of NAC,'
15–64.

5 With regard to how one might identify and analyse feminists and feminist
activism, notably in 'non-feminist' eras, I have found Iris Marion Young's
article insightful. See 'Gender as Seriality: Thinking about Women as a
Social Collective,' *Signs* 19, 3 (1994): 713–38.

6 Interview with Peggy Hope-Simpson and David Hope-Simpson conducted
by Frances Early, 8 June 2000.

7 'Voice of Women Dialogue,' 168.

8 Ibid., 169.

9 Peggy Hope-Simpson quoted in Ball, 'Voice of Women,' 347–8.

10 See Heather Frederick, 'Pearleen Oliver: Indomitable Crusader for Human
Rights' (honours essay, Mount Saint Vincent University, 1994).

11 Interview with Lillian Wainwright conducted by Frances Early, 23 July
2000. David Hope-Simpson and Gordin Kaplan took turns serving as chair
of the Halifax CCCRH, and by 1961–2, Kaplan was a strong presence in the
national CCCRH. See Muriel Duckworth Papers, Public Archives of Nova
Scotia (PANS), MG 1, 2910, folder 4, Canadian Committee for the Control
of Radiation Hazards. CCCRH transmogrified into CND in February 1962.
Gary Moffatt, *History of the Canadian Peace Movement* (St Catharines, ON:
Grape Vine Press, 1969): 90–1.

12 Minutes, 23 Nov. 1960, Duckworth Papers, MG 1, 2900, folder 9, Minutes
Halifax Branch, PANS.

13 According to Gary Moffatt, Minifie's book was 'the spark that ignited the
Canadian peace movement.' See Moffatt, *Canadian Peace Movement*, 81–6.

14 Minutes, 7 Dec. 1960, Duckworth Papers, MG 1, 2900, folder 9, Minutes
Halifax Branch, PANS.

15 Ibid.

16 In this period of the 'feminine mystique,' while some women took up professions, especially ones in which women predominated – teaching, social
work, and nursing – most gainfully employed women, who represented
just over 20 per cent of the labour force in the region, were found in the
economy's growing service sector. See Margaret Conrad, 'The Decade of
Development,' in E.R. Forbes and D.A. Muise, eds., *The Atlantic Provinces in
Confederation* (Toronto and Fredericton: University of Toronto Press and
Acadiensis Press, 1993), 387–8.

17 Over the 1960s, other British women, who had lived through the war in
their home country and had emigrated to Halifax sometime afterwards
with their spouses, joined VOW, including Dorothy Ball, Barbara Allt, and
Jo Shephard.

18 The phrase 'society of outsiders' was not used by VOW women, but it describes how they began to understand themselves in relation to the larger community. The phrase was coined by Virginia Woolf in her now classic feminist antiwar polemic *Three Guineas* (1938). Woolf's original intent in using the concept was to challenge women to face forthrightly their oppressed position within a patriarchal world – the base of which Woolf asserted was built upon militarism – and to take action to liberate themselves through a separatist consciousness and separatist institutional arrangements.

19 Alasdair M. Sinclair, *The Economic Base of the Halifax Metropolitan Area and Some Implications of Recent Population Forecasts* (Halifax: Institute of Public Affairs, Dalhousie University, 1961).

20 Oliver was a founding member of the NSAACP (1945), and Duckworth joined as soon as she arrived in Halifax.

21 Written communication from Judith Fingard to Frances Early, 18 May 2001.

22 Judith Fingard, 'Women's Organizations and Community Development in the History of Halifax' (public lecture presented to the Halifax branch of the Canadian Federation of University Women, 23 March 2000), 12. See also Judith Fingard's essay 'Women's Organizations: The Heart and Soul of Women's Activism' in this volume. For an in-depth study of women's contributions to the two world wars in Nova Scotia, see Sharon M.H. MacDonald, 'Hidden Costs, Hidden Labours: Women in Nova Scotia during Two World Wars' (masters thesis, Saint Mary's University, 1999).

23 VOW members took turns serving as delegates to LCW meetings, but no one enjoyed the task. Both Hope-Simpson and Duckworth recall that most of the women in attendance felt mildly scornful of or even hostile to the VOW peace message. Hope-Simpson's recollections also stress the presence of many military wives at LCW events. Author's interviews with Peggy Hope-Simpson, 8 June 2000, and Muriel Duckworth, 6 June 2000.

24 VOW was eventually forced to cancel this campaign, however, when the Canadian Peace Institute (CPI) directors informed Voices that because of negative publicity about their organization, potential contributors were dissociating themselves from the CPI.

25 A VOW conference in Toronto in September 1961 featured the concept of a 'world peace year.' Immediately after the meeting ended, U.S. women peace activists who had attended the conference sought out influential men in academic and media circles to back the proposal. Within less than a month the proposal, reconceptualized by this male lobbying group as International Cooperation Year, was circulating among diplomats at the United Nations. Prime Minister Jawaharlal Nehru of India brought the idea to the

Assembly, which voted in favour of designating 1965 as ICY. See press release on VOW World Peace Year (national office), Duckworth Papers, MG 1, 2901, VOW Correspondence and Papers, folder 2, 1961, PANS.

26 See Muriel Duckworth to Dr A.N. Hunt, 27 Aug. 1964, Duckworth Papers, MG 1, 2901, VOW Correspondence and Papers, folder 5, 1964, PANS, and Barbara Stewart to Mrs Shirley Duggan, 2 Feb. 1965, ibid., folder 6, January to April 1965. Muriel Duckworth's written communication to Frances Early (September 2000) explains that VOW Halifax hoped to draw more women into the peace cause; in her opinion, Duggan and her sorority pulled out because of their conservative Cold War views.

27 *The Voice of Women: The First Thirty Years*, directed and produced by Margo Pineau and Cathy Reeves (Full Frame Film and Video, 1992).

28 Minutes, 6 Nov. 1961, Duckworth Papers, MG 1, 2900, folder 9, VOW Minutes, Halifax Branch, PANS.

29 Author's interviews with Duckworth, 7 June 2000, and Hope-Simpson, 8 June 2000.

30 *Voice of Women Bulletin Maritime Branch* 1, 4 (1962): 4. Duckworth Papers, MG 1, 2931, folder 1, VOW Maritimes Area, Branch Bulletins (VOW Halifax), PANS.

31 'Vietnamese Women Visit Canada' (July 1969), Duckworth Papers, MG 1, 2932, folder 7, Speeches, Briefs, Reports, PANS.

32 Ball, 'History of the Voice of Women,' passim.

33 The Halifax group helped women in Fredericton, New Brunswick, headed by Norah Toole, to establish a branch in 1967. Through a 'Maritimes branch' organizational structure, Halifax Voices also kept in touch with Atlantic region members in Newfoundland and Prince Edward Island.

34 'Voice of Women Dialogue,' 171.

35 See, for instance, Lawrence S. Wittner, *Rebels against War: The American Peace Movement, 1933–1983* (Philadelphia: Temple University Press, 1984), 230–1, and Susan Lynn, *Progressive Women in Conservative Times: Racial Justice, Peace, and Feminism, 1945 to the 1960s* (New Brunswick, NJ: Rutgers University Press, 1992), 101–2.

36 *Speak Truth to Power: A Quaker Search for an Alternative to Violence. A Study of International Conflict* (Philadephia: American Friends Service Committee, 1955). Muriel Duckworth commented in an interview on the importance of this essay: '*Speak Truth to Power*, I believe, has had a very profound effect on [the Voice of Women's] central theme of non-violence as a way of life. It has permeated a lot of social policy strategies such as mediation, conciliation, labor relations and the idea of consensus.' In 'Voice of Women Dialogue,' 174–5.

37 Dorothy Norvell to Lester B. Pearson, 10 April 1962, Duckworth Papers, MG 1, 2901, VOW Correspondence and Papers, folder 3, 1962, PANS. See also Ball, 'Voice of Women,' 364.

38 Mrs S.T. Norvell, Jr, to Dr Doris Hirsch, 27 Nov. 1964, Duckworth Papers, MG 1, 2901, VOW Correspondence and Papers, folder 5, 1964, PANS. Norvell's ideas link her to a pacifist tradition in the United States that found expression not only in Quaker circles, but also in secular peace groups such as the War Resisters League (WRL), founded in 1924, by pacifist theoretician Jessie Wallace Hughan. In the era immediately following the First World War, Hughan argued for the creation of a militant minority committed in peacetime to an 'out-and-out' aggressive pacifist movement 'to fight all war.' Hughan's ideas became the bedrock of WRL philosophy and have influenced and been taken further by other pacifist groups and theoreticians. See Frances H. Early, 'Revolutionary Pacifism and War Resistance: Jessie Wallace Hughan's "War Against War,"' *Peace and Change* 20, 3 (1995): 307–28.

39 Vigil for Peace announcement, Duckworth Papers, MG 1, 2901, VOW Correspondence and Papers, folder 3, 1962, PANS.

40 Clipping, *Halifax Chronicle-Herald*, 2 Nov. 1962, in ibid. Green, a member of Conservative Prime Minister John Diefenbaker's cabinet, was not a proponent of nuclear arms for Canada, and Voices took advantage of their early-1960s 'ladylike' image to meet with him (and other politicians who would listen to them) as frequently as possible. In February 1962, Green visited Halifax to open a Model Security Council Meeting for young people. Afterwards, he met with a VOW delegation for forty-five minutes, urging the group to encourage women of other nations to work through their own governments for peace. 'The total impression,' a VOW report stated, 'was one of mutual respect and friendliness, though not complete agreement.' Within a year, however, the Liberals were in power and Prime Minister Pearson's new policy of nuclear arms acquisition was in place. Meetings such as this one with Green became a thing of the past. VOW was thereafter in the 'ban-the-bomb' camp, and politicians gave the group a wide berth. See 'Halifax VOW Members Talk with Howard Green,' in *Voice of Women Bulletin Maritime Branch* 1, 4 (1962): 2, Duckworth Papers, MG 1, 2931, folder 1, VOW Maritime Branch Bulletins, PANS.

41 See particularly, Veronica Strong-Boag, 'Peace-Making Women: Canada 1919-1939,' in Ruth Roach Pierson, ed., *Women and Peace: Theoretical, Historical and Practical Perspectives* (London: Croom Helm, 1987), 471–504.

42 Fran Maclean spoke about the influence of her religious values on her peace work in an interview conducted by Judith Fingard on 11 November 1997.

43 Report from the Human Relations Committee (6 pages), appended to 25
    May 1962 Minutes of the VOW Halifax Annual Meeting, Duckworth
    Papers, MG 1, 2900, folder 9, VOW Minutes, Halifax Branch, PANS.
44 Ibid., 2.
45 For instance, Muriel Duckworth helped to found the Nova Scotia NDP, and
    she and Peggy Hope-Simpson have both run for public office under the
    NDP standard.
46 Fran Maclean to Ella Manuel [chair of VOW Halifax], 17 March 1963, Duck-
    worth Papers, MG 1, 2901, VOW Correspondence and Papers, folder 4,
    1963, PANS. Emphasis in the original.
47 Elizabeth Reddick and Maxine Gough to Ella Manual, 26 March 1963, in
    ibid.
48 Catherine Verrall to VOW Halifax, 7 March 1963, in ibid. In 1967, Verrall
    wrote an articulate and angry letter to *Maritime Magazine* at CBC about her
    right to protest publicly and peacefully in a demonstration against the U.S.
    prosecution of the Vietnam War, a right she felt was being denied to her by
    'anti-protest' forces. See Catherine Verrall to *Maritime Magazine*, 22 April
    1967, Duckworth Papers, MG 1, 2901, VOW Correspondence and Papers,
    folder 11, January to May 1967, PANS.
49 There is some confusion as to when the Inter-racial Council was founded.
    Maxine Gough in a telephone conversation with Frances Early, 17 May
    2001, recalls that members of the Human Relations Committee constituted
    themselves as the Inter-racial Council after most of them resigned from the
    Voice of Women in March 1963.
50 Minutes, passim, VOW Halifax, Duckworth Papers, MG 1, 2900, folder 9,
    VOW Minutes, Halifax branch, and 2901, VOW Correspondence and
    Papers, passim, PANS. See as well Nancy Lubka, 'Ferment in Nova Scotia,'
    Queen's Quarterly 76, 2 (1969): 213–38. Historian Doug Owram notes that
    SUPA emerged out of Combined Universities Campaign for Nuclear Disar-
    mament when that group folded in 1964. Owram also notes that SUPA was
    'explicitly' New Left and saw peace and social issues as interrelated. See
    Doug Owram, *Born at the Right Time: A History of the Baby Boom Generation*
    (Toronto: University of Toronto Press, 1996), 220. On the founding of the
    Black United Front and Pearleen Oliver's role in this organization, see Fre-
    derick, 'Pearleen Oliver,' esp. 18–19.
51 Hattie Prentiss, 'Halifax Peace Action Committee,' *Halifax Voice of Women
    Newsletter*, 1 June 1968, 9, Duckworth Papers, MG 1, 2931, folder 7, VOW
    Halifax Newsletters, PANS. Prentiss reported archly that 'men in the Hali-
    fax area, doubtless long frustrated by the clarion Voice of Women, have
    been able to join the chorus recently with the advent of the Halifax Peace
    Action Committee.'

52 See the comprehensive and insightful study of WSP by Amy Swerdlow, *Women Strike for Peace: Traditional Motherhood and Radical Politics in the 1960s* (Chicago: University of Chicago Press, 1993). Swerdlow's assertion that the effectively articulated motherist ideology of WSP prefigured feminist 'second-wave' perspectives resonates with the parallel history of VOW's journey from an aggressive maternalist politics in the 1960s to an outspoken and incisive liberal/radical feminist politics in the 1970s and beyond. Also useful are two studies about North American women's social-change work in which the authors argue for the political effectiveness of maternalist politics in varied circumstances. See Joan Sangster, 'The Role of Women in the Early CCF, 1933–1940,' in *Beyond the Vote*, 118–38; and Eileen Boris, 'The Power of Motherhood: Black and White Activist Women Redefine the Political,' *Yale Journal of Law and Feminism* 2 (Fall 1989): 25–49. I have found Joan Sangster's concept of 'militant mothering' in relation to the socialist women that she examined in the Cooperative Commonwealth Federation (CCF) during the interwar period germane in analysing VOW's assertive, almost adversarial, maternalist political style in the 1960s, particularly in the latter 1960s, when the organization moved leftward politically.

53 Lyn Rodley, 'Visit of Dagmar Wilson,' *Halifax Voice of Women Newsletter*, 1 June 1968, 8, Duckworth Papers, MG 1, 2931, folder 7, VOW Halifax Newsletters, PANS.

54 9 Sept. 1968 Minutes, VOW meetings, Duckworth Papers, MG 1, 2900, VOW Minutes Halifax Branch, folder 9, 1968, PANS.

55 'Brief Presented by the Voice of Women of Halifax to the Royal Commission on the Status of Women in Canada,' 12 Sept. 1968, 5, Duckworth Papers, MG 1, 2932, Speeches, Briefs, and Reports, folder 6, PANS.

56 Ibid., 5–6.

57 Interview with Elizabeth Mullaly conducted by Frances Early, 4 August 2000.

58 Marion Douglas Kerans, *Muriel Duckworth: A Very Active Pacifist* (Halifax: Fernwood Publishing, 1996), 160–1, and interview with Muriel Duckworth, 7 June 2000.

59 See Prentice, et al., *Canadian Women*, esp. ch. 4, 'The Unfinished Revolution,' 288–407. For essays that stress the persistence of social reform and left-wing women's activism in the 1940s and 1950s in the United States, see Meyerowitz, ed., *Not June Cleaver*. On U.S. leftist women's peace work, see Amy Swerdlow, 'The Congress of American Women: Left-Feminist Peace Politics in the Cold War,' in Linda K. Kerber, Alice Kessler-Harris, and Kathryn Kish Sklar, eds., *U.S. History as Women's History: New Feminist Essays* (Chapel Hill: University of North Carolina Press, 1995), 296–312.

60 Ella Manual to Muriel Duckworth [1965], Duckworth Papers, MG 1, 2901, VOW Correspondence and Papers, folder 8, May–Dec. 1965, PANS.

61 Duckworth commented in the 1 June 1968 *Halifax Voice of Women Newsletter* that 'we have to keep developing our rationality and our caring.' See Duckworth Papers, MG 1, 2931, folder 7, VOW Halifax Newsletters, PANS. *The Rebel Passion* was the title British writer Vera Brittain chose for her history of peace pioneers (1964). Her brilliant antiwar autobiographical book on the First World War generation in Britain, *Testament of Youth* (1933), influenced many readers, including Peggy Hope-Simpson and Muriel Duckworth, towards pacifism. Peggy Hope-Simpson, 'My Outlook on Life as a Young Person,' 7 June 2000 (written communication to Frances Early); Duckworth interview, 7 June 2000; and Ella Manual to Muriel Duckworth [1967], Duckworth Papers, MG 1, 2901, VOW Correspondence and Papers, folder 11, Jan.–May 1967, PANS.

A Fragile Independence:
The Nova Scotia Advisory Council on the Status of Women

JANET GUILDFORD

The Nova Scotia Advisory Council on the Status of Women (NSACSW) was, like its counterparts at the national level and in other provinces, a response to the *Report of the Royal Commission on the Status of Women* published in 1970. Since its creation in 1977, the NSACSW has conducted research on the status of women and provided advice and information to successive provincial governments, as well as a variety of services to women and women's organizations.[1] It has had to negotiate complex relationships among governments and women's groups, and has constantly tested the limits of its autonomy – with very mixed results. The advisory council exists at the pleasure of the government, and its members are appointed as individuals. While the government has ensured representation from all geographic areas of the province – and to a lesser degree from the diverse ethnic and racial groups that make up the province's population – the council has no direct links with community-based women's organizations in Nova Scotia.[2] Tensions have regularly developed over the relationship – or lack of relationship – between the council and women's organizations. At times, particularly in its early years, the council met with considerable success in improving the status of women; at other times it experienced frustration and failure.

In its first decade the NSACSW was preoccupied with bringing Nova Scotia law into conformity with the recommendations the Royal Commission on the Status of Women and the Canadian Charter of Rights and Freedoms. In the late 1980s, under the presidency of Francene Cosman, the agency experienced years of frustration with government inaction, but set the stage for what many regard as its 'golden age' under the leadership of Debi Forsyth Smith, who achieved the highest profile among its presidents. During her presidency the major focus was on issues relating to the safety and security of women – issues such as male violence against women, sexual harassment, and pornography. Although the council enjoyed considerable autonomy during Forsyth Smith's presidency, it was not able to maintain its independence from the provincial government. In 1996 the council – and the Nova Scotia women's community – lost a highly publicized struggle over appointments with Eleanor Norrie, the Liberal minister responsible for the status of women. As a result, the NSACSW was merged with the Women's Directorate, a provincial government agency that advised on issues relating to the status of women in the civil service. Since the merger, the council has continued to perform its advisory, research, and educational roles, although generally it has assumed a lower public profile.

A study of the Nova Scotia Advisory Council on the Status of Women provides us with an opportunity to explore one of the major institutions of the second wave of feminism and offers one small window on the relationship between feminists and the state. Advisory Councils on the Status of Women were established at the national level and in most provinces in the years following the *Report of the Royal Commission on the Status of Women* (1970). They are still operating in all four Atlantic provinces, in Quebec, Manitoba, the Northwest Territories, and the Yukon. The Ontario advisory council, established in 1973, was eliminated in the early 1990s by Premier Mike Harris's Conservative government. British Columbia did not create an advisory council, but has had various ministries with responsibility for the status of women – most recently, a minister of state for women's equality. The Saskatchewan government eliminated the Women's Secretariat, its version of an advisory council, in the winter of 2002. The story of the various provincial agencies charged with responsibility for the status of women is complex because councils, secretariats, and directorates were frequently established, changed, and dissolved. The general trend since the 1990s, however, has been towards dismantling them.[3]

Provincial councils have as yet received relatively little attention from historians. Yet such councils respond to and attempt to influence provincial government policies that directly affect women in their daily lives in areas such as social assistance, education, labour standards, and minimum wages. It is interesting to note that many of the trends, activities, and frustrations associated with the NSACSW are quite similar to the patterns identified nationally and in the province of Ontario, the most studied of the provinces.[4] The relationships between advisory councils and governments have consistently been characterized by contradictions and tension. As agencies funded by governments to promote democratic advocacy for improving the status of women and for opening up government to women's voices, they have fought an uphill battle. Council members often found that if they tried to push their autonomy too far they met with intractable resistance. The preoccupation many councils have had with achieving autonomy from the governments that fund them mirrors second-wave feminist concerns for independence and has shaped their activities. In spite of these tensions, advisory councils, including the NSACSW, have had some very important victories in advancing a liberal feminist agenda and ensuring that the status of women has remained on the public agenda.

The First Ten Years

In April 1975 Nova Scotia appointed a seven-member Task Force on the Status of Women to study the position of women in the province and to make recommendations to address the provincial implications of the recommendations of the federal Royal Commission on the Status of Women.[5] Although the mandate of the task force was to study how to bring the province into line with the recommendations of the royal commission, it can also be understood as part of Nova Scotia's recognition of International Women's Year (IWY) in 1975. In February 1975 the provincial government appointed a group of eighteen women from across the province as the Nova Scotia IWY Steering Committee. Kathryn Logan, a young Liberal, became the full-time provincial coordinator for IWY.[6] The task force and the steering committee shared a budget and often worked closely together. Logan attended the first meeting of the task force members, for example, and two weeks later the task force and the steering committee held a joint meeting.[7]

When the task force released its report, *Herself / Elle-Meme*, in March 1976, it recommended that the province establish a Ministry of State for the Status of Women 'to give women a strong voice at the highest level of decision-making in our province.'[8] The IWY Steering Committee had already made the same demand, as had the Nova Scotia Women's Action Committee, a group established in September 1975 to ensure the spirit of IWY continued.[9] Instead, the Nova Scotia government established the Nova Scotia Advisory Council on the Status of Women to 'advise the Minister [responsible for the status of women] upon such matters relating to the status of women as are referred to the Council for consideration by the Minister' and 'to bring to the attention of the Minister matters of interest and concern to women.'[10]

The NSACSW was not the province's only response to status of women issues. Earlier in 1975 it appointed an Interdepartmental Committee on the Status of Women (IDC), comprised largely of female senior civil servants, to address women's policy issues within the government. The IDC was an important institution, and it had a long and varied impact on the history of the NSACSW. In the months leading up to the creation and appointment of the advisory council, the IDC did considerable preparatory work, especially the development of a legislative package known as Bill 102 – An Act to Amend the Statute Law Respecting Women – which changed nineteen laws that had been found to discriminate against women. The IDC advised the provincial government on legislation and on its relationship with women within the civil service and provided research support for ministers attending intergovernmental meetings. Throughout most of the 1980s, the IDC reviewed issues such as employment and pay equity, recreational opportunities for women, family violence, child-care needs, and sexual harassment. The IDC also contributed to the establishment of the provincial government's Women's Directorate in 1988.[11]

Many of the fifteen members of the NSACSW selected by the government, including Elizabeth Crocker, the first president, were closely associated with the incumbent Liberal Party.[12] The concept of diversity was narrower in 1977 than it has since become, and was limited to the representation of Catholics and Protestants and urban and rural women; one man was also appointed.[13] Kathryn Logan, formerly IWY coordinator, was appointed executive director. Although the administrative work of establishing committees and procedures absorbed considerable energy during the council's first year of operation, members quickly identified a number of issues they hoped to address. Members worked on a range of issues including women's health, women in the labour force, the expansion of women's access to training and education, and daycare. Another immediate concern was leadership training to encourage women's participation in electoral politics and public affairs.[14]

Receiving top priority was matrimonial property law. The need for married women's property law reform had been dramatically demonstrated to Canadians by the *Murdoch* case. When Irene Murdoch, an Alberta farm wife separated from her husband in 1968, she was denied a half interest in the family farm. Although Murdoch received a lump sum maintenance payment in 1973, the judge's ruling explicitly failed to recognize her economic contribution to the farm, a decision upheld by the Supreme Court of Canada.[15] Late in 1975 Susan Ashley, the legal advisor to the Status of Women Task Force – and in April 1977 one of the first women appointed to the advisory council – warned in *The 4th Estate*, a progressive Halifax weekly, that Nova Scotia law would allow a replay of *Murdoch*. She argued that the province needed 'legislation stating that property acquired during marriage is considered to be held jointly by both partners.'[16] In December 1977 the council established a Legislative Committee to propose legislation that would at the dissolution of a marriage recognize women's unpaid labour. Until new legislation was passed in 1980, the committee worked tirelessly to ensure women's interests were served, meeting with ministers and other members of the legislature and cooperating with the Interdepartmental Committee on the Status of Women.[17]

In October 1978, just a year after the first meeting of the council, a new Progressive Conservative government was elected in the province. The election was probably the council's first reminder of its lack of autonomy. It not only got a new minister, Terry Donahoe, but also a new president, Elizabeth Anne Roscoe, a twenty-eight-year-old Halifax lawyer.[18] Although the council continued to pursue an agenda of legal reform, research, and community consultation, Donahoe proved to be a much more interventionist minister than his predecessor, Liberal William MacEachern. In November, he assigned the council a very demanding agenda. He asked members to draft a suitable legislative package for the 1979 session of the House of Assembly, instructed them to develop a talent bank of women qualified for public appointments, and told them that the council must improve the public image and understanding of status of women issues and structures both within government and among the general public.[19] Over the next year he also asked the agency to cut back in two key areas relating to language and meetings. He quashed the policy of bilingualism that had been adopted by the council, reduced the number of meetings from six to five each year, and reduced the per diems paid to members.[20] In September 1979, Donahoe expressed his dissatisfaction with the way the agency had carried out its educational role, arguing that many people in the province did not understand the council's role, and that the council did not understand what was going on around the province with community groups. He 'directed' the NSACSW to undertake a comprehensive review of all the organizations in the province, including men's and women's groups, to make a list and to establish and keep contact with these groups.[21]

By the spring of 1980 Donahoe's involvement with the work of the NSACSW had fallen off, and the council expressed disappointment when he did not attend the annual meeting in Wolfville, at which women from thirteen women's groups presented briefs. It was also disappointed that he postponed the appointment of a new president following the resignation of Roscoe in November 1979 after only one year in office.[22] By the time Donahoe appointed Dr Florence Wall president in October 1980, the grumbling about the council's inaction had become public. In November, *Atlantic Insight* published an article entitled 'What ever happened to the Status of Women?'[23]

The appointment of Wall signalled a change in the direction of activities. Until that time, the NSACSW had been preoccupied with legal reforms, especially the matrimonial property legislation, and the general process of assuring that Nova Scotian legislation reflected the recommendations of the Royal Commission on the Status of Women. Wall's presidency began with a rethinking of the council's function. In February 1981 a program committee identified three themes as a focus: the needs of women with disabilities in the workforce, women's unpaid work, and the disappearance of women as volunteers.[24] The council also committed itself to more educational activities, establishing a quarterly newsletter and meeting with provincial women's organizations.[25] Its profile was very low during the next year or so. Wall resigned for health reasons in January 1982, and once again there was a delay of several months before a new president was appointed. At a special meeting in April the council once again expressed frustration to Donahoe about its lack of 'clout.'[26]

Francene Cosman was appointed president of the NSACSW in the spring of 1982. Her presidency represented the end of the first phase of the agency's life and was a period of intense dissatisfaction among members. Despite her extensive political experience – she had served on Halifax County Council from 1976 to 1979 and then had become Bedford's first mayor – her presidency was marked by frustration.[27] After a few years of significant changes in legislation affecting women, the Nova Scotia government, like its counterparts across the country, had become less willing to promote reform. As the national political agenda shifted further to the right, feminists were increasingly treated as just another lobby group, and found it more and more difficult to influence either the political agenda or policies affecting women.[28] Donahoe continued to be erratic in his attention to the council. After considerable delays during which he did not act on matters such as the appointment of members, he would schedule a meeting and suggest an entirely new direction for the work of the council.[29] At a meeting in February 1984, when representatives from the three parties in Nova Scotia were invited to address the council, Alexa McDonough, leader of the NDP, and A.M. Cameron, Liberal leader, both participated, whereas the governing Conservatives only sent a letter.[30]

Many members who welcomed Cosman in 1982 had been serving for several years and brought considerable experience and energy to the work. Individual women and women's organizations had also become accustomed to bringing their concerns to the council, and its agenda became larger and more diverse under Cosman's leadership. Additionally, many individual women used the council as a resource for finding services they needed, and referrals had become an important element in the day-to-day work of the staff. The council increased its research and publication efforts, preparing briefs, reports, and pamphlets on a wide range of issues, including the needs of widows and disabled women, women on social assistance, daycare, the impact of part-time employment on women, the provincial labour standards code, affirmative action, and access to postsecondary education. The goals of the research and publication program included improving women's access to services as well as improving the services themselves. The most significant new area of focus was violence against women, a concern that would become increasingly central over the next decade. The related issue of pornography also became a major concern, in response to the large number of letters and phone calls on the subject.[31]

Canada's adoption of the Charter of Rights and Freedoms in 1982 created new challenges for the NSACSW. Many of Nova Scotia's laws had to be changed in order to conform to the new rights guaranteed to women by the Charter. In 1983 the council developed a Plan of Action that included a comprehensive package of legislative reforms.[32] The plan passed very slowly through the bureaucracy. By April 1984 it had been analysed by all departments; at the June council meeting Donahoe announced that it had been accepted by provincial cabinet and asked the council to identify its priorities.[33] In response, employment issues and economic development were identified as the areas most in need of immediate attention.[34] The *Halifax Mail-Star* published a five-page report on the Plan of Action, which advocated new policies to

curb drug and alcohol addiction among women, eliminate sex stereo-
typing from school textbooks, and increase opportunities for women to
work in traditionally male occupations, as well as a host of improvements in the areas of health, the family, education and training,
employment and economic development, and participation of women
in the public service and politics.[35]

At the end of her first term as president, Cosman complained that the
credibility of the council 'as a voice to be listened to and respected has
not significantly affected changes in legislation.'[36] It was not for lack of
trying. The council had presented briefs to commissions and task forces
on pension reform, family benefits, the impact of micro-electronics on
women's employment and occupational health and safety, part-time
work, employment equity, pornography, and changes to the Divorce
Act. Despite constant complaints, the minister had been very slow at
appointing new members to council when terms expired. Nonetheless,
Cosman accepted a second appointment as president in June 1985.

At the time of Cosman's re-appointment, the NSACSW informed
Donahoe that a number of issues internal to its operation needed
urgent attention. 'As members of a revitalized Council, with lots of
fresh enthusiasm,' they wanted reassurance that there would not again
be long delays in appointments, and they wanted an immediate
appointment to replace the Acadian member whose term had expired.
They also told the minister that there was a dire need for a regional
fieldwork coordinator and that the funding for this position had
already been approved. 'When can we make the appointment?' they
asked. They expressed both the urgency regarding the appointment of
a full-time staff researcher and their frustration at the delay in resolv-
ing changes sought in the structure of the council. Finally, they were
concerned some members were not attending meetings, and asked the
minister how he planned to address the problem.[37]

For several months it looked as though the situation was improving.
Donahoe reacted quickly to members' concerns. By September Pauline
d'Entrement had been appointed as a new member, a part-time
regional fieldwork coordinator was hired, and the minister invited the
council and the Interdepartmental Committee on the Status of Women
to revisit the implementation of the Plan of Action.[38] However, the
government's Management Board refused to fund a researcher, a decision the council found very frustrating. Progress on the Plan of Action
to address the Charter was also agonizingly slow. In April 1985 Cosman expressed her hope that Nova Scotia could have legislative

change without court battles and argued that the laws of the province must conform to the Charter.[39] Donahoe was not encouraging. In September he told the *Chronicle-Herald* that it would take years before the Plan of Action would be reflected in Nova Scotian communities, but he believed that it did commit the provincial government to a general policy direction designed to improve women's condition by fine-tuning laws and encouraging profound changes in society's attitudes towards women.[40]

During this time the Council was working hard to build stronger relationships with the women's community. The organizations and institutions of the second wave of feminism were well established in the province by the late 1980s, but these community-based women's groups had no formal relationship to the government-appointed Advisory Council. The tensions created by the NSACSW's lack of autonomy and issues of representation were perennial problems. However, without strong support from the women's community the council remained a weak and isolated voice for change.

Conflict and Controversy

In January 1986 the appointment of Brian Young as the new minister responsible for the status of women inaugurated a period of intense conflict and public controversy for the NSACSW. Although Young agreed to meet on a regular basis with the council, and research and lobbying campaigns on housing and family violence continued, no action was taken on the restructuring of the council.[41] At his first meeting with them, members told Young that they wanted representation on the Interdepartmental Committee on the Status of Women, a staff researcher, and a more effective structure, which members defined as a smaller council that met monthly, and one where appointments were made in a timely fashion and represented the diversity of Nova Scotia women.

In the fall of 1986 a frustrated Cosman resigned to considerable publicity, hoping her resignation would be a catalyst for change. She claimed that the council 'lacked clout' and that she was tired of trying to prod Premier John Buchanan's Tories into action on women's issues.'[42] Even though the council presented over thirty briefs to government during her presidency, it saw no action, and this ineffectiveness cost valuable support. Sue MacLeod, writing in *Atlantic Insight* in December 1986, claimed that the women's community had long ago 'written off' the council.[43] Three weeks after her resignation, Cosman joined the Liberal Party. Interestingly, in 1998 she herself became minister responsible for the status of women in John Savage's government.[44]

Despite their scepticism, women's organizations in the province supported Cosman's protest and quickly met to plan their response. In addition to sending a letter to Brian Young criticizing the provincial government for its inaction on women's issues, the group laid the groundwork for a further meeting at which the Women's Action Committee of Nova Scotia (WACNS) was formed. Modelled on the National Action Committee on the Status of Women (NAC), the WACNS was completely independent of government and developed a very different structure from that of the advisory council, with elected regional representation from women's organizations across the province. For several years WACNS successfully lobbied provincial politicians at its annual meetings and pursued a range of issues, both independently and in collaboration with the advisory council. Although WACNS ceased to be active by the late 1990s, many of its feminist activists continued to lobby for improved policies and programs for women through newer organizations such as Feminists for Just and Equitable Public Policy (FemJEPP), established in 1998.[45]

Cosman's resignation and the support she received from the women's groups in the province were important. She was the fourth president to resign during the council's first decade, and its credibility as a voice for Nova Scotia women was severely compromised as a result. For all practical purposes, the annual WACNS lobbies took over the advisory council's role of advising the provincial government about issues affecting women. In these circumstances, the council, under the temporary leadership of its chair, Irene Swindells, warned the minister that 'credibility is now the most important consideration – both the credibility of the government of Nova Scotia and the credibility of the Nova Scotia Advisory Council on the Status of Women.'[46]

Debi Forsyth Smith's Presidency

In a remarkable turnaround, the fortunes of the council were restored by the appointment of Debi Forsyth Smith, a popular television consumer affairs reporter, as president in March 1987. She brought to the job excellent public relations skills and good connections within the Conservative Party of Nova Scotia.[47] Equally important, during her presidency the women's community in Nova Scotia was well organized and capable of effective collective action. Forsyth Smith was highly regarded by women's groups, who felt she made a real effort to develop relationships with the women's community.[48] In the spring of 1992, for example, she publicly supported the protests of WACNS against the proposed $1.6 million cut to federal funding for women's programs.[49] During her tenure as president, the council also benefited from considerable continuity within its membership. Its budget increased every year during her presidency, from $407,238 in 1988–9 to $542,340 in 1992–3.

Forsyth Smith was, undoubtedly, the agency's highest-profile president. A steady stream of press releases issued from the council office and were picked up by the media. Forsyth Smith was always available to the local press for comment on women's issues inside and outside Nova Scotia. She even received kudos from notoriously anti-feminist *Frank* magazine, which claimed in 1988 that 'she has performed a really Herculean feat – pulling the advisory council out of the humiliation it had suffered – right across the country to a point where it is respected and recognized for the kind of work she had done.'[50]

The new president was especially effective at bringing violence against women to public attention, an issue that feminists in Canada were working hard to address. She began her campaign in October 1990 by calling on police to be more effective in their response to domestic disputes.[51] In February 1991, following a period where four women had been murdered by their spouses, she raised the issue in the media again, calling on the provincial government to do something about domestic homicide.[52] The council's report on sentencing for sexual assault, released in the summer of 1991, provides a good example of the kind of attention the agency was receiving in this period. At a well-attended press conference organized by the council, Sherry O'Brien, a sexual assault victim, told her personal story.[53] Forsyth Smith strongly criticized judges, lawyers, and police for not taking the crime of sexual assault seriously enough. A story in the *Globe and Mail* reflected her concern, claiming that 'Nova Scotia's male-dominated judiciary treats sex offenders less harshly than deer poachers and robbers.'[54]

For the next few months Forsyth Smith kept the issue of violence against women in the public eye.[55] There was extensive press coverage of observances on the second anniversary of the Montreal Massacre. As part of these ceremonies the advisory council publicized the names of six Nova Scotian women who had been murdered in 1991.[56] Forsyth Smith publicly criticized the municipal governments in Queens County and Mahone Bay for refusing to take part in the observances. She also kept pressure on the provincial government, publicly criticizing Community Services Minister Marie Dechman's comment that domestic violence was a result of the depressed economy.[57] In May 1991 the provincial government announced a program designed to reduce family violence and plans for a study of domestic homicide.[58]

At the same time that the provincial family violence program was announced, the NSACSW publicly argued that North Sydney Police Chief George Brown was acting in appropriately when he accused feminist groups of making up statistics on the abuse of women to justify their existence. The council took the complaint to the Nova Scotia Police Commission, where it hit a number of snags. First, the commission claimed that the council had lost the opportunity to file a complaint as it had not done so within thirty days of the incident. Forsyth Smith responded that the thirty-day limit did not allow women's organizations enough time to prepare complaints.[59] The case dragged on amidst procedural wrangling and public debate. In the meantime similar complaints had also been laid against three other police officers, a Dartmouth constable, a New Glasgow sergeant, and a Sydney sergeant. In early March 1992 Nova Scotia Supreme Court Justice Walter Goodfellow ruled that the Nova Scotia Police Review Board had exceeded its power in extending the time for an investigation into the complaint and that the advisory council was not entitled to lay the complaint. Although the complaint was dropped, the publicity kept the issue of violence against women high on the public agenda.[60]

The advisory council also took an active role in supporting a group of women patients who alleged they had been sexually abused by a Halifax physician, Ralph Loebenburg. In the early 1990s the agency received between sixty and eighty complaints against doctors around the province. Although fourteen women testified against Loebenburg, he was exonerated by a Provincial Medical board inquiry. When the board later appointed a subcommittee to look into the issue of sexual abuse of patients by doctors, it decided not to seek the opinions of victims.[61] The success of the council in keeping the issues of sexual abuse and violence against women in the public eye, despite frequent rebuffs, owed much to national efforts on these issues, but it also reflected the ability of Forsyth Smith, the council, and other provincial women's organizations to respond to local concerns and to use the media effectively.

The NSACSW continued to pursue a wide range of women's health, human rights, political, and workplace issues. In 1989 Forsyth Smith participated in a press conference with lesbian and gay rights activists to agitate for the inclusion of sexual orientation in the provincial Human Rights Act.[62] In 1990 the council successfully persuaded the provincial government to cover the prosthesis costs for mastectomy patients.[63] The same year, it began to work with a new Black women's network.[64] In the early 1990s the underrepresentation of women in electoral politics continued to be an ongoing theme in the work of the advisory council. Its annual meeting in April 1991 was held in conjunction with the Winning Women Political Skills Forum. Six months later, the council published *Votes for Women: A Political Guidebook for Nova Scotia Women*. Women's labour force issues also remained high on the agenda. In 1991 the council published a report on the province's part-time workers, three-quarters of whom were women, which argued that benefits, pensions, and labour standards protection must be improved.[65] It presented thirty-three recommendations to the Nova Scotia Pay Equity Commission, arguing for the elimination of historic and systemic pay discrimination against women.[66] It also undertook important research on young women, published as *Attitudes, Behaviour and Aspirations: A Report on Young Women*.[67] In 1992 this concern with young women prompted Forsyth Smith to ask the Halifax County–Bedford District School Board to reconsider its abandonment of a proposal to set up daycares in two high schools.[68]

Long-awaited changes in the structure and administration of the advisory council occurred during Forsyth Smith's tenure. In 1987 and 1988 both staff and the council itself were restructured. A researcher was hired. The numbers of members was reduced from fourteen to eleven (excluding the president) to conform to the federal electoral districts in the province, the number of meetings was increased from five to seven each year, and an orientation manual for new members was developed.[69] Among the most far-reaching of the structural changes discussed in the late 1980s was the question of how to achieve a better representation of the diversity of Nova Scotian women. In 1987, Forsyth Smith told the Standing Committee on Human Resources that women's groups had raised the issue of diversity and that the council was considering ensuring representation for Native and disabled women.[70] Under the Advisory Council Act, the government had the right to select and appoint members. Those pressing for reform argued that only by giving the members a much greater role in the selection process and asserting a greater autonomy than the council had previously enjoyed could more diverse representation be achieved. At the same time, members developed a new selection process for the presidency – one that would ensure they would play the central role in choosing Forsyth Smith's successor.

In February 1993 Debi Forsyth Smith resigned from the presidency of the NSACSW to become a member of the provincial cabinet before unsuccessfully seeking the Progressive Conservative nomination in the suburban Halifax riding of Timberlea-Prospect.[71] Her legacy was significant, and within the women's community in Nova Scotia, her presidency is remembered as a high point for the advisory council. There is considerable evidence from both the public record and agency's own internal documents to sustain that view. During her presidency the council was able to keep women's issues in the public eye, keep the ear of government, and maintain effective relationships with the provincial women's community. The council adopted procedures designed to enhance its autonomy from government, particularly its ability to select its own president. Forsyth Smith's resignation inaugurated a period that tested the ability of the Nova Scotia Advisory Council on the Status of Women to maintain this autonomy.

An Attempt to Control the Appointment Process

The appointment of a new president went smoothly. The council recommended that the position go to Katherine McDonald, a Halifax lawyer and long-time activist with Planned Parenthood; this recommendation was swiftly approved by the new Liberal provincial government.[72] McDonald was touted as the first non-partisan NSACSW president. Under her leadership, the council embarked on a comprehensive process of community consultation and restructuring designed to provide greater representation for historically disadvantaged groups in Nova Scotia. As part of this process in 1993 the council undertook a very extensive review of its programs and structures and entered into consultations with the women's community regarding their views of the agency.

The consultations determined that public perceptions of the advisory council varied significantly. At one extreme, some saw it as partisan window-dressing for government inaction, while others saw members as radical feminists, 'bra burners and against men.' Some respondents believed the presidency was a springboard to electoral politics, as it had been for former presidents Francene Cosman and Debi Forsyth Smith.

The former location of the offices, in a high rise on the Halifax water-front, was criticized as inaccessible and intimidating; much more satisfaction was expressed for the new more modest premises above a shopping mall. The strongest support was for the council's research and publications and for the information provided by staff to people who phoned the office. Fifty recommendations were developed to address concerns expressed during consultations. The most pressing was to ensure the diversity of both the council and the staff.[73]

While consultations with women's groups in the province were being conducted – the results of which were published as *Who Will Speak for Us? A Consultation Paper with Nova Scotia Women* – the council, with some help and advice from representatives of the women's community, hammered out a new appointment process.[74] This process had been discussed during both Cosman's and Forsyth Smyth's presidencies, and issues of representation and autonomy had been concerns. In 1993 the NSACSW made dramatic changes to the appointment procedure, which were intended to offer much greater representation to the organized women's community within the province and to the diversity of women in the province. In their deliberations, members noted that neither a First Nations woman nor a self-identified lesbian had even sat on the council. According to Brenda Beagan, a member of the newly appointed Community Advisory Committee, the 'status of women [council] was regarded by many as an elite government body, filled with government appointees.'[75] As seven of the twelve seats were vacant, the Community Advisory Committee wasted no time in recommending that the council create 'designated' seats on the basis of which groups most needed representation. The committee believed that the most thoroughly alienated were Black and Native women, and recommended that they each receive two seats. Lesbians, Acadian women, and women with disabilities were each given one, for a total of seven. The council accepted these suggestions and began the application procedure. After placing advertisements for the specially designated appointments, and sending out 800 application forms, the agency received 164 applicants, 52 of them from designated groups. On 12 August 1994 the new members were appointed.[76]

The focus on community consultation and internal restructuring lowered the public profile of the NSACSW and absorbed the time and attention of both members and staff. Between 1993 and 1996 it produced only ten publications, a small number compared to the nine in 1992 and the eleven in 1991. At the same time, it had to cope with a meaner political climate. In November 1995, Finance Minister Bernie Boudreau announced the NSACSW faced a tough provincial review because 'we have a hard time quantifying the contribution [it] makes.'[77]

The advisory council became news again in April 1996, when Eleanor Norrie, minister responsible for the status of women, ignored the procedure, so painstakingly developed just two years earlier, in making new appointments.[78] McDonald told a press conference 'we're making a last ditch effort to maintain independence,' and accused Norrie of violating the agreement signed in 1994.[79] The criticisms of the minister were symptomatic of a very antagonistic relationship between Norrie and McDonald. Moreover, the minister was well aware that there was some dissatisfaction with McDonald's leadership, and she was able to use the tension it generated as an opportunity to restructure the government's agencies working in the area of the status of women.

In June 1996, when Katherine McDonald applied for a second term as president of the NSACSW, Eleanor Norrie turned her down. Her term would end on 31 July 1996. Later that summer, Norrie announced her plans to merge the NSACSW with the Women's Directorate of the Nova Scotia government. McDonald expressed fears that 'the council will simply be swallowed by government,' and complained that the cabinet committee that began to look at women's issues and funding in 1994 had not sought the input of council members or women's groups.[80] Although members of the council and the women's community vigorously protested Norrie's decision, the proposed merger was implemented. Even the conservative *Halifax Chronicle-Herald* editorialized that 'another watchdog has been euthanized.'[81]

The merger brought together two agencies with long experience in representing women's issues to the provincial government. The Women's Directorate had been created in 1988 by the minister responsible for the status of women to address women's issues such as affirmative action and to review government policy to identify gender-biased impact inside the provincial government. At the time the Women's Directorate was created, the minister had reassured the NSACSW that the two bodies were not in competition with one another and that other Canadian provinces had already established similar bodies. Much of the Women's Directorate's research focused on internal government administrative matters such as employment equity within the provincial civil service. In addition to briefing the minister and promoting a wide variety of initiatives regarding policies affecting women, the directorate also continued to serve in its staff role to the

Interdepartmental Committee on the Status of Women, which in 1991 was given a new mandate and a new name, the Interdepartmental Committee on Women's Issues (CWI).[82] Although largely comprised of more junior civil servants with less responsibility for policy than the senior civil servants who had sat on the Interdepartmental Committee on the Status of Women, the CWI was an important networking and educational vehicle, until it dwindled away in 1995. Most of its programs were designed to improve conditions for women working within the civil service.[83]

By 1989–90 some overlap between the work of the NSACSW and the Women's Directorate was beginning to emerge. The Women's Directorate began publishing research and educational materials such as a statistical handbook on women in Nova Scotia and a newsletter, *About Women*, intended for a provincial audience. Forsyth Smyth repeatedly expressed her concern to the deputy minister responsible for the status of women about potential overlap, but when the council suggested that it meet with directorate staff to discuss cutbacks in federal funding, the deputy minister responded that, while she felt informal liaison was good, a formal meeting was outside her terms of reference. Consequently the council never took its concerns directly to the staff of the Women's Directorate.[84]

Certainly both the advisory council and the Women's Directorate were established to advise the provincial government on issues relating to the status of women, and both reported to the minister responsible for the status of women. However their relationship to government was, in theory at least, quite different. The NSACSW was intended to be relatively autonomous from government – although the extent of this autonomy had to be constantly renegotiated – while the Women's Directorate was part of the provincial government.

The new agency that resulted from the amalgamation of the council and the directorate had both a different structure and a slightly different mandate than either of its predecessors. Brigitte Neumann, formerly a senior staff member of the Women's Directorate, became the acting executive director of the advisory council. Her role was to continue her advisory function for the minister responsible for the status of women and to provide support for the NSACSW. The position of the president of the council was eliminated, and leadership was vested in the chair. Patricia Doyle Bedwell, a Mi'kmaw lawyer and professor with several years experience on council, was the first chair of the merged agency. She expressed optimism at the time of the merger, claiming that the council and the Women's Directorate had often duplicated efforts, research, and policy development, and adding that the merger would provide more researchers and support staff.[85] Since the merger, the council has continued to operate in all areas of its mandate. It has conducted research on a number of issues of concern to women, presented a series of briefs to government, and offered a variety of services to women's organizations in the province. Among community-based women's organizations such as the provincial coalition FemJEPP there was considerable doubt about the ability of the advisory council to continue to represent the concerns of women in the framework of the newly merged agency. However, community-based women's groups remain firmly committed to the survival of the council; they regard its ongoing presence as evidence that the provincial government retains a commitment to addressing women's issues.

Since 2000 rumours of the elimination of the NSACSW have continued to surface, and there can be little doubt that the existence of the council as a relatively autonomous body is in jeopardy. Early in 2000, Liberal and New Democratic MLAs claimed that the provincial Conservative government led by John Hamm planned to eliminate the NSACSW in its April budget. In March, Jane Purves, minister responsible for the status of women warned that there would be changes to the council. Doyle Bedwell responded that the council provides 'a vital function to women throughout the province' and expressed her hope that the institution would survive the budget cuts.[86] It did survive the 2000 budget, but in the summer of 2001 it faced a new threat, as a merger with the Nova Scotia Human Rights Commission was proposed. Although opposition to the merger was unanimous among those who presented their views, rumours of the council's demise persist. As of 2004 the council had survived the threats, and it prominently celebrated its twenty-fifth anniversary at Government House on International Women's Day, 8 March 2002.

Advisory Councils on the Status of Women across the country have been an important mechanism for second-wave feminists, and the history of these agencies has a lot to tell us about the relationships between and among various levels of government and women's organizations, about the nature of the state, and about the policy process. Former Liberal finance minister Bernie Boudreau was right when he said that the work of the Nova Scotia Advisory Council was hard to quantify. In that respect, it is like a great deal of women's work – vital, but difficult to measure. The most obvious value of the advisory coun-

cil is as a concrete symbol of the Nova Scotia government's commitment to improving women's status in the province. Although this
preliminary overview of the history of the council does not purport to
offer an evaluation of its effectiveness, there have certainly been times
in its history when its influence as an advisory body has shaped legislative change. Its recommendations regarding matrimonial property
law reform and the Plan of Action on the Charter of Rights and Freedoms, adopted by the Conservative government in 1985, are two very
significant examples. The relationship between successive councils
and provincial governments has been consistently characterized by
conflict and disagreements about the former's autonomy. The council's
attempt to take control of the appointment process between 1993 and
1996 provides the clearest illustration of the limits of its autonomy.

The NSACSW is a government-appointed advisory body: it exists
and functions at the pleasure of the government. On the whole, conflicts about its independence have produced positive change, and
through the successful demands of its members the agency has, at various times throughout its history, increased its budget, found the
resources to do important research on a plethora of subjects, increased
the diversity of women's experiences represented on council itself, and
created new structural forms and administrative procedures. The role
of the advisory council in providing information and referrals for individual women with personal problems is not mandated by legislation
or envisioned as part of its role, but it has nonetheless been a vital
function of the council and its staff at least since the early 1980s.
Despite its almost continual struggles and frustrations, the persever-
ence and persistence of the Nova Scotia Advisory Council on the
Status of Women has furthered the aspirations of women in Nova
Scotia.

NOTES

Access to the Minutes of the Nova Scotia Advisory Council on the Status of
Women was granted through a research agreement under the Freedom of
Information and Protection of Privacy Act. I want to express my gratitude to
Brigitte Neumann, acting director of the Nova Scotia Advisory Council on the
Status of Women, for her generous support and guidance through this process.

1 An Act to Establish an Advisory Council on the Status of Women, Statutes
  of Nova Scotia, 1977, c 3.

2 Nova Scotia Advisory Council on the Status of Women Chronology of Order-in-Council Appointments, NSACSW 1999. The exceptions to this pattern were the seven appointments made in September 1994 under an autonomous selection process developed by the council. These will be discussed in more detail later in this chapter.

3 Discussions on PAR-L, a women's research listserv based at the University of New Brunswick, during the winter of 2002 were very helpful in piecing this information together. The PAR-L Web site provides good information on government services and programs for women in Canada. See http://www.unb.ca/PAR-L/policy2.htm. Alberta appears not to have had on advisory council.

4 See, for example, Judith E. Grant, 'Women's Issues and the State: Representation, Reform and Control,' *Resources for Feminist Research* 3 (1988), special issue on *Feminist Perspectives on the Canadian State*, 87–9, and Sue Findlay, 'Canadian Advisory Council on the Status of Women: Contradictions and Conflict,' and 'Feminist Struggles with the Canadian State, 1966–1988, in ibid.; Jill Vickers, Pauline Rankin, and Christine Appelle, *Politics as if Women Mattered: A Political Analysis of the National Action Committee on the Status of Women* (Toronto: University of Toronto Press, 1993).

5 See Christine Eisan, 'A Catalyst for Change: The Nova Scotia Task Force on the Status of Women' (honour essay, Mount Saint Vincent University, 2003).

6 *The 4th Estate* (Halifax), 26 Feb. 1975, 20.

7 Minutes of the Nova Scotia Task Force on the Status of Women, 3 April 1975, 22 April 1975, Public Archives of Nova Scotia (PANS), RG 44, vol. 177, no. 1.

8 *Herself / Elle-Meme: Report of the Nova Scotia Task Force on the Status of Women* (Halifax: Nova Scotia Department of Social Services, 1976), 72.

9 *The 4th Estate*, 7 Jan. 1976, 9; 17 March 1976, 5.

10 An Act to Establish an Advisory Council, s. 4 (1).

11 NSACSW Resource Centre, 'History and Accomplishments of the Women's Directorate' (typescript prepared by Christine Corston, n.d. [ca 1993]).

12 The number of council members was not determined by the legislation.

13 I have not conducted biographical research on the members of council, but many of the members have had sufficient public profile to permit some generalizations. The NSACSW minutes and press clippings provide brief biographical information for some members.

14 NSACSW Minutes, 12 Oct. 1977–24 Oct. 1978. During this period the council met almost monthly.

15 Alison Prentice, et al., *Canadian Women: A History*, 2nd ed. (Toronto: Harcourt Brace, 1996), 439–40.
16 *The 4th Estate*, 24 Dec. 1975, 4–5.
17 NSACSW Minutes, 3 March 1978, 19 May 1978, 20 July 1978, 18 Jan. 1979, 20 April 1979, 22 March 1980.
18 Crocker resigned in the fall of 1978 'to go into private business.' NSACSW Minutes, 1 Sept. 1978, 24 Oct. 1978.
19 NSACSW Minutes, 17 Nov. 1978.
20 Ibid., 17 Nov. 1978, 19 Jan. 1979.
21 Ibid., 19 Sept. 1979.
22 Ibid., 16 Nov. 1979, 27 June 1980. The groups presenting briefs included the YWCA, a coalition of women's groups, Bryony House, Prepared Child Birth, Better Obstetric and Neonatal Decisions in the New Grace, the Canadian Sociology and Anthropology Association, Women's Institutes of Nova Scotia, Dalhousie University Faculty, the Canadian Research Institute for the Advancement of Women, Nova Scotia Women's Action Committee, Nova Scotia Women and the Law, Mount Saint Vincent University, Saint Mary's University Women's Caucus, and the Nova Scotia College and University Association's Status of Women Committee.
23 NSACSW Minutes, Special Meeting, 27 Oct. 1980, 24 Nov. 1980.
24 Ibid., 18 Feb. 1981.
25 Ibid., 24 April 1981.
26 Ibid., 21 Jan. 1982, 30 April 1982.
27 *Halifax Daily News*, 1 Nov. 1999, 4.
28 Findlay, 'Feminist Struggles with the Canadian State, 1966–1988.'
29 NSACSW Minutes, 27–8 Sept. 1982.
30 Ibid., 16 Feb. 1984.
31 Ibid., 27–8 Sept. 1982, 28 Oct. 1982, 1–2 Dec. 1982, 29–30 Sept. 1983, 17–18 Nov. 1983, 5–6 April 1984.
32 Ibid., 17 Jan. 1983.
33 Ibid., 5 April 1984, 18 June 1984.
34 Ibid., 27–8 Sept. 1984.
35 Newspaper clipping scrapbook, NSACSW Library (hereafter NSACSW clipping), *Halifax Mail-Star*, 19 June 1984.
36 NSACSW clipping, *Port Hawkesbury Scotia Sun*, 6 March 1985.
37 NSACSW Minutes, 27–8 June 1985.
38 Ibid., 18-19 Sept. 1985.
39 NSACSW clipping, *Halifax Chronicle-Herald*, 17 April 1985.
40 NSACSW clipping, *Halifax Chronicle-Herald*, 12 Sept 1985.
41 NSACSW Minutes, 15–16 Jan. 1986.

42 Sue MacLeod, 'Tories and Women's Issues: An Advisory Council's Troubles' *Atlantic Insight*, 8, 12 Dec. 1986, 9–10

43 Ibid.

44 *Halifax Daily News*, 1 Nov. 1999, 4. Cosman did not run in the July 1999 election due to the recent death of her husband. She has not ruled out a return to politics.

45 Author's interviews with Deborah Trask, Nov. 1999, Linda Christiansen-Ruffman, December 1999.

46 NSACSW Minutes, 6 Nov. 1986.

47 Forsyth Smith was criticized by a Liberal member of the Standing Committee on Human Resources for speaking at a Progressive Conservative function. She responded that she was attending an event for women and that she also attended NDP and Liberal functions. Nova Scotia, *Annual Report Standing Committee on Human Resources* (Halifax: Queen's Printer 1987), 31.

48 Forsyth Smith claimed that WACNS was supportive. She told *Frank* 'My constituency is women,' adding that Ann Bell, the president of the Newfoundland and Labrador Advisory Council recommended that she ingratiate herself with women and the media if she wanted to prove she could work under governments of various political stripes. NSACSW clipping, *Frank* 1, 11 (5 May 1988).

49 NSACSW clipping, *Halifax Daily News*, 2 April 1990.

50 Ibid., *Frank* 1, 11 (5 May 1988). Forsyth Smith was not without critics, however. See, for example, the *Halifax Chronicle-Herald*, 11 June 1991, where a letter to the editor from Betty Kimber, a long-serving member of the Halifax Local Council of Women, claimed that Forsyth Smith's credibility had fallen to a new low.

51 NSACSW clipping, *Halifax Daily News*, 22 Oct. 1990.

52 NSACSW clipping, *Halifax Mail-Star*, 16 Feb. 1991.

53 NSACSW clipping, *Halifax Chronicle-Herald*, 4 July 1991, 5 July 1991; *Sunday Daily News*, 7 July 1991; *Yarmouth Vanguard*, 12 July 1991.

54 NSACSW clipping, *Globe and Mail*, 4 July 1991. The same issue carried an editorial supporting the council's report, as did the *Daily News*, 5 July 1991.

55 NSACSW clipping, *Halifax Chronicle-Herald*, 18 and 21 Feb., 9 April 1991; *Halifax Daily News*, 20 Feb. and 25 March 1991; *Globe and Mail*, 21 Feb. 1991; *Cape Breton Post*, 5 March 1991; *Liverpool Advance*, 6 March 1991; *Chronicle-Herald* (Valley Bureau), 8 March 1991; *Yarmouth Vanguard*, 8 March 1991.

56 NSACSW clipping, *Chronicle-Herald*, 22 and 28 Nov., 5 Dec. 1991; Six Nova Scotian women were murdered in 1991: Emma Ann Paul, Carla Strickland, Bernice Whiffen, Kelly Whynot, Theresa Maureen Carrick, and Barbara

Anne Parrish. *Halifax Daily News*, 5 and 7 Dec. 1991; *Amherst Daily News*, 20 Nov. 1991.

57 NSACSW clipping, *Halifax Chronicle-Herald*, 8 March 1991; *Halifax Daily News*, 8 March 1991, *Cape Breton Post*, 20 June 1991. Forsyth Smith disagreed with Dechman, stating that 'things like a poor economy or alcoholism can act as a catalyst to violence,' were not the cause of violence.

58 NSACSW clipping, *Halifax Daily News*, 8 May 1991; *Halifax Chronicle-Herald*, 8 May 1991.

59 NSACSW clipping, *Halifax Chronicle Herald*, 5 April, 16 April 1991.

60 NSACSW clipping, *Cape Breton Post*, 18 April 1991; *Globe and Mail*, 13 Aug. 1991; *Halifax Chronicle-Herald*, 11 March 1992.

61 NSACSW clipping, *Halifax Chronicle-Herald* 5 July 1991; *Halifax Daily News*, 5 Oct. 1991.

62 NSACSW Minutes, 14–15 April 1989.

63 NSACSW clipping, *Halifax Daily News*, 8 June 1990.

64 Ibid., *Halifax Chronicle-Herald*, 2 March 1990.

65 NSACSW clipping, 5 July 1991; *Halifax Daily News*, 5 Oct. 1991.

66 NSACSW clipping, *Yarmouth Vanguard*, 27 Nov. 1990.

67 NSACSW clipping, *Halifax Daily News*, 1 Dec. 1990. The same story also appeared in the *Halifax Chronicle-Herald*, 1 Dec. 1990.

68 Ibid., *Halifax Chronicle-Herald*, 15 April 1992.

69 NSACSW Minutes, 1–2 Sept. 1987, 7–8 April 1988.

70 Nova Scotia, *Annual Report of the Standing Committee on Human Resources*, 1987, 31.

71 NSACSW clipping, *Halifax Chronicle-Herald*, 2 March 1993.

72 McDonald's appointment attracted considerable media attention because she was the first non-partisan president.

73 Dian Day, *Who Will Speak for Us? A Consultation Paper with Nova Scotia Women* (NSACSW, 1994).

74 Day, *Who Will Speak for Us?*

75 For a discussion and analysis of the new selection process see Brenda Beagan, '"Diversifying" the Nova Scotia Advisory Council on the Status of Women: Questions of Identity and Difference in Feminist Praxis,' *Atlantis* 21, 1 (1996): 75–84.

76 Ibid.

77 NSACSW clipping, *Halifax Daily News*, 1 Nov. 1995.

78 Ibid., 26 April 1996; *Halifax Chronicle-Herald*, 26 April 1996.

79 NSACSW clipping, *Halifax Chronicle-Herald*, 23 April 1996.

80 NSACSW clipping, *Halifax Daily News*, 16 July 1996; *Halifax Chronicle-Herald*, 16 July 1996.

81 *Halifax Chronicle-Herald*, 17 July 1996.

82 'History and Accomplishments of the Women's Directorate.'
83 Author's interview with Brigitte Neumann, Feb. 2000. Neumann regards the creation of an effective sexual harassment policy for the provincial government as the directorate's most important accomplishment in its first five years.
84 NSACSW Minutes, 27 Oct. 1988, 9–10 March 1989, 14–15 April 1989; NSACSW papers, Letter from Debi Forsyth Smith to Cathy MacNutt, 7 June 1989; Letter from Cathy MacNutt to Debi Forsyth Smith, 15 June 1989; Neumann interview.
85 NSACSW clipping, *Halifax Daily News*, 2 Sept. 1996, 4.
86 Ibid., *Halifax Chronicle-Herald*, 24 March 2000, A4.

Contributors

Wanda Thomas Bernard, Director of the School of Social Work, Dalhousie University, and community advocate, is currently examining the impact of racism and violence on the health and well-being of Black men, their families, and communities, in Halifax, Calgary, and Toronto, with the support of the Canadian Institute for Health Research.

Frances Early, Department of History, Mount Saint Vincent University, is the author of the prize-winning *A World without War: How U.S. Feminists and Pacifists Resisted World War I* (1997) and co-editor of the anthology *Athena's Daughters: Television's New Women Warriors* (2003).

Jeanne Fay, School of Social Work and Dalhousie Legal Aid Service, Dalhousie University, specializes in the practice of poverty law and the formulation of social policy and has been an anti-poverty activist and advocate since 1969.

Judith Fingard, Department of History, Dalhousie University, has written extensively on the history of class, race, and gender in Halifax including *Halifax: The First 250 Years* (1999) with Janet Guildford and David Sutherland.

Frances Gregor, School of Nursing, Dalhousie University, is interested in how gender organizes women's participation in nursing, voluntary health organizations, and informal caregiving. She is currently researching the role of the St John Ambulance Brigade after the Halifax Explosion of 1917.

Janet Guildford, Departments of History, Mount Saint Vincent University and Saint Mary's University, and Beach Meadows Research Associates, is co-editor with Suzanne Morton of *Separate Spheres: Women's Worlds in the 19th-century*

Maritimes (1994) and co-author with Judith Fingard and David Sutherland of *Halifax: The First 250 Years* (1999).

Suzanne Morton, Department of History, McGill University, is the author of the Halifax-based study *Ideal Surroundings: Domestic Life in a Working-Class Suburb in the 1920s* (1995) and *At Odds: Gambling and Canadians, 1919–1969* (2003).

Shirley Tillotson, Department of History and Women's Studies Program, Dalhousie University / University of King's College, is the author of *The Public at Play: Gender and the Politics of Recreation in Postwar Ontario* (2002) and is writing a history of charitable fundraising in twentieth-century Canada.

Illustration Credits

Duckworth, Muriel (Private Collection): Muriel Duckworth

Province of Nova Scotia: Debi Forsyth Smith

Nova Scotia Archives and Records Management (NSARM), Provincial Archives of Nova Scotia, Bollinger Collection: Bride and attendants, #4853-4; Researcher at the Atlantic Fisheries Experimental Station, #472-3; Fish packers, #4970-20; X-ray technician #479-46; Shopping at the Dominion Store #4876-1; Retail clerk, #495-5

NSARM, Provincial Archives of Nova Scotia, Halifax *Herald* Collection: A patient at the Children's Hospital, 1956-026; Canadian Girls in Training banquet, 1963-1170; White Cross volunteers, 1964-2522; Halifax Coloured Citizens Improvement League Queen, 1965-1115; Debutantes' Ball, 1965-3005; Mount Saint Vincent University students and faculty, 1963-1845; Taxi driver, 1965-2296; Junior League's Bargain Box, 1962-160; Abbie Lane, 1965-2339; Pearleen Oliver, 1967-0151; Institute of Women of the African Baptist Association meeting, 1963-2038; St John Ambulance Home Nursing Brigade members, 1964-0111; Baking for the Hadassah Fair, 1966-1247; Indian Night, 1967-0174

NSARM, Provincial Archives of Nova Scotia, MG1: 'Women and Work' Workshop, Vol. 1439, #25

NSARM, Provincial Archives of Nova Scotia, Robert Norwood Collection: African–Nova Scotian women, 0759-0787

Sisters of Charity Archives Mount Saint Vincent: Sisters of Charity nursing sister with Sister John Elizabeth

Index

´ceau de bib´ thèques   ork